SLAVES IN THE NEW TESTAMENT

SLAVES IN THE NEW TESTAMENT

LITERARY, SOCIAL, AND MORAL DIMENSIONS

J. ALBERT HARRILL

FORTRESS PRESS

MINNEAPOLIS

Cover art: Relief of two slaves turning an olive press. Roman relief. Museo Archeologico Nazionale, Aquileia, Italy. © Scala / Art Resource, N.Y. Used by permission.

Cover design: Kevin van der Leek Design Inc.
Interior design: Zan Ceeley

Library of Congress Cataloging-in-Publication Data

Harrill, James Albert.
    Slaves in the New Testament : literary, social, and moral dimensions /
    J. Albert Harrill.
        p. cm.
    Includes bibliographical references and indexes.
    ISBN 0-8006-3772-0 (hardcover : alk. paper) — ISBN 0-8006-3781-X (pbk. : alk.
        paper)
    1. Slavery in the Bible. 2. Bible. N.T. 3. Slavery—Religious aspects—Christianity.
    I. Title
HT915.H32 2005
225.8'306362—22
                                                2005024272

The paper used in this publication meets the minimum requirements of American National Standard for Information Sciences—Permanence of Paper for Printed Library Materials, ANSI Z329.48-1984.

Manufactured in the U.S.A.
09   08   07   06   05   1   2   3   4   5   6   7   8   9   10

For David

The God who, in America, is declared to sanction the impious system of slavery—the annihilation of the marriage institution and the sacrifices of all human rights—is my ideal of the devil.

—William Lloyd Garrison

If it were a matter to be determined by personal sympathies, tastes, or feelings, I should be as ready as any man to condemn the institution of slavery, for all my prejudices of education, habit, and social position stand entirely opposed to it. But as a Christian . . . I am compelled to submit my weak and erring intellect to the authority of the Almighty. For then only can I be safe in my conclusions, when I know that they are in accordance with the will of Him, before whose tribunal I must render a strict account in the last great day.

—John Henry Hopkins (1792–1868), Episcopal Bishop of Vermont

CONTENTS

ACKNOWLEDGMENTS

This book is the result of nearly a decade of research. During that time, I have gathered quite a few debts. The Alexander von Humboldt Foundation awarded a Research Fellowship (2002–2003) to work at the pleasant setting of Münster, Germany, in the Westfälische Wilhelms-Universität, Evangelisch-Theologische Fakultät, Neutestamentliches Seminar, where Prof. Dr. Dietrich-Alex Koch was my gracious academic host. The National Endowment for the Humanities offered a Summer Stipend (1999) at a crucial stage of the project's initial conception. Indiana University and DePaul University each supported the project enthusiastically, with research leaves as well as summer research grants. The Institute for Advanced Study at Indiana University, Bloomington, gave a congenial office space to me as a Visiting Scholar (1999–2000). I presented earlier versions at meetings of the Society of Biblical Literature, the Studiorum Novi Testamenti Societas, the North American Patristics Society, the Association of Chicago Theological Schools (ACTS) New Testament Discipline Group, the Boston Theological Institute New Testament Colloquium, and "After the Body: An International Conference on Religion, Culture, and Gender" at the University of Manchester, England. A number of scholars offered direction, helpful advice, and criticism sharpening the focus and articulation of my thesis: David Brakke, Ellen Eslinger, James Grossman, Robert Jewett, Martin Rese, Richard P. Saller, Stephen J. Stein, Steven Weitzman, and Lawrence Wills. I am grateful to all these people and institutions.

Portions of this work originally appeared in various journals and edited collections, revised, expanded, and adapted for use here with a large amount of previously unpublished research and new directions. Two sections of the introduction come from "Using the Roman Jurists to Interpret Philemon: A Response to Peter Lampe," *ZNW* 90 (1999): 135–38 and a few pages of "Paul and Slavery," in *Paul in the Greco-Roman World: A Handbook* (ed. J. Paul Sampley; Harrisburg, Pa.: Trinity Press International, 2003), 575–607. Chapter 1 was first published as "Paul and the Slave Self," in *Religion and the Self in Antiquity* (ed. David Brakke, Michael L. Satlow, and Steven Weitzman; Bloomington: Indiana University Press, 2005), 51–69; and chapter 2 as "Invective against Paul (2 Cor 10:10), the Physiognomics of the Ancient Slave Body, and the Greco-Roman Rhetoric of Manhood," in *Antiquity and Humanity: Essays on Ancient Religion and Philosophy Presented to Hans Dieter Betz on His 70th Birthday* (ed. Adela Yarbro Collins and Margaret M. Mitchell; Tübingen: Mohr [Siebeck], 2001), 189–213. I have adapted "The Dramatic Function of the Running Slave Rhoda (Acts 12.12-16): A Piece of Greco-Roman Comedy," *NTS* 46 (2000): 150–57, for incorporation as the first section of chapter 3. Chapter 5 was originally published as "The Vice of Slave Dealers in Greco-Roman Society: The Use of a Topos in 1 Timothy 1:10," *JBL* 118 (1999): 97–122; chapter 6 as "The Domestic Enemy: A Moral Polarity of Household Slaves in Early Christian Apologies and Martyrdoms," in *Early Christian Families in Context: An Interdisciplinary Dialogue* (ed. David Balch and Carolyn Osiek; Grand Rapids, Mich.: William B. Eerdmans, 2003), 231–54; and chapter 7 as "The Use of the New Testament in the American Slave Controversy: A Case History in the Hermeneutical Tension between Biblical Interpretation and Christian Moral Debate," *Religion and American Culture* 10 (2000): 149–86. I thank the publishers for their kind permission to reprint and the peer referees (some of whom remain anonymous to me) and editors for their valuable criticism on previous drafts. For translations of Greek and Latin sources, I used the LCL editions, altered when not sufficiently literal for my purposes.

A personal note of gratitude goes to the people who have been there throughout the ups and downs: Mary Jo Weaver, Steven Goldman, and Kathy Rexrode. This book is dedicated to David Brakke, with my heartfelt gratitude for the many ways he has sustained me over the fifteen years of our partnership.

INTRODUCTION

Imagining Slaves

Slaves in the Ancient Literary Imagination

How did the early Christians think about slaves? In this book, I argue that they did so through the literary artifice of conventional figures and stereotypes familiar from ancient literature, handbooks, and the theater. Such stock characters included the domestic enemy, the comic, the trickster, the elite, and the faithful slave. Although modern scholars often consider such New Testament figures as the maid Rhoda (Acts 12:13-16) evidence for the "liberating" participation of slaves in early Christian communities, a careful study of the evidence shows them to be literary characters drawn from the ideologies that supported Roman slavery.

I advance this thesis primarily through close readings of particular passages in their ancient context, in order to trace the development of literary themes or social types. I work strictly as a historian; that is, I do not advocate a "faith" solution to or a theological position on the question of slavery and the Bible; such questions are best left to Christians, theologians, and ethicists to answer. But I do deny that appeals to "what the Bible says" can serve as a foundation for Christian moral arguments, because such appeals do not explicitly acknowledge the agency and contingency of the interpreter.[1] Rather, any critical interpretation of the New Testament must start by situating the early Christian writings firmly in the literary, social, and cultural world of the early Roman Empire. Indeed, this book argues that the *Roman* context is particularly helpful in bringing clarity to difficult texts and in moving scholarship beyond tired, old clichés about the Bible and slavery that repeat unexamined presuppositions born of the modern abolitionist era. On the other hand, I do not argue that the resulting interpretations are the only valid ones. The professions of history and of biblical studies have happily moved beyond the objectivism of seeing historical facts naively, as prior to and independent of interpretation. Asserting an interpretative hegemony can no longer be intellectually justified. This should press us into caution, not despair.[2] We have gained some historical knowledge about ancient slavery that makes some interpretations from the abolitionist era (surveyed in chapter 7) impossible. Even if a reader disagrees with my exegesis at points, I hope that she or he nonetheless would see the value of exploring how an ancient Roman audience and its slaveholding culture would have heard the early Christian passages about slaves.

Rejecting the old "biblical theology" approach, I occasionally use early Jewish sources, such as Philo of Alexandria and Josephus, as a manifestation of Roman culture, seeing the integration of the Jewish material as a necessary part of good scholarship on ancient history. The problem with biblical theology is its totalizing interpretative framework that sets up an artificial cultural dichotomy between "Judaism" and "Romanness" (often conflated into "Hellenism") as code words masquerading as historical entities. The aim of that kind of scholarship is to urge the distinctiveness of Christianity against its "pagan" environment, a distinctiveness that it allegedly shared with ancient Israel.[3] Unlike other scholars who separate early Christianity from early Judaism or classical culture, and who compare the different "social worlds" to see how they are alike and how they differ, I study early Christianity as fully a part of and implicated in the ancient world. For this reason, I integrate Greek, Roman, and Jewish materials throughout all the chapters directly into my exegesis, rather than isolating them in some introductory "background" chapter. This volume, then, is an essay in biblical interpretation and hermeneutics, not a factual survey of slavery in the New Testament or early Christianity generally.[4]

Let me sketch the book's main thesis. I argue that early Christian writings reflect, participate in, and promote the literary imagination about slaves and the ideology of mastery widely diffuse in the ancient Mediterranean, which supported what the Romans called *auctoritas*. *Auctoritas* denoted the quality of actual power in the individual person (the *auctor*) granted by the willing compliance of subordinates and the esteem of one's colleagues, in contrast to the transactional power from governmental magistracies, social status, or family name. The value was deeply moral, belonging to the cultural milieu of masculinity and competition in Rome's conflict culture.[5] By *ideology* I mean language that colludes with, supports, and makes sense of the current structures of authority and domination that a particular society uses to construct and maintain its social "reality" and in which writers can participate even if the collusion is not altogether conscious.[6] This focus on ideology avoids the pitfall of claiming that authorial intention alone controls "the meaning" of a text. As Dale Martin writes, "I may wish to speculate about what Paul *thought* he was doing, but that speculation does not have the power to settle the question of what he was *actually* doing."[7] Because the Romans traditionally perpetuated their moral values through the retelling of example stories (*exempla*), the use of slaves and masters as literary figures was commonplace and a natural referent for the early Christians accustomed as Romans to use such language for self-definition and the construction of a religious community.[8]

The book is organized by corpora of texts, roughly in chronological order, and by theme. The first two chapters examine the Apostle Paul. Chapter 1 offers an exegetical study of Romans 7, one of the most important and controversial passages on the self in the Christian Bible. I side with a number of scholars who take the subject to be a fictive "I," a technique of speech-in-character (*prosōpopoiia*), and examine what remains unclear in this reading: Why a *slave* is chosen for the persona. Chapter 2 analyzes the rhetoric of the accusation, preserved in 2 Cor 10:10, that Paul was a religious fraud. I argue that the invective conforms to physiognomic conventions of what a "weak bodily presence" signified in ancient Mediterranean culture—the slave. I then connect the slave physiognomics to Roman ideologies of masculinity and manhood.

Chapter 3 is a study of Luke–Acts. I investigate the comedy of slavery in fictional characters that mock slaves. Rhoda, the slave maid in Acts 12:13-16, has been seen by modern scholars as a classic example of a touch a realism that lends authenticity to Luke's narrative. However, I argue that Luke has created an artificial stock figure from Roman comedy, a highly conventionalized sequence of narrative. Rhoda is the "running slave" (*servus currens*) whose function is to siphon implausibility from the scene, by which the subsequence action could be made to seem more real. The second figure is the dishonest manager ("steward"), subject of the most difficult of all the parables in the Gospels to understand (Luke 16:1-8). A solution lies in reading the action as that of a parasite (*parasitus*) playing the clever slave (*servus callidus*). The *servus callidus* was the template that defined and measured the form of all tricksters in ancient drama. This association held even for dramas that focused on nonslave characters. I argue that the parable of the Dishonest Manager contains clear narrative tags signaling this particularly Roman dramatic convention. But the function was more than mere comic relief. I interpret the Dishonest Manager as part of a narrative sequence leading to the Rich Man and Lazarus (16:19-31), and so I find problematic the scholarly habit of taking either parable out of its Lukan context to find its "real" historical meaning. The Dishonest Manager and the Rich Man and Lazarus form a literary diptych that contrasted two complementary modes of comedy, the farcical and the naturalistic. Read in this way, the dishonest manager thus acts as a catalyst that provokes important insights from more serious and complex characters in the literary artifice. In other words, both Rhoda and the dishonest manager are made up and play to ancient slave-holding tastes and sensibilities.

The fourth and fifth chapters examine the deuteropauline material on slavery. Chapter 4 surveys early Christian domestic codes that exhort believing slaves as moral agents *and* believing masters as subordinates of another Lord (Col 3:22—4:1; Eph 6:5-9; *Epistle of Barnabas* 19.7; *Didache* 4.10-11).[9] Although New Testament scholars have found irresistible a popular form of argument that these *Haustafeln* "upset" the domestic hierarchy of the ancient family and of slavery, I argue that they borrow the three didactic themes of justice, accountability, and piety widely diffuse in classical topoi on household management and best exemplified in the ancient handbook tradition on agriculture. A figure that previous scholarship has not thought to consider is the elite slave "bailiff" (*vilicus*) overseeing the estate in the place of the absentee estate owner (*pater familias*).[10] In the household codes, the Christian master is exhorted as a *vilicus*, in charge of a household yet also subordinate to another. Continuing the investigation of the deuteropauline letters, chapter 5 interprets the curious reference to "slave traders" in 1 Tim 1:10. I explore the cultural stereotypes surrounding the slave-trading profession in classical antiquity. In early Christian self-definition, *slave traders* functioned as a stock term of abuse and pointed not to actual people dealing in slaves but to the use of stereotyping to get a congregation to think about opponents as correspondingly vicious.

The final two chapters address the legacy of the New Testament. Casting my net wider than the New Testament canon in order to gain a fuller picture of early Christianity, I analyze in chapter 6 early Christian apologies and martyrdoms that condemn the ordinary household slave as an instigator of family corruption, the "domestic enemy" par excellence. As in the case of the term *slave trader*, I argue that the language is more literary artifice than social reality. In the process, I call into question recent scholarship that sees martyrdom as a discourse that undermines ancient ideologies of the family. By looking at tales of slave martyrs, and of slaves who betray their Christian owners in early Christian apologies, I find that martyrdom did not entirely contest the prevailing ideology of the family in the case of slavery. Elements of that ideology do appear in the moral polarity of "the slave" as either the domestic enemy or the faithful companion.

Chapter 7 shifts to the modern era and examines the use of the New Testament in the religious debate over legal slavery in antebellum America, offering several hermeneutical reflections on the book as a whole. I trace patterns in nineteenth-century exegesis that illumine a fundamental paradox in American religious culture—between literalism and moral intuition as opposing ways to read the Bible. The moral imperative of antislavery fostered an interpretative approach that found conscience to be a more reliable guide to Christian morality than biblical authority. Antislavery/abolitionist exegesis constituted an early form of biblical criticism that promoted more critical readings of the Bible, which prepared the way in the United States for the eventual reception of German higher criticism. My study thus illustrates the complicated relationship between the historical-critical interpretation of the Bible and Christian debate over moral issues, which carries implications beyond my case history of slavery. This book offers a hermeneutical challenge to the noble dream that biblical criticism can settle Christian moral debate, especially on family values.

Because a complex topic like slavery requires a diversity of interpretative approaches, as a historian I try out different methods in order to discover which best addresses the questions that a specific passage raises. Consequently, I do not conform my research to a consistent application of a single methodology or model. For example, I explore recent directions in gender studies and cultural theory, build on insights from literary approaches, do a great deal of social history, and pay close attention to what rhetorical analysis can yield. My approach is thus eclectic.[11]

In sum, this book investigates in detail representative examples of the main kinds of evidence in the New Testament (and elsewhere) used to recover early Christianity's "challenge" and "answer" to ancient slavery.

The findings show how difficult such claims are to maintain historically. Such references are *literary figures* that confirmed ideological stereotypes and bland moralistic polarities that slaveholders and those associated with the slaveholding orders of Roman society created and maintained. The evidence cannot support readings that purport to find early Christianity's moral unease with ancient slavery.[12] Unfortunately, we cannot correct New Testament passages that appear to be immoral, even when the interest to do so serves the noblest of aims.

Modern Literary Imagination: The Stories of Onesimus

But there were real slaves among the early Christians, and we know one of them by name—Onesimus. Surely, one might think, in this case we can avoid stock figures and types and get some actual historical information about a flesh-and-blood Christian slave. Unfortunately, matters are not so simple. Modern literary imagination is just as capable as ancient literary imagination of producing a fiction. Many of the so-called stories of Onesimus behind Paul's Letter to Philemon are more stereotype than history.

Modern biblical scholars prove to be as reliant as ancient authors on stock characters to "think with" when they use the Roman slave law of a "runaway" (*fugitivus*) or a "truant" (*erro*) to "explain" the text of Philemon.[13] Because Philemon is perceived in the history of interpretation to be the single most important text for understanding slavery and the Bible, I outline here the methodological difficulties with this approach, which has created multiple and conflicting stories of Onesimus. Current scholarship offers four different and competing reconstructions of the situation that Paul addresses: (1) the "runaway slave" hypothesis (the standard view); (2) the "intercession" hypothesis; (3) the "dispatched slave" hypothesis; and the hypothesis that Onesimus was not a slave but rather Philemon's brother (for this last view, see chapter 7). Unfortunately, none of these hypotheses solves all of the exegetical difficulties of Paul's shortest extant letter.[14]

Onesimus as Runaway Slave

The "runaway slave" hypothesis assumes the letter to be what patristic commentators since John Chrysostom (fourth century) said it was—an epistle requesting the Christian slaveholder Philemon to take back his runaway slave Onesimus, who, after doing damage, theft, or some other wrong, had somehow met Paul in prison and had been baptized.[15] We know that ancient slaves fled their masters and typically sought asylum in a temple or at a statue of the emperor (Achilles Tatius, *Leucippe et Clitophon* 7.13), went underground in a large city (Cicero, *Epistulae ad Quintum fratrem* 1.2.14), joined marauding bands of maroon gangs in the countryside (Athenaeus, *Deipnosophistae* 265d–266e), or tried to enlist in the army under a false identity (Pliny, *Epistulae* 10.29–30).[16] Yet Onesimus, it is alleged, took none of these options (or was captured before he had a chance to do so) and either found himself (by remarkable luck) thrown into the same prison cell as Paul or took refuge among the associates of Paul.[17] Subsequently, Paul converted Onesimus—becoming his "father during my imprisonment" (Phlm 10)—and then sent Onesimus with the letter, back to the master Philemon.

Supporters of the runaway-slave hypothesis often draw an alleged parallel with the correspondence of Pliny the Younger (*Epistulae* 9.21 and 9.24) about an errant freedman being returned to his patron Sabinianus.[18] Pliny, after being convinced of the freedman's "genuine penitence," says that he gave the man a very severe scolding and warned him firmly never to make such a request again, in order to frighten the errant runaway (*Ep.* 9.21). But this comparison creates more difficulties than solutions. Paul, in contrast, does not say what we would expect of a situation involving a runaway: he does not ask Philemon (as Pliny does of Sabinianus) to forgive or have pity upon the fugitive.[19] Pliny talks to Sabinianus about having scolded the runaway, pardoned his crime as foolish, and gotten genuine penitence and reassurance that it will not happen again, which is not what Paul says to Philemon about Onesimus. And, in any case, Pliny discusses a freedman and not a slave at all. The story of Onesimus the runaway slave looks more and more to be a fiction of Pauline interpreters.

The Intercession Hypothesis

In recent decades, several New Testament scholars have cast doubt not only on the Pliny parallel but also on the entire runaway-slave hypothesis. This leads to the second interpretation, the "intercession" hypothesis, which claims that Onesimus did not simply run away to freedom but ran specifically to Paul for his intercession after some misdeed. Onesimus could not have been a criminal runaway because he does not fit the definition of a *servus fugitivus* in Roman slave law.[20] This argument has changed the discussion in the exegesis of Philemon, prompting a number of exegetes to reassess the runaway-slave hypothesis, the *opinio communis* on the letter.[21] This legal approach is understandable, given the importance of law as a Roman institution and its coherence as a body of evidence, but in the reconstruction of a historical context against which to read the letter it is misleading. In antiquity, as today, law codes were not positive indicators of social practice. The claim that Onesimus was not a runaway slave may be correct, but the law codes do not provide good evidence for it.

The argument against calling Onesimus a *fugitivus* uses the academic opinions of three professional Roman jurists, each of whom agreed that the intentionality (*animus*) of the slave should be determinative to decide such a hypothetical case. The jurist Proculus declared a slave "who, having in mind that his master wished physically to chastise him, left to seek a friend whom he persuaded to plead on his behalf" not a "runaway" (*fugitivus*) but a "truant" (*erro*) (*Digesta* 21.1.17.4). The jurist Vivianus declared a slave who left his master to go home to mother "in the hopes that a mother's entreaties would better extenuate some wrongdoing of his" not a *fugitivus* but an *erro* (*Dig.* 21.1.17.5). The jurist Paulus declared a slave who "runs away to a friend of his master to seek his intercession" not a *fugitivus* but an *erro* (*Dig.* 21.1.43.1). According to some New Testament scholars, since Onesimus fled not to freedom but to Paul to seek intercession for some misdeed, he was merely a delinquent "truant" (*erro*) and not a criminal "runaway" (*fugitivus*).[22]

The first methodological question with this exegesis concerns the difficulty of making monolithic claims about Roman slave law. A survey of the *Digesta of Justinian* reveals that the legal technical term "runaway slave" (*servus fugitivus*) carried multiple and conflicting definitions, on which the jurists themselves did not agree. The bulk of the legal source material derives from the work of the famous jurist Ulpian (*Dig.* 21.1.17), who quotes previous jurists whom he respected. According to Ulpian, Aulus Ofilius defines a *fugitivus* as a slave "who remains away from his master's house for the purpose of flight (*fugae causa*), thereby to hide himself from his master" (*Dig.* 21.1.17.pr.).[23] Cassius Longinus says simply that a *fugitivus* is "one who with deliberate intent (*certo proposito*) leaves his master" (*Dig.* 21.1.17.2). Labeo defines "a truant (*erro*) as a petty fugitive (*pusillus fugitivus*) and, conversely, a fugitive (*fugitivus*) as a great truant (*magnus erro*)" (*Dig.* 21.1.17.14). Ulpian, however, disagrees with such simple definition and recommends nuance in meaning: "If we wish to be accurate, we define a truant (*erro*) as one who does not actually run away (*qui non quidem fugit*) but frequently indulges in aimless roaming and, after wasting time on trivialities, returns home at a late hour" (ibid.). Yet, following a senatorial decree that quotes the *lex Fabia*, he reverses this opinion: "*Fugitivus* should be interpreted as covering an *erro* as well" (*Dig.* 11.4.1.5). Another jurist, Callistratus, calls for even greater gradation, distinguishing among *fugitivus simplex* and *fugitivi* of other kinds (*Dig.* 11.4.2). The *Digesta*, then, records a complex historical development (over a period of at least two hundred years) for the technical term *servus fugitivus*, whose final definition could not be found without resorting to excessively fine distinctions in reasoning. As intellectually stimulating as such hairsplitting may have been for the Roman legal minds, its relevance for the exegesis of Philemon is difficult to see.

This difficulty leads to a second, larger methodological question about the use of legal evidence in historical inquiry. Our access to the opinions of the various classical jurists is dependent largely on the sixth-century Justinianic compilation, the *Corpus Iuris Civilis* (containing the *Digesta* or *Pandectae, Institutiones,* and *Codex*). Justinian promulgated the ambitious project for two incompatible reasons: to preserve the best of classical literature and yet to reform and set out law in his own day. He ordered the compilers to alter the texts, confident that no contradictions would be found that an acute mind could not reconcile.[24] The synthetic and prescriptive nature of the legal source material should caution against its uncritical use as social description in the exegesis of any Pauline letter, or in doing history. To accept juridical definitions of a *fugitivus*, which classify a runaway only in law and in theory, is methodologically questionable because legal codes, at best, provide only inexact knowledge about social practice and, at worst, can build a highly misleading model of slavery.

There is a third methodological caution. The jurists (known as *iurisprudentes* or *iurisconsulti*) wanted general rules precisely because they did not have to participate, either as advocates or judges, in the practice of law. In pursuit of truth and its theoretical systematization, jurists were academic lawyers whose training and modes of argument were not the same as those of advocates, the practicing attorneys in actual court paid to use rhetoric to win their clients' case. This distinction between academic law and the practice of law is fundamental: "In academic law the facts are clear whereas the law is often uncertain; in the practice of law, usually the facts are uncertain but the law clear. A large part of the practice of law lies in the handling and ascertaining of the facts."[25]

The deliberations of the jurists were academic games having little to do with the practice of law. Cicero, not a jurist but an advocate who actually practiced law in court,[26] protests:

> The jurists (*iurisconsulti*) often divide up into an infinite number of parts what is really based on a single principle, either for the purpose of deception, so that their knowledge may seem greater in amount and more difficult to acquire, or else, as is more likely, through lack of skill in teaching; for an art consists not merely in the possession of knowledge, but also in skill in imparting it to others. (*De legibus* 11.19 [47])

In another work, Cicero attacked the jurists and their profession as lacking "prestige (*dignitas*), much less public support," because their decisions were based on knowledge that had "no value outside Rome and not even at Rome during the vacation" (*Pro Murena* 28–29). To be sure, the passage reveals satire and stereotypes the great republican jurist Ser. Sulpicius Rufus, who was an accuser appearing in the trial of Murena, Cicero's client. Yet, granted its polemical status, the passage nevertheless demonstrates the plausibility such satire and stereotyping commanded before an ancient audience.[27]

The rhetorician Quintilian accepted this stereotype of jurists. The jurists, he writes, "have preferred to become specialists in *formularii*, or 'legal hacks' (*legulei*), as Cicero calls them, on the pretext of choosing a more useful branch of study, whereas the real motive was its comparative easiness" (*Institutio oratoria* 12.3.11). The literary sources, in contrast to the legal, provide a control against uncritical reading of the *Digesta*. If Cicero and Quintilian conducted their daily affairs in Rome with little contact or regard for the technical deliberations of the *iurisconsulti*, then provincials like the Apostle Paul and Philemon would have had even less contact with or concern for such minutiae.

Even the jurists acknowledged their own irrelevance in the actual practice of slavery. Vivianus writes, "the common belief of laypeople (*quod plerumque ab imprudentibus*), which is that a slave who without the master's consent stays away for a night is a *fugitivus*, is not true; one has to assess the slave's purpose in so acting (*ab affectu animi*)" (*Dig.* 21.1.17.4). Vivianus admits that his ability to discriminate a merely delinquent truant (*erro*) from a criminal runaway (*fugitivus*) results from his professional training and not his observation of slavery. The jurist disdains both social actualities and the common sense of amateurs.

Such amateurs would have included practicing attorneys, judges, and Roman imperial magistrates. Roman magistrates in particular were not legal experts but had wide discretionary powers in local jurisprudence, and this was not unintentional. Under the early Principate, central and provincial administration was a government without a bureaucracy. For non-Romans and provincials especially, the use of either Roman law or indigenous legal customs was uneven and opportunistic, depending on whichever best suited a litigant's interest, and followed the rule of "self-help" rather than depending on magistracy enforcement; "the police" in the sense of an institutionalized municipal service did not exist in antiquity. The law was in actuality a mixed bag of Roman, Greek, and local influences, and varied according to the region and the idiosyncrasy of the magistrate.[28]

These difficulties make the use of the Roman jurists to interpret Philemon problematic. Such mistreatment of the evidence is symptomatic of the larger methodological mistake of relying on law exclusively for one's understanding of ancient slavery. In the end, the hypothesis that Onesimus was not a runaway slave based on juridical definition of *servus fugitivus* does not hold. This finding, however, does not preclude a necessary reassessment of the "runaway slave" hypothesis to explain the social situation of the letter. Rather, we need to relocate the issue of slavery in the letter from a predominately legal question to one that stems from social, economic, and familial considerations.[29]

Even if one accepts the intercession hypothesis, it nonetheless brings us back to the same doubts about the runaway-slave theory: Why does Paul not scold and rebuke Onesimus for leaving the household without permission? Why does Paul's letter not share the same tone as Pliny's letter to Sabinianus? Pliny's letter is, after all, the main example offered as a request for intercession.[30] The distinction between a runaway *fugitivus* and an intercession-seeking *erro* existed only in the minds of the jurists. There was no substantial difference in the actual practice of ancient slavery. Both slaves had run away and deserved punishment. In the end, then, the intercession hypothesis is but a variation on the runaway-slave hypothesis and leaves still unanswered the original problem, that Paul's tone lacks a rebuke of Onesimus.

Onesimus as Dispatched Slave

One answer is the "dispatched slave" hypothesis. It holds that Onesimus did not *run away* but *was sent* to Paul by Philemon.[31] There is encouraging precedent for such a scenario. In Philippians, Paul thanks the congregation for sending Epaphroditus (who may have been a slave or freed-man) to "minister to my need" (Phil 2:25). Paul acknowledges that "I have been paid in full and have more than enough; I am fully satisfied, now that I have received from Epaphroditus the gifts you sent" (Phil 4:18). Perhaps Onesimus served in a function on behalf of Philemon's congregation similar to that of Epaphroditus on behalf of the congregation at Philippi.[32] Rome had no penal system, because incarceration was not a punishment but a detention before trial or execution. Guards generally threw the accused into any available strong room or secure hole and left issues like feeding, clothing, and other needs to the criminal's friends or family to supply, with bribery being common.[33] Especially in rural areas, apprehended runaway slaves and freeborn victims of kidnapping often found themselves thrown into the private slave prisons (*ergastula*) on estates of wealthy landowners, never to be heard from again.[34] Early Christian congregations would have known the dangers that an imprisoned Paul faced and at least on one occasion (recorded in Philippians) sent a representative with money and other gifts to sustain Paul while in prison. Onesimus could have served Paul as a servant, scribe, letter carrier, personal assistant, or a combination of all these things. The occasion of the letter would be, in this scenario, Paul's carefulness in not detaining the slave either whom Philemon had lent him or who went away to Paul on his own accord.[35]

We have abundant examples of such cases, especially in the letters of Cicero, who was notorious for keeping his friends' letter carriers too long. "You too," reminds Publius Cornelius Dolabella in a letter to Cicero, "on your part, honorable and courteous as you are, will see that the letter-carrier I have sent to you may be enabled to return to me, and that he brings me back a letter from you" (Cicero, *Epistulae ad familiares* 9.3). "I have been rather slow," writes Cicero to his friend Atticus, "in sending back your letter-carrier, because there was no opportunity of sending him" (Cicero, *Epistulae ad Atticum* 11.2). And Cicero apologizes: "What is happening here you may gather from the bearer of your letter. I have kept him longer than I should, because every day I am expecting something fresh to happen, and there was no reason for sending him even now, except the subject on which you ask for an answer" (Cicero, *Att.* 11.3).[36]

A papyrus letter dated 12 September 50 c.e. provides further support. Mystarion, an Egyptian olive planter, asks Stotoëtis, a chief priest, for the rapid return of his slave Blastos.

Mystarion to his own Stotoëtis, many greetings.
I have sent to you my Blastos for forked(?) sticks for my olive gardens. See then that you don't detain (*kataschēs*) him. For you know that I need him every moment (*hekastēs hōras*).[37]

Two verbal parallels, clear in the original Greek, are immediately apparent. First, Mystarion asks not "to detain" (*katechein*) Blastos, and, similarly, Paul admits that he wants "to detain" (*katechein*) Onesimus (Phlm 13). Second, Mystarion emphasizes that he needs Blastos each "moment" (*hōra*); likewise, Paul explains the need ("usefulness"; Phlm 11) to keep Onesimus for a "moment" (*hōra*; Phlm 15). These similarities suggest the same kind of story: A slave was sent to aid a friend. The slave Onesimus must be sent back as soon as possible, so Paul writes a letter to say the importance of not delaying the return of Onesimus. This scenario explains the absence of any rebuke on the part of Paul for the slave's actions and the lack of remorse on the part of Onesimus for wrongdoing.

Doubts nonetheless remain about this prehistory for the letter. One might object, for example, that the pledge Paul makes to "repay" any wrongdoing (Phlm 18) seems to support the runaway-slave hypothesis, or at least the idea that the fault lies with Onesimus. But Paul could refer to a number of things here—such as the *peculium* that Onesimus had at his disposal (which in law technically belonged to the master), the additional cost of keeping Onesimus from his regular duties at home, or the lost wages that the slave would have earned for his master had he not stayed away so long—but the text is too brief to be certain. One reply to this objection is that the radical change of a slave's religious commitment without his master's permission, and the slave's possible pledge of *peculium* in that conversion, could be taken as a wrong by a slave to the master.[38] Perhaps Paul was anticipating this reaction. He does not write that any wrong has actually taken place. Paul uses the subjunctive mood: "*if* he has wronged you at all, or owes you anything, charge that to my account" (Phlm 18), meaning possibly "not to the slave's account" (or *peculium*). Arguably, then, the hypothetical language implies that the wrongdoing was a perceived, not an actual, condition.[39] Paul addresses the letter to several people, including the church in Philemon's house (Phlm 2), to raise the honor-shame stakes to that of a public hearing, in the agonistic code of face-to-face rhetorical encounters. Paul pressures

Philemon by making a public plea, before the entire house church, to strengthen his hypothetical language.[40]

The exegetical problems are due in part to Paul's diction, which is unusually deferential and circumspect: "I preferred," he writes, "to do nothing without your consent, in order that your good deed might be voluntary and not something forced" (Phlm 14). On one interpretation, the "good deed" that should be "voluntary and not something forced" is manumission and/or granting Paul domestic authority over Onesimus. "Perhaps for this reason [Onesimus] was separated [or, 'went away'] from you for a while, so that you might have him back forever, no longer as a slave but more than a slave, a beloved brother—especially to me but how much more to you, both in the flesh and in the Lord" (Phlm 16). The phrases "more than a slave" and a brother "in the flesh and in the Lord" may imply that Paul hopes to secure the manumission of Onesimus,[41] a possibility that Paul's ending the letter with a note of confidence supports somewhat: "knowing that you will do even more than I say" (Phlm 21). Paul first denies the validity of Onesimus's prior slave relationship with Philemon ("no longer a slave") and then substitutes a fraternal bond in its place ("a beloved brother"). Paul wants Philemon to accept Onesimus in accordance with the apostle's terms, making the slaveholder acknowledge Paul's mastery over Philemon's domestic affairs. By calling himself a "father" of Onesimus, Paul asserts rhetorical authority over Philemon's legal right to determine the future of his slave Onesimus.[42]

Onesimus as "Apprenticed" Slave

To reconstruct what future Paul wants for Onesimus, I suggest a new hypothesis. This reading identifies the letter's genre (its style, contents, and function) in a particular kind of document. That document was the "journeyman apprentice" contract, such as those among the documentary papyri found at Oxyrhynchus, in Roman Egypt, especially associated with weavers and the textile industry. I argue that the letter asks Philemon to let Onesimus be apprenticed to Paul for service in the gospel (cf. Phlm 13). The value of this exegesis is its focus on the letter's future (its purpose and function) rather than on its prehistory (of which very little can be known).

Paul describes his relationship to Philemon as a "partnership" (*koinō-nia*) (Phlm 17 and 6). He uses technical formulations of a formal written appeal (9-10, 19) and asks for the "good deed" to be by consent and "not something forced" (14). Paul addresses Philemon with affective language—"coworker," "friend," and "brother" (1 and 7)—and expresses "joy" over the love (7) upon which Paul bases the whole proposition. Paul asks, "let me have this benefit" (20), asserting confidence in success (21) and the concrete expectation of a meeting (22). Paul also uses other formulae standard in apprentice contracts. Apprentice contracts contain a "command" for the slave to obey (cf. 8) (which Paul does not impose on Philemon but would on Onesimus), a reference to the slave "doing service" under the agreement (13), and the assumption that the proposed apprenticeship will turn a "useless" slave (one unskilled in any particular trade) into a "useful" one, both to the master craftsman and to its original owner.[43] Apprentice contracts end with the usual penalty clause by which the master craftsman guarantees assumption of any debts that might accrue (19) (such as missed sick days, loss of work due to truancy, and so forth) and the promise to return the slave, using the language of receipts (12). These parallels suggest that the Epistle to Philemon is a letter of recommendation: Paul recommends Onesimus for apprenticeship in the service of the gospel, an explicit "appeal" (10). Important to his appeal is Paul's enumeration of the slave's credentials (10). Onesimus, Paul notes, has already become "my child" (10), proven to be "useful" whereas before he was "useless" (11), and to be already a "beloved brother" (16). Onesimus, therefore, extends Paul's own self and should be received accordingly (12). Paul emphasizes also the creditworthiness of Onesimus (18-19). In short, Paul wants Philemon to entrust the slave with new responsibilities, as a business partner.[44]

I propose this new hypothesis to explain the letter in full knowledge that doubts may still remain. This exegesis suggests that Paul used stock formulae of slaves in apprentice contracts, probably familiar from his manual labor associated with the weaving industry, to "think with," perhaps without realizing the wider cultural habit in which he participated. But many of the parallels that one could draw from the documentary papyri read more like phrases used in ancient slavery generally, not technical "formulae" of apprentice contracts alone.[45] And the shift from literary genre to social description of the "story" in the letter's prehistory gives one pause, because it takes the stock caricatures of slaves in apprentice contracts (an ideology of masters) to be neutral reporting of objective "facts" about Onesimus.[46] The same doubts expressed above regarding the runaway-slave hypothesis remain: How did Onesimus and Paul end up in the same prison? By remarkable luck? And why would any ancient slave have gone voluntarily to a prison?

Apprentice contracts, in the end, express the narrow manner in which ancient slave owners judged both slaves and their actions, consisting of a bland moralistic division into "the useful" and the "the useless," and so are ideology, not social description.[47] Such material is not evidence of Onesimus's "story" but of Paul's participation and deep implication in ancient slavery. It does not tell us whether the historical Onesimus was really "useful" but that Paul thought about slaves in terms of stereotype and bland moralistic polarities. Even if the journeyman-apprentice hypothesis holds (and it might), the affective language is still a cliché. Paul still treats Onesimus instrumentally, as a "thing" to be transferred, owned, and used. Although we can invent stories of Onesimus that help the text seem more moral, the letter gives no hint that Paul or Philemon listened to what Onesimus may have wanted to do; we, in fact, have no evidence of what Onesimus wanted or what decision he made. No matter which story of Onesimus they tell, even the most imaginative modern historians cannot restore to this Christian slave his voice or agency. There is no story that Onesimus tells. Paul considers Onesimus's wishes to be unimportant, at least not important enough to mention to Philemon. The idea that Onesimus wanted any other life than working for Paul seems an unthinkable proposition in the letter. The slave literally is a "living tool" caught between two "masters" deciding on the use of his services.

I discuss Onesimus as a flesh-and-blood slave only as a prelude to the aim of this book. In the pages that follow I talk less about real slaves and more about stock character types that the ancient writers created. One might object that literary conventions are conventions precisely because they reflect real life. Such claims, however, are more often asserted than proved. Our first test case will be Romans 7, in which Paul impersonates a slave who is dominated by the wrong master. This "I," as we shall see, is a discursive, literary speech-in-character that is a product of the particularly Roman ideology of mastery known as *auctoritas*.

1

THE SLAVE SELF

Paul and the Discursive "I"

The Problem

The Apostle Paul considers the inner subjectivity of a slave in Romans 7, one of the most important and controversial passages on the self in the Christian Bible. The traditional reading, which goes back to Augustine, credits Paul with centering his attention on the split internal to the individual and the resulting incapacity of the self to carry out its own will. Augustine first took the passage to depict the introspective conscience of the unregenerate human, and later came to identify Paul's words, assumed to be autobiographical, with his own agonizing struggle against sin, described in the *Confessions*. Interpreting his own conversion retrospectively, in light of the Platonic myth of the soul (its alienation from the good and its return), Augustine created from Romans 7 a normative model of the religious self, which in Western culture has become the archetype for inquiry into the individual, influencing Thomas Aquinas, Martin Luther, John Calvin, and the Protestant Reformation, as well as Søren Kierkegaard and Sigmund Freud.[1] Biblical scholars advancing this psychologizing model of the self assume that the mythical picture of bondage and helplessness in Romans 7 is direct testimony of Paul's interior, subjective religious life. The claim is that the voice is both personal and realistic.[2]

Viewing Paul's letters from the perspective of Greco-Roman literary conventions, however, sharpens the problem of this psychologizing approach to the ancient Christian self. One of the successes of modern biblical criticism is the discovery that there is little indication that Paul

understood himself or the typical convert to be a person who had previously agonized under a subjective sense of incapacitating guilt. In the
rare places where Paul speaks about his former life in Judaism, he does
so with pride (Gal 1:13-14; Phil 3:4-6).[3] It is therefore unlikely that the
first-person singular in Rom 7:7-25 is Paul voicing his inner struggle of
his "preconversion" experience, or that it includes the apostle at all.[4]
While the particular identification of the *egō* ("I") does not matter to my
argument—my point is that the persona is enslaved—I follow current
scholarship that identifies Paul's subject as a fictive "I," specifically, the
technique of "speech-in-character" (*prosōpopoiia*) familiar from Greco-
Roman rhetoric and literature, which I find to be the most convincing
explanation of the text.[5] The question that I bring to the text is how an
ancient *Roman* audience would have most likely heard Paul's discursive
"I," especially in a letter whose opening words assert a slave persona:
"Paul, a slave of Jesus Christ" (Rom 1:1).

Speech-in-Character and the Slave Persona

Prosōpopoiia is the introduction of a character whose speech represents
not that of the author but that of another person or an invented persona.[6]
The technique played a central role in the hypothetical situations posed
for declamatory exercises, the preliminary rhetorical drills in formal
Roman education, which closely followed Greek teaching methods. The
teacher (*grammaticus* or *rhetor*) would ask the student to compose poetry
or prose, for the purposes of recitation, by imagining what a certain type
of person would say to another in a given situation. The identification of
the speaking voice and characters formed particular reading habits attun-
ing the student's ear to standard interpretative conventions of oral speech
used in written texts, teaching him or her to ask "Who is speaking?"
—a critical skill in an ancient culture where readers faced texts containing dialogues that had no punctuation, no word division, and nothing to
indicate change of speakers. Importantly for our study of Romans 7, the
exercise figured prominently for training in letter writing.

The technique of speech-in-character is commonplace in Greek and
Roman literature. The best evidence comes from Cicero, Quintilian,
and the extant handbook *progymnasmata* (preliminary rhetorical exercises).[7] Aelius Theon of Alexandria, a rhetor of the first century C.E.,
explains in his handbook that speech-in-character consists of both cases
in which one invents through conventional diction the character (*ēthos*)

of a known person (*prosōpon*) and cases in which one invents both the *ēthos* and the person. In the latter case, the student conforms the words of the invented persona—the self—to fit the moral habits and inner dispositions of a recognizable stock type, often taken from Greek and Roman drama, such as a husband, soldier, braggart, barbarian, or the slave.[8] While to me the argument that Paul employs this latter case of speech-in-character to invent both the *ēthos* and persona of the "I" in Romans 7 is convincing,[9] what remains unclear in this reading is why a *slave* is chosen for the persona.

Paul writes, "I delight in the law of God in my inmost self (*kata ton esō anthrōpon*), but I see in my members another law at war with the law of my mind, making me captive to the law of sin that dwells in my members" (Rom 7:22-23). As many commentators have shown, Paul refers to the Greek philosophical concept of an "inner" versus an "outer" human being, an idea of the self that originated from Platonic tradition, going back to the ninth book of the *Republic*.[10] Scholarship emphasizes that although the Platonic tradition identifies the "inner human being" with the *psychē* (soul), *nous* (mind), or *pneuma* (spirit), Paul considers the "inner human being" not to have a higher status than the "outer human being" but thinks that both are two aspects of the same *anthrōpos*, a non-dualistic entity.[11] What commentators overlook in their analysis of "Pauline anthropology" is that Paul does not describe a generic or "typical" *anthrōpos* but one pointedly characterized as enslaved, having specific connotations in the slaveholding culture of Roman imperial society. In the rush to analyze the Platonic "background" of Pauline theology, there has been no serious inquiry into why Paul chooses the persona of the slave as his model of the *anthrōpos* containing both an "outer" and "innermost" self.

At first glance, the slave seems an unlikely model of the *anthrōpos*, if we follow the formal definitions of the slave in Greek philosophy. Aristotle and his epigones claim that the slave does not have the very "inner self" that Paul's speech-in-character requires. Aristotle writes that because the slave is deficient in many human essentials, such as emotion, virtue, reason, and deliberative powers, the slave is only a partial (outer, bodily) self whose actions are incomplete. Since the slave's actions are incomplete, the slave is and ought to be an "animate tool" (*empsychon organon*) of someone else.[12] After arguing the inherent naturalness (goodness) of slavery, Aristotle raises the subsequent, independent question of whether some slaves are "natural" slaves. His comments on this second topic are, to be sure, scattered and inconsistent, but his overarching theme is clear: the relationship of master and slave in the family is the paradigm that grounds and naturalizes all human relationships of domination.[13] Later Hellenistic and Roman writers, particularly among the Peripatetic school, develop Aristotelian ideas of the natural slave into a coherent theory with detailed elaboration and systemization in technical handbooks on physiognomics, as we shall see in the next chapter. In this theory, the slave's body, by virtue of its very anatomy, is biologically built for servitude. The natural slave is a deficient *anthrōpos*, without the faculty of reason, a human subspecies assimilated to irrational beasts requiring taming and domestication.

Greeks in general defined the slave, like the animal, in terms of its body alone. A common word in Greek for "slave" was simply "body" (*sōma*); other ancient terms included "boy" (Greek *pais*; Latin *puer*), "rogue" (that is, someone who needs a whipping: *mastigia*; *verbero*), "garbage" (*katharma*), and "man-footed creature" (*andrapodon*), the last term derived from a common word for cattle (*tetrapodon*).[14] The somatic vocabulary reflects a cultural habit that tended to define the slave by its (my use of neuter is pointed) outer corporality alone—a mere "body." The semantic and philosophical evidence, therefore, makes Paul's case of a speech-in-character, in which an invented slave persona communicates thoughts from an "innermost self" (and not, as we would expect, the flesh or bodily members), curious. Significantly, the passage in Romans 7 expresses no need to argue that "the slave" has an innermost self. Paul simply presumes that a slave character would naturally have one, and proceeds with the speech. If Paul expected that his encoded Gentile readers (Rom 1:5-6, 13; 15:15-16) would immediately associate the speech-in-character with a recognizable stock type whose special trademark was the innermost self and would thereby catch his wider meaning about baptism, "the slave" seems a poor choice. In classical Greek philosophy, ideology, and even vocabulary the slave has neither a "self" nor an interior experience.[15] The passage does not make sense in the philosophical history-of-ideas context of standard biblical commentary.

Examining Romans 7 in a context wider than Greek philosophy makes Paul's choice of an enslaved *anthrōpos*, to depict the inner and outer aspects of the religious self, more intelligible. Key is attention to different social constructions of the slave in classical culture, focusing on Roman and not Greek (Athenian) ideologies of slavery. The focus on Roman sources serves as a methodological control against exclusive reliance on Aristotle or Plato to interpret the passage and its ideas of slavery. In contrast to Aristotelian ideas of the slave being only an outer "body" without interior rationality or agency, the main Roman (Stoic) ideology required the ideal slave to possess reason and virtue (*logos* and *aretē*).[16]

Roman law recognized the slave to have inner subjectivity and moral agency. Influential on this principle were Stoic ideas of common humanity, organic cosmology, and fate.[17] A condition of fate and not of nature, slavery in Roman legal categorization belonged to the law of nations (*ius gentium*), by which, contrary to nature (*contra naturam*), one person is subjected to the power (*dominium*) of another. Remarkably, this case is the only one in the entire extant corpus of Roman private law in which the *ius gentium* and the *ius naturale* are in conflict.[18] The legal material reveals also the enormous importance of slaves in commercial and other acquisitions. The centrality of trusted managerial slaves on rural estates, which Roman agricultural writers emphasize (see chapter 4), parallels the urban household situation envisioned in the legal texts.[19] Partly because masters employed their slaves as de facto agents, Roman law lacked a concept of agency in the modern sense of a free person representing another—one reason why a slave was often more useful to his master in business transactions than a free client. The importance in the Roman economy and society of trusted slaves who often worked independently and in locations outside the master's hometown rests on an ideology that the master did not need to supervise every decision a slave agent made. The Roman notion of mastery defined the ideal slave not in terms of obedience to individual commands of the master but in terms of having accepted the master's wishes so fully that the slave's innermost self could anticipate the master's wishes and take the initiative. Romans did not want automatons for their slaves.[20]

The Slave as Automaton and the Art of Authority

Roman moral philosophy used the slave automaton and the comedy of its ineffectiveness to teach the art of authority. The *Life of Aesop* (*Vita Aesopi*) offers an illustration. Although the legendary figure of Aesop originates from the early Greek period, the extant biography was written no earlier than the time of the Roman Empire. The *Life of Aesop* is a romance based on themes found in the fables, a repository of slave-savant anecdotes about Aesop and his hapless master, Xanthos, a so-called philosopher.[21]

A recurring theme of the biography is Aesop's philosophical game of cat and mouse with his master. Xanthos looks for excuses to beat his slave. Aesop, in turn, evades punishment by his ingenious "misunderstandings" of the orders, repeatedly receiving opportunities to lecture his master on the meaning of self-control and proper household authority. This willful misbehavior frustrates Xanthos (and his wife) so completely that Xanthos finally orders Aesop to act like an automaton, to do nothing more or less than what his commands literally demand. Of course, this move only leads to further situation comedy as Aesop takes his master exactly at his word. Going to the baths, Xanthos instructs Aesop, "to pick up the oil flask." Aesop picks up the flask but not the oil. Xanthos orders the slave home to "cook lentil" for a dinner party. Aesop tosses a single legume into the cooking pot. Xanthos tells Aesop to give his dinner guests "something to drink, right from the bath." Aesop returns with a pitcher full of bathing swill. Succeeding in driving Xanthos nearly mad, Aesop explains that his demonstrations are the same a philosopher would use with students: "You shouldn't have been so precise in laying down the law, and I would have served you properly. But don't feel sorry about it, master. The way you decreed the law to me will be useful to you, for it will teach you not to make mistakes in the classroom. Statements that include or exclude too much are no small mistakes." The moral is that one's subordinate has a self. When they want subordinates to act as automatons—that is, without a self—masters have only themselves to blame for the resulting chaos in the household (and in the classroom). To be properly served, the master needs the slave to have agency and to take some initiative from interior subjectivity. The farcical comedy of the *Life of Aesop* teaches the moral philosophy of proper mastery.[22]

That mastery was *auctoritas*, which routed power through patterns of personalized influence rather than through abstract institutions such as bureaucracy, wage labor, or public office. The Latin term—whose force was something like "influence" or making known one's will based on mutuality—was, as the Greek senator and historian Cassius Dio remarked, quintessentially Roman and untranslatable (Dio, *Roman History* 55.3.5). As I noted in the introduction, *auctoritas* denoted a quality of real power in the individual that colleagues and social lessers granted by willing compliance. The value was deeply moral, belonging to the cultural habit of aristocratic competition. Roman government was based on the concept.[23]

The emperor Augustus had underscored the term as the central characteristic of his rule, asserting that he "surpassed all others in *auctoritas* while possessing no more official power (*potestas*) than those who were colleagues of his in each magistracy" (*Res Gestae* 34.3).[24] Spectacles of Augustan providential "realities" of power (*imperium*) for awe and emulation filled public space throughout the Roman world, in monumental architecture, art, coinage, epic literature, and emperor worship. Augustus, whose very name carried religious and divine connotations, was proclaimed the ultimate guarantor (*auctor*) of peace and stability after decades of civil war. By deliberately emphasizing *auctoritas* as his governing concept in the restoration of the *res publica*, Augustus made clear his intention to provide leadership higher and more moral than that of just a functionary or magistrate. He played upon culturally charged themes in both public and private discourse.[25] In that discourse, an aristocratic adult male achieved honor (*dignitas*) and mastery (*auctoritas*) from the successful domination of others. Rome's fundamentally hierarchical society envisaged slavery as the absolute in a continuum of domination and subordination.[26]

This personalized view of power recognized subjectivity in the slave. *Auctoritas* was achieved in specific, concrete events in which the slave expressed acceptance of the master's point of view so fully as to anticipate the master's wishes. Rather than merely following individual orders in mechanical fashion, the good slave (*servus frugi*) completed and developed what the master had only suggested or even unconsciously desired— a task that in the practice of Roman slaveholding encouraged the actual slave to develop moral intuition.[27] This social construction imagined the slave with an internal faculty of assent, a function of reason. The ideology reflects the Stoic philosophy of *prohairesis*, which detached an essential self from the outer body ("the flesh") and identified it with an interior moral subject understood to be personal and individualized.[28] The Stoics stressed the importance of the self to such an extent that some scholars are tempted to say that they even discovered the concept.[29]

Personalization of the slave with this kind of subjective self is a central tenet in the Roman discourse of authority. Ancient authors discuss the hard work and constant maintenance that such mastery over a self requires. Epictetus warns his aristocratic students—teenaged masters themselves, and future householders—against allowing their happiness to depend upon the constant obedience of their slaves. "Nothing is got without a price," lectures the Stoic teacher. "And when you call your slave boy, bear in mind that it is possible that he may not heed you, and again, that even if he does heed, he may not do what you want done" (Epictetus, *Encheiridion* 12.2). In actual practice, mastery does not always work.

Slaves do not always conform their innermost self to the master's will. Additionally, the moralist Plutarch recounts the "famous case" of a slave resisting mastery to illustrate a lesson about foolish chatter. Ironically, the case involves an orator. Plutarch writes:

> Pupius Piso, the orator, not wishing to be troubled, ordered his slaves to speak only in answer to questions and not a word alone. Subsequently, wishing to pay honour to Clodius when he was a magistrate, Piso gave orders that he be invited to dinner and prepared what was, we may suppose, a sumptuous banquet. When the hour came, the other guests were present, but Clodius was still expected, and Piso repeatedly sent the slave who regularly carried invitations to see if Clodius was approaching. And when evening came and he was finally despaired of, Piso said to his slave, "See here, did you give him the invitation?" "I did," said the slave. "Why hasn't he come then?" "Because he declined." "Then why didn't you tell me at once?" "Because you didn't ask me that." (Plutarch, *Moralia* 551d–e; Helmbold, LCL)

The anecdote resembles the episode discussed above in the *Life of Aesop* and is further evidence that the "automaton slave" is a stock comic type. Plutarch goes on to contrast the back talk of such a "typical Roman slave" with the poetic line an Athenian slave would say to his master, the moral of the story being that people often talk in habituated banter rather than with intelligence.

Cicero provides an additional example. He pleads:

> What law, what decree of the senate, what edict of the magistrates, what pact or agreement or even, if I may speak of the civil law, what will, what judgments or stipulations or formulae of agreement and contract could not be weakened and pulled apart, if we wanted to twist the substance to suit the words and leave unaccounted for the intentions, reasoning, and *auctoritas* of those who wrote the document? By god, everyday household language will make nonsense, if we try to pounce on each other's words; ultimately there would be no household authority (*imperium domesticum*) if we allowed our slaves to obey us in accordance with our words, and not comply with what we understand from the words.[30]

Cicero uses the private discourse of household mastery to illustrate by analogy the public discourse of *auctoritas*. He and the other authors above show the prevalence of *auctoritas* in Roman culture across the board, from education and moral philosophy to law, rhetoric, and religious/political ideology.

This cultural context is critical for the interpretation of Romans 7 because Paul uses the ideology of *auctoritas*, with its model of the slave self, to influence his Roman audience. Establishing this thesis requires locating Roman cultural influence not only on Paul himself but also on early Christians broadly, since Paul's encoded audience, though Gentile, is not "Pauline" in the sense of having the apostle as its founder. Paul had not visited Rome and had not established any of the congregations in that city (see Rom 1:10-15). Comprehensive examination of the Roman imperial context of early Christianity is beyond the scope of my exegetical study, and it hardly needs repeating.

The Parable of the Talents/Pounds

As a prelude to the exegesis of Romans 7, one example of what I find to be the best source outside of the Pauline material must suffice: the parable of the Talents/Pounds.[31] In Matthew's version, a man "going on a journey" summons three slaves and entrusts talents to each "according to his ability" (Matt 25:15). Predictably, and almost as a setup, the slave having the least ability, and so entrusted only with a single talent (his inherent character flaws made explicit in the narrative's introduction), fails to prove his usefulness and worth. While the slave complies with the literal commands, he is "useless" because he has not internalized the master's will that the ideology of *auctoritas* required. Ironically, the paralysis causing the slave to act like an automaton stems from fear of merciless punishment for failure to obey, his master being characterized as a "harsh man" (25:24-25). The slave hides the money in a hole, whereas his more able fellows go out and trade with the talents to make more (25:16-18). The master, in Matthew's reasoning, rightly rewards the entrepreneurship of the good slaves, who receive more responsibility in the household and "enter into the joy of [their] master" (25:21-22), and punishes the bad. "You wicked and lazy slave!" the master yells at the terrified piece of chattel. "You knew, did you not, that I reap where I did not sow, and gather where I did not scatter? Then you ought to have invested my money with the bankers, and on my return I would have received what was my own with interest" (25:26-27). The master then gives the slave the beating of his life: "As for this worthless slave, throw him into the outer darkness, where there will be weeping and gnashing of teeth," the master said, employing domestic torturers used regularly for such purpose (25:30).[32]

The author of Matthew makes explicit his contrast of the "good slave" (who shows loyalty to an absent master) and the "bad slave" (who does not), two stock types in tales of *apsente ero* (when the master's away) familiar from ancient comedy. This contrast echoes what Cicero and Plutarch say above and is a further example story (moral exemplum) of the distinctively Roman ideology of *auctoritas*—personalized power channeled through the master's ethos. The bland moralistic division into good and bad, which the slave parables of the Synoptic Gospels advance, makes the connection to Roman slaveholding ideology (and its stock of comic slave types) even more likely.[33]

The Art of Authority in Paul's Gospel

The principal concept of *auctoritas* influenced Paul's gospel as well. As did Augustus, Paul claims that the root of his authority is, quite simply, his deeds. Paul connects his authority to apostolic activity (converting Gentiles and establishing congregations) and not to official rights (*exousia*, power) granted by the title or office of "apostle" (2 Cor 3:1-3; 1 Cor 9:4-6, 12, 18; cf. 1 Cor 8:9).[34] Part of the historical meaning of Paul's Letter to the Romans, as Stanley Stowers has shown, comes from imagining how readers in Paul's day would have received this gospel in the context of the Augustan revolution and its developing ideology of declining morality, divine wrath, and hopes of a golden age (compare Rom 1:18-32). Paul's message appealed not because it introduced new moral values into the wider "pagan" culture but because it played on politically and culturally charged themes that all readers met daily on the images of coins, in public monuments, and in everyday discourse, transcending ethnic boundaries of Jewish, Greek, and Roman.[35] I argue that Paul integrated the contemporary moral value of *auctoritas* and its particular model of the slave into his gospel to urge a new social allegiance in dialogic relation to the old, pre-converted self.[36] In Romans 7, the Apostle Paul uses the specifically Roman cultural imagination of the slave to help himself and his Gentile audience think through what happens to the religious self, the *anthrōpos*, before and after the ritual of baptism. In other words, to borrow Lévi-Strauss's famous formulation, Paul found slaves "good to think with."[37]

Romans 7 and the Slave Self

Convincing to me is the thesis of Stanley Stowers that the *anthrōpos* in Rom 7:7-25 refers to a Gentile, and not a "universal," self. The subject of Rom 7:7-25 is a representation of the Gentile situation described at the outset of the letter (Rom 1:18-32), punished by God for idolatry with slavery to the passions (*epithymiai*). In this way, Paul's speech-in-character appropriates the caricature, in Hellenistic Judaism, of Gentiles as morally degenerate. The perspective is not philosophical anthropology (the human essence), but what we would call ethnic cultural stereotype. Yet, as Stowers shows, the persona Paul so carefully constructs is more specific than "Gentiles." That *anthrōpos* represents someone caught between two cultures, torn between the passions of an idolater and the law of the one true God. The specific persona is a Gentile attracted to Judaism, what modern scholars would call a "God-fearer."[38] Central to Paul's argument is the Greek and Roman model of self-division (*akrasia*), its classic expression being Medea's great monologue (Euripides, *Medea* 1021–1080).[39] Paul, then, depicts the religious quest of his encoded reader— the Gentile attracted to Judaism, who undergoes (and should undergo) an agonizing crisis of identity, especially when confronted with the Pauline gospel.

The importance of these exegetical issues lies in the fact that they raise directly the question of what interpretative categories we should use for an adequate reading of Paul's letter. Whereas Stowers focuses on the moral philosophy of self-mastery, and others examine the presence of Platonic themes, my aim is to relocate the issue of the religious self in Romans 7 from a predominately philosophical question to one that stems from considerations of mastery and slavery in Roman ideologies of power. I take the prevailing metaphor in the passage seriously. I am challenging New Testament scholarship that downplays or dismisses outright the importance of the slave language.[40]

Paul incorporates Roman slaveholding ideology, the cultivation of the interior motivation of the slave by *auctoritas*, into his discussion of baptism (Rom 6:6-14) and into his speech-in-character (Rom 7:14-25). The opening chapters establish interior motivation as a central theme in Paul's definition of the religious self. First, a set of antitheses (concerning God's impartiality) underscores the point: "visible" (*en tō phanerō*) versus "in secret" (*en tō kryptō*); "on the fleshly surface" (*en sarki*) versus "from the heart" (*kardias*); "literal" (*en grammati*) versus "spiritual" (*en pneumati*) (Rom 2:28-29). Next, Paul reassures his readers that Christ has redeemed them from a curse: by agreeing to go to and die on a cross, Christ displayed trust (*pistis*) in God and his promises, and in so doing generated a proper relationship with God on the model of Abraham's faithfulness to God and the covenant (Rom 3:21-33). The term *pistis* (faith) here carries the sense of faithfulness or trust ("obedience"), not "belief" as in the traditional theological reading.[41] Paul then encourages his readers to think about their participation in the Christ event during the ritual of baptism, knowledge being an explicit warrant for the exhortations: "We know that our old self was crucified with him, so that the body of sin might be destroyed, and we are no longer enslaved to sin (*douleuein hēmas tē hamartia*)" (6:6).[42] Paul asks rhetorically:

> Do you not know that if you present yourselves to anyone as obedient slaves (*doulous eis hypakoēn*), you are slaves of the one whom you obey, either of sin, which leads to death, or of obedience (*hypakoēs*), which leads to (God's) righteousness (*dikaiosynēn*)? But thanks be to God that you, having once been slaves of sin (*douloi tēs hamartias*), have become obedient from the heart (*hypēkousate de ek kardias*) to the standard of the teaching to which you were entrusted, and that you, having been set free from sin (*eleutherōthentes de apo tēs hamartias*), have become slaves of (God's) righteousness (*edoulōthēte tē dikaiosynē*). (6:16-18)

The slave speech-in-character of chapter 7 follows, leading into chapter 8, where Paul expresses apocalyptic knowledge that "creation itself will be set free from its slavery to decay and will obtain freedom" (Rom 8:21). Paul portrays "creation" (8:19) as a person enslaved to the wrong master and suffering under Sin's domination, one of four agents (including the Spirit [8:26], God [8:31-33], and Christ [8:34]) personified as friends having all emotions in common.[43] The whole section (Romans 6–8) argues against Gentile adherence to the law, by pairing the law with slavery under Sin.

Redemption from the Persona of Sin

In this context, sin is not something the self does (as in a "crime"), but a personalized demonic power that victimizes the self by residing in the self's fleshly "members" (where sinful passions are located) when the self hears the holy law.[44] The Gentile self remains devoted to God's law but is nonetheless powerless to achieve what it wants, even doing the very opposite of what it avoids (7:18-19). The conflict is not between two different selves, nor two selves at different levels—such as the "rational self" (*nous*) and "irrational self" (*sōma*) in the Platonic tradition—as though one were under the power of Sin and the other not. Both "innermost self" and "members" are two facets of the same self that is "sold under sin" (6:14).

Paul does not, then, simply repeat Platonizing concepts of the self but thinks in terms of a whole *anthrōpos* (both *nous* and *sōma*, but without the flesh [*sarx*] that will be saved). To be sure, there is an apocalyptic dualism, but not in anthropology. Paul speaks about two different laws—the holy law of God and a demonic law (not just "another law") called the "law of sin," which resides in the outer members of the religious self. The speech-in-character declares allegiance and delight in the first (7:22) and then reports discovery of the second (7:23). The eschatological hope of salvation is not *release of the soul* from the body but *redemption of the self* (the pneumatic *sōma*) from the "law of sin and death" (8:2) for enslavement to God, where it belongs.[45] The problem is not slavery per se, but slavery to the wrong master.

The slavery is also partial and chaotic. The demonic power of Sin possesses external "members" but not the "innermost" part of the religious self, which still delights in the law of God. For this reason, Paul reminds his readers that baptism does not bring a complete end of sinning (in the judicial sense of committing crimes and vice; hence the moral exhortation in Romans 14–15) or manumission from Sin itself (in the participationist sense of a demonic power). The apocalyptic drama imagined has the religious self caught in the eschatological tension of "already and not yet," forced to work against its will like a captured war slave, but already experiencing partial effects of God's redemption because of baptism.[46] Set against an enemy in battle (*antistrateuomenon*) and captured as prisoner of war (*aichmalōtizonta*; cf. 2 Cor 10:3), the self is locked in close-arms combat (Rom 7:23). Paul's imagery of face-to-face fighting corresponds to the visual representation of armed conflict in Greece and Rome that localized all actions to immediate partners or opponents, limited to the reach of the person's limbs and weapons (depicting the individual as part of a comprehensive whole, such as providential Destiny [Fortuna; Tychē]). In Roman depictions, as opposed to Greek, brute physical strength of the enemy loses out to superior technical skill and static loyalty.[47] Paul incorporates the Roman visual representation of close-arms combat into his mental construct of apocalyptic battle. The sustained military imagery typecasts the "I" character as captured but still having a punch, and the loyal hope of ultimate victory, in its self.

Paul's letter evokes the military culture of Rome by use of another cultural symbol—*auctoritas*. The apocalyptic drama personalizes God's power and authority over Sin and other demonic war enemies. Gentile converts are captives of Sin, slaves whom God has now "bought with a price" (see 1 Cor 6:20; 7:23). In Paul's gospel, Christ had demonstrated *pistis* (faithfulness, trust, obedience) to God. Converts must likewise accept God's point of view so fully as to anticipate the divine personal will and to make it effective in the world, even when the Eschaton is not yet present. This theme corresponds to the classical Roman topos of the "faithful slave," who acts and dies on behalf of her or his master (*de fide servorum*).[48] For Paul, baptism is the concrete ritual moment moving the catechumen away from an "I" (the subject of the individual as the normative locus) and toward identification of that subject with Christ. Comparable to the Stoic theory of *oikeiōsis* (appropriation, or taking as one's own), this transference of subjectivity is believed by Paul to be a direct consequence of a transformation in the individual self. The Pauline view of God's mastery recognizes the subjectivity and agency of the converted religious self and sees that true authority consists not in obeying individual commands—as in the automaton who misunderstands, and who obeys only literal instructions of the law—but in total directness toward God.[49]

Paul's overarching combat language echoes themes not only in Jewish apocalyptic eschatology and Roman military culture but also in ancient Mediterranean terms generally that symbolized slavery with the language of "death" and "life." The classic statement comes from Roman law and its discussion on the etymological root of the Latin word for slave: "Slaves (*servi*) are so-called, because generals have a custom of selling their prisoners and thereby preserving (*servare*) rather than killing them: and indeed they are said to be *mancipia*, because they are captives in the hand (*manus*) of their enemies" (*Digesta* 1.5.4.2–3). In Pauline understanding, catechumens present themselves *as if* they were brought from death to life (6:13; note the baptismal cry in 8:15; cf. 7:25), with baptism participating in Christ's death and resurrection. The theme of "being dead to" also confirms for ancient studies the interpretative value of modern definitions of slavery as a "social death."[50] In addition, Paul's theological statements on baptism connect directly to his paraenesis later in the letter, a central plank of which is obedience to Rome's governing authorities (Rom 13:1-7). The paraenesis further confirms Paul's full participation and deep implication in the Augustan imperial ideology of *auctoritas*.[51]

Conclusion

Paul, in the final analysis, does not present a polemical argument against slavery as an ideology or institution in the Roman world. The dramatic persona of "the slave" served Paul as a rhetorical device for thinking about community, social categorization, hierarchy, and one's relation to the divine. The subject of Paul's speech-in-character (Rom 7:14-25) presented for an ancient Roman audience a recognizable stock voice of the slave self. Defining *pietas* in his gospel, the apostle uses the slave, and especially the trope of the faithful slave (*de fide servorum*), to "think with." Paul offers the slave experience of disassociation by change of owners as a metaphor for the situation of Gentile converts. The metaphor also corresponds to the Stoic philosophy of *prohairesis* (volition) that urged the integrity of the individual self in the face of moral slavery to the passions. Paul could not have been unaware that Gentile converts could not completely forget their former life in paganism. Using stereotypes about slaves familiar from wider "pagan" culture, Paul aims to help his encoded Gentile readers move into a dialogic relation with their old, pre-converted selves. The juxtaposition of two worldviews—the bad enslavement under Sin's domination and the good enslavement under God's *auctoritas*—allows each worldview to throw light on the other. The juxtaposition of one culture over against another is a fundamental feature of self-definition in Paul.[52] Of course, the slave is a common representation of the other, and of a person caught between two cultures.

The specific persona in Romans 7 is a captured war slave who undergoes an agonizing crisis of identity because it is alienated from its rightful owner. Every facet of the *anthrōpos*, both inner and outer, responds. Like all slaves, the persona is answerable to its new master (the demonic power Sin) with its body. The slave cannot control or prevent the violence inflicted on its body; it can only learn to withstand by a known passive strategy of disguised resistance common among all slaves, a "hidden transcript" of slave resistance that the "public transcript" of *auctoritas* created.[53] The persona is compelled to follow the new master, but in its external bodily members alone and only in habitual, mechanical obedience to individual commands (to the law of Sin) like an automaton. The subject of the slave's self takes solace in not letting Sin have *auctoritas* over it. A passive commodity of Sin, the persona delights in a different law (the holy law of God) inwardly. Its innermost self perseveres unwaveringly in total directness toward its true master (God), as a good and faithful slave (and Roman soldier) should, even when the master is not yet present. The enslaved self, though captured, retains its capacity to fight and its inner, subjective agency. Paul thus thinks of "the slave" in terms of *auctoritas*, the quintessentially Roman idea of personalized power.

The figure of the slave provides a powerful and compelling idiom through which to articulate Christian community formation and self-definition precisely because early Christians shared with wider "pagan" society the same set of cultural assumptions, literary tropes, and social stereotyping of the slave. As a metaphor for the transformation of the religious self by baptism "from death to life" existing within the eschatological tension of the Parousia being not yet present, the experience of enslavement was perfect for an ancient audience. Like a slave, the Pauline convert experienced the violent psychological force of personal upheaval, the social dishonor of turning away from one's family and traditional culture, and the natal alienation of losing one's whole past identity—getting a new name, having to learn a new language and worldview, and forming new (fictive) kinship relations.[54]

For the wider question of whether we can know anything about the private, hidden, or unconscious selves (that lie behind public constructions of ancient self-identity), the implications of this exegesis are limited, however.[55] Before making broad claims from first-person narratives about the accessibility of the self in religious sources, we must do close reading of the texts. Often those texts present voices that prove, in the end, not to be reflexive of the authorial self but to be artificial and literary. The extent to which Paul's statements can reasonably be said to provide a context for the idea of the self in early Christianity is hindered in part because the modern idea of self—as a unique individual, a possessor of a "real" or an "authentic" personality rather than a "bearer of character traits that are assessed in reference to general moral norms"— has no obvious equivalents in ancient Greek or Latin. The term "self" is also normatively and sometimes politically charged in modern discourse, particularly in reference to freedom and slavery. The definition of a slave as a "person" or "self" often leads too quickly into assertions about the recognition of moral and political rights for slaves, and evidence of ancient criticism of the institution of slavery.[56] Ideas such as that of "personality" and "self" need to be taken as part of a whole context, in the specific cultural milieu under study, and not just in isolation.[57]

The findings do, however, draw attention to the notion of voice as a literary construction. For our study of Paul, the most obvious connection to the larger question of the religious self in antiquity lies in the analytic categories of the "public transcript" (the voices of masters) and the "hidden transcript" (the voices of slaves). These categories, however, should not be taken as absolutely separable in the Pauline material. No evidence survives from antiquity that reflects the voices of slaves or their point of view that can then act as a methodological control on the evidence generated by Roman slaveholding society.[58] The so-called hidden transcript of "playing the automaton" would not have been very hidden to Paul's Roman audience. The act was well known in the ancient comedy of the "bad slave," which slaveholders created for their "public transcript" of domination, as Plutarch and the *Life of Aesop* prove.[59]

In the end, Paul's representation of "the slave" consists of a bland moral polarity of good and bad and is an artificial construction serving Roman slaveholding ideology. The apostle's speech-in-character uses such stereotyping to influence congregations, which would have only strengthened prejudices that his Gentile readers already held about the morality of control, domination, and abuse of human chattel. We learn, therefore, how Paul uses voice as an essential tool in his construction of the slave self. Yet, personifying the speech and character of a slave was not without risks for a freeborn adult male in the ancient world. It left him open to invective by rivals and opponents. In the next chapter, I examine how early Christian opponents questioned Paul's legitimacy to manhood and *auctoritas* by calling his speech and body "slavish," the use of slave physiognomics.

2

THE SLAVE BODY

Physiognomics and Invective against Paul

Having discussed Paul's use of slave speech, I am ready to examine his and his opponents' view of the slave body. The question leads us to the rhetoric of the accusation, preserved in the New Testament, that Paul was a religious fraud.[1] The most important instance of this accusation is 2 Cor 10:10, in which Paul reports invective against him that questions the legitimacy of his body and *logos*: "For they say (*phēsin*), 'His letters are weighty and strong, but his bodily presence is weak (*parousia tou sōmatos asthenēs*), and his speech contemptible.'"[2] Yet what exactly did Paul's opponents mean when they accused him of having a "weak bodily presence"? Why does Paul include the invective as part of his own defense? These exegetical questions remain unresolved among biblical scholars.[3]

Previous scholarship assumed the meaning of 2 Cor 10:10 to be obvious, no discussion being needed beyond noting that the physical description, presumably neutral, showed Paul suffering from chronic illness.[4] In a mode of exegesis that would become standard, many commentators interpreted the reference in light of the literary portrait in *The Acts of Paul and Thecla*, which describes Paul as short, bald, bow-legged, and with a crooked nose.[5] Although the assumption grew that this portrait was negative and typical of "the ugly Jew," a few commentators as early as Alfred Plummer and Rudolf Bultmann challenged the standard opinion and argued that the reference in 2 Cor 10:10 to Paul having a "weak bodily presence" was not a neutral description of Paul's physical appearance but a piece of rhetorical invective against Paul's moral character.[6] The questioning of the consensus encouraged other scholars to examine the passage more closely and to take it seriously as invective. Walter Schmithals developed a "pneumatic" interpretation, based on his reconstruction of Gnosticism, that Paul's "weak bodily presence" referred to what his opponents saw as a deficiency in "spiritual" ("pneumatic") powers, an exegetical solution that gained support among several scholars.[7] Ronald Hock suggested instead an economic approach, focusing the charge on Paul's decision to work with his own hands: Paul's lack of high social status as an artisan appeared "weak" and "servile" to the upper orders of Roman society.[8] Hans Dieter Betz turned the discussion toward an appreciation of the philosophical tradition and located the charge within the Socratic-Cynic tradition of disputes between philosophers and Sophists.[9] Other scholars, notably Peter Marshall, returned to the moral interpretation of Plummer and Bultmann, arguing that the accusation points to the "weakness" in Paul's character as a community leader when he acts as a "servile flatterer."[10]

In this chapter, I offer a new interpretation of 2 Cor 10:10 that builds on the Socratic-Cynic philosophical connections pioneered by Betz and the moral approach of Marshall. My argument is twofold. First, I suggest that the invective against Paul in 2 Cor 10:10 conforms to physiognomic conventions of what a "weak bodily presence" signified in the ancient Mediterranean—the body of a slave. The use of such physiognomics in political invective aimed to question an enemy's legitimacy to manhood by calling him slavish. Second, I contend that Paul chose to quote this invective because it served his apologetic goal to reveal the mistake of relying on outward appearances. Paul's apology in 2 Corinthians 10–13 belongs to a wider cultural conflict between Sophists, who rely on physiognomics to persuade, and Socratic-Cynic philosophers, who do not. The Sophistic gender construction of manhood through slave physiognomics becomes intelligible when we enter the cultural logic of a slaveholding society. In such a logic, the aristocratic adult male was not a man unless he acquired the honor (*dignitas*) that resulted from successful domination of others, in the particularly Roman sense of *auctoritas* that we defined in the last chapter. Commanding a strong bodily presence was essential for a man to hold legitimate claim to political office as well as to the three roles assigned to him in the family: husband, father, and master. Paul's enemies were trying to discredit him by alleging that he had a "weak bodily presence" betraying his naturally slavish inferiority.

The first section below examines the naturally slavish body in art, epic poetry, the philosophy of Aristotle, the professional physiognomic handbooks, dramatic slave masks, runaway-slave notices, and literary sources contemporaneous with Paul. The next section explains this physiognomic representation as part of a Greek and Roman rhetoric of manhood: the physiognomic distinctions between the slave body and the free body were not about actual slaves but were really aimed at sorting legitimate men (who rightfully dominate others) from illegitimate slavish impostors. The final section grounds this argument exegetically in Paul's philosophical defense of 2 Corinthians 10–13 by relating its military imagery (2 Cor 10:1-6) to Socratic-Cynic traditions praising Odysseus for taking the *schēma* of a slave during the siege of Troy.[11] My thesis, therefore, connects the work of Betz to that of the classicist Maud Gleason, who suggests that notions of gender identity in certain Roman authors, particularly the Sophists, "depend on polarized distinctions . . . that purport to characterize the gulf between men and women but actually serve to divide the male sex into legitimate and illegitimate players."[12] I propose that a similar phenomenon appears for the Roman physiognomic polarity of free and slave, which has little to do with actual slaves, but only between free men and slavish free men, and of which 2 Cor 10:10 is a specific example. In other words, the reference is *literary*, not social, description.

The Physiognomics of the Naturally Slavish Body

Physiognomics, the pseudoscience of reading an individual's body to detect character, status, or destiny, influenced Greek and Roman constructions of the female, the barbarian, the beast, and the slave as fixed character types.[13] Archaeological evidence shows such influence going back to the early Greek period. Attic vase paintings, for example, typically portray the free body with upright carriage, robust chest, broad shoulders, and well-proportioned frame, while depicting the slave body in a humiliating, crouched posture that is almost hidden, with diminished height, and with gestures frozen at some menial task for the master.[14] The bodily inversion contrasts the strong and the weak, two opposing ethical types. Whereas the free body displays strength, dignity, and heroic character in the ideal citizen, the slave body exhibits weakness, dishonor, and baseness in the lowly slave.[15] Such paintings reflect the ancient physiognomic principle that a weak bodily presence signifies a slave.

This physiognomic principle is present also in the earliest extant Greek literature. In Homeric epic, physique often reveals the natural division separating nobles and ignobles. For example, when Odysseus examines the Achaeans as they sail close to home, the commoner Thersites dares to pass as a prince. His body, however, betrays him: "He was bandy-legged and went lame of one foot, with shoulders stooped and drawn together over the chest, and above his skull the hair went up to a point, thinning at the top" (*Iliad* 2.216–219). Thersites' posture of stooped shoulders and drawn-in chest resembles the weak bodily presence of the crouching slaves in Attic vase paintings. Odysseus's father has the inverse body type. Despite old age, squalid condition, and tattered clothing, Laertes still possesses signs of strength and nobility: "You seem in no way like a slave either in build or stature. You look like a king" (*Odyssey* 24.252–253). The dramatic function of the scene operates on the presupposition that slaves "look" weak and small.[16] Yet an ironic reversal of this principle is also present in Homer. During the siege of Troy, it is reported, Odysseus had adopted the *schēma* of a slave (and of a beggar), allowing him to sneak into the city unnoticed by all except Helen (*Od.* 4.240–250). This exploit, deemed heroic, led to the fall of the stronghold. The episode presents a counterexample to physiognomic principles operative in other places of the narrative and is important for understanding why Paul would quote in 2 Cor 10:10 the invective that his enemies hurl against him, as will become clear below.

Greek assumptions about the slave exhibiting an inferior bodily presence find their first extant formal definition in the philosophy of Aristotle. As I pointed out in chapter 1, Aristotle reasoned that the "natural slave" (*kata physin doulos*) is a "tool that breathes" (*empsychon organon*) and is deficient in *aretē* and *logos*.[17] Defining the natural slave as a kind of "thing" (*ktēma*) to be owned, Aristotle claimed that its body, by virtue of anatomy, is biologically built for servility. He writes:

> And also the usefulness of slaves diverges little from that of animals; bodily service for the necessities of life is forthcoming from both, from slaves and from domestic animals alike. The intention of nature therefore is to make the bodies of the freemen and of slaves different—the latter brawny for necessary service, the former erect and unserviceable for such occupations, but serviceable for a life of citizenship (and that again divides into military service and the occupations of peace); though as a matter of fact often the very opposite comes about—slaves have the bodies of freemen and freemen the souls only; since this is certainly clear, that if freemen were born as distinguished in body as are the statues of the gods, everyone would say that those who were inferior

deserved to be these men's slaves; and if this is true in the case of the body, there is far more just reason for this rule being laid down in the case of the soul, but beauty of the soul is not so easy to see as beauty of the body. It is manifest therefore that there are cases of people of whom some are freemen and the others slaves by nature, and for these slavery is an institution both expedient and just. (*Politics* 1.2 [1254b25–35]; Rackham, LCL)

Although brawny in physique, the natural slave nonetheless is humble in bodily presence, like a beast of burden, and lacks the true essence of real strength defined by Greek liberty and heroic military service. In contrast, the adult male Athenian citizen commands by his "upright posture" (*orthon*) an essence so powerful as to be divine (*ousian einai theian*).[18]

Aristotle's theory of biological determinism for natural slaves, however, did not convince all in ancient Athenian society. Euripides and other Greek playwrights told stories of captured and enslaved nobles that suggested slavery to be an accident of fortune, not a determination of nature.[19] (Even Aristotle himself admitted, as I mentioned above, that not all enslaved persons were natural slaves; a freak of nature often gives a slave body type to a citizen and a free body type to a slave.) Yet the plays represent such Euripidean nobles incapable of lowering themselves, and so they retain their freedom even in captivity, whereas slaves who aspire to noble ends never manage to reach the full stature of dignified individuals.[20]

Athenians in general, then, defined slavery in terms of the body. Demosthenes, for example, differentiates the slave and the free by the degree of corporal punishment: "Slaves are responsible in person (*sōma*) for all offenses, while the freeman, even in the most unfortunate circumstances, can protect their persons" (*Adversus Androtionem* 55; repeated in *In Timocratem* 167; *De Chersoneso* 51). In fact, the repeated physical abuse of the whip broke down and reshaped the bodies of slaves, thereby creating in actuality the slave body that ideology required.[21] An enslaved person was deemed not a whole human being but merely a "body," which helps explain why the word *body* (*sōma*) is one in the Greek vocabulary for *slave*, a synecdoche that appears in Hellenistic Jewish writing (LXX Gen 36:6; 2 Macc 8:11) and in the New Testament (Rev 18:13, referring to slave cargo).[22]

Aristotle's theory of natural slaves, with its biological determinism, persisted into Hellenistic and Roman times and received detailed elaboration in the technical handbooks on physiognomics.[23] Although the earliest extant physiognomic handbook survives under Aristotle's name, and authorities like Pliny the Elder (*Naturalis historia* 11.273–74) and Diogenes Laertius (5.25) in the Roman era had assumed that Aristotle composed such a treatise, modern scholarship has shown the handbook to be a pseudepigraph, written in the third century B.C.E., and an epitome of two Peripatetic writers, often collectively called "Pseudo-Aristotle."[24] The work offers an eclectic method that was produced to correct previous methodologies. Its first author (chaps. 1–34) catalogs a series of twenty-two moral types (such as the Flirt, the Debaucher, the Irascible, and the Well-Born) and the signs by which each may be recognized, drawn from analogy with stereotypes seen in different ethnicities and animal species. The second writer (35–74) shows more concern for detailed reading of the body and its individual parts to discover inferences about personal character, stressing the importance of male and female types.[25]

For the physiognomics of the ancient slave body, the first author is more useful. He calls physiognomics the "skill" (*technē*) of detecting the "signs" (*semeia*) in the human body, and the professional physiognomist one who "draws his data from movements, shapes and colors, and from habits as appearing in the face, from the growth of hair, from the smoothness of the skin, from the voice, from the condition of the skin, from parts of the body, and from the general character of the body" (Ps.-Aristotle, *Physiognomonica* 2.806a28–34). The author teaches that "freedom of the soul follows freedom in the appearance of the body," which means loose-knit and agile shoulders, feet, and thighs (4.811a1–4). The servile and cowardly is the inverse of this loose and well-portioned body form, with bent body carriage constrained in movement, stiff shoulder blades, thick thighs, oversized forehead (3.807b5–12). A zoological method drawn from animal traits to detect inferior moral types is advised: red hair, for example, indicates "bad character; witness the foxes" (6.812a16–18). A ruddy complexion marks a "shameless man" whose figure is "not erect but inclines to stoop forward" in downcast, servile fashion (3.807b29–34). "Those people whose hair groups up and curls back are free-spirited (*eleutherioi*); witness the lions," whereas "those whose hair inclines to grow down from the head toward the nose are servile (*aneleutheroi*); this is appropriate, as the appearance looks slavish (*douloprepēs*)" (6.812b35–813a2).[26] The downcast hair enhances the subject's dishonor as the inferior other. Quite literally, the subject is faceless. Interestingly for our study of invective against Paul, this physiognomic method aims to detect slavish traits not necessarily in actual slaves—as if serving as some kind of owner's manual for slaveholders—but in freeborn people.

This Peripatetic tradition to detail the physiognomic signs of the slave body or, more precisely, the slavish freeborn body, finds particular use among Sophists in their invective against the flatterer as a moral type. In the tradition of the Second Sophistic (period after 60 C.E. when showpiece orators flourished), the Sophist and physiognomist Polemo of Laodicea writes that "small and shifty eyes" betoken the flatterer, a very wily and servile character who says one thing while secretly doing its opposite.[27] The flatterer lacks integrity in body and morality. Other servile traits that betray him and other inferior freeborns include "thick legs and heels," betokening "stupidity, insufficiency of understanding, and the natural character of slaves (*servorum mores*)."[28] Rather than an actual observation and measurement of slave legs and heels, the physiognomy is a rhetorical attempt to use slave anatomy (which in the physiognomic handbook tradition is invariably male) as a moral construct separating freeborns, and specifically freeborn men (which I shall argue below), into legitimate and illegitimate players.[29]

Servile typecasting of inferior freeborns is found not only in Polemo but also in a fourth-century C.E. anonymous Latin physiognomic treatise. Its author states that thick and heavy legs denote bad persons who lack moderation and shame, and who have a "servile character."[30] The author itemizes additional features like a small nose and blue eyes (with tiny pupils) signifying a deceitful, thieving, procrastinating, and "slavish disposition."[31] These features draw on those deemed deficient from the perspective of ancient Mediterranean culture: pale white complexion, blue (*glauci*) eyes, thick legs, and red hair. The traits are neither Greek nor Roman but *barbarian*, characteristic of dwellers on the world's remote edges—Celts, Scythians, and Thracians, for example—who are believed to be ill-tempered, rash, stupid, and otherwise culturally inferior because of alleged deleterious effects of their cold, northern climes.[32] The physiognomic theory, therefore, constructs the slave body as foreign and intrusive. It collapses the slave and the barbarian as the same moral type and connects both with vice, criminality, and a weak bodily presence.

Negative stereotyping connecting the slave with a weak bodily presence also appears in another important area of Greek and Roman culture—drama. Because dramatic slave figures (their gestures and masks) resemble iconic slave representations found in the physiognomic handbooks, many investigators have argued for a direct causal relationship, with the physiognomics influencing the playwrights and other artists involved in stage production.[33] Yet one can also imagine influence going in the opposite direction, from the playwrights to the physiognomists. We should question an assumption common among scholars that prescriptive writers influence imaginative writers (and artists generally).[34] Whichever the causal direction of influence, however, the representation of slaves in drama provides another piece of evidence alongside the physiognomic that a "weak bodily presence" signaled a slave or slavish man in Greek and Roman culture. Slaves, like other characters in New Comedy (such as grandpas, pimps, excellent youths, old women), were readily identifiable by their costume, their *schēma*. In the prologue to one of Plautus's plays, for example, the god Mercury refers to his "slave's getup (*servile schema*)" (*Amphitruo* 116–17).[35] More than any other costume piece, the mask (which covered the whole head) indicated this *schēma*. The mask represented a moral type based on Greek and Roman cultural assumptions and prejudices about the free and the slave. Comic slave masks in particular aimed to encourage the audience to equate the slave and the barbarian, and to laugh at both. Masks in archaeological reliefs show a striking contrast between the handsome countenance of the excellent youth and the hideous grimace of the slave.[36] Yet it is the Roman rhetorician Iulius Pollux who supplies the best extant description of slave masks. Analogous to the representation in the physiognomic handbooks, nearly all of the slave masks in Pollux's list are red-haired, and several have ruddy faces.[37]

This preponderance of the color red in the slave masks is curious and demands deeper analysis beyond noting its correlation with the prescriptive remarks of physiognomic authors, which only begs the larger question of what cultural significance the color red had in Greek and Roman society. Why would a red face signify a slave and somebody slavishly weak? One possibility is ethnocentric views of what is geographically normative. A ruddy face may betoken barbarity as a servile foreigner from the north whose pale white skin burns easily under the hot Mediterranean sun. Yet this hypothesis rests on the unexamined presupposition that actual observation of many (sunburned) ethnic foreigners, such as Celts or Scythians, in the Mediterranean slave population led to such representation of slaves in drama and in physiognomic handbooks. By situating slave physiognomics in its ethical and political context, I aim to suggest that this representation has a broader ideological function. The representation, I argue, has less to do with what actual slaves looked like (to their masters on the farm and home) and more to do with a rhetoric of manhood in Greek and Roman society. The ruddy face, particularly in Stoic ethics of Paul's day, marks the loss of manhood through the vices of excessive anger, fear, and lack of self-control. Seneca, for example, writes that the angry man looks "insane," his whole face being "crimson with blood that surges from the lowest depths of his heart" (*De ira* 1.1.3–4). To allege that a man had a red face was to question his manhood and so his legitimacy to dominate others. Such a man was infantile, womanish, slavish—a weak bodily presence.[38]

The ideological construction of the slave body as a weak bodily presence enforces a somatic hierarchy of manhood present also in runaway-slave notices, a source that many scholars rarely consider for purposes other than documentary because of an unexamined presupposition that it provides realistic, neutral descriptions of slave bodies. This "realistic" approach assumes that the vivid, personal detail and poignancy in many of the notices serve practical purposes of advertisement and so could reflect nothing other than accurate representation without idealization. Yet, as Dominic Montserrat argues, the descriptions in fact conform to perceived somatic norms and idealizations about the slavish and the free male body. In one of the most detailed of the extant runaway notices, originating from third-century C.E. Oxyrhynchus, the fugitive slave (whose name is lost) is described as

> an Egyptian from the village of Chenres in the Arthribite nome, utterly ignorant of Greek, tall, skinny, clean-shaven, with a [small] wound on the left side of the head, honey-complexioned, rather pale, with a wispy beard—in fact, with no hair at all to his beard—smooth-skinned, narrow in the jaws, long-nosed. By trade a weaver, he swaggers around as if he were someone of note, chattering in a shrill voice. He is about 32 years old. (*P. Oxy.* 51.3617)[39]

The language does more than facilitate apprehension of the fugitive. It enforces a somatic hierarchy by reducing him to a passive object laying illegitimate claim to manhood and deserving domination, as Montserrat explains:

> Naturally some of the bodily details are included here for entirely practical purposes, but there is a sub-text to their inclusion. Because he is a slave, he cannot be a 'real man', and the adjectives applied to the body of this anonymous slave serve both to set him physically apart and render him ridiculous. He is ugly and beardless, and thus infantile, although 32 years old; and like a child he goes around jabbering away as though he has delusions of grandeur.

Stress is also placed on the man's Egyptianness and his ignorance of Greek, and in general the whole text recalls the derogatory descriptions of indigenous Egyptians in writers such as Juvenal.[40]

One possible reason for this enforcement of a somatic hierarchy, especially in the Roman period, may be a tension in free male self-definition caused by the Roman urban institutionalized practice of manumission, which rendered the slave body and the free body potentially the same.[41] Such a paradox makes intelligible the need to emphasize patently slavish traits in this slave trying to run toward freedom. Toward this end, the runaway notice attacks the legitimacy of the fugitive's body and *logos*, precisely the two charges in the invective against Paul in 2 Cor 10:10.

Literary sources confirm also the use of slave physiognomics in the Roman period to maintain a somatic hierarchy between the slave and the free. Josephus writes that emperor Augustus sent a certain Celadus to check the face of an impostor posing as a prince. Celadus had no sooner set eyes on him than he "detected the points of difference in his face, and noted that his whole person had a coarser and servile appearance" (*J.W.* 2.106–108) (= *Ant.* 17.332–334). Philo of Alexandria assumes a slave had a "naturally slavish body," the coarse physical strength of which Philo uses as a rhetorical topos while also advancing the potentially contradictory idea that one's body does not determine one's ultimate status of freedom or slavery (*Prob.* 40).[42] Apollonius of Tyana, the hero of an ancient romance, argues that the body of a Greek boy from Arcadia, the Peloponnesian heartland, was nonbarbaric in ethnicity because the child "possessed all the good looks that Arcadians wear even in the midst of squalor" and was "by no means slave-like in appearance" (Flavius Philostratus, *Vita Apollonii* 8.7.12).[43] In another romance, by Chariton, physical beauty indicates high birth and nobility: "A person not freeborn," states one protagonist, "cannot be beautiful" (*De Chaerea et Callirhoe* 2.1.5).[44] Some Roman writers generalize such perceptions of the slave body to typecasting entire foreign populations as exhibiting properties of natural slavery; the "Jews and Syrians," writes Cicero, are people "born to be slaves" (*De provinciis consularibus* 5.10). Livy claims that "all Syrians" because of their "servile dispositions (*servilia ingenia*)" are better fitted to be slaves than warriors (35.49.8; see also 36.17.5–6).[45] These various examples show that a number of literary authors in the Greek and Roman world made a physiognomic connection between somatic inferiority—a weak, ugly bodily presence—and the condition of natural slavery.

Invective and the Greek and Roman Rhetoric of Manhood

One way upper-order Romans enforced somatic hierarchy was through invective. Yet the invective was rarely directed at slaves per se but rather at freeborn men, often political enemies, perceived to be slavish. Physiognomic distinctions between slave and free, therefore, had little to do with social description of actual slaves and more to do with the ancient rhetoric of manhood. The servile/free-looking dichotomy as a mask for disputes about manhood was operative in Greek and Roman thinking across the board, from oratory and history to moral philosophy, comedy, and satire.

The judicial oratory of Cicero provides rich examples of such physiognomic distinctions in Latin invective. Attacking L. Calpurnius Piso Caesonius, one of the consuls in office at the time of his exile in 58 B.C.E., Cicero focuses his invective on ridicule of Piso's deceptive facial features, which under physiognomic scrutiny betoken servility:

> Do you begin to see, monster, do you begin to realize how men loathe your impudence? No one complains that some Syrian or other, some member of a crew of newly-made slaves, has become Consul. We were not deceived by your slavish complexion (*color servilis*), your hairy cheeks, and your discolored teeth; it was your eyes, eyebrows, forehead, in a word, your whole countenance, which is a kind of silent speech of the mind, that pushed your fellow-men into delusion. This was how you tricked, betrayed, inveigled those who were unacquainted with you. There were but few of us who knew of your filthy vices, the crassness of your intelligence, and the sluggish ineptitude of your talk. Your voice had never been heard in the forum; never had your wisdom in council been put to the test; not a single deed had you achieved either in peace or war that was, I will not say famous, but even known. You crept into office by mistake, by the recommendation of your dingy family busts (*imagines*), with which you have no resemblance save color. (*In Pisonem* 1; Watts, LCL)[46]

Cicero accuses Piso of inconsistency, underscoring Piso's "slavish" complexion, hairy cheeks, rotten teeth, and inept speech as physiognomic signs pointing beyond the deluding mask of Roman *gravitas* with "one eyebrow soaring into your forehead and the other tucked down to the level of your chin" (*Pis.* 14). The invective encourages the audience to typecast Piso by caricatures familiar from Roman comedy; Piso's grave facade mimes the mask of the *senex iratus*, which bears no relation to the wretch behind it.[47] Piso's complexion, however suggestive of low birth, caused nobody to look at him as un-Roman before Cicero's speech; in fact his countenance made a deceptively favorable impression upon those who (before Cicero) attempted to do physiognomy on him.[48] Yet Cicero hopes to correct this error by revealing Piso as a monster by invective that reduces him to an animal, the antitype of the well-groomed Roman aristocrat.[49] Piso's teeth are said to be rotten, his beard unshaven, and his "slavish" complexion black like grimy ancestor masks (*imagines*) darkened with soot.[50]

But why does Cicero assume black to be a "servile color"? After reading the representations in the physiognomic handbooks and in the comic slave masks, we would expect a reference to ruddy. Proposed explanations include interpreting the black color reference either ethnographically, as a marker of Syrians whom Cicero judged proverbially slavish, or economically, as a sign of outside work (under the hot Mediterranean sun) deemed servile by upper-order Romans.[51] While these are possible, it is more probable that the reference to Piso's "black face" continues Cicero's calculated use of stock characters familiar from Roman comedy. Typically servile, the stock characters of the parasite and the flatterer have masks of dark complexion, which is a mark of cowardice in the physiognomic handbooks.[52] This interpretation holds because Cicero's invective against Piso's "slavish complexion" is part of his larger polemic against Piso's close associations with Epicureans, whose cultivation of friendships often led to charges of servile flattery.[53] Importantly, Cicero's invective is not evidence that Piso actually had a black face or otherwise looked like an ethnic Syrian. Rhetoric is not physical description. Invective need not be true but only point to real or imagined defects in an enemy's character by comparison with similar defects in shameful stock figures.[54] Cicero himself advises, in cases where an opponent has lived a blameless life or has a long-standing reputation, that an orator could concoct a charge that he has been "concealing his true character" (*De inventione rhetorica* 2.10.34).[55] This finding casts doubt on using 2 Cor 10:10, as much New Testament scholarship has done, as evidence for Paul's physical appearance.

An analogy, therefore, between this invective and that against Paul in 2 Cor 10:10 appears. Cicero's invective attacks the inconsistency of Piso's bodily presence, once having looked stern and authoritarian but now unmasked (by Cicero) as weak, slavish, and lacking true manhood. As Cicero claims Piso's face had a *gravitas* that was only a masquerade for his inner depravity and "sluggish ineptitude of speech," so also the rival apostles claim Paul's "weighty and strong" letters were only a masquerade for his truly "weak bodily presence" and "contemptible speech." Another similarity is the use of formal comparison (*synkrisis*) of credentials as a mode of invective.[56] The language does more than expose criminality. It makes Piso (and Paul) the object of all contempt, a man deprived of the attributes proper to a free citizen.[57]

Cicero's goal is to see Piso "abject, despised, scorned," reduced to a slavish creature that "peers into every corner and quakes at every whisper, that lives mistrustful of itself, without voice, liberty or authority, stripped of consular pride, a shivering, trembling, fawning, wretch" (*Pis.* 99). Such is physiognomic description of the weak, cowardly appearance of the natural slave.[58] In another speech, Cicero condemns Piso's "unkempt, boorish, sullen figure" that would lead anyone to "call him stockish, insipid, tongue-tied, a dull and brutish clod, a Cappadocian plucked from some slave-dealer's stock-in-trade" (*Post reditum in senatu* 14). The term *Cappadocian* meant a natural slave, a mockery in Greek and Latin invective similar to calling someone a "jail-bird Greekling" (*ergastulo Gracchus*) or a rustic "Phrygian."[59] Ancient invective often combined animal and slave metaphors in this fashion, as when Horace condemns certain men by writing, "O you mimics, you slavish herd!" (*Epistulae* 1.19.20). For Paul, a similar accusation of servility may have arisen over his admission to "have become all things to all people" (1 Cor 9:22).[60]

The reason to blame such behavior is its absence of manhood. Rhetorical handbooks provided Roman youths guidelines on how to look like real men. Mistakes that Cicero cautions against are base and unmanly actions that result from "a cowardly, slothful, servile, or womanish spirit" (*Tusculanae disputationes* 2.55). Dignity of demeanor is crucial. "There should be no effeminate bending of the neck," Cicero exhorts, "no twiddling of the fingers, no marking the rhythm with the finger-joint. He will control himself by the pose of his whole frame, and the vigorous and manly attitude of the body" (*De oratore* 59). Quintilian warns against shrugging one's shoulders, for it "produces a mean and servile gesture, which is even suggestive of dishonesty when men assume an attitude of flattery, admiration or fear" (*Institutio oratoria* 11.3.83). Furthermore, Quintilian advises learning the dramatic gestures that comedy employs to distinguish among "slaves, pimps, parasites, rustics, soldiers, harlots, maidservants, old men stern and mild, youths moral or luxurious, married women and girls" (*Inst.* 11.3.74), providing further evidence of the use of dramatic stereotypes in Greek and Roman oratory. An orator must secure dignity through specific gesticulation, such as carrying one's head erect, "for a droop suggests humility (*humilitas*)" (*Inst.* 11.3.69). The oratorical handbooks stress repeatedly the fragility of manhood; youths must master and maintain a strong bodily presence in order to become and remain legitimate men. Attacks against one's outward appearance and speaking ability, as in 2 Cor 10:10, must be interpreted in light of these cultural "beliefs about deportment as a system of signs that reveal both one's self-control and one's fitness to rule others."[61] In Greek and Roman invective, to accuse a person of a weak bodily presence and deficient speech is to call that person a slavish man unfit for public office or otherwise to dominate others.[62]

In addition to invective in judicial oratory and to advice in rhetorical handbooks, we find in the genre of history plenty of material that typecasts a target as physiognomically servile, demonstrating the widespread use of the convention. Such material appears regularly in narrative episodes about life under tyranny, in which men assume weak bodily demeanors pretending "assent by expression of their faces, which most readily play the slave" (Quintus Curtius Rufus, *Historiarum Alexandri* 8.4.30). The historian Tacitus condemns the servility of upper-order Romans who even while holding consular rank willingly become slavish men under the emperor Tiberius. "At Rome," he laments, "consuls, senators, and equestrians were rushing into slavery (*ruere in servitium*). The more exalted the personage, the grosser his hypocrisy and his haste" (*Annales* 1.7). Under Nero, upper-order Romans were also "quick to flattery," but a few like Seneca exhibited "frankness" more often than "servility" (*Ann.* 15.61). While some men, like Vitellius, were able to "screen servile knaveries (*servilis fallacias*)" behind political masks and office (*Ann.* 12.4), others, such as Otho, gained political power by overt flattery. "Otho did not fail his part," writes Tacitus, "He stretched out his hands and did obeisance to the common soldiers, threw kisses, and played in every way the slave (*omnia serviliter*) to secure the master's place" (*Historiae* 1.36), referring to the failures of the year of the four emperors (68–69 C.E.). These historical exempla teach that a weak demeanor in aristocratic leaders is slavish and leads to a loss of Roman manhood, and even to the stasis of civil war.

The condemnation of slavish appearance appears also in moral philosophy. Most of the philosophical examples belong to moral preaching against the flatterer and his weak bodily presence. Aristotle exhorts that "flatterers are always servile, and humble people flatterers" (*Eth. Nic.* 4.1125a), a view that continued into the Roman period.[63] Seneca, for example, warned that wealth and success can only bring "flatteries

instead of facts" and "cringing obsequiousness (*obsequium servile*)" substi-
tuted for frankness and loyalty (*De beneficiis* 6.30.5).[64] The term *obsequium*
alludes to a legally enforced act of servile deference that in addition to
specific work duties (*operae*) Roman freedpersons had to perform for
their former masters, now patrons.[65] The image is one of weakness, self-
debasement, and cowardice, the loss not only of manhood but also of
humanity, reflecting the literal meaning of the Latin term for flattery
(*adulatio*), which means the fawning or cringing of a dog.[66] Plutarch
says that such cringing flatterers are "freeborn by freak of fortune" but
"slaves by choice" (*Moralia* 13c). Before the town council of Prusa, Dio
Chrysostom boasts as proof of his own manhood that he never flattered
a tyrant (even the emperor Domitian) with a "single ignoble or servile
word" (*Orationes* 15.8), and he condemns flatterers as "altogether servile," reminding his audience that the term *slave* (*doulos*) applied originally not to chattels (either purchased or homebred) but to the freeborn
"man who lacked a free man's spirit (*aneleutheros*) and was of a servile
nature (*douloprepēs*)" (*Or.* 15.29). Being captured does not make a man a
slave, Dio claims, but rather being "insignificance in appearance, servile,
unsleeping, never smiling, ever quarreling and fighting with someone,
very much like a pander, who in garb as well as character is shameless"
(*Or.* 4.96). Likewise, Epictetus claims that a "deed of sale" does not make
one a slave (*Diatribai* 4.1.8) but the self-degradation of acting slavish,
especially while lovesick (*Diatr.* 4.1.15–18). In a similar fashion, Philo of
Alexandria writes that "fawning and flattery and dissembling, in which
the words are at war with the thought, are utterly slavish" (*Prob.* 99). All
these examples demonstrate that flattery and inconstancy were physiognomic signs of the slavish man whose ignoble gestures and weak bodily
presence served as a rhetoric topos for the antitype of manhood in Greek
and Roman moral philosophy.[67] Such moral preaching assumes a rhetoric of manhood similar to that in the moral exempla of historical literature and in the invective of judicial oratory aimed at typecasting an
enemy as physiognomically servile.

An exception, however, is found in the writings of Seneca the Younger.
He argues against using superficial signs as indicators of character. He
writes:

> This same standard, as I have remarked, is to be applied to things as well as to
> men; virtue is just as praiseworthy if it dwells in a sound and free body, as in
> one which is sickly or in bondage. Therefore, as regards your own virtue also,
> you will not praise it any more, if fortune has favored it by granting you a sound

body, than if fortune has endowed you with a body that is crippled in some
member, since that would mean rating a master low because he is dressed like
a slave (*ex servorum habitu*). For all those things over which Fate holds sway are
chattels—money, person, position—they are weak, shifting, prone to perish,
and of uncertain tenure. (*Epistulae morales* 66.23; Gummere, LCL)

Several issues are apparent. First is the assumption that a weak body is
a slave body, an equation that Seneca tries to dissuade his reader from
making; a master simply "dressed like a slave" does not necessarily make
him slavish. Second is Seneca's criticism of the (to his mind, misguided)
physiognomic habit of attempting to discover temperament and character from outward appearance. A third observation is that this preaching
against slave physiognomics has less to do with actual slaves and more with
the superficial judging of freeborns to detect whether virtue is present.
Importantly, although Seneca dislikes physiognomics, he nonetheless by
his protest shows its persistence in Roman culture. The passage by Seneca,
therefore, further demonstrates the use of slave physiognomics as a mask
for disputes about manhood that was operative in Roman thinking.

Other genres in which we find the charge of servility applied to weak,
freeborn males include ancient comedy, a source noted previously in
regard to Cicero's invective against Piso, and satire. The best example is
the parasite, a figure familiar from New Comedy and its adaptation in the
Roman *palliata*, which is the subject of chapter 3. The parasite fawns and
flatterers his social betters, runs "to play the slave (*praeservire*)" (Plautus,
Amph. 126), and acts as if he has made a voluntary "self-sale" to a master
(Plaut. *Persa* 145–146; *Stich.* 172, 195).[68] His gestures, such as hurrying at
the bidding of another, convey a weak bodily presence. The parasite is
also an important moral type in Roman satire. Lucian of Samosata wrote
a whole work devoted to the figure, entitled *The Parasite*, in which the
author lampoons the conflict between philosophy and rhetoric by making the shamelessly sponging parasite a rival of the Philosopher and the
Sophist for the favor of a rich patron. Yet it is another satire of Lucian
that provides his best extant physiognomic portrait of the slavish body as
an unmanly body. In a prose dialogue of a dream sequence involving the
figures Sculpture and Education, Lucian contrasts the dignified appearance of great teachers and the demeaned appearance of artisans devoid
of eloquence or learning. Education exhorts:

On the other hand, if you turn your back upon these men so great and noble,
upon glorious deeds and sublime words, upon a dignified appearance (*schēma*

euprepes), upon honor, esteem, praise, precedence, power and offices, upon fame for eloquence and felicitations for wit, then you will put on a filthy tunic, assume a servile appearance (*schēma douloprepes*), and hold bars and gravers and sledges and chisels in your hands, with your back bent over your work; you will be a groundling, with groundly ambitions, altogether humble (*tapeinos*); you will never lift your head, or conceive a single manly (*andrōdes*) or free (*eleutheron*) thought, and although you will plan to make your works well-balanced and well-shapen, you will not show any concern to make yourself well-balanced and sightly; on the contrary, you will make yourself a thing of less value than a block of stone. (*Somnium* [*Vita Luciani*] 13; Harmon, LCL) [69]

What the character shows concern over is the "servile appearance" of freeborns (in particular, potentially that of the narrator), not that of actual slaves. Lucian employs the physiognomics of the ancient slave body to reinforce a Roman rhetoric of manhood. The "slave-looking" and "free-looking" dichotomy functions to divide not the slave and the free but freeborn males into legitimate and illegitimate players. With the language of physiognomics, the passage articulates the fragility of manhood. Once a man falls into a weak, servile appearance, his mind and character become correspondingly slavish. Interestingly, Lucian uses the same term to describe this demeaning state (*tapeinos*) that we find in Paul's apology (2 Cor 10:1; cf. 11:7).

The language of physiognomics, however, did not convince all Greek and Roman authors, as I noted above in the case of Seneca. Many were skeptical about its accuracy, disbelieved it outright, or noted its notorious failure in the case of Socrates. Epictetus asks rhetorically, "Surely everything is not judged by its outward appearance only, is it?" and answers, "Therefore, neither are the nose and the eyes sufficient to prove that one is a human being, but you must see whether one has the judgments that belong to a human being" (*Diatr.* 4.5.19–21). Pliny the Elder comments on the physiognomic handbook attributed to Aristotle, "For my own part, I am surprised that Aristotle not only believed but also published his belief that our bodies contain premonitory signs of our career" (*Naturalis historia* 11.273). Despite Pliny's high regard for Aristotle as a "great master of the sciences," he declares flatly that "I think this view unfounded" (*Nat.* 11.273–274). Cicero reports the story of a certain physiognomist named Zopyrus "who professed to discover the entire characters and natures of people from their body, eyes, face, and brow" and who stigmatized Socrates as "stupid and thick-witted because he had not got hollows in the neck above the collar-bone," prompting a loud guffaw of disbelief from the Socratic disciple Alcibiades (*De fato* 10). [70] These examples reveal doubts about physiognomics as pseudoscience. As in the case of Zopyrus, the language of physiognomics could backfire on a speaker. Quintilian provides another anecdote about the failure of physiognomics to persuade, one especially relevant because it is used in a rhetorical context of invective. In his wider discussion of personal ridicule in judicial oratory, Quintilian advises caution because jokes, especially about looks, may recoil upon the orator. He recounts one law case debating the free status of an individual. The accusing orator, Sulpicius Longus—who, Quintilian reports, was "extremely ugly"—argued that the defendant must be a slave because he even had the "face of a slave." The defending orator, the famous Domitius Afer (whom Quintilian admired), replied, "Is it your profound conviction, Longus, that an ugly man must be a slave?" (*Institutio oratoria* 6.3.31–32), making Longus the butt of his own joke.[71]

We find, therefore, the use of physiognomics in a variety of literary genres, showing it to be a topos in the Greek and Roman rhetoric of manhood, which not all authors believed. This finding provides a new interpretative context in which to read the invective against Paul in 2 Cor 10:10, which questions the legitimacy of his body and *logos*. The language conforms to conventions and techniques of character assassination common in Greek and Latin invective. By questioning the legitimacy of Paul's body and *logos*, the rival apostles tried to get the Corinthians to think of Paul not as an individual but in terms of his alleged group affiliation with slavish men generally, like parasites and flatterers, deemed unfit to rule either family or community.[72] Paul is said to be "crafty" and one who took the Corinthians in "by deceit" (2 Cor 12:16). Paul responds by refraining from boasting, except of his weakness, "so no one may think better of me than what is seen in me or heard from me" (2 Cor 12:6), parodying the use of physiognomics to discredit him. "We rejoice," he writes, "when we are weak and you are strong" (2 Cor 13:9).

While the physiognomics of the ancient slave body provides an interpretative context for the invective against Paul, it nonetheless leaves several exegetical questions unresolved. Why does Paul report this invective in the first place? Perhaps he had to acknowledge it openly in order to refute it. But this solution only begs a second, larger question: Why does Paul encourage and even rejoice in the charge that he looks slavishly weak? One could simply note it as one among several instances in which Paul designates himself a "slave of Christ," but such analysis is not deep enough for the complex issues involved in the specific invective under study. Curiously, Paul accepts his opponents' charge that his bodily presence is weak, and he even boasts of his bodily weakness in a catalog of hardships (2 Cor 11:23-29), which includes subjection to repeated floggings. This corporal idiom did not mean heroic battle scars. Paul's "whippability" betokened his dishonor and servility, the boasting of beatings being exactly what Paul says it is: the boasting of things that show his weakness.[73] Although Paul does not choose the *schēma* of a slave—his opponents give it to him, perhaps because of his beatings—he nonetheless adopts the slave *schēma* as his own. Why does Paul boast of looking like a slave? This question leads us back to the work of Hans Dieter Betz, who argues that the tactic conforms to a Cynic apology in the Socratic tradition.

Cynic-Socratic *Apologia* and Paul at War

The letter fragment known as 2 Corinthians 10–13, as Hans Dieter Betz has shown, conforms to an apology within the Socratic-Cynic tradition.[74] Paul presents himself in the *schēma* of the Cynic philosopher, who appears "humble (*tapeinos*) when face to face" before the Corinthians but "bold when away" (2 Cor 10:1).[75] Paul employs military imagery showing that the stakes of the conflict have been raised above conventional warfare. "We do not wage war according to human standards (*kata sarka*)," he warns the Corinthians, "for the weapons of our warfare are not merely human, but they have divine power to destroy strongholds" (2 Cor 10:3-4). Such strongholds include "arguments and every proud obstacle raised up against the knowledge of God" (10:4-5). Paul threatens, further, to "take every thought captive to obey Christ," with a readiness "to punish every disobedience when your obedience is complete" (10:5-6), referring to the standard practice in the ancient world of enslaving prisoners of war in the wake of successful battles and sieges.[76] As part of his apology, Paul reports invective against him that questions the legitimacy of his body and *logos*.

This is a curious apology, since Paul renounces any proclamation of the gospel by means of rhetoric, patently denying the compatibility of a rhetorical defense (*apologeisthai*) with "speaking in Christ before God" (2 Cor 12:19). This renunciation, as it unfolds in the letter, is not of *all* apology for the gospel but only of a specific kind, the rhetorical art of persuasion that the Sophists craft. This rejection of apology in its *rhetorical* sense draws on the Socratic tradition, in which Socrates is presented as refusing to defend himself on Sophistic terms before the Athenian jury. Based on this famous episode, the Socratic tradition preserved in Plato and other writers proceeds to divide the art of "apology" into two kinds: (1) forensic speech, which operates with the techniques of rhetorical debate by which the Sophists aimed at persuading; and (2) the philosophical defense speech, which uses the Socratic method of *elenchos*, the ultimate goal of which is not persuasion but understanding. By using a philosophical apology, Paul attempts to expose the fallacy of the Sophistic kind that his opponents craft, in order to defend himself against charges that he acquired his apostolic office illegitimately and was, in short, a religious fraud.[77] Given that, as we saw above, Sophists like Polemo and orators like Cicero incorporated physiognomics into their rhetorical speech, drawing on comedic figures as fixed moral types, it is not that surprising to find Paul's opponents also employing this Sophistic mode of invective.

An important exegetical decision that supports this hypothesis regarding the influence of Socratic tradition on Paul is to read 2 Cor 10:1, "I who am humble (*tapeinos*) when face to face with you, but bold (*tharrō*) toward you when I am away," not as a restatement of the invective in 10:10 but as a reply to it.[78] Paul introduces the oxymoron of being "humble/servile" (*tapeinos*) and "bold" (*tharrein*) as part of his philosophical apology conforming to a Socratic tradition, appropriated by the Cynics, in which the philosopher, particularly Socrates, is described as "humble" (*tapeinos*). Interpreted in this Cynic-Socratic philosophical tradition, the pair "humble" (*tapeinos*) and "bold" (*tharrein*) assumes a positive value in Paul's cultural context. Paul draws on philosophical discussions of the appropriate *schēma* (fashion, manner) of the philosopher and the Cynic habit of self-deprecating irony to place his defense in terms used in the conflict between philosophers and Sophists.[79] I argue that Paul attacks rhetorical Sophistry for its particular use of physiognomics, specifically of the slavish body, by which his rival apostles tried to question Paul's manhood and right to dominate others. In this way, Paul belongs to a philosophical tradition that criticized physiognomics because of its encouragement of persuasion by superficial judgment based on stereotypes from comedic drama. Paul parodies such superficial judgment in his "foolish discourse" (2 Cor 11:21—12:10), in which he boasts of his "weakness," perhaps modeled upon performances of mimes as "fools" and "leading slaves" in Greek and Roman comedy.[80] Here, Paul shares the skepticism about the accuracy of physiognomics described above and, in like fashion, tries to make his opponents' use of physiognomics backfire. Paul exhorts the Corinthians not to "put up with it when someone makes slaves (*katadouloi*) of you" (2 Cor 11:20).

While this interpretative approach leads to a better understanding of curious terms such as the humble-and-bold pair in Paul's apology, it nonetheless does not explain all the diction. Why, for example, does Paul choose to frame his apology with intense military imagery (2 Cor 10:1-6)? How does assuming a "humble/servile" *schēma* relate to successful tactics in siege warfare? Paul warns the Corinthian congregation that he wages war "not according to human standards" because he has "weapons" not "merely human" but with "divine power to destroy strongholds" (2 Cor 10:3-4). This military imagery demands closer attention and connection to Paul's anti-Sophistic response to the invective in 2 Cor 10:10 attacking his body as slavishly weak in appearance.

Fortunately, Abraham Malherbe provides just such a connection.[81] Building on Betz's research, Malherbe suggests that the background for Paul's martial imagery, and specifically the use of a servile *schēma* to defeat strongholds, is part of a tradition that goes back to a well-known exploit of Odysseus described in Homer's *Odyssey*, one of the most important in the Trojan War. During the siege of Troy, Odysseus adopted the *schēma* of a slave to score a crucial military victory: "Flagellating himself with degrading strokes" and "flinging a wretched garment about his shoulders" to "look like a slave," Odysseus "crept into the wide-wayed city of the men he was fighting" where they were "all taken in" (*Od.* 4.240–250). Whereas the Socratic tradition came to see Odysseus representing a certain type of moral sage, the Sophists, most notably Gorgias, attacked Odysseus as cowardly and unscrupulous. Gorgias's student Antisthenes, however, defended Odysseus by comparing the military tactics of Odysseus and of Ajax. While Ajax lay snoring, Antistheses argues, Odysseus saved him by using "servile weapons (*douloprepē hopla*)," the rags, scars, and overall weak bodily presence that fooled the enemy.[82] War tends not to be a matter of appearances, Antisthenes reminds his audience, and despite Ajax's previous mockery of Odysseus's slave *schēma*, Odysseus in the end proved to be the better warrior.[83] As Malherbe shows, Paul in 2 Cor 10:1-6 appropriates this Antisthenic tradition, as developed by the Cynics in the Roman period, to counter charges against his consistency, courage, and strength.[84]

To be sure, the echo of Odysseus is not exact. Paul, unlike Odysseus, does not flagellate himself. But I argue that Paul's reference is *literary*. It need not correspond factually in every detail for the allusion to hold. Paul is quite willing, for example, to overlook (and change) details in other textual allusions and echoes, such as his peculiar handling of

Deut 30:12-14 (in Rom 10:5-10) and his allegorical reading of Genesis
that reverses Jewish tradition (in Gal 4:21—5:1). Paul has a penchant
for a *pesher*-style commentary on passages, focusing his attention on tag
phrases that connect to his own current situation, rather than paying
strict adherence to wooden readings.[85] While his opponents use the physiognomics of the slave body to question the legitimacy of Paul's personal
body and *logos,* Paul defends himself by taking the tag of the slave *schēma*
that connects his struggle to that of Odysseus, a famous counterexample
of the danger that confidence in outward appearance brings to strongholds under siege.[86]

Conclusion

Rather than a neutral description of Paul's physical appearance or evidence of so-called gnostic influences on Pauline Christianity, the reference to Paul's "weak bodily presence" and "contemptible speech" in
2 Cor 10:10 is best interpreted as slave physiognomics. The charge is
rhetorical and attacks Paul's moral character as a servile flatterer. The
invective draws on commonplace character-assassination techniques,
such as found in Cicero's invective against Piso, which typecast an enemy
as "looking" and "talking" like a natural slave. As part of his apologetic
strategy to build an anti-Sophistic response in the Socratic-Cynic tradition, Paul quoted this invective to expose the fallacy of its logic. In effect,
he wanted the charges to backfire, exposing his rivals as the true religious frauds. Paul's apology in 2 Corinthians 10–13 thus belongs to the
wider cultural conflict between Sophistic rhetoric, which relied on physiognomics, and Socratic philosophy, which did not.

   The physiognomics of the naturally slavish body is found in a variety
of classical sources: art, epic poetry, the works of Aristotle, the professional physiognomic handbooks, dramatic slave masks, oratory, history,
and runaway-slave notices. Such description purports to characterize the
gulf between the slave and the freeborn, but actually serves to divide the
freeborn male sex into legitimate and illegitimate players. The slave–
free polarity articulates a rhetoric of manhood achieved, in the logic
of a slaveholding society, through the successful domination of others,
which the Romans called *auctoritas.* Romans, and those emulating their
values, charged a male enemy with a "weak bodily presence" to label
him a slave and so to question his *ability to rule.* Slave physiognomics was
a discourse in the ancient ideologies of masculinity that was key in face-

to-face encounters with a rival, especially used among the Sophists. Not all ancient thinkers agreed with this use of physiognomics, however, and Paul was one of them.

3
THE COMEDY OF SLAVERY
IN STORY AND PARABLE

The last two chapters examined the evidence in Paul's letters for the rhetorical use of slaves as devices for invective and speech-in-character. Now we turn to the Gospels. As in the case with Paul, my goal is not to provide an encyclopedic inventory of all references to slaves but instead to trace the development of a theme. My interest lies in dramatic function and narrative context. In framing the question this way, I draw on the recent study of slavery and ancient comedy by the classicist Kathleen McCarthy, who suggests that what is needed is not a finer gauge for separating "the genuine" author from the "distracting accretions" of later redaction but "a way of theorizing the text as we have it."[1] I focus on two biblical stories by the same author, that of Luke–Acts, the second of which poses greater interpretative difficulties. The first is a slapstick bit of situation comedy, the "running slave" Rhoda (Acts 12:13-16). The parable of the Dishonest Manager (Luke 16:1-8) is more challenging, and many interpreters find it insoluble. In each case, I argue that artificiality in plot clearly signals a literary characterization of Roman slave comedy. Neither pericope depicts a real-life story from Mediterranean peasant society.

The Running Slave Rhoda (Acts 12:13-16)

Rhoda, the slave maid (*paidiskē*) in Acts 12:13-16, has been seen as a classic example of a touch of realism that lends authenticity to Luke's narrative. The vivid and precise detail of her flighty joy supposedly presents such a candid snapshot of her individuality and eccentric

Christian faith that it could only come from a historical source, perhaps the eyewitness reminiscence of Rhoda herself.[2] While less willing than earlier commentators to accept the description in its final form as factual, more recent scholars still perpetuate the goal of discerning the historical core behind the account and continue to read it as a piece of realistic drama.[3] Many, to be sure, have detected in the scene the presence of other elements, such as comedy and extraordinary suspense, but this idea is downplayed or subordinated as further evidence of realism; a few discount the idea as a modern reading.[4] Nonetheless, a consensus emerges: Rhoda's dramatic function in the narrative is to heighten realism. Some scholars then discover a further theological theme of liberation: Rhoda's genuine, assertive behavior to speak her mind "breaks down" the oppressive hierarchy between master and slave—revealing Luke's supposed subversion of slavery as a social institution—and the subsequent vindication of Rhoda's speech as trustworthy authenticates and uplifts the Christian witness of women (cf. Gal 3:28).[5]

What scholars advancing the "realistic" thesis overlook is the possibility that Luke has created a highly conventionalized sequence of action elaborated not to uplift slaves (or women) but to entertain with humor that dishonors them. In his important study offering the literary genre of ancient fiction as a more plausible background against which to read Acts, Richard Pervo departs from the consensus and explains the character Rhoda as "like a figure from New Comedy."[6] If Pervo is right, what remains unclear in this hypothesis is *which* specific stock figure. The formulaic nature of Rhoda's running routine provides a clue. Her situation and behavior correspond to those of a *servus currens*, the comic "running slave" familiar from Greek New Comedy, its adaptation in the Roman *palliata*, and its iconography in artifacts such as frescoes, mosaics, and terra-cotta figurines. Far from being a realistic representation that indicates Luke's use of some historical source, Rhoda is a running cliché of Greco-Roman situation comedy. Her function is to intensify the anticipation of the reader, to develop irony (inasmuch as the reader has more knowledge of the situation than do the characters), and to provide comic relief at a critical juncture in the narrative when all seems lost. Luke creates the artificial character, Rhoda, to heighten the audience's desire for a more realistic effect in the scene that follows, the appearance of Peter before the apostles.

The persona of the *servus currens* is among the most stylized, and most familiar, characters in the Roman *comoedia palliata* (comedy in Greek dress) extant in the plays of Plautus and Terence,[7] having its origins in

New (and Middle) Comedy.[8] The "running slave" was funny (to ancient Greeks and Romans) because it complicates artificially a simple messenger scene. A slave hurries onto the stage, breathless from haste and excitement, pretending to push aside invisible persons who crowd the street. He has unexpected, urgent news (good or bad) for another character, usually the master. In a monologue, he declares the extraordinary value of the news and its awesome effects, particularly on the personal interests of both master and slave. For being the first to tell, the slave anticipates a handsome reward such as extra food, special privileges, or manumission, which makes him deliriously happy. Yet a protracted delay always occurs, caused primarily by the melodramatic antics and backchat of the running slave, who is too frustrated and distracted to notice the business at hand.[9]

We know *servus currens* to be a technical term of Roman comedy, because ancient playwrights identify it as such. Terence's *The Self-Tormentor*, for example, has a prologue that lists the character among Plautine commonplace dramatis personae:

> Be fair—give me permission to put across a quiet comedy in silence, so that we don't always have to have a Running Slave (*servus currens*), an angry Senex, a greedy Parasite, an impudent Sycophant, a miserly Leno, all acted with the greatest noise and maximum effort. (Terence, *Hauton timorumenos* 35–40)[10]

Interestingly, the Plautine stock characters from which Terence distances himself are what he had produced two years earlier (161 B.C.E.) in *Eunuchus* (which brought him instant success), whose prologue justifies the use of clichés like the Running Slave (*servus currens*), the virtuous Matron, a wicked *Meretrix* (prostitute), a greedy Parasite, and a braggart *Miles* (soldier) (*Eun.* 35–37).[11] Although not as extreme as some of Plautus's examples, the Terentian cases of the running slave nevertheless use conventional motifs characteristic of the Plautine *servus currens*, and are just as unrealistic.[12]

Whether Plautine or Terentian, the *servus currens* had multiple functions. Socially, it dishonors slaves by stereotyping them as infantile adults whose puerile self-absorption and unmanly lack of emotional control invariably retard their own efforts to do even the most straightforward of duties asked of them.[13] Culturally, the humor reifies traditional Greco-Roman moral values about slavery and manhood as polar opposites, suggesting that to run at another's bidding is emasculatingly servile.[14] Artistically, the scene facilitates an iconographic portrayal of physiognomy signifying irrationality in the slave: the determined run, the splay and contortion of the body, and the grotesquely labile posture of a lunatic.[15] Dramatically, the running slave heightens suspense. George Duckworth distinguishes among three kinds of suspense: (1) suspense that is *uncertainty* because neither the spectators nor the other characters have foreknowledge of the slave's message (the Plautine technique); (2) suspense that is *anticipation* because the spectators learn the news immediately upon the entrance of the slave and the characters soon thereafter (another Plautine technique); and (3) suspense that combines anticipation and *irony* because the spectators know from earlier action of the drama what the announcement of the slave will be and have more knowledge of the situation than do the characters (the Terentian technique).[16]

The slave Pinacium in Plautus's *Stichus* is illustrative. He rushes on stage wildly exuberant, still holding his fishing gear from the previous scene, and shouts:

> No, not Mercury, the fabled messenger of Jove, e'er brought his sire so sweet a message as that I now bring my mistress. Oh, this breast of mine is brimming with delight and delectation! It likes me now to deal in naught but high hyperbole. The charms of all things lovable and lovely do I convey, and my heart doth overflow its banks and teem with joy. Push on, Pinacium, prick on thy feet, and fructify thy words with deed—now art thou empowered to win thee fame and praise and honor—and aid thy mistress all bereft who anxiously awaits the coming of Epignomus, her husband. Quite as beseems her does she love that husband, long for him ardently. (*Stichus* 274–283; Nixon, LCL)

Pinacium then elaborately prepares himself for action: "On now, Pinacium, as thou dost please, run as thou likest! Care not a straw for any man alive! Elbow them all from thy path! Clean them out and clear the road! Be it a monarch that blocks thy course, up and land that monarch on his neck!" (*Stic.* 284–287). The parasite of the play, Gelasimus, sees the steamrollering slave flailing his bait and tackle to brush aside imaginary people, and he makes an aside, "What the deuce makes the little friskyromper so fond of running? He's carrying a rod, and a basket and a bit of tackle" (*Stic.* 288–289). Too self-absorbed to notice Gelasimus, Pinacium stops to think about how the servility of running compromises his own self-importance: "And yet, methinks, 'twere more fitting for mistress to petition me and send me envoys and gifts of gold and a four-horse chariot for transportation. No indeed, travel afoot is not for me. So back I go forthwith" (*Stic.* 290–292). He then struts back to his starting point and pontificates:

I hold it proper that I be approached myself, that I be appealed to. Canst think, forsooth, that what I now know is but a trifling thing of no account? Why, such good news from the port am I reporting, such bounteous bliss am I returning with, that mistress herself, unless informed, could hardly venture to pray it of the gods. And now am I to be a porter of such news, unasked? It suits me not, 'tis not my notion of a manly part. I feel it more befits a message such as mine that she come meet me and beseech that I impart it. Hauteur sits well on those whom fortune favors. (*Stic.* 293–299)

Pinacium soon comes back to (partial) reality, girds himself with the bravado of the best Olympic athletes, and dashes home, where he hammers on and eventually gets into a fight with the door:

And yet, on second thoughts, how could she know that I know this? Ah well, I see I must return, speak out, unfold it all, and sweep away her sorrow, over-top the good deeds of my sires and top off mistress' woes with an unexpected, timely blessing. Those efforts of Talthybius I'll scrap, and hold all messengers in scorn. Likewise I'll try my stride for the Olympic games. But what a rotten place to run! This track's too short. How do I regret it. What ho! I see the door is shut. I'll go and knock. Open up this door and do it double-quick! Throw it open wide, wide! No more dawdling! The appalling slackness of this house-hold! See how long I have to stand and knock! Busy, are you, taking naps? I'll find out which is stronger, this door or these elbows and feet. Ugh! I wish this door had run away from home, so as to be let in for some good sound disci-pline. I'm exhausted from pounding. Now for a knock-out! There! Curse you! (*Stic.* 300–314)

Pinacium eventually pounds his way into the house. Yet he is so breathless and eager to spill out his news that he has difficulty in composing himself enough to deliver it, only to suffer verbal abuse from other characters, including his mistress, who chastises her slave for acting shamefully. This abuse is like that in similar scenes of other plays in which the *servus currens* is accused of having "confounded talk" (Plautus, *Asinaria* 446), speaking nonsense (Terence, *Phormio* 840–846), being "drunk" (Terence, *Eun.* 655), or acting psychotic (Terence, *Adelphi* 300–325). The knocking at a door and the frustrating delay of an answer elaborate a formulaic part of the comic apparatus.[17]

The situation comedy was so popular among Roman audiences that there are even scenes in which a character plays the character of *servus currens*. Plautus inserts such metatheater in the midst of a play whose plot revolves around the failure to distinguish slaves from masters, a Saturna-lian inversion of slave characters posing as free people and free charac-ters as slaves. In the play, one of Hegio's sons has been taken prisoner in a battle with the Eleans, the other stolen by a runaway slave who sold him at four years of age. Hegio is in great anxiety to recover the captured boy, thinking the other one long lost, but a parasite named Ergasilus spots the son, along with the fugitive who stole the younger boy, at the harbor. Elated over his good fortune, the character turns to the audience and does a comedian's stand-up routine announcing his intention to be the only one in the play to do the slave's part right:

> Supreme Jupiter! You save me and enrich me with wealth. Boundless abundance, yes, sumptuous abundance do you bring me! Praise, profit, play, merriment, jollity, feasting, a parade of victuals, eats, drinks, satiety, delight! Never will I come begging to a human being again, I now resolve it. Why, I can advance my friend and ruin my foe, now that this delightful day has loaded me with its delightful delightfulness! I've landed a legacy stuffed fit to burst, and no strings attached! Now for a race up to old Hegio here. I'm bringing him all the happiness he craves of heaven, and more, too. Now I have made up my mind; I'll put my cloak over my shoulder in the same way that comic slaves (*comici servi*) do and run, so that I'll be the first one from whom he hears this news. And I hope to get food forever and ever for my information. (Plautus, *Captivi* 768–780; Nixon, LCL)

The antics of the parasite Ergasilus provide comic relief from the disconcerting actions of earlier scenes. The serious dilemmas of the plot become for Ergasilus mere obstacles to dinner. The metatheater proves awareness by poet and public of the established conventions of the *servus currens*.[18]

The conventions of the *servus currens* provide the best interpretative context in which to read the actions of the slave Rhoda in Acts. The scene is a private house, the *oikia* of "the mother of the John whose other name was Mark" (Acts 12:12). Peter's arrival at the gate and the subsequent behavior of Rhoda are anticipated by the previous scene of Peter's disbelief at what he sees (Acts 12:9) and his experience of disorientation (cf. Acts 12:11). This preparation serves to increase the urgency and importance of Rhoda's message. Rhoda's entrance, prompted by Peter's knocking at the gate (Acts 12:13), makes direct reference to both the slave's haste (*eisdramousa*) and her announcement (*apēngeilen*). Her extreme joy (*apo tēs charas*) makes her too distracted simply to open the door for Peter (Acts 12:14), so determined is she to be the first to tell the others inside that the person they pray for is at hand. An ancient audience familiar with the *servus currens* stock figure would have likely seen Rhoda's flighty delight as a sign not of her faith but of her lust for a reward such as extra food or even manumission, the ultimate prize imaginable that motivates slave exuberance.

There is the invariable delay caused by her own melodramatic antics, which disturb those inside from prayer. Upset from being bothered, the other characters frustrate Rhoda by saying, "you are out of your mind" (*mainē*), but Rhoda vents her indignation and talks back (*diischyrizeto houtōs echein*), only to be told that she is seeing things (Acts 12:15).[19] Here, Rhoda's reaction conforms to the stereotype of the "running slave" who imagines invisible people in the street and dares to lecture social betters, including the master. The dramatic use of melodrama to delay the delivery of the message, rather than the usual (male) determination to get people out of the way, displays a female slave's rendition of the *serva currens* scene.[20] The tension of urgency does not stop with Rhoda's impulsive decision to the deliver her message at all costs. There is delayed recognition of the obvious solution: she fails to fetch the caller, Peter, who continues all the while to knock at the gate (Acts 12:16), so distracted is she from the business at hand. She ignores the very person standing nearby about whom she frantically runs.

In Acts for a brief moment Rhoda holds the narrative spotlight, and blows it. Such is the blunder of a "running slave,"[21] often a "protatic" character who introduces incidental dialogue and then disappears from the scene, never to reappear.[22] The dramatic effect is suspense, but of neither uncertainty nor surprise, for the reader already knows that Peter has been miraculously rescued and is really at the gate. Luke heightens a specific kind of suspense aimed at the reader—anticipation—and so creates irony caused by the incongruity between the words of the drama and its accompanying situation, which is understood by the reader but not by the characters doing the action. In this function, the narrative of Acts displays the Terentian technique.[23]

Yet why does Luke include a *serva currens* at this particular point of his narrative and not elsewhere? As a highly conventionalized sequence of action, the "running slave" is an instance of a phenomenon characteristic of New and Roman Comedy, which was developed, paradoxically, when the prevailing taste in art and literature was toward greater realism.[24] The device created tension between the sense of the artificial and the desire for a more realistic effect in the scenes to follow. The resultant paradox provided one of the greatest opportunities for irony and intertextual humor in ancient literature. In his excellent study of the *servus currens*, Eric Csapo explains, "An ironic posture towards artifice is typical of the 'realistic style' in any era: when an artist cannot do without an artificial device, he can at least label it, expose it and place it at a moral distance."[25] The sequence is a piece of escapist comedy that siphons implausibility from the scene, by which the subsequent action could be made to seem more real.[26]

As several commentators have observed, Luke's intention is to parallel the Rhoda scene in Acts with the events in the Gospel immediately following Jesus' resurrection in order to represent the indirect heightening of the miraculous: the first witness to Peter's release is a woman (Rhoda), whose report, like that of the women who went to Jesus' tomb, is not believed (Acts 12:13-15; cf. Luke 24:11).[27] According to Pervo, the use of entertainment and especially humor in scenes when all seems lost for the characters is critical to the plot development of Acts, since Luke's goal throughout the narrative is to hold the interest of his audience.[28] The insertion of a stock *serva currens* scene in Acts 12, a critical turn in the narrative when all believe Peter to be dead, is one way Luke uses humor to do just that. By providing comic relief, the author aims to heighten anticipation in the audience for a more realistic effect in the following scene, the apostles' encounter with the miraculously rescued Peter (Acts 12:16b-17), and by parallel their encounter with the resurrected Christ (Luke 24:13-53). Rather than advancing a theme of liberation that subverts slavery, Luke reinforces its institution and ideology by making Rhoda a running cliché that encourages laughter at her as a moral inferior even when her news is true.

The Dishonest Manager (Luke 16:1-8)

While the story of Rhoda represents a fairly uncomplicated running-slave routine and a straightforward bit of slapstick comedy, the Dishonest Manager poses more of a challenge. In fact, the parable is arguably the most difficult in the New Testament. The elite steward (manager, *oikonomos*) of a rich master faces charges of squandering the property and is under the threat of imminent dismissal. He laments his troubles in a monologue but resolves to control the situation. He decides to use his last *oikonomos* opportunity to gain the friendship and hospitality of his master's debtors. Lying about his authorization to act on behalf of his master, he summons the debtors one by one and instructs each to reduce his own debt by a set amount in the ledger. The master learns of the deception and—surprise—praises his "dishonest manager" (*oikonomos tēs adikias*) for acting "shrewdly" (*phronimōs*) (Luke 16:1-8). Appearing only in Luke, the narrative presents a rogue who betters his master, and is rewarded for it.

The amorality of praising a dishonest rascal for his shrewdness has simply been unacceptable to interpreters who seek moral, theological, or edifying lessons in all of Jesus' parables. Adolf Jülicher denounced attempts to explain away the problem through allegory and declared the parable the *crux interpretum* among all in the Gospels. A hundred years later, the designation still stands.[29] To clarify this difficult text, we should follow its comedy, as we did with Rhoda above.

My analysis below examines the parasite (*parasitus*) in ancient theater, connects it to the persona of the clever (trickster) slave (*servus callidus*), and argues that both dramatic types are combined in Luke's dishonest manager, as they are in Roman comedy generally. The last section considers farce in light of naturalism, its counterpart comedic mode, and reflects on the social effects of farce in Roman imperial society, and the reasons for its dramatic production. My thesis is that the parable shows strict adherence to a limited set of conventions used to give precise knowledge about the fictive world represented. The dishonest manager is the parasite playing the *servus callidus*.

The Comic Stage Parasite

A professional sponger type, the Parasite appears not only satire, but also in philosophy, rhetoric, writings of the Second Sophistic, and the anecdotes of symposium literature.[30] Roman comedy especially uses the persona of the *parasitus* as a stock character, having its ancestry in the *kolax* (flatterer, toady) and *sykophantēs* (swindler) of New (and Middle) Comedy.[31] Precisely because New Comedy shows his character and art (*technē*) to be so completely a product of stereotype and comic conventions, the parasite is more explicitly artificial than other dramatic types. The parasite's great flexibility for episodic adventure provided one of the richest sources of thematic development in ancient comedy. Conforming to Greco-Roman ideological constructions of masculinity as normative and generic, the characterization of the parasite is invariably male and includes a number of stereotypical traits. He cannot exist without a host, transacts business as a cheap hireling/agent, sees parasitism as a career, takes after the slave on the level of comic convention, has a penchant for absolutes and extremes, and relocates to new hosts when resources from the current one are gone.[32]

First, the parasite needs a host. Driven not so much by greed as by fear of poverty, the comic parasite is willing to be a lackey for anyone providing a meal and a household welcome. The obsession renders him a cheap hireling, doing passable work in various tasks but mainly serving one or several patrons regularly as agent or financial manager. J. O. Lofberg explains the characterization in Plautine comedy:

> The most easily employed agent that a family of wealth could find was naturally the parasite. Men of this profession admitted that they were available for any service. The parasite Artotrogus is sent by Pyrgopolynices to conduct the *latrones* that he had collected to Seleucus. The wife of Epigonus sends the family dependent (parasite) Gelasimus to the harbor for news of her husband. The parasite in the *Asinaria* is his master's clerk. Curculio is a very efficient agent for Phaedromus. He goes on a mission to borrow money for his *rex*. To further the latter's interests he steals an important seal ring, connives at a forgery, and is ready to serve as witness in a "shady" affair. . . . This identification of the parasite with the sycophant was but natural. The only essential difference was in the remuneration they received. This very difference rendered the parasite a much more "comic" character than the sycophant. . . . And since they are practically alike in methods, availability, and general character, and since the parasite was an established convention in the New Comedy, a playwright could easily motivate his presence in a comedy by letting him serve as Jack-of-all-trades.[33]

As an elite steward, the parasite transacts business for his master—running errands, acting as agent, and collecting debts (Plautus, *Bacchides* 573–576). He drafts financial instruments, collects payments, and takes receipts for all family members, placing him often in the awkward but comic position of having to serve two masters, typically the father and the son, pitted against each other (cf. Luke 16:13).[34] Yet the parasite does his best work in deceit, for which he receives praise—"Ah, you're the one and only artist at this business" (Plautus, *Asin.* 748; full context, 746–809)— and often drafts contracts for youths in schemes to pay for their furtive love affairs. The parasite, then, has a reputation for underhandedness, typically as clerk or agent of a wealthy household, the same occupation as Luke's dishonest manager.[35]

Second, the parasite cannot stop being a parasite. He is incapable either through situation or temperament to do real work and earn an independent living. He prefers material satiety over freedom and considers parasitism his only possible career.[36] The parasite Saturio, for example, claims that his parasitical vocation follows proud ancestral tradition.

He boasts:

> The ancient and venerable vocation of my ancestors I continue, follow, and cultivate with constant care. For never a one of my ancestors was there who didn't provide for his belly as a professional parasite. My father, grandfather, great-grandfather, great-great grandfather, great-great-great grandfather, and his father, too, always ate other folks' food, just like mice, and not a soul could beat 'em at voraciousness. Yes, and their family surname was Hardheads. It's from them I inherit this profession and ancestral position of mine. (Plautus, *Persae* 53–61; Nixon, LCL)

Parasitism, then, is a family business. Saturio's careerism goes even further, to promote the parasite's voluntary destitution on principle. "A parasite with his own money," he philosophizes, "is a ruined man: he instantly hankers to begin banqueting, to gobble things down at his own expense, if he has the wherewithal. It very well behooves a parasite to be a destitute Cynic (*cynicum esse egentem oportet parasitum probe*)—let him have a flask, strigil, cup, sandals, cloak, and a purse having next to nothing for the sole delectation of his very own household" (Plautus, *Pers.* 118–126).[37] This philosophizing belongs to the general penchant of the parasite for reciting pretentious scruples (Plautus, *Curculio* 349).[38] That the "hungry parasite" sponges off others at the cost of his being his own man is also a piece of gender farce. The parasite fancies himself a member of aristocratic society but lacks the acquired honor (*dignitas*) and mastery (*auctoritas*) that resulted from the successful domination of others, which Roman ideologies of manhood required of aristocratic males.[39]

Third, although technically a free professional type, the parasite is nonetheless a slave on the level of comic convention. Like slaves, the parasite receives verbal abuse as a moral inferior (rascal, *improbus*) and by his own admission is no more than a surrogate body of his master (*integumentum corporis*: Plautus, *Bacch.* 577–611). The emphasis on food and corporal constitution contributes to the reduction of the parasite to a mere body. He is an infantile adult (e.g., the chronic bed wetter in Plautus, *Curc.* 413–417), feminized male (called "Missy" in Plautus, *The Captives* 69–76), and animalized (dubbed as "mice," "dogs" in *Capt.* 77–90). This dehumanization includes the slaveholders' habit of no-naming their inferiors. Parasites often do not bear actual names but homonyms of and dehumanizing puns on the dramatic type they represent; most do not have names at all, only being called *Parasitus*.[40] Such monikers function as synecdoche, in which appetite is put for the whole of the character, and promote servility in the parasite. The parasite calls himself a "freedman" of his master (Plautus, *Curc.* 413), offers his body "for sale" in mock slave auction (Plautus, *Stic.* 193–236), and "chains himself" to anyone providing a meal (Plautus, *Curc.* 384–412; *Asin.* 912–918; *Menaechmi* 79–109). This verbal abuse, emphasis on the body, no-naming, and servile diction all characterize the parasite as a slave, not a "man," according to ancient ideologies of masculinity and manhood.[41]

Fourth, the parasite cries much and often, having a penchant for extremes and absolutes. His monologue is an important dramatic technique for this characterization. He bemoans his lack of free dinner as a sign of supreme failure in the moral world order. The monologue responds hysterically to scenes of disaster, often of the parasite's own making, such as brokering a deal that does not go through, being discovered to squander the property of the master, or falling into some mishap that results in host abandonment. The parasite wails, "Oh Lord, I'm dead, dead, beyond a doubt, without one human obligation," often sees no other option but suicide (Plautus, *Stic.* 497–504), and exclaims again, "I am a dead man! I can barely see! My teeth are full of rheum, my jaws are bleary-eyed with hunger! Such a state as I am in, all from lack of food, from intestinal fatigue!" (Plautus, *Curc.* 317–319).[42] He complains repeatedly that the loss of a host reduces him to the level of a rodent, forced to nibble only twigs and brambles (Plautus, *Capt.* 185–190), and he blames his personal shortfall on a world conspiracy (*Capt.* 461–497; see also 134–137). He cries over his lack of dinner as equal in suffering to the calamities befalling more serious and fragile characters (152–153), philosophizes on the cruel reversal of fate (142–145), and bemoans holidays when hosts leave town as national disasters (82–84).[43]

The interior monologue of Gelasimus, the parasite of Plautus's *Stichus*, is illustrative of the dramatic technique involved. Plagued by mockery and depressed by isolation, he cries out:

> I am a miserable man; dire misfortunes have befallen me. Alas! It is my possessions that have made me a miserable man—countless drinks quite dead and gone—and all the poor dead dinners I have mourned, besides—and all the draughts of mead, aye, and noonday meals that I have missed within these last three years! Alas, alas, sorrow and suffering have made me old before my time; I am almost dead and gone myself from hunger. (*Stic.* 209–216)

The comedy is obvious even to the slave maid standing nearby, who laughs: "He's just the funniest fellow ever, when he's ravenous" (*Stic.* 217). The monologue allows the audience to eavesdrop and follow the parasite's interior dilemmas with increasing empathy (e.g., 631–640). The disaster threatens to carry spectators, both inside and outside the story, away toward a more serious world. But the blunt stereotypes and clear absurdities introduced in the parasite's monody anchor an otherwise distressful situation back in the comic artificiality of farce.[44]

Fifth, the parasite stands ready to transfer his attentions to a new host when resources from the current one appear about to be exhausted or denied. Regaining composure from the full horror of having no more free dinners, the parasite invariably refocuses his attention to damage control involving intrigue. The frank declaration and formulaic routine are both utterly familiar and yet satisfyingly different every time. His machinations frequently target the households of potential hosts or that of his old host. Seizing his opportunity, the parasite Gelasimus, for example, exclaims with glee, "I've consulted my books; I'm absolutely sure I can hold my patron, I'll be so comical," and takes on the role of the comic trickster (*Stic.* 454–455). The parasite's true loyalty, though, lies with his own stomach, not with his host. The routine even serves as a commonplace in moral philosophy. Plutarch writes, "The flies do not stay after the good food is gone, nor the retainers after their patron's usefulness is gone" (*Moralia* 94c).

While amusing, the topos of the parasite does more than offer mere comic relief. The parasite is not, as previously thought, always an "inorganic" character inessential to the plot, having a superfluous or only an incidental relationship to others in the play. Rather, the parasite is a catalyst who provokes important insights from more serious and complex characters in the narrative. His monologue presents an ironic world vision, a moral commentary upon the motives and actions of the aristocratic elite. Although lacking nobility himself, he expects noble conduct from others, especially the rich, being a sounding board for their hypocrisy and greed. As a stock character whose personality does not alter with circumstances, the parasite is not developed for the sake of humor alone but serves to measure the fragility and unpredictability of the more realistic persons in the foreground. Understanding this dramatic function and narrative structure allows the interpreter to bridge the otherwise puzzling gulf between a play's humor and its serious content.[45]

In sum, the parasite is a play on conventions specific to Roman slave comedy. The figure is literary, a professional type of trickster. This finding leads to the template that defines and measures the form of all tricksters in ancient drama, the *servus callidus*.[46]

The Clever Slave

The persona of the *servus callidus* (clever or wily slave) is one of those stock tricksters in ancient literature who make fools of the rich, perhaps the most picaresque in Roman theater, going back to the early Latin *palliata*, drawing on models from New and Middle Comedy, and achieving classic form in Plautus, who is our main extant source.[47] The comedy for Romans lay in the farce of a slave as hero (or rather, antihero) displaying the *calliditas* that reversed the natural moral order. Although *calliditas* can be complimentary in Latin, it usually is not, having far more frequently the sense of cunning, craft, slyness, and artfulness in the negative moral sense (like its English translation "shrewd"). The term denotes the (underhanded) practical wisdom of social inferiors or the cunning of animals.[48] In this way, the Latin term is equivalent to the Greek *phronimos*. The *servus callidus* rules the world of farce, yet his schemes ironically work to reinforce his domestic subordination and to keep his servile position secure so that he can cause more general mischief.[49] This is why his machinations never aim to achieve his own manumission. The clever slave does not wish to leave the household of his master and does not accept freedom, "not even three freedoms," for the chance to concoct some mischief (Plautus, *Casina* 504–505).[50] The trickster's routine has no goal other than farce, going exactly nowhere in dramatic terms, a cycle of skits rather than some linear teleological development from problem to resolution. The clever slave is a literary artifice created by masters, not social reality of how slaves actually behaved or wished they could behave.[51]

The comedy begins by a setup. The *servus callidus* holds a position of responsibility in the master's household, such as manager. Then, a domestic crisis, love triangle, or just plain incompetence (or outright squander) calls for the slave's need of quick cash. In a monologue, the clever slave bewails all being lost, asks himself what to do (often lacking farsightedness), and has to devise his plan on the spot.[52] The monologue cultivates empathy for the bold intrigue, recruiting the audience as an ally of the deceiver. A good example is the clever slave Tranio. He announces:

> The god Jupiter Almighty is after us, with all his might and power, and bound to ruin me and young master Philolaches for good! Our hope is gone; Confidence can't be found; not even Salvation herself can save us now, even if the goddess wanted to! I just saw such a huge mountain of trouble and misery at the harbor! Master's back from abroad, and I myself, Tranio, am bound for ruin! (*to the audience*) Anyone want to make a bit of fast money by taking my place at an execution scene? . . . (*to the son*) Hush, hush! I'm the man to

cook up a shrewd plan for you. Will you be satisfied, if I fix it so that when
your father arrives, he'll not only keep out of the house, but run as fast as he
can to get out of the neighborhood? (*to the other household slaves*) You guys, go
inside now, yes you! Hurry, clear away this stuff! (Plautus, *Mostellaria* 350–390;
Nixon, LCL)

Even the exception proves this dramatic rule. The unusual role of
cooperating and not deceiving the master confuses the *servus callidus*,
who knows nonetheless that he has to swindle *somebody* in the play
(Plautus, *Asin.* 249–266).[53]

To get out of the pickle, the clever slave impersonates authority figures, misleads about his authorization to act as an agent of others, and
forms alliances with social betters.[54] Successful hoodwink involves "fleecing the master" (Plautus, *Bacch.* 239) and "disemboweling the old man's
purse" (Plautus, *Epid.* 183, see also 187, 158–163). The slave boasts of
single-handedly taking his master, philosophizes on the virtue of shrewd
intelligence, and champions his own labors as comparable to that of generals, mythological heroes, and immortals.[55] The slave's giddiness bal-
ances his despair in previous soliloquies, steadying the play as it sails
along its farcical course to exactly nowhere, in dramatic terms.[56] Illustrative is Chrysalus, the clever slave who exclaims:

Here I am, one worth his weight in gold. Here I am, a guy who should have a
gold statue erected in his honor. Why, I have done a double deed today, and
have been graced with double rewards. The old master—how cleverly I did
take him in today. See how much he was fooled! Clever as the old master is, my
crafty arts pushed him and made him to believe me in everything. . . . There's
nothing more worthless than a slave without brains. He's got to have a very
powerful intellect. Whenever a scheme is needed, let him do it from his own
intellect. Not a single person can be worth anything, unless he knows how to
be both good and bad. He must be a rascal among rascals, rob robbers, steal
what he can. A guy that's worth anything, a guy with a fine intellect, has to be
able to make himself versatile. He must be good with the good and bad with
the bad; whatever the situation calls for, that's what he's got to be. (Plautus,
Bacch. 640–660; Nixon, LCL)

After discovering the trick, the master (for his part) threatens terrible
punishment and torture. The playwright applies the usual gallows
humor, but in the end the slave is always pardoned. Praise of *calliditas*
follows, either by the slave himself, the master, the other characters, the
playwright, or a combination of all these voices. An example of a master
praising a clever slave is this dialogue from Terence:

[Syrus]: Dear me, Sir, so you commend slaves who deceive their masters?
[Chremes]: If done in the right situation, certainly I commend them.
(*Haut.* 537; Sargeaunt, LCL)[57]

The master's praise of the slave's *calliditas* resets the comic cycle and so is an important dramatic element; it is neither "ironic" nor a throwaway line. The praise can be genuine because the trickster's routine does not challenge anything. The episode does not permanently alter the hierarchy of master and slave, nor does it reverse their essential relation of domination and subordination. The slave's puerile attitude diffuses the scheme's venality and disarms potential danger of real rebellion or permanent reversal of power in the household and wider society. The clever slave, like the comic parasite, never challenges the authority figures against which he rebels, and his monologue does not represent the point of view of actual slaves or recover the lost voices of the poor, oppressed, and marginalized in ancient society. The intrigue of the rogue had no edifying moral or psychological lesson for an ancient audience. It presented the comedy of farce.[58]

The Farce of the Dishonest Manager

The farce of the parasite playing the clever slave provides the best interpretative context in which to read the language and action of the dishonest manager. The parable's protagonist is a mediocre, cheap hireling identified only by his servile domestic service (*oikomonos*), an agent who sponges off a rich man (*plousios*) (Luke 16:1). The manager faces accusations of squandering the master's property, which must be true because, from his determined personality developed in the monologue (16:4), we would expect a fight or at least some denial of false charges. Told to deliver the account books and in anticipation of his imminent dismissal (16:2), the manager imagines the worst of his horrors—having do real work, or real begging. He clearly does not want dismissal from the rich man's household. Like a parasite, the dishonest manager cannot exist without a host.

The dishonest manager speaks in absolutes and extremes, which corresponds to the cries of a parasite. "What will I do? (*ti poiēsō*),"[59] he blubbers to himself. "I am not strong enough to dig, and I am too proud to beg" (16:3), enunciating his own worst fears of manual labor and poverty. The language is exaggerated, but also stylized to a specific comic type. The first protest of being too delicate to dig is a deliberate absurdity on the part of the author. Practically everybody in antiquity, even women and small children, could and did dig in the underdeveloped economy of agriculture (Columella, *De re rustica* 2.2.13), in which the mass of the population labored at or near subsistence level.[60] A lazy excuse not to work, the protest was proverbial in ancient comedy and mocked a moral inferior's personal dislike for the manual labor that everybody below the elite aristocratic orders had to do.[61] The manager's second excuse of being "too proud to beg" expresses bald hypocrisy, principles recited merely to justify unethical behavior. Pride over (the indignity of) freeloading in "other people's homes" (16:4) is a common theme of the parasite, whose stock includes playing an object of ridicule—the comic *scurra* (jester) in a rich patron's service—for his own self-interest, in order not to have to beg for the necessities of life.[62] The manager assumes the facade of his social betters, pretends membership in aristocratic society, and takes on airs above the mass that had to work for a living. But an ancient audience familiar with Roman comedy would have seen through his ridiculous and empty show.

The manager resolves to shift loyalties to new hosts now that resources from the current one are about to be denied. He declares, "I have decided what to do so that, when I am dismissed as manager, people may welcome me into their homes" (Luke 16:4). This plan involves the dishonesty of accounting alchemy that the man hopes will turn his base predicament into gold. Jesus, the narrator of the parable, explains:

> So, summoning his master's debtors one by one, he asked the first, "How much do you owe my master?" He answered, "A hundred jugs of olive oil." He said to him, "Take your bill, sit down quickly, and make it fifty." Then he asked another, "And how much do you owe?" He replied, "A hundred containers of wheat." He said to him, "Take your bill and make it eighty." (Luke 16:5-7)

The debts reported in the parable are preposterously inflated, indicative merely of a certain order of magnitude and exaggerated for comic effect.[63]

The numerical hyperbole provides but one clue to the story's artificiality. The interior monologue parodies a classical literary model of deliberation, which is the *self in dialogue*. The manager first entertains and then rejects certain courses of action, and this rejection is a crucial preliminary to the reaching of a conclusion. The monologue contains inferential *reasoning*, not simply reasons for acting. The reasoning resembles Aristotelian and Stoic accounts of motivation, which explain action by reference to an "impression" (*phantasia*) that generates an "impulse"

(*hormē*). As a dramatic device, the interior monologue creates a sense
of time—the ability to weigh advantages of future courses of action in
light of one's own past experience—and signifies the exceptional isolation in which the figure finds himself at this moment. He has no one
with which to share his dilemmas but himself. Importantly, the mental
image of digging and begging does not shake the manager's core values or beliefs. The impression does not generate the impulse to get an
actual job, to seek any alternative careers, or to work for himself. We find
no deliberation here *about* the goals of his life; these remain fixed. The
single-mindedness reveals the manager's inability to be anything other
than a perpetual, or at least a serial, houseguest, and the inner dialogue
with the self parodies serious deliberations of the self in Greek epic and
tragedy. Seeking not employment but hospitality, he is a professional
sponger and cannot change his tune. His soliloquy chants the mantra of
the comic stage parasite. The manager is, therefore, characterized as an
artificial, stock figure whose parasitical personality does not alter with
circumstances.[64]

Another narrative tag to the parasite is the manager's technique of
friendship attainment. He is said to act *phronimōs* (shrewdly; 16:8), a term
appearing in anti-Epicurean polemic. A brief word study explains the
link. The adverb refers frequently to the cunning of animals (Aristotle,
Historia animalium 612a3–b1; Ps.-Xenophon, *De equitum magistro* 4.20) and
the practical, streetwise wisdom of people "of less repute" (Plato, *Apology*
22a). The term carries furthermore a military sense of prudent battle
stratagem often involving a trap, and it describes the virtue of Odysseus
and similar archetypes of craftiness.[65] As such, *phronimos* enters the language of moral philosophy. Although Aristotle had argued against the
identification of practical wisdom (*phronēsis*) with knowledge, in Hellenistic times those thinkers informed by Peripatetic theories of character
types regarded *phronēsis* to be one of the four cardinal virtues, opposite
of the vice of *mōros* (folly). In this regard, Epicurus was reputed to exhort
the use of *phronēsis* in friendship attainment because of the virtue's ability, by tempering the inrush of random atoms, to render a person independent of fate. The emphasis on friendship led to the caricature of
Epicureans as proverbial flatterers and parasites, as I noted in chapter
2. The parable participates in the Roman gender farce of a man crying
over the compulsion to get a real job and the anti-Epicurean satire of a
person declaring control over fate by means of *phronimos* to cultivate a
household welcome from potentially new friends.[66]

In addition to the parasite's routine, Luke's miniature drama also conforms to the intrigue of the *servus callidus*.[67] The past performance of the manager has rendered him vulnerable to charges of squandering, his dishonesty already known by others. The squandering has to be reported to the master (*houtos deblēthē autō*), characterized as a rich fool (cf. the parable of the Rich Fool, Luke 12:13-21) who is the last to know about his misplaced trust and his own stupid inattention. The *servus callidus*, likewise, makes fools of the rich—"fleecing them" and boasting about it to others—exposing aristocratic reputations for mastery (*auctoritas*) as an open joke. The parable has an interior monologue that draws in the hearers as an ally of the deceiver, also a Plautine technique. The master's threat to fire the manager is not carried out. The *servus callidus* endures threats that are there precisely in order *not* to be carried out. The gallows humor reminds the spectators that the slave's ability to get away with his outrageous misbehavior is limited to the stage.[68] The manager uses shrewdness to control his fate, to aid others with quick cash, and to fulfill his freeloading dream—that is, of being subordinated. All these tags mark a character as artificial and dramatic, acting the part of the "clever slave" who aims single-handedly to reverse setbacks and to control events (but never to secure his own independence or freedom).

Moreover, the manager serves as an example of intelligence in the *underhanded* use of money but ineptitude in its *proper* use. He approaches potential hosts and anticipates the handsome reward of hospitality (Luke 16:4), the massive debts indicating the value of the wealth at stake in the parable's story world. The dishonest manager misleads the debtors about his authorization to reduce their debts, and his accounting shiftiness extends to doctoring the account books in the debtors' handwriting, not his (16:6-7). In the same way, the comedy of the clever slave involves impersonation, lies about permission to act as an agent, and alliances with social betters. The dishonest manager is caught in his dishonesty, and the master—by the rule of farce—praises him for the scheme. The clever slave, correspondingly, is always pardoned too readily in the end, being the rogue who "makes good" by "being bad," receiving the applause of his master, fellow characters, the narrator, and the audience (Plautus, *Epid.* 733–734), analogous to a modern show about mischievous pets. The master's praise in the parable, therefore, would not have been puzzling to an ancient audience familiar with Roman comedy.

I have summarized the dramatic sequence of the Roman comedy in such detail because it clarifies precisely what modern commentators find so opaque (and morally embarrassing) in the parable: the master's explicit praise and implied pardon of his dishonest manager. In her important study, Mary Ann Beavis mentions Plautine comedy but focuses instead on the slave *picaro* theme in the fables of Aesop, a parallel less direct than that of the clever slave and the parasite.[69] Also, her insistence on the manager's being a literal slave in the story has opened Beavis's work, and that of Bernhard Heininger, to sharp criticism, which unfortunately has encouraged many scholars to discard the thesis wholesale.[70] We need to refocus attention on the clear dramatic conventions and tags, and to contextualize the parable in the farce of the parasite *playing* the clever slave.

Why is Luke using this mode of comedy? One ready answer is that such comedy enhances the entertainment value of the parable for a Greek and Roman audience.[71] But the narrative does more than entertain. It exhorts the hearer to play the burlesque of the dishonest manager in daily life, puzzling biblical commentators, theologians, and other modern readers expecting a moral lesson. Why does Jesus (the narrator) exhort the disciples and the hearer to "make friends for yourselves" by means of shrewdness in "unrighteous mammon" (16:9)? As many commentators have observed, shrewdness (*phronimos*) does not ordinarily indicate a Christian virtue in Luke or the New Testament generally.[72] And the subsequent exhortations (16:8*b*-13) appear to turn the parable's meaning in different and several directions, seeming to be an awkward addendum of originally unrelated gnomic sayings linked up by catchwords (e.g., *adikos* in Luke 16:10 and 11).[73] However, I argue that at least some of the gnomic exhortations have an essential relationship to the parable's play to the reader. The social effects and properties of Roman farce give clarity to this difficult text.

The Social Effects and Properties of Roman Farce

There were two modes of Roman comedy that juxtaposed moral values and literary values in dialogic tension. The first mode was the fantastic comedy of rebellion, which valued stylized language, slapstick bits, and stereotyped characters over realism. It favored the *form* of the dramatic conventions over the play's *content* (and any moral norms that civic life and tradition ascribed to that content), meaning for a play with slave characters that the content of slavery took secondary meaning to the form of dramatization, characterization, and monologue. Trickery was given pride of place. The domination of the master turned from unstable to chaotic. The trick was revealed. But the plot led exactly nowhere, in dramatic terms. Despite his *calliditas*, the *servus* remained a slave, looking forward to another round of trickery without consequences. Nothing changed the characters' situation or fundamental relation to each other.[74]

Roman farce operated in tandem with its complementary mode, the naturalistic comedy of manners. Naturalism championed aristocratic values and social hierarchy as an organic part of the divine moral order. It called attention to the content of the story rather than to the story itself, aiming to make the miniature world of the play as real as possible. The point was *autopsy*, as if the spectators were spying on real life with their own eyes rather than watching a play performed by actors (more on autopsy in chapter 6). The idealized realism functioned as hegemonic discourse, showing that the way things are must be the way things ought to be. In sharp contrast to the plots of farce, those in the naturalistic mode made resolutions and changed the characters' place in the story world. Key was the recognition scene (*anagnōrisis*), which revealed the author's attitude toward justice, truth, and moral norms: families are reunited, marriages contracted, the faithful rewarded, and the bad receive just punishment. Naturalism and farce did not argue against each other but self-consciously uncovered through their polyphonic juxtaposition how one language and worldview sounded and looked to another language and worldview, a relationship that resembles what Mikhail Bakhtin calls dialogism.[75]

In addition, the naturalistic comedy of manners and the fantastic comedy of rebellion display what the political theorist James Scott has called "the public transcript," the actions and words that dominant and subordinate groups use in open interaction. Farce is not the "hidden transcript" that represents a critique of power spoken behind the back of the dominant. Roman imperial society was fundamentally hierarchical and authoritarian, and everyone was subordinated in some sense. In particular, aristocratic males had to define themselves and their communities by continual contesting of status and *auctoritas*, the distinctively Roman form of personalized authority that we explored in the introduction and the preceding two chapters. Slavery in this context was the extreme in a social continuum of *auctoritas*, in which mastery over chattel slaves functioned to articulate larger issues of domination and subordination.[76]

The farce of the *servus callidus* had specific social effects on its Roman audiences. Most of all, the fantastic comedy of rebellion responded to the spectators' desire for fictive, carefree authority and rebellion in their own lives, within the Roman social continuum of domination and subordination. In her excellent study of slavery and the art of authority in Plautine comedy, Kathleen McCarthy explains:

> The clever slave in comedy serves as a talisman against anxieties having to do specifically with slavery but also, more broadly, against the anxieties that arose from the constant need to jockey for position in the many minutely graded hierarchies that ordered Roman society. The clever slave presents a character who is specifically marked with the attributes of slavery and yet stands for all those who are actually or potentially subordinated to others (in other words, the whole audience). . . . Since comedy is part of Rome's "public transcript," it makes sense that the citizen population used this opportunity both to reassert their difference from slaves (and, in doing so, reaffirm the essential meaninglessness of slave resistance) and to enjoy under the cover of this very difference the liberatory release (without ever having to admit that they, not just their slaves, were in need of such release). . . . One of the most powerful reasons for putting the relationship between master and slave on center stage to stand for all relationships of domination is that slavery poses in an extreme form the problem that competing subjectivities create for the effective practice of domination.[77]

McCarthy appropriately criticizes romantic notions of social subversion where none existed. She also corrects previous "safety valve" theories of comedy and slavery, which had interpreted fictive rebellion as a Saturnalian "overthrow" of the everyday Roman value system designed by dominate members to release potential social unrest among subordinates (such as sons and slaves). Because these plays were performed at civic religious festivals and publicly funded by magistrates, it is unlikely that they expressed a "hidden transcript" of the slaves (or others similarly oppressed) without a voice in public life.[78]

An ancient audience would have likely heard the parable of the Dishonest Manager not as the subordinate critique of power but as the "public transcript" and literary artifice of masters. The stylized and artificial form of the language, characterization, and trickster-routine drama signals the parable's utter conventionality. In the exhortations that follow, Luke plays the farce to the audience. The author writes, "For the children of this age are more shrewd in dealing with their own generation than are the children of light. And I tell you, make friends for yourselves by means of dishonest wealth so that when it is gone, they may welcome you in the eternal homes" (16:8-9). The Lukan Jesus exhorts his disciples—and so "Theophilus" (the intended reader; Luke 1:1) and the hearer—to identify with and play the dishonest manager in their own lives. The initial exhortations (Luke 16:8-9) have an essential relation to the parable because they play to anxieties in the audience that arose from the constant need to jockey for position in the continuum of domination and subordination that ordered Roman society. People could succeed in hierarchical society by being similarly shrewd.

There is another narrative element to consider. Jewish wisdom declared God to be the maker of both the rich and the poor (Prov 10:22; 22:2; Sir 11:14, 29), that diligence earns riches (Prov 10:4), that wealth is a "gift from God" (Eccl 5:19), and that "rich men endowed with resources" were honored in their generations as the "pride of Israel" (Sir 44:6-7). Wealth is called "good" as long as it remains untainted by sin (Sir 13:24). In Ecclesiastes (Qoheleth), the Teacher (appearing in the role of "a king over Israel") declares that he acquired wealth through his wisdom, that is, "shrewdness" (Eccl 2:1-24).[79] Varying a saying in Proverbs, Ben Sira praises the value of a clever slave (Sir 7:21; 10:25; cf. Prov 17:2). The wisdom tradition thus reflects Jewish cultural participation in the reversal-of-fortune topos of slave characters diffuse throughout Aramaic and Greek culture. Importantly, the topos need not involve literal slaves. For example, stories of the foreign royal court have as their hero the elite Judean who faces intrigue and so also needs to win by his or her wits (e.g., Daniel, Bel and the Dragon, Esther).[80] And there is the cycle of stories about the famous Joseph son of Tobias that the historian Josephus narrates (*Ant.* 12.160–187). Joseph makes a great deal of wealth under the Hellenistic Ptolemies, earning the Tobiads high status as Judea's leading clan (rivaling the Hasmoneans) through the shrewdness of tax farming. He gains tax-farming rights by his wit—getting King Ptolemy to laugh at a joke at the monarch's expense (12.178–179)—and uses the newly acquired wealth "to make permanent the power which he now had, thinking it prudent (*phronimon*) to preserve the source and foundation of his present good fortune (*eutychias*)" (12.184). Such stories taught that social charm and sagacious learning alone will not help Judeans living in a Gentile world. Judeans, especially aristocratic courtiers (servants) of a foreign king, must practice a shrewd wisdom to be successful. We see from these stories the presence of the "clever slave" topos from New Comedy integrated into the Jewish sapiental tradition. The literature of both Aramaic and Hellenistic Judaism already had incorporated the commonplace in pre-Maccabean times.[81] From this evidence we find a possible explanation for our problem above, why the assorted gnomic exhortations are placed awkwardly next to Luke's parable. Luke is casting a "sideways glance" from his own language and worldview (Roman comedy) at what he believes to be the language and worldview of Jesus' teaching (Jewish wisdom). The author makes a free dialogic association of two different cultures. The narrative result is awkwardness, because Jewish sapiental traditions about shrewdness in wealth actually contradict Luke's theme of wholesale condemnation of the rich by God.

Bakhtin's idea of dialogism also clarifies Luke's purpose in crafting a particular parabolic sequence. The Dishonest Manager appears just before the Rich Man and Lazarus (16:19-31). The two parables form a literary diptych, self-consciously juxtaposing contradictory languages and worldviews, putting on display the dialogic tension of farcical and naturalistic theater. The Rich Man and Lazarus has the plot mechanism of the afterlife, which displaces the burlesque of the Dishonest Manager into a "realistic" scene—God's concern for the poor and punishment of the rich (16:23-28). The graphic (and comic) torment presents "empirical," autoptic witness ("in Hades"; 16:13) that ultimate recompense is inescapable in God's justice of the poor. The rich man gets the punishment that the dishonest manager so richly deserves.

The Dishonest Manager ends with the master implicitly agreeing to forgo punishment while explicitly being unreconciled to the breach of his authority. Injustice and chaos prevail in playful tandem.[82] The fantastic comedy of rebellion siphons implausibility from the narrative and serves as a measure for the realism and naturalism in the scene to follow. The dishonest manager functions as a catalyst for the recognition scene involving the more fragile and serious character of the rich man in the Lazarus parable. The burlesque of farce tries to accomplish indirectly what a narrative completely in the naturalistic mode could never do: the seduction of escapist entertainment gets a Roman audience to accept Luke's gospel about the poor. Importantly, the *form* of the Dishonest Manager's farce lies in tension with the *content* of the Rich Man's recognition. By this polyphonic counterposing of farcical and naturalistic theater, Luke creates discourse that condemns wealth in Christian discipleship on a par with Jesus' condemnation of the Pharisees as "lovers of money" (16:14). In this way, the theatrical artifice of the rich man and his dishonest manager links to the more serious and "realistic" rich man and Lazarus. The narrative cycle of judgment against the rich has been rising in a crescendo since the parable of the Prodigal Son, moving the hearer—especially the rich hearer—to accept the truth of Luke's didactic message about wealth and poverty.[83]

Conclusion

Neither the slave Rhoda nor the dishonest manager is an example of a "real" person in ancient Mediterranean peasant society. Both are dramatic fictions of Roman slave comedy. The drama encouraged early Christians to laugh at slaves as moral inferiors. Like a Roman playwright, the author of Luke–Acts modulates rapport between a character and the audience. Empathy with the literary characters encoded as slaves alleviated anxieties about subordination and domination in the readers' own lives, who, after hearing Luke–Acts, had to return to their daily routine of negotiating the continual contesting of status and personalized authority (*auctoritas*) required to define person and place within Rome's fundamentally hierarchical culture. By their utter conventionality and artificiality, the scenes are *literary*, not social, description. The language is hegemonic discourse. It would have had persuasive power on a Roman audience to promote generous support of the poor. Luke thus integrates Roman slave comedy because its didactic value was useful to his vision. But that vision did not include the subversion of cultural assumptions, literary tropes, and social stereotypes about slaves and masters. Instead, Luke's concern was wealth and poverty in Christian discipleship, and the social implications of rich patrons (sc. "most excellent Theophilus" [*kratistos Theophilos*]; Luke 1:3; Acts 1:1) entering his congregation. Luke crafted fictional slave characters to entertain and to exhort a Roman audience.

The character of the *servus callidus* from his role as manager (*oikonomos*) functions as a stock elite slave. Did other New Testament authors, besides Luke, use the figure of the elite slave as a didactic theme? This question leads us to the next chapter on the household duty codes.

4

SUBORDINATE TO ANOTHER

Elite Slaves in the Agricultural Handbooks and the Household Codes

Did early Christians really subvert the ideologies of slavery in classical culture? Many modern students of the household codes (what Luther called *Die Haustafeln*) think so and have found irresistible a popular form of argument that amounts to a red herring. The argument has a standard formula. The scholar declares as a fact that the household codes undermine or at least challenge the ideology and institution of slavery. He or she then digs into the data to come up with "proof" that the slave is indeed treated as a moral agent and the master as not really dominant. Why else are slaves addressed *at all*? Why else are masters told to treat their slaves "justly" and "fairly" and reminded of their own *subordination* to another Lord ("master," *kyrios*)? The formula ends with some ringing piece of theological triumphalism to the effect that the household codes, especially those in Colossians and Ephesians, are unique— a "remarkable leveling of the ordinary relations between masters and slaves," an implicit "subversion" of the pagan ethical norm, and a "revolutionary step beyond Hellenistic house-table ethics."[1] As Richard Hays writes, "When masters are told to stop threatening their slaves because 'you have the same Master in heaven, and with him there is no partiality' [Eph 6:9], a theological image is invoked that unsettles the conventional patterns of master-slave relations."[2] Hays, like other scholars, finds an essentially Christian core in the otherwise "pagan" debris of the *Haustafeln*, precious gems for Christian theology today repudiating slavery.[3] The domestic codes are seeds of egalitarianism sown in the apostolic age, whose flowering in nineteenth-century abolitionist Christianity eventually destroyed the harmful sin of slavery.

But this view merely retells the nineteenth-century "seed growing secretly" hermeneutics that even antislavery and abolitionist writers came to recognize as specious (as I note in chapter 7). More important, the broad generalizations about ancient slavery are simply wrong. They overlook the evidence of ancient agricultural handbooks, which address slaves directly and remind the local farm master (or *vilicus*; bailiff) of his subordination to a greater lord, the *pater familias*.[4] In this chapter I argue that the agricultural handbooks reflect the culture of prescriptive literature in which the early Christian household codes also participate. What appears initially as unique Christian teaching ends up actually being part of a handbook topos in Roman slave management.

Although earlier commentary assumed the domestic codes to be unique to Christianity, or at least Judaism, scholars now recognize the literary form as having originated from Hellenistic discussion "on household management" (*peri oikonomia*) following the tradition of Aristotle's *Politics*.[5] Aristotle takes the city-state (*polis*), which could stand for any social group, to be a body. His dissection of the body politic finds its essence to be the basic "couplings" of the family—husband and wife, father and children—in a relation of patriarchy that the "obvious" pairing of master and slave legitimizes as "natural" (*Politics* 1.1252a17–1253b14). Importantly, the individual is not theorized within this system but is defined in terms of family associations only, which are already in a fundamental hierarchical structure.[6]

Aristotle does not write that the essence of political rule is slavery, however. He mentions household management only as an excursus to his main theme of political knowledge, an important point to remember. The *Politics* is a polemical work written in large part to refute rivals and opponents who use Plato to assert that political rule ("rule of a *polis*," the Greek city-state) is no more than advanced household management skills. In order to separate political rule (*to politikon*) from household rule (*to oikonomikon*) and mastery (*to despotikon*), Aristotle classifies household management as a distinct branch of science (*epistēmē*), analogous but not identical to monarchy. Aristotle thus develops Plato's extension of the Socratic method of "division" (*diaeresis*) from ideal Forms to social affairs and human institutions, which Plato did in order to acquire technical knowledge about what previously had been a matter of opinion.[7] Plato taught that Athenians needed to learn the "science" of the statesman in order be true masters at home. Masters should order slaves with a simple command (*epitaxis*), like a lawgiver (*Laws* 6.776–777e). On this point Aristotle disagrees with his teacher. Instead of command, masters should rather use "admonition."[8] Aristotle observes that nearly all people, including other slaves, give commands to slaves. The wealthy, for example, often appoint a trusted slave as a steward (*epitropos*) who orders slaves directly and teaches them in the tasks they must perform. This elite slave, Aristotle reminds his audience, rules other slaves but is not really a "master" (*despotēs*). The real master is not one who just commands slaves or instructs them in their work but who has the actual character, not merely the science (*epistēmē*), to rule slaves, being the cause of their virtue (1.1260a33–b8). Ideally, the master's own character is "stamped" upon the steward, who then represents the master. The master sets the elite slave in charge of other slaves while yet remaining their ultimate lord.[9] Political science is not the same as the master's science.

The position of the elite slave in Aristotle's definition of the master, which Hellenistic and especially Roman agricultural handbooks develop, provides a promising parallel for the ethical warrant of "being subordinate to another" in the early Christian household codes. Previous commentary had noted the goddess Fortuna (being a "greater Lord" to all) as the only known parallel to the Christian warrant, an exception often used to prove the so-called rule that the Christian exhortations are unique.[10] The discussion below indicates otherwise.

Early Christian Household Codes for Masters: Colossians and Ephesians, the *Epistle of Barnabas*, the *Didache*, and the *Doctrina Apostolorum*

A distinct corpus, the household codes appear in the deuteropauline epistles and the writings of the so-called Apostolic Fathers, dating from the end of the first century c.e. and into the second. They contain moral reasoning different from that of the Apostle Paul. In his undisputed letters, Paul avoids simple, apodictic commands in favor of indirect persuasion and siding with everyone. This polyphonic style of moral reasoning allows multiple voices to be heard, including nonhegemonic ones; Paul's admonitions cannot be reduced to rules.[11] The household codes, however, are rules and can be divided into two basic groups. One contains rules for slaves alone (1 Peter, 1 Timothy, Titus). The second group has rules both for masters and for slaves (Colossians, Ephesians, the *Didache*, the *Doctrina Apostolorum*, and the *Epistle of Barnabas*).[12] Because they are more misunderstood in current scholarship, the texts of the second group are the subject of this chapter and are collected in Table 1.

Table 1. Synopsis of Early Christian Household Codes
for Slaves and for Masters

Colossians 3:22—4:1	Ephesians 6:5-9
Slaves (*hoi douloi*), obey your earthly masters (*tois kata sarka kyriois*) in everything (*kata panta*), not only while being watched and in order to please them, but wholeheartedly (*en haplotēti kardias*), fearing the Lord (*ton kyrion*).	Slaves (*hoi douloi*), obey your earthly masters (*tois kata sarka kyriois*) with fear and trembling (*meta phobou kai tromou*), in singleness of heart (*en haplotēti tēs kardias*), as you obey Christ; not only while being watched, and in order to please them, but as slaves of Christ, doing the will of God from the heart ("self") (*ek psychēs*).
Whatever your task, work from the heart ("self") (*ek psychēs ergazesthe*), as done for the Lord (*tō kyriō*) and not for people (*ouk anthrōpois*), since you know that from the Lord (*apo kyriou*) you will receive the inheritance as your reward; you serve (*douleuete*) the Lord (*tō kyriō*) Christ.	Render service (*douleuontes*) with enthusiasm (*met eunoias*), as to the Lord (*tō kyriō*) and not to people (*ouk anthrōpois*), knowing that whatever good (*agathon*) we do, we will receive the same again from the Lord (*para kyriou*), whether we are slaves or free (*eite doulos eite eleutheros*).
For the wrongdoer will be paid back for whatever wrong has been done, and there is no partiality (*prosōpolēmpsia*).	
Masters (*hoi kyrioi*), treat your slaves (*doulois*) justly (*dikaion*) and fairly (*isotēta*), for you know that you also have a master (*kyrion*) in heaven.	And masters (*hoi kyrioi*), do the same (*ta auta poieite*) to them. Stop threatening them, for you know that both of you have the same Lord (*ho kyrios*) in heaven,
	and with him there is no partiality (*prosōpolēmpsia*).

Table 1 (*continued*)

DOCTRINA APOSTOLORUM 4.10-11	DIDACHE 4.10-11	EPISTLE OF BARNABAS 19.7
		Be subject [pl.] to your masters (*kyriois*) as to a replica (*hōs typō*) of God, with respect and reverential fear (*en aischynē kai phobō*).
Do not order [sing.] your male slave (*servo*) or female servant (*ancillae*) in your anger (*ira*), who hope in the same Lord (*eundem dominum*);	Do not order [sing.] your male slave (*doulō*) or female servant (*paidiskē*) —who hope in the same God—out of bitterness (*en pikria*),	Do not order [sing.] your male slave (*doulō*) or female servant (*paidiskē*) out of bitterness (*en pikria*) —since they hope in the same God—
let [them] fear both the Lord and you (*dominum et te*).	lest they stop fearing the God who is over you both (*ton ep amphoterois theon*).	lest they stop fearing the God who is over you both (*ton ep amphoterois theon*).
For he [Christ] comes not to call according to personal status (*personas*), but those in whom he finds in the Spirit.	For he does not come to call according to personal status (*kata prosōpon*), but those whom the Spirit has prepared.	For he did not come to call those according to personal status (*kata prosōpon*) but those whom the Spirit had prepared.
You slaves (*vos servi*), moreover, be subject to your masters (*dominis*), as a symbol (*formae*) of God, with respect and trembling (*cum pudore et tremore*).	And you [pl.] who are slaves (*douloi*) must be subject to your masters as to a replica (*hōs typō*) of God, with respect and reverential fear (*en aischynē kai phobō*).	

A synoptic comparison of the New Testament household codes reveals that Ephesians redacts Colossians to preclude certain interpretations. The vague, even quasi-philosophical exhortation to treat slaves "justly (*dikaion*) and fairly (*isotēta*)" (Col 4:1), which might be read as a call for general manumission or even criticism of slavery,[13] is made less abstract by the more straightforward, clear command: "Stop threatening them!" (Eph 6:9). The clarification ends ambiguity over what "justice" and "fairness" might mean. Believing masters are plainly to "do the same things" to slaves (Eph 6:9): to facilitate as leaders the delivery of the very goods that the preceding sentence promises all believers (Eph 6:8). In the desire to shore up the authority of non-household Christian leaders and to shut up women and slaves, the author of Ephesians takes a more pragmatic tone by prohibiting angry speech by male masters. To strengthen the command's force, the warning about God's impartiality is moved from the section concerning slaves (Col 3:25) to that concerning masters (Eph 6:9), here the only persons directly accountable to the Lord.[14] The motive for obedience is introduced by an appeal to common sense (*eidotes hoti*, "knowing that"); on this point, Ephesians closely parallels the whole Colossian section (Col 3:22—4:1).[15] The author advocates behavior for masters not because he, an author speaking with a certain authority, says they should, but because it is behavior that people already know, practice, and take for granted as obviously right.[16] The so-called First Admonition of the second-century-C.E. Stoic philosopher Hierocles may also be relevant here: "A slave will be well treated by one who considers how he would like to be treated by him if he were the master, and himself the slave."[17] The reciprocity ethic connects the main warrant of subordination to the same Lord who ultimately dominates everyone (Eph 6:9; Col 4:1). The theme of accountability is presented not as new information but as a reminder of catechetical knowledge from baptism.

The author of Ephesians expands the definition of the "good slave" beyond the category of labor. Good slaves not only do particular jobs "wholeheartedly" (*en haplotēti tēs kardias*: Col 3:22; Eph 6:5) and "from the self" (*ek psychēs*: Col 3:23; Eph 6:6) but must also accept their subjugation (not just labor) with "enthusiasm" (*eunoia*; Eph 6:7). *Eunoia*, a virtue of general goodwill appearing in stock acclaim for faithful slaves and an important element in ancient ideologies of mastery (especially Roman *auctoritas*), intensifies the personalized domination of human masters.[18] Whereas Colossians exhorts slaves to "work" from the self (*ek psychēs*) (Col 3:23), Ephesians says that they must "be a slave" (*douleuontes*) from the self (*ek psychēs*) and conform that self to the will (*thelēma*) of the master (Eph 6:6-7), a more sweeping and generalized admonition. After all, merely focusing on the individual task at hand was a known slave strategy of theatricality and resistance known as "playing the automaton," as the example of Aesop in chapter 1 showed. Slaves are told to imagine in their minds (*psychē*, self) the eyes of their earthly masters upon them as the gaze of the very Lord, which forces them to obey "even while not being watched" (Eph 6:6; Col 3:22). Following ancient optical theory of vision as a power penetrating the object, the exhortation adapts a particularly Roman idea of conscience developed among the Stoics (especially Seneca) under the early Roman Empire, when aristocratic behavior under the external gaze (such as that of the emperor) became increasingly condemned as mere theatricality. One should imagine being watched by a great moral authority such as a Cato, and to act according to this mirror in the self.[19] Philo uses the theme in the episode of having Moses exhorting bullying shepherds about doing good even while not being watched, reminding them of the "heavenly eye of justice" (*Mos.* 1.55–56). Building on this tradition, the author of Ephesians identifies the will (*thelēma*) of the human master with that of the Lord more clearly than Colossians does and targets paraenesis more squarely on the slave's inner self (*psychē*) as an object to bind and so to control. Literally, mastery is wrestling *psychē* out of the slave.

It is important to realize the agonistic scenario that Ephesians develops. The hope that the *psychē* of slaves will be defeated with minimal effort, before potential struggles begin, is not apocalyptic but mundane. The language participates and is implicated in ancient ideologies of slavery that view mastery as a contest (*agōn*) establishing and maintaining a hierarchy of domination and subordination. Power is personalized to the winner. Slaves, who are supposed to lose, must acquiesce "from the self" (*ek psychēs*). Those who refuse, asserting their own selves, are viewed as "bad." In other words, the "good slave" contains yet does not possess a self, being an extension or "vessel" of the master's body.[20] Interestingly, Greek binding spells in curse tablets (*defixiones*) also target the *psychē* (among other body parts), where the hope of victory is thought to lie. The curses in athletic, amatory, and especially judicial *defixiones* aim to bind the *psychē* of an opponent, rival, or love interest in order to incapacitate the victim before the *agōn*. The choice of this target reflects beliefs in antiquity about the *psychē* as a cognitive faculty and the source of desire and personal motivation. To constrain the *psychē* is to bind the victim's competitive drive and will to fight back.[21]

Fear (*phobos*) is no longer sufficient for slaves—they must show the added reverential deference of "trembling"—and it is redirected from the Lord (Col 3:22; verbal form) to the master (Eph 6:5; a more concrete substantive), which heightens the theological basis for slaveholder authority.[22] Divine "payback" is turned from a note of warning of severe punishment for the wrongdoer (Col 3:25) into a sentence about the rewards for the good slave (Eph 6:8), a criticism of the Colossian use of threats as a motivational tool for slave obedience (cf. Eph 6:9).[23] The reward promised is no longer a single "inheritance" (Col 3:24) but a succession of returns, each corresponding to a slave's good deed (*agathon*).[24] When the earner will get the goods is unclear. The future tense could mean in this life (less abuse, more food, better clothing) soon after the good deed, or in the next. The former is more logical because the author promises a succession of rewards instead of a one-time "inheritance." Rather than saying that Christ will come on the Last Day to bring the collective "blessings of the inheritance" to all who are saved, the author of Ephesians assigns the future dimension of reward individually.

Baptismal catechesis (originally oral) came to be set down in other early Christian writings around the same time as or relatively soon after the composition of Ephesians. The relevant treatises, the *Epistle of Barnabas*, the *Didache*, and the *Doctrina Apostolorum*, survive in the disparate corpus known as the Apostolic Fathers, some of the most important literary remains outside the New Testament.[25] These so-called Apostolic *Haustafeln* on slavery share the commonality of a "Two Ways" section with exact verbal parallels thematically similar to, but literarily independent of, the Colossian/Ephesian domestic codes.

An anonymous writing later ascribed to the companion of Paul in Acts, the *Epistle of Barnabas* was treated as Scripture in some early Christian circles (especially in Alexandria, Egypt) and came to be included among the writings of the New Testament in one of the most important New Testament manuscripts (Codex Sinaiticus).[26] Most scholars date the work to around 130 C.E., and some view *Barnabas* as a homily in an epistolary framework.[27] The subject matter, however, is not merely hortatory but instructional. To be sure, the author claims not to be a "teacher" (1.8; 4.9), but this denial—"we" are only "taught by God" (*theodidaktoi*; 21.6) and not like "them" taught by people—is itself a rhetorical trope used to bolster academic authority and to avoid connotations of suspicious originality, familiar from other proto-orthodox Christian writers (such as Irenaeus).[28] In fact, the stated goal of the work is to turn the reader into one "who has learned" (*mathonta*; 21.1). And pedagogical techniques of ancient education drive the whole treatise. At crucial points the author says, "Pay attention!" (7.4–6; 15.4; 16.8), "Learn this! (5.5; 6.9), "We should look closely" (11:1), "This means" (11.11), "Let us pursue the question" (14.1), and "You ought to perceive" now (13.3). He addressed his pupils with the metaphor of a father, calling them "children" (7.1; 9.7; 15.4; 21:9), an idiom of Jewish sapiential teaching.[29] He embraces rhetorical questioning and diatribe,[30] repetitious illustrations of his point (12.1-11), and pedantic simplification (17.1), including one elementary math lesson (9.7), so that "you may understand" (6.5) the teachings. He even praises the success of his pedagogy: "No one has learned (*emathen*) a more reliable lesson from me" (9.9); "Here you have a perfect lesson" (10:10). The author quotes passages of Scripture not to encourage actual reading of the Old Testament but to present a distillation of the "firm teachings" (*dogmata*) of Moses (10.1; 10.9) in an epitome or handbook fashion, which controls Scripture (LXX) and quite possibly replaces it in practice. Other teachings called "traditional" (4.9; 19.1; 21.1) but different from Scripture are also being transmitted. One set piece of previously written "knowledge and teaching" (18.1) "given to us" as a guide (19.1) is the "Two Ways" section (18–20), whose advice on slavery is excerpted (19.7).

The modern debates about the *Didache* and the *Doctrina Apostolorum* are not over genre—both clearly are compiled manuals or handbooks of Christian life, and so I do not have to repeat that argument—but over their dates.[31] The *Doctrina Apostolorum* (*De Doctrina Apostolorum*) is a Latin translation of an ancient Greek original (no longer extant), which presents its teachings as coming from the apostles of Jesus.[32] The provenance of the Greek original is unknown. Its date cannot be determined with certainty; maybe it is before the third century C.E.[33] The *Didache* was edited probably in Syria-Palestine around 100 C.E., though its source material certainly comes from traditions much older. Some scholars date its final composition earlier (50–70 C.E.), even before some of the books of the New Testament were written; others argue that the sources of the *Didache* were also used in the construction of the Gospels (especially Matthew).[34] These debates over dating do not speak to our question, however, since neither Matthew nor any extant Gospel contains domestic codes. The answer to our question about the synoptic relation of the Apostolic *Haustafeln* must lie elsewhere.

Almost every conceivable way in which to answer the synoptic question of *Barnabas*, the *Didache*, and the *Doctrina* has been suggested. Early modern interpreters, for example, tried to uphold the priority of the *Epistle of Barnabas* by establishing that its author used the Ephesian *Haustafel* as the ultimate source,[35] but scholars today find this idea of literary dependence on Ephesians (or, alternatively, Colossians) implausible because no verbatim agreements of any kind extend for two words or more. I accept the common view of a documentary hypothesis, which holds that all three texts stem ultimately, yet independently, from a basic (but lost) document, a Jewish-Hellenistic "Two Ways" manual.[36] Dating to the first century C.E. or perhaps earlier, the manual must have been written, Jewish in character and substance, and related to Hellenistic wisdom literature such as Sirach and Pseudo-Phocylides. It must have also been a rather loose compilation of community rules, prohibition lists, virtue and vice catalogs, traditional gnomic sayings on Jewish piety, and eschatological *synkrisis* (comparison of fates between the pious and the impious) possibly for Gentile proselytes in the Greek synagogue. The documentary hypothesis holds that *Barnabas* copied from a recension of the Jewish Two Ways Manual, only slightly Christianized; a second Christian recension, which had a more topical organization, was the source of the Two Ways in the *Didache* and in the *Doctrina,* respectively, each of which used the second Christian recension independently of each other (see Table 2 on page 95).[37]

The question I want to explore is not, however, the textual transmission but the literary and social contextualization of the specific admonitions that the domestic codes have in common. The Apostolic *Haustafeln* contain several verbatim parallels. The first is a grammatical adjustment of number in the verb, possibly an indicator of the intended audience of the Two Ways paraenesis. The address is singular for the master, plural for slaves, and then switches back to the singular (*Barn.* 19.7; *Did.* 4.11; *Doctr.* 4.11). In fact, the prohibitions are all in the singular save those for slaves, an exception suggesting the intended audience to be a *pater familias* and his *familia* (retinue of household slaves)—individual aristocratic households. At least in *Barnabas* this is explicit. At the end of the Two Ways, the author singles out "those of you who are in high positions" as the intended addressees (*Barn.* 21.2)—the aristocratic elite of social superiors and civic authorities who would no doubt have been among the largest slaveholders in a city.[38]

There is also an absolutism in moral prohibition, which attends a theological warrant. The master must never command slaves in "bitterness" (*pikros*) (*Barn.* 19.7c; *Did.* 4.10a) or "in anger" (*ira*) (*Doctr.* 4.10a) because it disheartens slaves' reverential fear of the Lord.[39] Abusive speech is believed to damage the authority of the Lord that ought to flow exclusively through the Christian master; the slaves presumably have no collective or personal experience of Christ outside their earthly lord. This teaching participates in an absolutism in the particularly Roman ideology of anger control that understands rage as a disease of the soul that disgraces the *dignitas* of the aristocratic adult Roman male. Many

**Table 2. Stemma of Early Christian Household Codes
for Slaves and Masters**

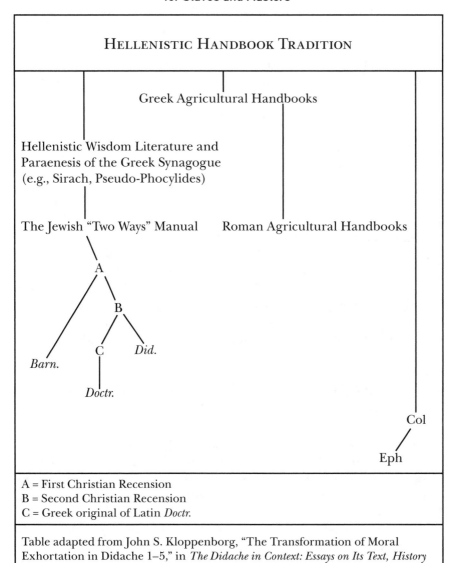

A = First Christian Recension
B = Second Christian Recension
C = Greek original of Latin *Doctr.*

Table adapted from John S. Kloppenborg, "The Transformation of Moral Exhortation in Didache 1–5," in *The Didache in Context: Essays on Its Text, History and Transmission* (ed. Clayton N. Jefford; Leiden: Brill, 1995), 92.

voices joined that of the Stoics to advocate nothing less than the categorical prohibition of all angry actions, speech, and feelings. This prohibition of rage cited the harmful effects of anger on the abuser, especially the loss of *dignitas* that personalized mastery (*auctoritas*) over subordinates required, and prescribed the therapy of daily self-examination.[40] Curiously, neither *Barnabas*, the *Didache*, nor the *Doctrina* recommends stratagems for anger control; no "therapy" technique is offered. Perhaps the authors assumed that the audience would clearly understand what they meant, or they were simply repeating their sources without deep reflection on the details. In any case, the use of "bitterness" (*pikros*) is a Septuagintal idiom locating rage on the visceral level of bodily taste, touch, and feeling deep in the inner self (*en pikria psychēs*).[41] The exhortation appears in a list of biblical sins of the tongue (*diglōssos, diglossia, proglōssos*; "double tongued," "hasty of tongue"), now placed within eschatological warnings about the mouth as a "deadly trap" and apocalyptic injunctions of the need to be "pure within" (*Barn.* 19.7–8). The human mouth is seen as a dangerous orifice of pollution and sin.

In comparison to *Barnabas*, the *Didache* and the *Doctrina* are less eschatological, better topically arranged, and modeled more explicitly after the Decalogue—absolutist, Moses-like prohibitions.[42] This "Torahization" of the Two Ways calls the Christian master a "replica" (model, *typos*) of God (*Barn.* 19.7b; *Did.* 4.11; *Doctr.* 4.11 [*forma*]), which may refer to Genesis 1.[43] The master's inability to control his rage diminishes his own *dignitas*, dissipates the "reverential fear" (*phobos*) in his slaves, and drives the hierarchy of divine creation into chaos. Violating the prohibition of abusive speech becomes tantamount to breaking "Torah" and so separates the entire congregation from God. Masters remembering their subordination to God, who is *ep amphoterois* (over both) "you and your slaves," prevents this disaster, which is the same moral reasoning of the domestic codes in Colossians and Ephesians.[44]

An additional source, the *Shepherd of Hermas*, repeats the theme. It exhorts, "Confess that you have a master [or 'the Lord'], lest after making a denial you be delivered over to prison. If the outsiders punish their slaves for denying their own master ['lord'], what do you suppose the Lord who has authority over all things will do?" (Herm. *Sim.* 105.7).[45] If pagan slaves in pagan households act in such a way, then how much more so should Christian masters. This use of an a fortiori argument (a form of the "argument from unlike") conforms to the scheme of moral reasoning in the literary topos *de fide servorum* (on the loyalty of slaves) familiar from Roman handbook literature on practical ethics and elsewhere.[46]

Our synoptic comparison of the early Christian household codes from Table 1 (see pages 88–89) finds them all sounding the same warrant. Believing masters should behave in a certain ethical way because they "know" their own subordination—as "slaves of God." But no single text has literary priority. The lack of sufficient verbatim agreements between the Apostolic *Haustafeln* and the Colossian/Ephesian *Haustafeln*, together with the independent evidence of the *Shepherd of Hermas*, suggests against the hypothesis of a single "origin." Rather than seeking origins literarily, in a specific text, I propose a sociological origin, in the struggles of non-household leaders to gain power in early congregations. The codes, with their pointed warning to individual *patres familias* to obey a higher authority, were part of the control that non-household church leaders began to exert.[47] The idea of "subordination to another" does not *come from* a particular document but is the content of thinking characteristic of slave management widely diffuse in classical antiquity.

Important for this cultural history are the Greek and Roman agricultural handbooks. New Testament scholars rarely consider these sources. Yet the agronomists provide important evidence for how Greco-Roman audiences would have been accustomed to hear and use rules for masters and slaves.[48] Not only do the agronomists provide the most extensive discussion on household management in all extant Greek and Latin literature, but they also give explicit admonition to the elite slave bailiff (*vilicus*) placed in charge of the rural household, turning mastery into an *ars* (science, Gk. *technē*), a teachable system. I want to be clear, however, that I not claiming that the writer of Colossians (or any other early Christian author) necessarily read the agricultural handbooks described below. Instead, I contend that the agricultural handbooks represent a broad cultural tradition that early Christian household codes share.

The Ancient Handbook Tradition

Before examining the agronomists in detail, we need some history of ancient handbooks as a genre of literature. The earliest evidence for handbooks is literary allusions, mostly in Plato's dialogues, to *hypomnēmata* (explanatory notes) by a teacher (or one of his epigones) for student use, which at least from the fifth century B.C.E. onwards were superseded by handbooks.[49] Covering topics like rhetoric, medicine, and early Greek science, these handbooks seem to have originated from Sophistic and early Pythagorean circles, whose enthusiasm for polymathy, *mathematica* (things learned, known), and abstract studies influenced Greek education broadly. Believing all knowledge to relate to fundamental theorems and axioms, the Pythagoreans promulgated philosophical doctrines (*dogmata*) that came to be set down in writing; the first Pythagorean to write such a book of *dogmata* appears to be Philolaus (ca. 470–390 B.C.E.), a contemporary of Socrates. Related to the Pythagoreans were the Sophists, who likewise advocated encyclopedic learning and the popularization of scientific knowledge. Although the Sophists (above all, Protagoras) receive mockery in Plato's dialogues as pompous interlocutors of Socrates who claim to "know everything," their works nonetheless had significant impact within two generations after Plato, when Aristotle emerged as a central figure. From the early Pythagorean and Sophistic doctrines, Aristotle had students in his school (the Lyceum or Peripatos) compile histories on physics, mathematics, geometry, astronomy, medicine, and music. With his pedantic approach to knowledge, encyclopedic interests, and general classificatory schemes, Aristotle thus formalized the handbook as an authority and as a literary genre. The histories of Aristotle's students provided the source material for the derivative handbooks, manuals, and compendia that multiplied during the Hellenistic era.[50]

Modern historians of ancient science often divide Hellenistic handbooks into two types, the scientific treatise and the "popular" manual.[51] The latter can be identified as *popular literature*, because it expresses a certain aesthetic. That aesthetic values straightforwardness over subtlety, factual content over artistic form, and easy and continued engagement while demanding little of the audience.[52] Such manuals abbreviate and systematize a body of technical knowledge for daily applicability, often with an emphasis on the ethical qualities needed for success. Handbook composition did not aim for a disinterested or neutral view of fact collection. The compiler wanted to control the body of knowledge as a teachable system (Greek *technē*; Latin *ars*) for a wide audience, often of outsiders (laypeople, amateurs).[53] Ironically, the same Hellenistic culture that fostered the most significant scientific and technological achievements of the Greeks also fed the full development of derivative handbooks, manuals, and compendia ultimately responsible for the decline of ancient science. And, also ironically, the very Hellenistic institutionalization of science in national museums and libraries, such as those at Pergamum and Alexandria, contributed to this decline. The Macedonian monarchs, notably, the Ptolemies of Egypt, established these academic institutions to showcase their Hellenistic kingdoms as the location of "all knowledge." The great museums and libraries did not foster original scientific research for insiders within a single school, technology, or philosophical tradition. The politics of polymathy valued pedantic explication for outsiders, including the royal patron, a popular aesthetic. The main intellectual activities centered on handbooks and learned commentaries. Scientists and scholars in the Hellenistic "age of science" were often satisfied to read the "learned commentaries" or a standard handbook on a particular author, presented as the source of all knowledge, rather than to read the author's original works or to pay attention to new research. In professional fields like engineering and medicine, instruction by handbooks came to supplant teaching by oral tradition. Perhaps responding to the rapid change that Hellenistic culture brought to human knowledge, handbooks promoted the stability of old ideas transmitted from generation to generation with little change.[54]

As a genre of popular literature, ancient handbooks shared four main features. First, they were didactic, intended to teach rather than merely to exhort. Their style employed a single authorial voice, direct imperatival expressions, an emphasis on moral precepts, and a dry, undemanding prose that created the impression of plain factuality. Handbooks also versified their prose into poetry for reasons of didactics and popularization; Columella's agricultural manual included, for example, a didactic poem (*Rust.* 10). Didactics offered a reasoned, learned system (*ars, ratio, technē*) that replaced irrational instinct, such as "fear" (*timor, ira*), as the primary object of instruction.[55] The second feature was pragmatic. Rather than examining a technical subject on a theoretical level or for quasi-philosophical purposes, popular handbooks were "how-to" manuals presenting their material as commonsense ("obvious") advice. They emphasized practical matters such as careful, watchful diligence rather than mastery of technical knowledge. The assertion of giving practical advice was itself a literary topos, a conventional justification of didactics.[56] The third trait was a compositional structure one might call *conglomerate*. Such a work gathered excerpted sources of mostly unknown authorship (both anonymous and pseudepigraphic), which recorded all opinions that the compiler regarded as authoritative on a given subject, with no regard for originality and little for citation consistency or organic unity.[57] The compilers were not experts in the field and often not competent to decide among various authorities. They seem frequently not even aware that the views expressed are redundant, incoherent, or even contradictory, which is one reason why ancient handbooks are full of discrepant statements. This conglomerate style leads to the fourth trait. Compilers also tried to conceal their pillaging of earlier handbooks by suppressing the identity of their sources. They either imputed to early masters (such as Pythagoras or Plato) the views of teachers contemporaneous with themselves, or they relied on anonymity to make the claim of an authority higher than that of a named teacher, which tried to deflect interest in who wrote the opinion and to give the impression of truth and completeness. Reassuring the reader of an extensive "tradition," the compilers of the handbooks did not encourage readers to care where the teachings *came from* but only that they worked, were obviously true, and constituted the *technē* and *praxis* that every educated person ought to know.[58]

Relevant to our investigation of the domestic codes, in the Roman period handbooks had become the main source of and vehicle for all the knowledge having evident authority and obvious truth.[59] Indeed, the *Epistle of Barnabas*, the *Didache*, and the *Doctrina* participate in this fashion by being manuals. The Romans caught the Hellenistic handbook fashion with enthusiasm, and it surpassed all other forms of literary production. There were handbooks on public expression (rhetoric, grammar, letter writing, elementary school exercises [*progymnasmata*], declamation); law and jurisprudence (*institutiones* for law students, *digesta* for jurists); medical and natural science (biology, veterinary arts [especially of horses], zoology, mineralogy, botany, the herbalist arts, remedies for snakes and poisonous insects); geographic ethnography (climatology, physiognomics, "periplus" literature of coastal voyages); mechanical engineering (hydraulics, military artillery); architecture (aqueduct construction, shipbuilding, land surveying); the arts (music theory and performance, sculpture, gastronomy, cosmetology [a work falsely attributed to Cleopatra]); industry and manufacture (mining; metallurgy, dyeing and cloth weaving); religion and magic (divination, binding spells, oracles, astrology, dream interpretation); recreational pursuits (board games, prostitution); and agriculture. Agricultural handbooks were a major source of ancient teachings on household management (*oikonomia*). The principal motivation for the written codification of agricultural knowledge in handbooks during the Roman period was increased reliance on elite slaves to supervise properties in place of the *pater familias*.[60]

The first extant Greek agricultural handbook is Xenophon's *Oeconomicus*, a dialogue between Socrates and interlocutors, mostly the rich Athenian Ischomachus, on the organization of a household (*oikonomia*) and the skill of effective leadership as a body of knowledge.[61] The Romans read Xenophon's *Oeconomicus* widely and for the most part approvingly in their normative discussions of proper household management. Cato the Elder, not usually an admirer of Greek literature,[62] considered the *Oeconomicus* particularly helpful for Romans. The Roman philosopher Philodemus (whose library has been unearthed at Herculaneum) opens his discussion "on household management" with an outline of Xenophon's ethical teaching. Cicero found the *Oeconomicus* so valuable that he translated it into Latin around 85 B.C.E. (*De officiis* 2.87), making Xenophon's handbook accessible to Varro, Columella, Pliny the Younger, and Quintilian, who all quote or paraphrase Cicero's translation rather than the Greek original. The greatest differences between the Greek original and the Roman paraphrases appear, not surprisingly, in the discussion of slaves, with Xenophon molding slaves in positions of leadership after the models of their own masters but Roman authors invoking nostalgic exemplars from the remote past.[63] The widespread use of Xenophon's *Oeconomicus* by these authors reveals the work's importance in Roman formations of household management and ideologies of slavery.

Another Greek handbook is the Hellenistic work known as *Oeconomica*, included among the works of Aristotle but recognized even in antiquity as the work of epigones; modern scholars date the work to 325–275 B.C.E. The first book derives material largely from Xenophon's *Oeconomicus* and Aristotle's *Politics*, carefully defining *oikonomia* and distinguishing it from *politikē* in Peripatetic philosophy of its early phase (not yet influenced by Stoicism). Collecting anecdotes about royal treasury administration (currency, taxation, insurance), the second book has only a tenuous connection to the previous and appears to have been originally an independent treatise. The third book, extant only in a Latin translation (by the thirteenth-century canonist Guillaume Durand), rehearses rules for married and family life very similar to those outlined in the dialogue of Ischomachus in Xenophon's *Oeconomicus*, which the author used as a source. The work as a whole shows how connected the name of Aristotle was to the Hellenistic handbook tradition on household management.[64]

The Roman who "taught agriculture to speak Latin" is the illustrious Marcus Porcius Cato (234–149 B.C.E.), also known as the Censor (see Columella, *De re rustica* 1.1.12). Cato's *De re rustica* addresses a young man "thinking of acquiring a farm" (1.1) and is an assorted and haphazard compilation of previous authorities and advises not anyone involved in agriculture, but primarily the owner of a medium estate based on slave labor; it is not addressed to Roman senators. Heavily didactic and moralizing, imperatives predominate throughout, urging cultural renewal.[65] Cato advocates the moral values of republican farming to counter the dramatic social and economic changes caused by the considerable loss of Italian manpower in the devastation of the Second Punic War (218–201 B.C.E.), especially the huge extension of public land (*ager publicus*) into the provinces. Important for its relevance to the urban context of the early Christian domestic codes, Cato's conservative advice on slave management offers rules and duties for any household, whether urban or rural.[66]

The second Roman handbook, Varro's *De re rustica*, appearing a century later (37 B.C.E.), continues this republican moral tradition but through a highly systematic analysis of agriculture in entertaining dialogue form; the interlocutor's names are chosen after the various topics under discussion, with occasional puns.[67] Varro addresses the work as a whole to his wife Fundania (*Rust.* 1.1–4), who had just bought a farm (but only the first book concerns agriculture proper). Significantly, the interlocutors are not senatorial owners but belong to the lower aristocratic elite, equestrians concerned with the systematic and rational management of more modest properties (1.2.1; 1.2.10; 1.13.7; 1.18.8). Varro's geographic range is broad, speaking about practices in Spain, for example, and his work represents thinking on household management outside Italy.[68] Being encyclopedic and derivative, Varro excerpts previous authors verbatim (especially Cato, often without attribution) and treats the agricultural subject as a comprehensive and international science; the "bibliography" (1.1.8–11) lists mostly non-Roman authorities (Punic and Greek).[69] Varro draws, therefore, on an established tradition *de re rustica* widely diffuse in Roman culture and in the ancient Mediterranean.

In the mid-first century, Columella contributed his own *De re rustica* (60–65 C.E.), the third extant in Latin, in twelve books, making it the longest and most systematic agricultural handbook that survives from antiquity. Its main function is polemical, to attack the existence of huge estates (*latifundia*), a term that appears in literary sources precisely in this period, the mid-first century of the Common Era. Like his literary contemporaries Seneca the Younger and Pliny, Columella bemoans the *latifundium* as a sign of Roman opulence and degeneracy. The disapproval comes from the moral association of *latifundia* with gangs of chained slaves, often with criminal records, and with the downgrading of local citizen-farmers into a state of dependency akin to debt bondage.[70] Columella wants to replace the criminal vice of chained slave gangs with a more dignified (and "Roman") system of slave labor—the rule by *auctoritas* of a just and fair elite slave bailiff (*vilicus*) in control of his passions. To be sure, the chapters on the *vilicus* and his wife, the *vilica* (*Rust.* 11–12), are a later addition after the request of Columella's addressee Publius Silvinus and his students (1.*Pref.*2; 4.1.1) for more elaboration on the bailiff's functions (11.2), but the Roman readers' request and Columella's lengthy response show nonetheless the emerging centrality and importance of the elite managerial slave in Roman imperial society. Something of a literary convention in didactic literature, the request suited Columella's efforts to defend the reality of a large slave staff in Roman villas while also to reform agriculture back to Cato's moral ideal of republican farming (sc. "family") values. Columella underscores the importance of a good and faithful *vilicus* for the security and prosperity of the rural household (*familia rustica*), after the model of a good and faithful managerial slave in the urban household (*familia urbana*). His advice claims to come from a long-standing handbook tradition and from personal experience on his estates near Rome (3.3.3; 3.9.2), in greater Italy (6.1.1–2; cf. 7.2.3), the provinces of Cilicia and of Syria (2.10.18), and his native Baetica in southern Spain (2.15.2). To bolster the authority of his teachings further, he makes studied mention of prominent Greek, Punic, and Roman authors as associates (1.1.7–17), name-dropping Varro as a contemporary of his grandfather, for example (1.*Pref.*15). The didactic poetry in book 10 has a similar apologetic function.[71]

A helpful way to interpret the early Christian domestic codes is in light of the ideology of slaveholding represented in this ancient handbook tradition. The didactic paraenesis on slave management in the Christian *Haustafeln* and in the Roman agronomists is similar and, importantly, so is the moral warrant. Key is taking seriously the metaphor "slave of Christ" as a title of Christian leadership (e.g., Rom 1:1; Phil 1:1; Gal 1:10; Mark 10:43).[72] The warrant common among the Christian domestic codes identifies the believing householder as an elite slave, called the *vilicus* in Roman culture, who "knows" his and her own subordination to another Lord.

The Figure of the *"Vilicus"*:
Justice, Accountability, and Piety

The figure of the elite slave belonged to ancient discussions on household management (*oikonomia*) as far back as Aristotle and the Hellenistic handbook tradition, but for the Latin agronomists its importance reached a new urgency due to the centrality of managerial slaves in Roman society and economy, both rural and urban. According to the Roman farm handbooks, the elite slave bailiff (*vilicus*) has authority to command (*auctoritas ad imperium*) as the representative of the estate owner (*pater familias*), understood in the ideology to be an absentee proprietor (Columella, *Rust.* 1.8.3).[73] The figure of the *vilicus* is not just literary artifice or only connected to the farm; it also reflects a social reality, and one present in cities. Inscriptions attest to all kinds of *vilici* as urban managers and administrators of workshops, inns, libraries, baths, theaters, amphitheaters, sports teams, and the collection of taxes. This "*vilicus* system" in the city and on the farm organized slaves into a hierarchy of orders (*ordo*, rank), which imitated the pattern of inequality and differentiation among Roman citizens.[74] Fully developed with a juridical framework by the first two centuries of the Common Era, the *ordo man-*

cipiorum (series of slave ranks) had a threefold chain of command: the *procurator* (steward); *vilicus* (bailiff); and *praefectus, monitor,* or *magister* (overseer, foreman). Other designations also appear (*actor, atriensis, dispensator, institor*), whose specific function varies according to literary context and historical period. In contrast, Greek terms for managerial slaves (*oikonomos, epitropos, cheiristēs*) appear to be synonymous, denoting slave managers and administrators generally.[75]

According to the Latin agronomists, good housekeeping required power to be routed through patterns of personalized influence of a just and fair *vilicus* in control of his passions, acknowledged by the willing compliance of subordinate slaves and the esteem of his fellow elites. The construction and maintenance of this *auctoritas* in the *vilicus* promised productivity and security in investment farming and large-scale ranching of sheep and cattle. But the agronomists were not simply talking about investment and profit in agriculture (though they were doing that).[76] The exhortations countered, especially for Columella, moral degeneracy and criminal vice due to the dramatic economic and social changes in Italian agriculture since the late Republic. Handbooks used the farm (*fundus*) as a site for measuring the quality of traditional moral values in Roman urban society.[77] The Roman farming manuals connected to and reflected on the urban life in which they were compiled, which should answer the objection of some New Testament scholars who might question the relevance of using agricultural handbooks in any interpretation of early Christian household codes produced for and by urban congregations.

In Roman urban culture, the term *vilicus* evoked often the negative and comedic stereotype of the elite slave as tyrannical *rex* (king). Reference to the stock type facilitated warnings about servile brutality and lack of self-control in freeborn rulers. A stock bully, the *vilicus* terrorizes everyone under his control, rural and urban slaves alike. In a comedy by Plautus, the bailiff Olympio threatens his rival, an urban slave, with backbreaking work, countless floggings, nasty food, and cramped quarters if sent to the farm, and even gets the master's permission to carry out his threats. The urban slave retorts that Olympio should go back to his "own kingdom" and "own province," deriding the *vilicus* as a tyrannical "magistrate." Plautus thus evokes the antagonism between bailiff and field hand, a stock piece of Roman situation comedy. The threat of transfer from the *familia urbana* (urban household) to the *familia rustica* (rural household) was funny precisely because abuse on the farm by the *vilicus* was so proverbial. By the first century C.E. this comedic stereotype entered philosophical moralization on the general degeneracy of *latifundia*. The Stoic philosopher Seneca complains that rural estates in his day had become so large that a *vilicus* was a de facto proconsul and king. Seneca describes the *vilicus* as being accustomed to giving orders, with verbs like *imperare* (to command) and *iubere* (to order), speech more appropriate to a Roman magistrate than a household slave, no matter how elite. Such servile tyranny betrays a moral disgrace and loss of manhood in Roman estate owners unable to control their own households. Along these lines, we find Roman satire also using *vilicus* as a term of opprobrium for weak adult males, especially civic magistrates under tyrannical emperors. Juvenal, for example, mocks Rome's urban prefect under Emperor Domitian as the "*vilicus*" over an astonished city, a mere slave who may have power over fellow slaves but who actually is subordinate to another, the "*dominus et deus*" (Lord and God) Domitian. The extension of the figure of the *vilicus* beyond actual elite slaves to freeborn leaders appears also in the early Christian household codes, as we shall see below. In sum, a broad range of urban sources across the board uses the agricultural metaphor of the *vilicus* for debating tyranny, mastery, and the "realities" of imperial power. Importantly for our study of the household codes, this discourse uses (as a rule) direct address to slaves—obey only one person, the *vilicus*—and extends the metaphor to freeborn citizens.[78]

Responding to explicit apprehensions in Roman society about the *vilicus*, the Roman agronomists devote whole sections to the bailiff, borrowing from and adapting models in the Hellenistic handbook tradition. They try to build up *auctoritas* in the *vilicus* as an extension of the master's self. The teachings on slave management revolve around the three broad themes of justice, accountability, and piety.

Justice

Emphasis on justice goes back to the political philosophies of Aristotle and Plato. Plato's *Laws* contains the first extant "handbook" on slave management, and it is for a utopian city. The dialogue defines "proper treatment" (*trophē*) as doing no "violence" (*hybrin hybrizein*: outrage, insult, arrogant assault), because *hybris* diminishes the dignity of the abuser. Outlawing acts of *hybris* does not mean a prohibition of all corporal punishment for slaves, however. Reasonable whippings are said to be necessary and obvious *trophē*:

> We ought to punish slaves justly (*en dikē*), and not to make them conceited by merely admonishing them as we would free people. An address to a slave should be mostly a simple command: there should be no jesting with slaves, either male or female, for by a course of excessively foolish indulgence in their

treatment of their slaves, masters often make life harder for themselves, as rulers, and for their slaves, as subject to rule. (Plato, *Laws* 6.777d–778a; Bury, LCL)

"Just" and "equal" treatment of slaves means that slaves should be fed (but in smaller rations from the public food supply than what freeborn citizens shall receive) (*Laws* 8.848a), that slaves shall be punished for offenses in proportion to the crime committed,[79] and that slaves shall always receive floggings for their crimes (whereas citizens should be fined). The double standard of flogging for slaves and fines for citizens (6.777e) is the Platonic ideal of "justice," a so-called golden mean between the extremes of treating slaves like brutes and of overindulging them like free people.[80] Aristotle added the concept of "proportional" equality and "distributive" justice, which defined "just" (*dikaios*) and "equal" (*isos*) in terms of distribution of goods in proportion to one's social rank.[81]

Appropriate corporal punishment of slaves continued as an ideal into the Roman era. Following Greek philosophers, Cicero contended that Romans must distinguish different kinds of domination and subjection. A father must nurture his children with a readiness to obey, but a master must "coerce and break" (*coercet et frangit*) his slave (*De republica* 3.37) with the whip. Even Seneca the Younger, the Stoic urging "humane" treatment of slaves (*Epistulae morales* 47), defined that *humanitas* according to Roman standards of equality and justice, which are not ours. He recognized the need for moderate floggings (*De ira* 3.32), slaves forming the background of his larger discussion on child rearing in a hierarchical society where the act of beating and the whip had special potency.[82]

Among the Latin agricultural handbooks, Columella provides the fullest discussion of Roman justice. He tells owners to pay more attention to the slave's moral character when selecting a *vilicus*, listing a capacity to understand and do justice as the important job requirement. He writes:

> [The *vilicus*] should be not only skilled in the tasks of husbandry, but should also be endowed, as far as the servile disposition allows (*quantum servile patitur ingenium*), with such qualities of feeling that he may exercise authority without laxness and without cruelty (*neque crudeliter*), and always encourage some of the better hands, at the same time being patient even with those of lesser worth, so that they may rather fear his sternness than detest his cruelty. (*Rust.* 1.8.10; Ash, LCL)

The office of *vilicus* requires ethical principles of rule difficult to find even in social betters; honorable senators can easily become corrupted in consular magistracies that have analogous "supreme power" (*imperium maius*). The bailiff must strike a balance between cruelty and leniency—keeping people on task, praising the industrious, exhibiting patience with those who disappoint, eliciting the best work even from the worst, and showing restraint in punishment (*Rust.* 11.1.25–27). In short, slaves are to be *managed*, not simply ordered or beaten. "Such justice and care (*iustitia et cura*)," writes Columella, "contributes greatly to the increase of his estate" (1.8.18).

This teaching repeats advice familiar from previous handbooks. According to Varro, overseers and foremen should rule "with words" rather than whips, if they can achieve the same result. Cato avers justice to be paramount in the duties of the *vilicus*: the bailiff should keep "good order" (*disciplina bona*), prevent "household quarrels," reward good behavior "so others will want to do well," and give "proper punishment in proportion to damage done" (*pro noxa bono modo vindicet*). Instilling a sense of justice (*dikaion*) in trusted slaves to incorporate them into the *oikos* (household) as loyal partners is also a major theme of Xenophon's dialogue. Rather than a negative emphasis on chastisements or on treating all slaves alike, Ischomachus and his wife employ a proportional system of rewards and incentives, "equitable" and "fair" to each according to the quality of work, which is said to engender household security and productivity. Treating their slaves with laws intended for free citizens, Ischomachus and his wife hope to put slaves "on the path of honesty" (righteousness; *eis tēn dikaiosynēn*), a parallel to the exhortation to slaves and masters in the Jewish-Christian Two Ways. This tradition about justice provides evidence for reconstructing a plausible context in which an ancient audience, both Gentile and Jewish, would have heard exhortations on treating slaves "justly" and "equally" (Col 4:1).[83]

Philo of Alexandria provides an example of connecting this Gentile discussion of justice in slave management to an exposition of the Jewish law. Written in Alexandria, a city in which justice and "equal rights" had poignancy and a specific history for all residents (Jews, Greeks, and Greco-Egyptians), Philo's great series of commentaries on the Pentateuch (especially, *De decalogo*, *De specialibus legibus*, and *De vita Mosis*) provided a systematic and elementary introduction to the Jewish law that argued its practical harmony with Gentile jurisprudence in Roman Egypt. It functioned as a "handbook" (*institutio*, as the Romans would say) on the law for interested outsiders, Gentiles beginning to learn about Judaism, rather than for Jews.[84] In his *De decalogo*, Philo teaches that the brevity of the commandment on due parental honor conceals "many important and necessary laws" applicable to all forms of domination and subordination, including that of "slaves and masters" (*Decal.* 165). He interprets the Torah command as a real (as opposed to an allegorical) juridical principle of reciprocity in the duties of masters and slaves, with universal applicability in actual households:

> There are also other commandments given . . . some to slaves (*therapousi*), encouraging them to show an affectionate service towards their masters (*eis hypēresian philodespoton*), others to masters (*despotais*) recommending them to practice that gentleness and mildness (*ēpiotēta kai praotēta*) toward their slaves, by which the inequality of their respective conditions is in some degree equalized. (*Decal.* 167; trans. Young)

Philo offers a moral exemplum of this advice in the story of Moses killing the Egyptian taskmaster. According to Philo's account, Moses through words (*dia logōn*) repeatedly tried to convince the taskmasters "to show clemency and relax and curb the vehemence of their orders." Only after words had no effect did Moses resort to violence on the cruelest taskmaster of all, the act described as the height of justice (*Mos.* 1.40–44). None of these details are in Philo's source. The text of Exodus in the Bible describes Moses knowing his deed to be murder, because he looks to see that no witnesses are around and hides the body afterwards in the sand (Exod 2:11-12). Philo's redaction advances his wider encomium of Moses as a prophet-king and conforms the Pentateuch to Hellenistic moral prohibitions of the harsh commands of masters. Following ancient handbook tradition, Philo's exposition of the law is both instructional and hortatory.

The hortatory purpose is especially prominent in *De specialibus legibus*, which emphasizes justice toward slaves, the practice of self-control, and master restraint in harsh commands as the main ethical qualities needed for successful slavery:

> Let so-called masters (*hoi legomenoi despotai*) therefore cease from imposing upon their slaves (*doulois*) severe and scarcely endurable orders, which break down the bodies by violent usage and force the soul to collapse before the body. You need not grudge to moderate your orders. The result will be that you yourselves will enjoy proper attention and that your servants will carry out your orders readily and accept their duties not just for a short time to be abandoned through wearying too quickly, and, indeed, we may say, as if old age had prematurely overtaken them in their labors. On the contrary, they will prolong their youth to the utmost, like athletes, not those who fatten themselves up into full fleshiness, but those who regularly train themselves by exertion and sweat to train themselves, so as to be able to acquire the things necessary and useful for life. (*De specialibus legibus* 2.90–92; Colson, LCL)

Such advice could have come from a Cato or a Columella. Participating in classical ideologies of mastery, Philo generalizes the Pentateuch into a "handbook" for Gentiles to admire, understand, and identify as their own.

Philo follows a trajectory in Jewish Hellenistic philosophy, wisdom literature, and the paraenesis of the Greek synagogue.[85] The main resemblance to the Roman agricultural handbooks lies in Philo's hierarchical vision of human society as a *vilicus* system. Philo expands the meaning of *vilicus* (using the Greek term, *epitropos*) to include Jewish priests in the Jerusalem temple, judges at the bench, and governmental officials with delegated authority, which aims to educate the Gentile aristocracy in Roman Egypt about the subordination of elite Jews to another Lord, the living God.[86] The language of slavery in early Judaism, therefore, constitutes not some "different" or unique culture, as if the historian could place "Judaism" and "Hellenism" into separate containers.[87] Rather, the sources reveal the same literary topoi found in the agricultural handbooks, which is evidence for an overarching ideology on slave management diffuse throughout the ancient Mediterranean. Philo and other Jewish intellectuals use the literary figure of the elite slave to "think with" on particularly important and complex themes like justice, and to universalize the Jewish law for the wider, Gentile world.

Accountability

Related to justice is the second theme of accountability. In the Roman handbooks, the admonitions often appear in direct address to the elite slave, who may be understood as the intended reader.[88] The manuals tell the *vilicus* not to abuse his authority as a local master, warn about a day of reckoning, and remind him of his subordination to another. Columella recommends that "a careful master" (*diligens dominus*) shall visit the farm periodically to inspect the condition of the slaves, to see the progress of the work, and to take the *vilicus* to task for any shortcomings.[89] The *pater familias* shall inquire whether slaves "are receiving what is due to them under his instructions," whether their clothing is sufficient, and whether the food and drink are good "by tasting it himself" (*Rust.* 1.8.17). Columella's language is quasi-legal. Slaves shall be given "frequent opportunities" for hearings on complaints against superiors who treat them cruelly or dishonestly (*crudeliter aut fraudulenter*), a practice similar to that of Ischomachus and his wife (see above). Columella supports jurisprudence for slaves by his own personal example: "In fact, I now and then avenge those who have just cause for grievance (*iuste dolentes*), as well as punish those who incite the slaves to revolt, or who slander their taskmasters; and, on the other hand, I reward those who conduct themselves with energy and diligence" (1.8.18). Columella insists that the master learn the reasons for all punishments, ensure that they are just and fair, and remind the *vilicus* that he answers for all abuse. Knowing the behavior of "all cautious people (*omnibis circumspectis*)" appears as a warrant for the moral teaching, which connects a norm for behavior with "established custom (*sollemnia*)" of successful mastery asserted to be common sense. As with the early Christian domestic codes, Columella does not tell people to act in a certain way because he, the author with a certain recognized authority, says they should. Rather, he advocates behavior that "all cautious people" already do and take for granted as "established custom" because it is obviously right (1.8.16).[90]

In particular, the householder must ascertain the living conditions of slaves in the prisons (*ergastula*) on the estate. On this point Columella is adamant, because he believes elite slaves are still moral inferiors easily corrupted by absolute power. Prisoner abuse demoralizes the entire household and damages the master's *auctoritas*. He writes:

> The investigation of the householder should be the more painstaking in the interest of slaves (chained in *ergastula*), that they may not be treated unjustly (*iniuriose*) in the matter of clothing or other allowances, inasmuch as, being liable to a greater number of people, such as bailiffs (*vilicis*), taskmasters (*magistris*), and jailers (*ergastulariis*), they are more liable to unjust punishment (*iniuriis*), and again, when smarting under cruelty and greed (*saevitis atque avaritia*), they are more to be feared. (Columella, *Rust.* 1.8.17–18; see also 1.6.3)

Columella fears that abuse turns slaves disloyal, even outright rebellious. His teaching echoes an exemplum in accounts of the great slave wars of the late Republic, which blames slave rebellion morally and hierarchically, on the arrogant abuse of bad masters and overlords.[91] The cultural logic provides a context for the moral appeal of the household codes in the *Didache* and the *Epistle of Barnabas*. Interestingly, both Christian authors state categorically that a master's sharp, angry shouts do nothing but dull slaves to "stop fearing the God who is over you both" (*Barn.* 19.7; *Did.* 4.11). To be sure, loss of the slaves' reverential fear is said to take the whole congregation down the Path of Darkness. Yet the exhortation says something else just as terrifying to an ancient audience familiar with the legacy of Spartacus (73–71 B.C.E.) and of the two Sicilian Slave Wars (ca. 136–132 B.C.E.; ca. 104–100 B.C.E.). Abuse causes slaves to abandon fear of their masters, which brings all society to the brink of murderous revolt.

Piety

The third major theme is piety. In Roman culture, "piety" (Latin *pietas*) was a core virtue defining the essence of the family. *Pietas* was not merely obedience to some authority (such as a father) but fulfillment of one's family obligations as one party in a permanent reciprocal relationship. Being in a reciprocal state was (and is) not being equal—children were not understood as equal to their parents, for example—but rather being on one side of a reciprocal relationship of unequal power.[92] Each party observed its respective set of duties interwoven by mutual obligation and concern. This familial nuance of *pietas* is essential, especially in understanding its meaning in a Roman religious context. To be *pius* was to give offerings and reverence to a particular deity (or deities) in faithful devotion (*diligens*), especially in ritual, which maintained the link between the worshiper and the divine. The deity (or deities), in return, would and should offer reciprocal benefits—success, health, well-being—to the worshiper's family (as a unit) and, by extension, to the community. *Pietas* thus had a collective sense of linking an individual to a family, the family to the community, and the community to the divine. To be sure, the *pater familias* held the major responsibility in the family for establishing and maintaining *pietas*, to pray and sacrifice on behalf of the whole household. But when the owner was absent, as we shall see below, the *vilicus* assumed paternal duties on the estate, especially before the gaze of the other slaves.[93]

Presuming Roman estate owners to be absentee, agricultural handbooks give to the *vilicus* the roles normally reserved for the *pater familias*, including the fulfillment of domestic cult obligations to the ancestral household divinities. Columella writes that the *vilicus* must act as head of the *familia* as a surrogate *pater familias* and not participate in or allow any *superstitio* eroding the traditional values of the household and its cult. The *vilicus* shall "offer no sacrifice" except "by direction of the master" and "not welcome diviners (*haruspices*) and prophetesses (*sagae*)" onto the estate. Such religious frauds incite the "ignorant minds" of slaves through "empty fanaticism" (*vana superstitio*) to spend money and then to "shameful practices."[94] Columella employs *superstitio* and, by association, *religio* as labels for opposing moral polarities. The standard of *pietas* is the publicly paraded custom of Roman ancestral tradition (*mos maiorum*), *superstitio* being any worship outside that boundary. *Superstitio* is thus a slur against outsiders, who invade the home, charge fees for private divinations, and peddle "empty" religious knowledge—an intriguing parallel to the community rules against itinerate prophets in the *Didache* (*Did.* 11.4–12; cf. 2 Tim 3:6-7). In this way, Columella emerges as an active defender of the religious authority of Roman tradition and the domestic cult. His handbook functions to define and patrol the acceptable and the unacceptable on the estate: knowledge outside the domestic cult (and the handbook) threatens the stability of the household and of the master's *pietas* to ancestral gods.[95]

This advice follows that of Cato, whom Columella quotes. Cato advises that the *vilicus* observe only those religious rites authorized by the master, particularly those involving animal sacrifice and feasting. The *vilicus* must keep the feast days prescribed by the calendar of canonical festivals. And he must conduct the daily practice of the household cult, especially that of protecting boundaries at the crossroads, before the hearth, and over the farmland.[96] Under no circumstances shall the *vilicus* observe any nondomestic ritual observance. As with Columella above, the polarities of *religio* and *superstitio* frame the prohibition: the *vilicus* shall not consult illegitimate and exploitative ritual technicians, such as a diviner (*haruspex*), seer (*augur*), prophet (*hariolus*), or astrologer (*Chaldaeus*).[97] The unregulated ritual power of wandering diviners is a plague inflecting the body of the family. This advice may reflect anxiety among the estate owners that *vilici* were actually going to outside diviners for the discernment of future events, such as the master's death day or date of estate inspection, circumventing the authority of the handbook itself.

In any case, Cato's concern is great enough for the need to address the *vilicus* directly in the second person, a style characteristic of handbook writing.[98] One major section reminds the bailiff of the privileges of his rank, such the right to marriage. Cato reminds the *vilicus* that "you have a wife"—the female elite slave (the *vilica*, often wrongly translated "housekeeper") given to him as a "wife" by the *pater familias*—an implicit threat that master can take her away at will. Cato tells the *vilicus* to keep his *vilica* doing her job of supervising the domestic side of the farm operation. She is not to worship "without express orders of the master," though she may garland the hearth and pray before the *Lar* (divinity protecting the household) "for abundance," but only on the *Kalends*, *Nones*, and *Ides* of the month and certain festival days, the most ordinary of household rites that do not involve feasting.[99] This prohibition repeats Cato's point about the master marking the calendar for the entire household, an important tool in the Romanization of slaves. The *pater familias* at home, like the college of *pontifices* in Rome, regulates the everyday organization of public time, decides how the past is linked to the future, and establishes how family history is ritually celebrated and remembered.[100] The *vilicus*, as the master's deputy, must follow the official calendar, patrol for *superstitio*, worship the domestic cult, and—most important—uphold in fellow slaves the proper form of reverential "fear" that the master's *pietas* requires.[101]

Early Christian Household Codes as "Handbooks"

Because the *vilicus* was rife in the popular imagination, the stock figure was a natural referent for early Christian authors. We find the figure in Paul's use of a gnomic maxim on elite slave accountability, "It is a requirement of stewards (*oikonomous*) that they be found trustworthy" (1 Cor 4:2), and, from the Synoptic tradition, in the parable of the Faithful Slave, "put in charge of other slaves" (Mark 13:33-37; Luke 12:42-48; Matt 24:45-51), one of a series of parables on eschatological vigilance and watchfulness.[102] Continuing this practice, the writers/compilers of the *Haustafeln* select certain ethical material about elite slaves from wider classical culture, call it the "traditional" teachings of the church, and use it to bolster the domestic framework of their nonhousehold authority. The Lord is made the absent *pater familias* figure, and Christian masters are integrated into the figure of the *vilicus*. The word of Aristotle thus becomes the word of the Lord.

Both Colossians and Ephesians sandwich the codes between a series of ritual directives—prayer, singing psalms and hymns, and giving thanks to God (Col 3:15-17 [=Eph 5:19-20] and Col 4:2-4 [=Eph 6:18])—which are said to bind individuals into a collective "family." Worship is thus linked to familial obligations of mutual support. This conceptualization of the deity is the particularly Roman moral value of *pietas*. The deity is not omnipotent, arbitrary, or irresponsible, but rather a party with whom worshipers could negotiate and bind by a network of obligations, traditions, and rules. The relationship is "contractual" in the sense that the deity is seen as laid under an obligation by the mere act of doing certain behavior outwardly correct and in the right internal disposition. Christian slaves could and should expect reciprocal return from the Lord in exchange for their wholehearted work (*ek psychēs*) under their Christian masters (Col 3:23-24; Eph 6:6-8). Masters in turn agree to abstain from bitter commands, for the sake of upholding their slaves' reverential fear (*Barn.* 19.7; *Did.* 4.10; *Doctr.* 4.10), which affects the congregation internally and its covenant with God. Like the *vilicus* in the agricultural handbooks above, the Christian master is directed (in subordination to the higher Lord) to maintain the *pietas* that binds a particular deity to and keeps other deities out of the household.[103]

Colossians

The author of Colossians writes to discredit the authority of charismatics gaining popular support among the congregations at Colossae, news of which has reached sister churches in the neighboring cities of Laodicea and Hierapolis. The charismatics claim to have apocalyptic "visions" and a special relationship with angels as avenues of divine "wisdom." This wisdom advances a particular *philosophia* (best translated "religious praxis") of ascetic regimens, diet, and a calendar of special religious observances (Col 2:16-23), rules possibly Jewish in character. Despite the author's polemics, the teachers appear to be Christian insiders who quite possibly have a competing claim to the legacy of the Apostle Paul and of Epaphras, the community's founder (1:7; 4:12). Colossians condemns the "wisdom" of these charismatics by asserting its novelty, masquerade (merely "human commands and teachings"), and moral vice (2:22-23). The *oikonomia* language throughout the letter anchors the author inside God's purpose and family, and it caricatures the rivals as outsiders luring innocents from their rightful father and ancestral tradition. Being "empty deceit, according to human tradition," their *philosophia* takes people captive (*sylagōgōn*, steal as booty) (2:8). Such vituperation charges them with the crime of a vicious slave dealer, a moral and literary type of kidnapper to which we shall turn in the next chapter.

In a style characteristic of ancient handbooks, Colossians does not merely exhort but also instructs. The author writes for a wide audience: "warning everyone" and "teaching (*didaskontes*) everyone in all wisdom" (*en pasē sophia*), hoping to present "everyone mature in Christ" (Col 1:28). His pedagogical strategy is to teach "household" values in order to support a patriarchal understanding of the language of baptism (3:1-11). He invokes the name of "Paul" as a reminder of the educational, moral, and spiritual change in the self that the *domestic* setting of conversion brought to the believers. The Colossians were "once estranged and hostile in mind, doing evil deeds," but now stand "holy and irreproachable" before Christ, a status exalted and effective only if they "continue securely established and steadfast in the faith, without shifting from the hope promised by the gospel that you heard, which has been proclaimed" (1:21-23). The tradition, which the Colossians have already received at home, contains the "riches of assured understanding," "knowledge of God's mystery," and "all the treasures of wisdom and knowledge" (1:27; 2:2-3). Because "you have received Christ Jesus" at baptism, no more wisdom is required, and so, "Continue to live your lives in him, rooted and built up in him, and established in the faith, just as you were taught" (2:6-7). Instead of *charismata* (spiritual gifts), "tradition" is the only avenue of God's wisdom. Colossians is therefore conventional, and intentionally so.

The Colossian polemics urging "unity" under the one household of God, under one "Father" (Col 1:3, 12; 3:17), should be interpreted in this light. The author avers Christ to be the single "head of the body, the church," supreme over "every ruler and authority." He convicts the opponents of "not holding fast to the head" and so tearing the congregation asunder (1:18; 2:10, 15, 19) like a great carcass. The human body stands as a metaphor of the hierarchy, stability, and identity of the church. The grim metaphor of bodily mutilation signals a violation of those boundaries that separate family members from strangers, friends from enemies, citizens from aliens, patriots from traitors—which is familiar from historical narratives of civil war.[104] The "household" rhetoric brands the renegades as "domestic enemies" (on this term, see chapter 7, below) and reaffirms the legitimacy of "Paul," the pseudonymous author, and his "fellow slaves (*syndouloi*) of God" as the only authorized "ministers" (*diakonoi*) of God. Such nonhousehold apostolic ministers are stewards granted a "commission" (*oikonomia*) by the distant *pater familias* (1:25; 1:7; 4:7, 12, 15).[105] The "handbook" tone brands the charismatics, and any local patrons or householders who may support them, as working against the common sense of this hierarchy that even the non-Christian world finds valid and normal. All Christians must bind together as a single household under the *vilicus* and "bear with" one another in virtue and *pietas*, teaching and admonishing each other in "all wisdom" (3:13-16) as a unified *familia* in the *oikonomia* of God. The admonition that Christian masters remember their "subordination to another" tries to put local householders in their place under a larger hierarchy of church leaders. To paraphrase George Orwell, all Christians are equally slaves of God, but some slaves are more equal than others.

Ephesians

Ephesians repeats this emphasis on domestic hierarchy unified under the fatherhood of God, but generalizes without addressing any particular controversy or community. Its author aims to explain broadly how baptism integrates believers into God's family and plan (*oikonomia*) "built upon the foundation of the apostles and prophets" (Eph 2:19; see also 1:10; 3:9; baptismal references in 4:22-24). The epistle not only exhorts but also instructs novices in the "rich variety" of divine "wisdom" acquired only through the agency of church "ministers" (*diakonoi*) given the "commission of God's grace" (*oikonomian tēs charitos tou theou*) (3:2, 7, 10) to be stewards. The author of Ephesians heightens the emphasis on unity in Colossians by stacking slogans one upon another—there is one body, one spirit, one hope, one Lord ("master"), one faith, one baptism, and one God and Father of all (4:4-6; see also 1:22-23; 2:14-16)—a sequence that may describe early Christian worship. Ephesians generalizes what Colossians created for a specific occasion—the figure of the *vilicus* as a referent for the metaphor of "being subordinate to another," a topos widely diffuse in the Roman handbook literature.

Like Colossians, Ephesians imitates the ancient handbook style in a number of ways. It promises comprehensiveness, providing all the knowledge deemed important about a recognized authority at a single reading (3:4), with an emphasis on the moral qualities needed for success (e.g., 4:25-32): being "wise" means being moral (5:15-17). Such wisdom repeats what both the Hellenistic handbook tradition and the Jewish sapiential tradition said every educated person ought to know. The author of Ephesians hopes that the reader may have "the power to comprehend" the subject in all its dimensions ("the breadth and length and height and depth") (3:18-19). The letter is practical, trying to help householders become better masters while also educating them in the meaning of proper mastery in a larger hierarchy. It also tutors ordinary people, even slaves, in a "worthy life." And it aims to serve Christians as a vade mecum for generations to come (3:21; 4:1-2), perhaps even replacing Scripture (LXX). Its vocabulary of "mystery" notwithstanding, the letter's "wisdom" is mundane—rules for daily life, virtue/vice lists—not esoteric or theoretical speculation about the divine. According to the classification of two types that modern scholars of technical literature identify for ancient handbooks, Ephesians (like Colossians) resembles the "popular manual," not the scientific treatise.

Conclusion

To an ancient Roman audience, the early Christian household codes would have evoked the stock literary figure of the *vilicus*, which has ancestry in Greek and Hellenistic writings but is best illustrated by the agricultural manuals. Precedents in Jewish sapiential tradition and Philo applied this well-known literary figure for the Jewish law beyond reference to actual slaves, to freeborn religious authorities and household masters. Following these precedents, the *Epistle of Barnabas*, the *Didache*, and the *Doctrina*

Apostolorum functioned as "handbooks" for local Christian masters, as did Colossians and Ephesians. The language of the household portrays the emerging nonhousehold leadership as "domestic" and "traditional." Expanding the *vilicus* to freeborns is not an innovation, as I noted above with respect to Philo and Juvenal's satire of the urban prefect at Rome. Far from unsettling ideologies of slavery found in the wider Greek and Roman culture, the Christian writers incorporate the figure of the *vilicus* into their understanding of God's *oikonomia*. The use of the figure as a metaphor for freeborn masters expands the legitimacy of slavery as a totalizing ideology and implicates early Christianity more deeply in the social reality of the institution.

All three didactic themes of the *vilicus*, familiar from the agricultural handbooks, appear in the early Christian *Haustafeln*. First, there is a concern for justice. The Christian master is not to be abusive in his speech to slaves, for such injustice causes slaves to become rebellious and disloyal to the absent *pater familias*, God "the Father." Second, there is a concern for accountability. Masters must know their place and that they, too, are subordinate to a higher authority and will face a day of reckoning for abusive behavior. Third, there is a concern for *pietas*. Masters baptized into Christ are in charge of the domestic cult, centered on the Lord, and must avoid actions and influences that will turn the community (as a "household") from proper ritual adherence and obligations of reciprocity with the divine. They must remember their subordination and accountability to a higher authority. In sum, the Christian master is a *vilicus* who needs a handbook to learn his role in the "household of God."

5

THE VICE OF THE SLAVE TRADER

In the preceding chapter we examined the use of the *vilicus* motif in the early Christian domestic codes to remind masters of their "subordination to another" according to "God's purpose" (*oikonomia*). Now we consider another stock character, the slave trader, which evokes not the language of subordination but that of vituperation. This chapter explores the cultural stereotypes surrounding the slave trader (Greek *andrapodistēs*; Latin *mango*) in order to interpret *andrapodistai* in 1 Tim 1:10.

The Pauline author of 1 Timothy attacks the *auctoritas* of his opponents by claiming that their lives exhibit the immorality described in a list that groups slave traders with other criminals, in the presumed belief that their crimes have something in common (1 Tim 1:9-10). What exactly, however, slave traders have to do with the lawless and disobedient, the godless and sinful, the unholy and profane, the killers of mothers and fathers, the sexually immoral, the liars and perjurers, and "whatever else is contrary to sound ('healthy') teaching" is not explained beyond their being antitypes of the "just person" (*dikaios*). They all are "bad" because they all violate the law of God, which is "good" (1:8). Yet just how would slave dealers be acting against "the law" and moral custom in a society where the institution of chattel slavery and the practice of slave trading were seen as legal, moral, and necessary? Why did 1 Timothy assume the lawlessness and immorality of slave dealers to be obvious? In what ways did claiming that one's enemies took on the lifestyle of slave traders make effective polemic in Greek and Roman rhetoric? Answering these questions is critical for the interpretation of the biblical passage, since its author was using such stereotyping to influence his congregation.

Previous scholarship (following Str-B, 1:810–13) assumed "the law" to be Torah and the vice list to originate from the Decalogue. The term *slave traders* was then explained as coinciding with the violation of the commandment "You shall not steal," presumably meaning kidnapping.[1] In recent decades, however, scholars have suggested other possible sources, such as Greek and Roman virtue and vice catalogs.[2] The goal has been to explain the literary function of the vice catalog itself, rather than to reconstruct the cultural stereotypes of the figures listed.[3] This chapter expressly attempts a historical reconstruction of the latter.

Reconstruction of a cultural stereotype within a topos is no easy task and requires an initial methodological consideration. Not only must we inquire into how other, non-Christian authors understood the Greek term *andrapodistēs*, but we need also to examine the full range of terms used for those involved in the business of buying, selling, and trading chattel slaves. Because *andrapodistēs* occurs only once in the New Testament, we must move outside the New Testament to discover its meaning. Although ancient lexicography offers a logical starting point—claiming that *andrapodistēs* comes from two Greek words: the noun "man" (*andra-*) and the verb "to sell" ([*apo*]*didosthai*; said to be equivalent to *pōlein*)[4]— the attempt to define a word by the etymology of its component parts proves in the end linguistically illegitimate.[5] Using etymology as social description is even more misguided. As I demonstrate below, a survey of Greek literature shows *andrapodistēs* to be one term among many for a slave dealer or trader. Because many of these contexts use *andrapodistēs* in a derogatory way to condemn a merchant of an unscrupulous and lawless kind, as we find in 1 Tim 1:10, knowledge of these parallels is essential for understanding what the biblical author meant.

A crime catalog from Pollux parallels closely the list in 1 Timothy. The combination of various crimes under the same penal action helps to explain why *andrapodistai* appears in 1 Tim 1:10:

The names of crimes (*adikēmata*) against which there are private lawsuits and state criminal prosecutions: thief, burglar, grave-robber, pickpocket, adulterer, murderer (*androphonos*), highway robber, temple-raider, traitor, coward—about this one Plato [*Laws* 12.944b] says, "While the coward in battle wishes not to be named so in the judgment of all, he nonetheless is one who throws away arms." Aristophanes [*Nubes* 352] calls a coward by name—deserter, idle, ungrateful, impious (*asebēs*), vile, never served in military, refused to enlist, tyrant, slave trader (*andrapodistēs*), brewer of poisonous potions, taker of bribes, bandit, pirate, the sexually immoral (*pornos*), parricide (*patraloias*), matricide (*mētraloias*), savage, violent, slanderer, blackmailer. (Pollux, *Onomasticon* 6.151)

The words quoted in Greek transliteration above (except *adikēmata*) are identical to those in the vice list of 1 Tim 1:9-10 and provide six verbal parallels. Others, such as "slanderer" (*kakēgoros*) and "blackmailer" (*sykophantēs*), express types of liars (*pseustai*) and perjurers (*epiorkoi*) and so offer further parallels. Pollux and the author of 1 Timothy both place slave traders among murderers, the sexually immoral, parricides, matricides, the impious, and other people who violate the law.

In the vocabulary of ancient vituperation, "slave trader" (*andrapodistēs*) was a term of abuse. It functioned as a convenient stereotype within the topos for expressing contempt, one of many epithets—"corrupter" (*diaphthoreus*), "thief" (*kleptēs*), "bandit" (*lēstēs*), "highway robber" (*lōpodytēs*)—used to slander an opponent.[6] Often, however, the legal charge was more rhetorical than actual: only an assertion of, not an argument for, the opponent's criminality. Prosecution focused on condemning the quality or state of being criminal, which was to argue the obvious rather than on providing actual evidence of the defendant's guilt. Ancient rhetorical textbooks, such as the one by Hermogenes, named this strategy the use of *prejudicial* (or *characterizing*) *terms*. These terms designated stock characters familiar from New Comedy—dissolutes, adulterers, flatterers, farmers, generals—a form of oratory that emphasized character over argument, sometimes to the extent of rendering the argument invalid.[7]

Ancient orators knew well this kind of polemic, and many disapproved of it because of its irrationality. Isocrates, for example, while defending himself against the charge of corrupting youth, decries as specious this argument from vice rather than evidence:

> Ought you to believe a man who is so unscrupulous and so brazen that, having indicted me for teaching the kind of eloquence which enables people to gain their own advantage contrary to justice, he has not brought before you the slightest evidence of this but has dwelt from the beginning to the end of his speech on the iniquity of corrupting our youth—as if anyone disputed that, or as if it were necessary for him to prove what all men concede, instead of showing simply that I have been guilty of this offense? (Isocrates, *Antidosis* 89; Norlin, LCL)

The "corrupter of youth" charge, also used against Socrates (Plato, *Apology* 33a–b), is merely a stock piece of rhetoric that convicts the vice, not the defendant. The prosecutor is trying to use stereotyping, not evidence, to influence jurors. Isocrates claims that the "corrupter of youth" topos is analogous to indicting an opponent simply by labeling him a "slave dealer" ("kidnapper"):

> Why, if anyone were to bring this fellow to trial for kidnapping (*andrapodistēs*) or stealing or highway robbery, and, instead of proving that he had done any of these things, were to hold forth on the iniquity of each of these crimes, my opponent would reply that his accuser was mad and talked like a fool; yet he has, himself, used just such arguments and thinks that you do not see through them. I, however, believe that even the most simple-minded of people recognize that an accusation, to be convincing and to carry great weight, must not be one that may be employed equally well against the innocent, but one that can be applied only to the guilty. My accuser has made light of this fact, and has made a speech that is in no respect pertinent to the indictment. For he ought to have produced before you the speeches by which I corrupt my associates and to have named to you the pupils who have been debased by association with me. However, he has done neither of these things, but has rejected the most legitimate form of accusation and attempted to lead you astray. (*Antidosis* 90–91; Norlin, LCL)

Despite Isocrates' protest against the practice, litigants in Athenian courts often relied more on topoi than evidence. One of many convenient terms of abuse, *andrapodistai* was part of a stock accusation list used in Greek law courts to condemn opponents. It did not necessarily describe actual slave dealers.

Aristotle provides further evidence of this rhetorical condemnation. He reportedly reviled the Greek colony of Locri Epizephyrii (in south Italy) by claiming it "consisted of runaway slaves, lackeys, adulterers, and kidnappers (*andrapodistai*)" (*apud* Polybius 12.8.2–3; see also 12.9.5–9).[8] This is hyperbole; not all residents of the city were in these occupations, as Timaeus of Locri counters (Polybius 12.8.3–4). Timaeus calls Aristotle's charge "an effrontery" and "untrustworthy," a groundless attempt to slander an entire colony as a pack of rascals.

In a comedy by Aristophanes, the term *andrapodistai* slanders another pack of rascals—men. Aristophanes writes: "But we [sc. women] could show that many men do such things. And besides this, there are among you gluttons, burglars, buffoons, and kidnappers (*andrapodistai*), and even worse" (*Thesmophoriazusae* 815). The women use the string of abusive epithets to prove their superiority to men, an example of hyperbole. There is little regard for actuality, only stereotype.

The use of *andrapodistai* as a stereotypical term of abuse, therefore, often pointed not to actual slave dealers but to opponents as a way to brand them as correspondingly vicious. Cicero brands a certain tax collector as a *plagiarius* (kidnapper, slave trader) (*Epistulae ad Quintum fratrem* 1.2.6). Plutarch exploits the commonplace's rhetorical power to rebuke when he writes, "A dinner guest called the host who dined with him day after day 'kidnapper' (*andrapodistēs*) and 'tyrant' on whose account he had not seen his own table these many years" (*Moralia* 632f). Plutarch uses this story as an illustration of irony. By holding his guest hostage, the host made his (freeborn) guest a "slave" by depriving him of dinner with his own family at home. The guest censured the inhospitality of his host by branding him with the epithet "kidnapper," claiming that his host took on the vice of the slave trader who abducts (as a tyrant does) free citizens.

Because of their procurement of merchandise often from the free-citizen population, slave dealers were branded "kidnappers" (*andrapodistai*; Latin *plagiarii*), suspicious criminal elements who did not follow the legitimate use of the law even at the beginning step of the slave-trading process. When applied to a person or a group one disliked, this epithet functioned in Greek and especially Roman oratory to brand opponents as renegades—lacking proper *auctoritas* and so endangering the citizenship of compatriots and the orderly administration of society. In this way, ancient moral philosophy used the image of the slave dealer as an antitype of the virtuous and law-abiding person.

The language of 1 Timothy conforms to this rhetorical style. The author attacks his opponents, "some people" who have "deviated" and "turned to meaningless talk" (1 Tim 1:6), merely by evoking the characterization of stock criminals as part of his larger statement about the purpose of the law. The rhetoric contains a first proposition, "Now we know that the law is good, if one uses it legitimately" (1:8), and then a second, "This means understanding that the law is laid down not for the innocent but for the lawless and disobedient, for the godless and sinners, for the unholy and profane, for those who kill their father and mother, for murderers," and so forth (1:9-10). He attacks the lawlessness that breaks down the *oikonomia* in the Christian congregation. The author does not provide details, witnesses, or specific evidence of any kind to back up his allegation. Instead, the author rests his prosecution merely on the condemnation of criminality.[9]

Slave dealers displayed vice at every stage of the slave-trading operation, from the illegitimate acquisition and the deceptive selling of merchandise to the polluting result such sale had on places and people. In acquiring merchandise when legitimate sources such as war captives did not offer enough supply, they were not above kidnapping free citizens, a criminal act against the law of nations. In selling merchandise to unload slaves of questionable quality, slave dealers typically used deceptive speech and unhealthy practices, such as pseudomedical techniques to heighten a slave's sexual attractiveness. The result was considered "unholy"; it polluted the temples in which such sale frequently occurred and violated the holiness of the wrongfully enslaved people. As we shall see, Philo of Alexandria provides an example of connecting these Greek and Roman stereotypes to violations of the Jewish law. In keeping with Philo's precedent, the author of 1 Timothy draws on this topos in his effort to portray his opponents as "lawless" (1:9), as "liars" who are "deceitful" in their speech (1:6-7; 4:1-2), as motivated by "greed" (6:2-10), and as "unholy and profane" (1:10).

Lawlessness of Slave Dealers in Acquiring Merchandise

Vice tainted slave dealers at the first step in the process of slave trading, the acquisition of merchandise by suspicious means. Even before wheeling and dealing, slave traders received blame as "lawless" because of a black-market underclass who habitually procured chattel not through the legitimate slave supply abroad (such as foreigners or war captives) but through the illegal abduction of domestic freeborn compatriots (or their slaves). In Athenian law, slave traders caught in this nefarious activity were condemned as "kidnappers" (*andrapodistai*). "Piracy, kidnapping (*andrapodistikē*), tyranny, and the whole art of war," according to Plato, are all collectively known as "hunting by force" (*Sophist* 222c); "temple-robbers, kidnappers (*andrapodistai*), burglars, swindlers, and thieves are the appellations of those who commit these several forms of injustice" (*Republic* 1.344b). Athenian law grouped *andrapodistai* with thieves (*kleptai*), clothes stealers (*lōpodytai*), burglars (*toichōrychoi*), and pickpockets (*ballantiotomoi*) under the same penal judgment.[10] The law aimed to protect freeborn Athenians and their chattel slaves against illegal abduction for ransom or sale. In the ideology of Athenian democracy, this crime of kidnapping a citizen (or the slave of a citizen) was a particular abuse of Greek liberty.

In Roman law "kidnappers" (*plagiarii*) who procured merchandise by abducting upper-order Romans were similarly condemned as outlaws. Such lawless types were vicious pirates masquerading as legitimate slave dealers.[11] In his commentary on the Manilian Law, Cicero laments such piracy in the Mediterranean. "How many islands," he asks, "do you suppose were deserted, how many of your allies' cities either abandoned through fear or captured by pirates?" (*Pro lege Manilia* 11.32). "Need I lament the capture of envoys on their way to Rome from foreign countries, when ransom has been paid for the ambassadors of Rome? Need I mention that the sea was unsafe for merchants, when twelve lictors have fallen into the hands of pirates?" (12.33).[12] Although Cicero decries only criminal pirates who made the frequent abduction of freeborn Romans a profitable business—not legitimate slave merchants per se—the vice of this piratical underclass nonetheless tainted slave traders generally with the "kidnapping" stereotype. To both Roman and Athenian law, therefore, "kidnapper" was the criminal in the extreme sense, a manifest thief who robbed the state of its citizens.

Untrustworthiness of Slave Dealers in Selling Merchandise

In the second stage of the slave-trading process, retail sale in the marketplace, slave dealers received further opprobrium because their wheeling and dealing (of kidnapped or otherwise defective merchandise) did not follow the legitimate use of law, specifically the Roman law of sale. In Rome, the *curule aediles* issued edicts regulating market sales of slaves (and beasts of burden). Collectively known as the Aedilician Edict, this law increased the seller's liability, stereotyping slave traders as a group being "more concerned with making a profit or with underhanded dealing" (*Digesta* 21.1.44.1). The law required full disclosure of any defects in the merchandise:

> The aediles ordain that a slave of long standing is not to be sold as one newly enslaved. This edict counters the wiles of sellers; for the aediles ensure generally that purchasers shall not be circumvented by their sellers. Now many dealers are in the habit of selling as new slaves those who are not so in order to get a better price; for it is assumed that the more recently one has been enslaved, the slave will be more malleable, more trainable to his function, more responsive to direction, and more adaptable to any service; on the other hand, it is difficult to retrain an experienced slave or one of long standing and to mold his or her habits. And since slave dealers know that their customers will readily seek to purchase new slaves, they interpose those of long standing and sell them as new. In this edict, the aediles lay down that this is not to happen: accordingly, if such a sale be made to an unsuspecting purchaser, the slave will be returned. (*Dig.* 21.1.37)

Other defects to be disclosed were disease or unsound health, physical or mental disability, lack of talent, or the tendency either to wander off (*erro*) or to run away (*fugitivus*).[13] Each defect had to be declared directly on the advertisement placard (*titulo*) placed around the neck of a slave on the auction block (*catasta*). One particular quality in a slave that Roman masters prized was education, especially literary and memorization prowess. The literary slave (*litteratus*), as opposed to a slave merely literate (*litterator*), knew more than how to read and write: such a slave could craft the master's letters, audit the home and business accounts, recite the necessary poetry at social gatherings, and educate the children. Because a *litteratus* on the *catasta* brought a high price, slave dealers in the time of the early Empire notoriously showed little hesitation to list this capacity on the *titulo*, even if exaggerated or a downright lie.[14] Yet the jurist Ulpian (mid-second century C.E.) averred "defects of the mind, not of the body," to be nonetheless clear "defects in law and so a seller may not make false stipulations to hide them" (*Dig.* 21.1.4.3; also 21.2.32.pr.). In the marketplace, slave dealers who deceived their customers in any way were considered criminals under the Roman law of sale.[15]

This legal condemnation of unscrupulous slave traders, however, did not imply moral condemnation of the institution of slavery. Ancient slave dealers enjoyed a reputation similar to that of used-car sellers today: although the used-car seller functions as a standard example of an untrustworthy and unsavory person, users of the example do not mean to condemn the selling of used cars in general or even to suggest that *all* used-car sellers are so bad. Still, extreme caution in dealing with such people is warranted.[16] Slave dealing was seen as one of the more "sordid" forms of work that was beneath the dignity of those in the upper equestrian and senatorial orders. That some traders were freedmen contributed to the employment's dishonor.[17]

Slave dealers were notorious for caring more about the packaging than the quality of their merchandise. They were known to sell someone else's slave without consent or try to unload a troublesome slave by concealing defects. Indeed, the deceptive business practices of slave dealers became so infamous that their reference facilitated moral discussions about hypocrisy. When purchasing from slave dealers, the principle of civil law was caveat emptor. The young, vulnerable, and innocent needed education about them and other swindlers in the adult, outside world.

In a comedic drama, Plautus has an experienced business manager warn an innocent Curculio about the untrustworthiness of such snakes in the marketplace. The Forum at Rome, behind the Temple of Castor, contains "those whom you would do ill to trust too quickly" (*Curculio* 480), probably referring to slave traders who were known to hold auction there.[18] The presence of the temple must not mislead a potential customer to trust that the business dealings under its shadow are anything close to holy. In his Greek novel, Chariton has the experienced Dionysius tell the innocent steward Leonas who is trying to track down the dealer who cheated him into buying a freeborn girl as a slave, "This experience will make you more careful in the future. . . . [The dealer] was a kidnapper (*andrapodistēs*) and that is why he sold you someone else's slave in an isolated place" (*De Chaerea et Callirhoe* 2.1.7–8; see also 5.7.3–4).

Seneca offers a third illustration of caveat emptor. In the midst of a general discussion about hypocrites, he warns of the untrustworthiness of slave dealers:

> You may speak in the same way about all these dandies whom you see riding in litters above the heads of people and above the crowds. In every case their happiness is put on like the actor's mask. Tear it off, and you will scorn them. When you buy a horse, you order its blanket to be removed. You pull off the garments from slaves advertised for sale, so that no bodily flaws may escape your notice. If you judge a man, do you judge him when he is wrapped in a disguise? Slave dealers hide under some sort of finery any defect that may give offense, and for that reason the very trappings arouse the suspicion of the buyer. If you catch sight of a leg or an arm that is bound up in clothes, you demand that it be stripped and that the body itself be revealed to you. (*Epistulae morales* 80.9; Gummere, LCL)

The need for close inspection was great, especially when dealing with the best-known slave trader in first-century B.C.E. Rome, Toranius Flaccus. Liar, dishonorable merchant, and con artist, Toranius once sold to the triumvir Mark Antony a pair of slaves as twins, even though one came from Asia Minor and the other from Gaul. The two did not even speak the same language, further heightening the outrage. When Antony confronted Toranius for a refund, Toranius's lying speech deluded Antony into thinking that no fraud had occurred, only a rare, lawful buy of exceptional value (Pliny, *Naturalis historia* 7.12.56). Because of this and similar episodes, "Toranius, the slave dealer" entered Roman oratory. To call someone a "Toranius" or simply a "slave dealer" attacked an opponent as an exploiter of the vulnerable and innocent.[19]

This untrustworthiness in selling merchandise was seen to be motivated by greed. In his drama, Aristophanes includes "slave dealers" (*andrapodistai*) dwelling in the region of Thessaly, who operate solely "for the sake of gain" (*Plutus* 520). Lucian of Samosata speaks of "large sums" owed to slave dealers (*andrapodokapēloi*), who are proverbial creditors from whom no one ever expects debt relief (*Adversus indoctum* 24). This theme is part of the larger, moral condemnation of the "huckster" (*kapēlos*) who, as opposed to the "merchant" (*emporos*), lies to and exploits customers because of greed (LSJ, s.v.; see Lysias 22 [*Against the Corn-Dealers*], esp. 22.21).

Dealers in slaves also traded in other luxury goods such as gold, silver, jewels and pearls, fine linen, purple, silk and scarlet, scented wood, ivory pieces, incense and perfume, marble columns, and similar opulent imports.[20] Such luxury merchants received broad criticism for contributing to the moral vices of society: greed, gluttony, luxury, and lack of self-restraint. In addition, merchants, luxury or otherwise, received general condemnation for perjuring their religious promissory oaths made to close a commercial transaction.[21]

The ancient novel *The Life of Aesop* (*Vita Aesopi*) supplies one of the longest extant descriptions of the greed and untrustworthy speech of slave dealers, a work discussed in chapter 1, above. In the narrative, a slave dealer acquires the slave Aesop, an ugly dwarf. Searching for a buyer, the dealer goes to the island of Samos, a market known for its wealth, and decorates Aesop and his other slaves for sale:

> He dressed the harpist, who was good-looking, in a white robe, put light shoes on him, combed his hair, gave him a scarf for his shoulders, and put him on the selling block. But since the teacher had spindly legs he put a long robe and high boots on him so that the length of the robe and the protection of the boots would hide his ugly shanks, and then, when he had combed his hair and given him a scarf, he put him on the selling block. But he couldn't cover up or prettify Aesop since he was a completely misshapen pot, so he dressed him in a sackcloth robe, tied a strip of material around his middle, and stood him between the two handsome slaves. (*Vita Aesopi* 21)[22]

The narrative describes the slave dealer's actions to hide defects (clearly illegal under the Aedilician Edict) and his unethical attempt to decorate his slaves as a routine and regular part of the slave-trading retail business. The trouble with Aesop is that he is too ugly to cover up, so the dealer tries placing Aesop between two handsome slaves in the hope of unloading him. The dealer eventually does unload Aesop (without profit) onto the philosopher Xanthus, who admires the slave dealer's selling skill, but not for the reason the dealer anticipates. The philosopher explains to his students the trick to make the handsome slaves appear even more so:

"You see, this man had two handsome boys and one ugly one. He put the ugly one between the handsome ones in order that his ugliness should make their beauty more noticeable, for if the ugliness were not set in contrast to that which is superior to it, the appearance of the handsome ones would not have been put to the test" (*Vita Aesopi* 22).[23]

The Aedilician Edict and proverbial stories of its abuse by slave traders provide a promising context for the language in 1 Tim 1:10. The author borrows his language from cultural stereotypes in the Greek and Roman world. He attacks his opponents as "lawless and disobedient" (1:9) with untrustworthy speech (1:6-7). They have greedy intent (6:2-10) to sell their ministry as "sound" ("healthy") (1:10) while masking its defects from the "innocent" (1:9) in the marketplace of "divine training" (*oikonomia theou*) (1:4). The opponents, being masters of deception, take on the vice of slave dealers who violate the Aedilician Edict.

Yet the language of 1 Tim 1:10 does more than this. It groups the vice of slave traders right next to the vice of the sexually immoral (*pornoi, arsenokoitai*). This juxtaposition in the vice list points to a specific deception of slave traders, their pseudomedical attempts as pimps to heighten the appeal of their merchandise for immoral sex.

Slave Dealers and Sexual Immorality

In his preparation of slaves for retail sale, the ancient slave dealer was often seen as a pimp. Pagan moralists attacked this kind of slave trading as fueling the prostitution industry, male homoerotic prostitution being particularly criticized.[24] The perception was not inaccurate. As pimps, slave dealers were known to do cosmetic makeovers of their slaves, which helps explain how (beyond coincidence) slaves from opposite ends of the Mediterranean could have appeared to look like twins. The techniques were pseudomedical and not in the interest of a slave's health.

Pliny the Elder writes that "Salpe the midwife touched-up slave boys for market" by removing superfluous hair in order to make them more effeminate and so attractive to high-paying buyers (*Naturalis historia* 32.47.135). The process used tuna-fish blood, gall, and liver mixed with cedar oil, which had been stored in a lead box. "Superfluous hair" refers to *lanugo* (adolescent facial peach fuzz) as well as armpit hair; removal of such hair made a slave look younger and so was of particular concern for slave dealers: "Rubbing with ants' eggs prevents hair in the armpits of children," writes Pliny, "and slave dealers use blood that comes from the testicles of lambs when they are castrated to delay growth of peach fuzz (*lanugo*) on adolescents. Applications of this blood after the hair has been pulled out also do away with the rank smell of armpits" (*Nat.* 30.13.41). The depilation called for a recipe of animal blood, which gave the added bonus of an underarm deodorant. An additional method involved the use of "red-hot nutshells" to singe and so to soften the leg hairs of male slaves, which in the context of its usage on willing aristocratic youths the biographer Suetonius denounced as a shameless act of effeminacy and sexual vice beneath the dignity of a male Roman (*Divus Augustus* 68).

Roman authors condemn dealers' attempts to mask slave disease or deformity with drugs and cosmetics. Dealers do not practice the "sound" ("healthy") teachings of legitimate physicians. Paraphrasing the use of flattery (*adulatio*) in Plato's definition of rhetoric, Quintilian avers "the art of slave dealers" to be "a flattery of gymnastics (*exercitatrix*), for they produce a false complexion by the use of paint and a false robustness by puffing them out with fat" (*Institutio oratoria* 2.15.25). Plato actually does not mention slave dealers, but writes:

> Cookery, therefore as I say, is a form of flattery that corresponds to medicine, and in the same way gymnastics is impersonated by beautification, a mischievous, deceitful, mean, and ignoble activity, which cheats us by shapes and colors, by soothing and draping, thereby causing people to take on an alien charm to the neglect of the natural beauty produced by exercise. (*Gorgias* 465b; Lamb, LCL)

Plato has Socrates explain the confusion that results when the body, not the soul, dictates what is good. Quintilian in contrast takes this quotation about the vice of beautification and applies it exclusively to slave dealers. There is no reason to exclude slave dealers from Plato's identification of the perpetrators of this vice, but Plato himself does not make this exclusive connection. Quintilian's paraphrase of Plato exhibits a shift toward more intense prominence of and negativity toward slave dealers in the Roman context. This shift makes sense given the increasingly massive numbers of slaves pouring into the Italian and Sicilian slave markets as a direct result of the Roman wars of expansion in the middle and late Republic. The Romans experienced more contact with slave dealers than the Greeks before them.

Whether Greek or Roman, successful slave dealers had to possess some medical and pharmacological knowledge in order to exploit technology that cheated the lengthy period required in gymnastic body-building of their slaves. The slave dealers' obsession with the body, its anatomy and beauty, attracted attention from ancient physicians like Galen, who remarked on their procedures for stretching fleshy skin and other cosmetic surgery as well as their wrestling-coach-style classification of body types.[25] In rhetorical fashion similar to that of Plato and Quintilian above, Galen, as part of his general discussion of the usefulness of the parts of the body, criticizes slave dealers for confusing artificial, superficial beauty for proper, true beauty in the human body:

> And so, if you are seeking to discover the proper form for the eye or nose, you will find it by correlating structure and action. In fact, this is your standard, measure, and criterion of proper form and true beauty, since true beauty is nothing but excellence of construction, and in obedience to Hippocrates you will judge that excellence from actions, not from whiteness, softness (*malakotēsin*), or such qualities, which are indications of a beauty meretricious and false, not natural and true. Hence the qualities a slave dealer (*andrapodokapēlos*) would value in a body are not the same ones that Hippocrates would commend.[26]

This "softness" indicates youthful effeminacy, prized by slave dealers but scorned by Galen. The passage belongs to a classical tradition of a wider attack against luxury, found particularly in Stoicism. Interestingly, *malakoi* (effeminates) appears in the New Testament, coupled with *arsenokoitai* (sexual exploiters), in one of Paul's own vice lists (1 Cor 6:9).[27] The author of 1 Timothy agrees with this gender attitude and sexual ethic. First Timothy links slave dealers with "fornicators" (*pornoi*), "sexual exploiters" (*arsenokoitai*), and so associates—as Galen does—the vice of exploitative, immoral sexual behavior with the vice of slave trading.

Galen offers more intriguing details about slave traders' pseudomedical obsession with the body and its cosmetic presentation, further connecting the profession with sexual exploitation and the effeminate. Slave traders know effective procedures for using wheat flour to whiten the skin brilliantly, and they know the best detergents to clean and the most effective plasters to besmear the face. Those "slave dealers and women," Galen continues, "understand well" the effectiveness of uncooked barley gruel to cover up defects in complexion.[28] Although anecdotal, to be sure, this evidence nonetheless demonstrates the widespread use of the trope in medical as well as rhetorical contexts. The slave dealer's skill in deception and seduction caught the attention even of doctors, many of whom were, like Galen, slave owners themselves. Slave traders did not typically offer sound, healthy slaves but often tried to unload unsound, diseased ones.

The reputation of slave traders in cosmetics and expedient pseudo-pharmaceutical remedies appears in a wide range of medical contexts. Discussing the cosmetic properties of terebinth tree resin dissolved in oil, Pliny the Elder says, "Slave dealers are especially anxious to use this ointment for rubbing over the whole bodies of their slaves, with the object of correcting thinness; by walks afterward they loosen the skin of every limb, and they have the further object of making possible the assimilation of a greater quantity of food" (*Naturalis historia* 24.22.35–36). Apparently, the goal was to fatten up a slave to give the impression of health. Describing the uses of a certain lily plant, Pliny the Elder notes slave traders' knowledge of its pharmacology. Although its bulbous root, claims Pliny, does relieve colic and counteracts the bites of spiders, the root nonetheless also has unhealthy properties. It is "well known to slave dealers, for applied in sweet wine it checks the physical signs of puberty, and does not let them develop" (*Nat.* 21.97.170). The value that slave dealers (and their customers) placed on effeminacy in youth compounded their vice in the eyes of Roman moralists and helps explain the juxtaposition of "slave traders" with *pornoi* and *arsenokoitai* in the moralizing of 1 Tim 1:10. The medical contexts of Galen and Pliny provide background against which to read 1 Timothy's language of health and disease to describe the opponents—their teaching is not "sound" ("healthy").[29] The evidence makes 1 Timothy's casting of polemic in medical terms intelligible in an ancient context.

The most unhealthy vice of all was castration. When they could no longer check the physical signs of puberty, slave dealers were not above castrating their slaves to preserve youthfulness. The Roman emperors decreed laws against its practice by slave dealers. Domitian, for example, issued his edict out of both moral and economic concerns. He "prohibited the castration of males, and kept down the price of the eunuchs that remained in the hands of slave dealers" (Suetonius, *Domitianus* 7.2). Many upper-order Romans also condemned castration: "No more do boys mutilated by the art of a greedy slave dealer grieve for the loss of their ravished manhood, nor does a wretched mother give a penny to her prostituted infant for the haughty pimp (*leno*) to calculate" (Martial 9.5 [6]). Dealers mutilated and exploited slave boys for immoral sex. These vicious pimps extorted not only the boys' youth but also the love of their poor mothers.

The comedy of Plautus has one *leno* (pimp) be the target of a vice list. The *Pseudolus* has a scene in which invective aims to attack a slave dealer named Ballio, who sells slaves for prostitution. Ballio is called "sexually immoral," "criminal," "grave-robber," "villain," "business-partner swindler," "parricide," "temple-robber," "perjurer," "law-breaker," "corrupter of youths," "thief," "public defrauder," "dishonest," "morally foul," "filth," and "pimp" (*Pseudolus* 360). Although Ballio mocks and even encourages such vituperation, the terms catalog him and his profession among the most vicious in Roman society. Plautus develops this negative stereotype of the "pimp" in other plays. In *Captivi* he has a character condescend to the "dishonorable trade" of slave dealer in order to rescue his captive son (*Captivi* 98–100). In *Rudens* he writes a physiognomic portrait of the *leno*: "with a bald forehead, a good-sized fellow with a fat belly and beetle brows and a scowl, a detestable swindler that smells to heaven, curse him, chock-full of cursed vice and villainy, that had a couple of rather sweet things in tow" (*Rudens* 314–20).[30]

The specific viciousness of slave dealers was their sexual and economic exploitation of the innocent, which helps explain the juxtaposition of *andrapodistai* directly after *pornoi* and *arsenokoitai* in 1 Tim 1:10. The string of these three vices is not part of a random, monotonous series but forms a literary subgroup. The neighboring words on both sides of *andrapodistai* echo the term's prejudicial characterization of the slave trader as pimp who practices pseudomedicine and pseudopharmacology to make his merchandise appear "sound" ("healthy").

Slave Dealers and Violation of "Holiness"

The final phase of the slave-trading process, the result on people and places, was tainted with vice as well. While Greek and Roman laws and ethics condemned slave dealers with the sexually immoral as seditious and sordid, Greek and Roman religions denounced the result as sinful and "unholy." Such sexual immorality polluted the temples in which dealers held auction and violated the holiness of the enslaved. Castrated and otherwise sexually exploited people were damaged goods whose past participation in prostitution invalidated their future candidacy for pagan priesthoods. The castration and prostitution of an enslaved freeborn citizen was the height of religious sacrilege.

Herodotus tells the story of a certain Hermotimus who had been a war captive sold to Panionius, a slave dealer from Chios. Panionius belonged to the underclass of slave dealers who made their living "by the most sac-rilegious deeds"—the castration of Greek youths for sale to the Persians. Herodotus explains:

> Whenever he could get any boys of unusual beauty, he castrated them, and car-rying them to Sardis or Ephesus, sold them for large sums of money. For non-Greeks (*barbaroi*) value eunuchs more than others, since they regard them as more trustworthy. Many were the slaves that Panionius, who had made his liv-ing by the practice, had thus treated; and among them was this Hermotimus of whom I have here made mention. However he was not without his share of good fortune; for after a while he was sent from Sardis, together with other gifts, as a present to the king. Nor was it long before he came to be esteemed by Xerxes more highly than all his eunuchs. (*Historiae* 8.105)[31]

Religious language is used to condemn the vice of the slave trader. The term "most sacrilegious" (*anosiōtatos*) carries a sense of religious pollu-tion, with the technical meaning of "most unholy" or "most profaning." Herodotus condemns not *enslavement*, which he does not see as morally wrong (the Greeks also practice it), but *castration*. Herodotus expresses religious outrage at the slave dealer Panionius's eunuch-making prac-tices to suit not Greek but "barbaric" tastes. Castration is wrong because it is unsound (unhealthy), foreign, and irreligious. Herodotus uses the episode as a didactic illustration of the reversal of fortune in history. By chance Hermotimus happens to meet his former seller, Panionius, flat-ters him into trust, and exacts revenge (*Hist.* 8.106). The moral lesson is that one cannot escape punishment for religious sacrilege.

Seneca the Elder, in his work on declamation, records the use of the religious topos in a Roman context. He writes of one law-court speech in the case of a freeborn woman whom pirates abducted and forced into slavery as a prostitute:

> If I speak against her, it is not because I am moved by hatred for anybody. What hatred, what enmity can be felt for a woman whom none of her fellow citizens knew before she became a prostitute? I am swayed by regard for all the virgins on whom today a grave sentence is being passed if in this city no one can be found who is more chaste than a whore or purer than a murderess. The pirates kept you inviolate? A pirate, a pimp, a slave trader would not have left even a priestess alone. . . . Proclaim you are freeborn. What are you wait-ing for? (*Controversae* 1.2.9; Winterbottom, LCL)

A number of stock characters of vice, notably sexual perversion, appear in connection with slave traders: whores, murderers, pirates, pimps. Of particular interest is the charge that the woman in question has lost not only her virginity but also any chance of a priesthood. "Once you enter a brothel," charges the lawyer, "temples are closed to you. She is sullied by the kisses of her companions, bandied about amid the jest of drunken revelers, made to act now as a boy, now as a woman. From such a place not even a father can redeem her" (*Controv.* 1.2.10). The charge associates slave dealers with sexual vice and violation of gender. Importantly, the blame is on not the woman or her sexual clients but on the slave dealers who forced her into prostitution. The main problem is religious—slave dealers by their sexual and unholy vice profane indelibly a person's capacity for cultic purity.

Dio Chrysostom decries the presence of the slave trader as one among a number of intruders whose unholy vices (doing away with the laws, striking one another, committing murder, stealing the neighbors' property, committing adultery, and highway robbery) become contagious among the domestic population and signal depravity in the city (*Orationes* 52[69].9). A letter attributed to the Neo-Pythagorean holy man Apollonius of Tyana associates the slave trader with the thief, the bandit, and "every kind of criminal and sacrilegious person" (*Epistulae* 65).[32] Apollonius, according to his hagiographer, attacked the unholy practice of gladiatorial shows in Athens for which criminals of the lowest sort were bought at an expensive price and made to fight with one another. The list of criminals is similar to that in 1 Tim 1:10: "adulterers, the sexually immoral, highway robbers, pickpockets, slave traders (*andrapodistai*), and such like rabble" (Philostratus, *Vita Apollonii* 4.22). Apollonius refused to watch such perversity compounded by the participation of such wicked subjects as slave traders, normally the very ones who supplied contestants for the games. In the narrative, *andrapodistai* experience an ironic reversal of fortune, becoming themselves the twisted moral *monstra* of the arena that attract the fascination of gapers (*curiosi*).[33] Their human slaughtering makes Apollonius wonder why the goddess Athena had not already exited the Acropolis. The whole episode serves to heighten the need for and importance of Apollonius's moral and religious reforms. Without them Athens would be godless.

To Greek and Roman belief, slave traders belonged outside society in their element among slaves and the vicious *barbaroi* of the peripheral realms.[34] Their entrance into society brought moral and religious pollution. This use of religion to condemn the vice of slave traders is important to our study of 1 Timothy. It provides a social context in which to read 1 Timothy's language of cultic pollution: the false teachers are "unholy and profane" (1:9) as the Athenians and their conscripted criminals fighting as gladiators are "unholy," as the pirates who prostituted the woman above are "profane," as the slave trader Panionius is "most sacrilegious." The result of slave trading polluted temples and violated the holiness of people.

Philo of Alexandria:
Slave Dealers and Violation of Jewish Law

Ancient Jews shared the Greek and Roman cultural stereotype that slave dealers exhibited vice at every stage of the slave-trading process, from the lawless acquisition and the untrustworthy sale of merchandise to the resulting violation of holiness. Philo of Alexandria serves as an example of a Jew using the Greek and Roman stereotype in connection with the Jewish law. This connection belongs to Philo's larger project in his exegetical works to write a "handbook" on the Pentateuch for Gentiles, which I described in the preceding chapter.

First, according to Philo, slave dealers are bad because they are "lawless." In resorting to the kidnap of fellow Jews as merchandise, they violate the Covenant Code in the Pentateuch. Philo writes, "Anyone who thinks that kidnapped victims peddled for sale by slave dealers (*andrapodokapēloi*) become slaves goes utterly astray from the truth" (*Prob.* 37). In a discussion reminiscent of that concerning slave-dealer "lawlessness" in Greek and Roman contexts, Philo calls the slave dealer a kind of thief who steals the best of all the things that exist on the earth" who rightly deserves the most severe penalty of death (*Spec.* 4.13), citing the Covenant Code.[35] The LXX version, to which Philo most likely refers, changes the Exodus passage to conform to the wording in Deuteronomy that limits the violation to the kidnap of fellow Hebrews.

For Philo, such "kidnappers" deserve legal prosecution and judgment, the degree of which depending on the jurisdiction of the crime:

> The punishment against those who trade in slaves, if the captives belong to foreign nations, should be such as is adjudged by the court; if they are fellow nationals whom they have not only kidnapped but also sold, it is death without hope of reprieve. Yes indeed, for such persons are kinsfolk, bound by a tie bordering on blood relationship through a wider compass. (*Spec.* 4.19; Colson, LCL)

The jurisdiction of Jews kidnapping fellow Jews would fall under Jewish law. Philo vents his anger at these slave traders who operate by enslaving their compatriots:

> Indeed, we have known of some who improve on their inborn depravity and, developing the malice of their disposition to the point of implacability, have directed their slaving operation not only against those of other countries and other ethnicities but also against those of their own nation, sometimes their fellow citizens and fellow tribespeople. They disregard their partnership in the laws and customs in which they have been raised from their earliest years, customs which stamp the sense of benevolence so firmly on the souls of all who are not exceedingly barbarous or make a practice of cruelty. (*Spec.* 4.16)

Philo berates the "inborn depravity" of underhanded dealers who display a disposition to vice "to the point of implacability" and commit malice without end. Importantly, Philo does not launch his assault against all kinds of slave traders; those who acquire merchandise through the regular traffic of the legitimate slave supply (war captives and rightfully enslaved foreigners) never are said in ancient Jewish tradition to violate God's law (Lev 25:44-46; Josh 9:22-27; 1 Kgs 9:20-22; 2 Chr 8:7-10). Philo distinguishes clearly between "kidnappers" (*andrapodistai*) who violate the law and legitimate slave dealers (*andrapodokapēloi*) who do not. He writes:

> For the sake of an utterly unlawful profit they [sc. *andrapodistai*] sell their captives to slave dealers (*andrapodokapēloi*) or any chance comers to live in slavery in a foreign land never to return, never even to dream again saluting the soil of their native country or to know the taste of comforting hope. They would do wrong less if they themselves retained the services of their captives. As it is, their wrongdoing is doubled when they barter them away and raise up to menace them with two masters instead of one and two successive servitudes. (*Spec.* 4.17)

Philo condemns black marketeers and particularly those in that vicious underclass who abduct innocent victims from their own national freeborn population. As Plato and Greek orators had condemned *andrapodistai* of Greeks for violating Athenian law, and as Cicero had condemned Mediterranean pirates who kidnap ambassadors of Rome and lictors for violating the law of nations, Philo in turn condemns kidnappers of fellow Jews for violating Jewish law.

Second, according to Philo, slave dealers are bad because they are "greedy" and "untrustworthy" in speech. He applies to Jewish law the

Greek and Roman stereotype that the speech of slave sellers is untrustworthy because greed motivates them to lie. Philo points to the biblical
episode of the selling of Joseph into slavery (Gen 37:12-28), the brothers' lie about it to their father, and their delight in greed: "When they
[sc. Joseph's brothers] said that he [Joseph] had been sold, and showed
the price that had been paid, 'A fine business you have embarked on,'
he [Judah] said. 'Let us divide the profits. We have competed with slave
traders (*andrapodistai*) for the prize of wickedness'" (*Ios.* 18). Greed made
Joseph's brothers vicious and untrustworthy, competing in the vice of the
slave traders with whom they dealt. Philo asserts that "everyone with a
zeal for virtue is severe of temper and absolutely implacable against slave
traders who for the sake of a most unrighteous profit do not shrink from
reducing to slavery those who not only are freeborn but are of the same
nature as themselves [fellow Jews]" (*Spec.* 4.14). In an *a minore ad maius*
argument, Philo preaches the value of manumission on the master's virtue: "If it is a praiseworthy action for masters when masters for the sake
of benevolence do this for their homebred or purchased slaves, though
often they have brought no great profit, how great a condemnation do
they deserve who rob those who enjoy liberty" (*Spec.* 4.15). The vicious
greed of slave traders receives condemnation because it motivates the
traffic in stolen merchandise and the subjugation of freeborn Jews.[36]

Third, according to Philo, slave dealers are bad because their actions
result in the violation of holiness. In his discussion of slave traders, Philo
considers their psychology, imagining their possible moral rehabilitation, and the innocence of their unsuspecting customers. He writes:

> For they [sc. *andrapodistai*] themselves, as they know the former prosperity of
> those who are now in their power, might perhaps come to a better mind and
> feel a belated pity for their fallen state, remembering with awe how uncertain
> and incalculable fortune is, while the purchasers knowing nothing of their
> origin and supposing them to have generations of slavery behind them will
> despise them, and having nothing in their souls to incline them to that natu-
> ral gentleness and humanity which they may be expected to maintain in deal-
> ing with the freeborn. (*Spec.* 4.18)

Philo does not blame the purchasers of these illegal slaves; they are
innocent victims of sin. The fault lies squarely on the slave dealers who
because of vice "in their souls" violate the holiness of Jewish law.

Philo of Alexandria, therefore, provides a precedent for connecting
Greek and Roman stereotypes of slave traders to violations of the Jewish
law. In keeping with this precedent, the author of 1 Timothy attacks his

opponents by claiming that their actions and speech, like those of slave traders, violate the law of God.

First Timothy 1:10 and the Vice of Slave Dealers

The author of 1 Timothy attacks rival Christian teachers by encouraging prejudice and stereotyping in his congregation. He draws on the proverbial vice of slave dealers in Greek and Roman society as part of his larger effort to portray his opponents as engaging in obvious evil behavior at every stage of their operation.

The author of 1 Timothy uses *slave dealers* as a metaphorical term of abuse. The opponents are "lawless" (1:9) in their acquisition and peddling of merchandise. Their teaching is not from a legitimate source but from a "deviation" (1:6) into a black market of stolen members of the Christian household. Their instruction aims not toward the legitimate "love that comes from a pure heart, a good conscience, and sincerely faith" (1:5) and so violates the law of God. They are "liars" and "perjurers" (1:10) whose speech is untrustworthy, deceitful, hypocritical (1:6-7; 4:1-2). In this way, they are no better than slave traders who notoriously wheel and deal merchandise with undeclared defects and who proverbially perjure their religious oaths in the marketplace. Like slave traders, the opponents are motivated by greed, that "love of money," which is "the root of all kinds of evil" (6:10). The author of 1 Timothy emphasizes the specific evil of sexual immorality (1:10). The opponents prostitute "sound" ("healthy") teachings, as seedy slave traders pimp youths with unwholesome pseudomedical practices that actually promote disease.

Besides promoting disease, the opponents, like slave dealers, render places and people "unholy and profane" (1:10). They pollute the sacred space of the congregation and violate the holiness of believers. This language echoes the condemnation of slave dealers by Greek and Roman religions. The Neoplatonic philosopher Plotinus expresses similar moral and religious outrage when he writes:

> We must certainly not, either, attribute to the deliberate choice of stars and the decision of All, and to their rational calculations, what happens to the individuals subject to them. For it would be inappropriate for those divinities to plan human affairs so that some men become thieves, and others highway robbers, slave traders (*andrapodistai*), and temple raiders, and still others unmanly, effeminate in actions and emotions, and committing indecencies. So far from being appropriate behavior for gods, it would not even be appro-

priate for respectable men, or perhaps any kind of men, to do and plan things like this, from which they would get not the slightest benefit. (*Enneades* 4.4.50–51; Armstrong, LCL)

Plotinus is defending the stars against the charge that they make people do such unholy crime—not even respectable men would make them do this. The author of 1 Timothy articulates a similar theology when he defends the Christian gospel from association with the lawless teachers and their followers, people "godless" (*asebeis*), "sinful" (*hamartōloi*), and "lawless" (*anomoi*).

What Plotinus opposes is precisely what astrologers claimed about the stars. Ancient astrologers and those who sought their services understood human behavior to be fixed at birth from the configurations of planets and constellations. Mathematical calculations of these configurations provided horoscopes, which charted individuals' personalities, character traits, and futures—their lot in life. The widespread popularity of astrology in antiquity makes it a valuable source for determining widely held cultural values in the Roman period, values that may have influenced the composition of the New Testament.[37]

The professional Roman astrologer Vettius Valens produced one of few known handbooks (or "anthologies") on astrology in the Roman period. He blames kidnapping (*andrapodismos*) on the same planetary configuration that produces violence, tyranny, robbery, warfare, manslaughter, adultery, lies, banditry, perjury, and an extraordinarily long catalog of other violent vices.[38] Ptolemy, in his astronomical work, blames the vice of bandits and pirates, figures grouped together with slave traders, on the same planetary configuration (*Tetrabiblos* 3.13.159). The astrological vice list functions neither as *paraenesis* (since it believes character traits to be the innate lot of fate and so their rehabilitation irrelevant) nor *polemic* (since it blames not people but the stars, against which no human can fight), but as *education* about the actualities of life. Following the habit of the ancient handbook tradition, Vettius's language is didactic.

At first glance this pedagogical function in astrological texts looks to be a promising model for understanding the function of the vice list in 1 Tim 1:10 as teaching by "poster" fashion the invariable evil nature of life beyond the borders of Christian society.[39] Yet a better parallel proves to be Plotinus (see above), who aims to stop the idea that the stars (or the gods) cause criminal behavior. Wickedness results from those separated from the divine. Likewise, 1 Timothy argues that God is *not* the source of the "lawless" teaching of the opponents: the law of God is "good" (1:8).

The inclusion of "slave dealers" in the vice list, therefore, functions as part of an overarching strategy to influence opinion in the congregation toward acceptance of the author's gospel teachings and away from competing ones by rival preachers. The author of 1 Timothy hopes to get the congregation to think of these rivals not as individual people but in terms of their alleged group affiliation with the lawless and immoral. The author then tries to persuade by bolstering prejudice against the lawless and immoral with useful cultural stereotypes that he believes are valid from the perspectives of the whole Christian community and of the entire world. Yet, while the use of *andrapodistai* in the vice list of 1 Tim 1:9-10 functions to attack opponents, it does not function to attack the institution or ideology of slavery. Rather than revealing some alleged early Christian condemnation of slavery or the slave trade,[40] the language of 1 Timothy articulates attitudes commonplace among masters in the Roman Empire. The term *andrapodistai* was derogatory only in the sense of the slave traders' exploitation (economic and sexual) of free citizens, and of their proverbial abuse of the law. The ancient world believed in the moral goodness of slavery yet condemned the immorality of slave traders.

Comparative study of slavery as a phenomenon of Western history provides precedent for this attitude in other slave societies. In the nineteenth-century American South, proslavery apologists made slave-trader abuse of both Southern slave law and Southern decency a cause célèbre in their argument that slavery itself was not evil, only the cruelty of morally inferior masters and dealers, as I point out in chapter 7. Planters viewed the slave trader as a brute and antitype of the Southern gentleman—a "disgrace to human nature" and the combination of every bad character in Southern life: "an unscrupulous horse-trader, a familiar old-time tavern keeper, a superficially complaisant and artful hard-drinking gambler and an ignorant, garrulous and low politician."[41] After the Civil War, a Southern judge who had owned slaves wrote, "In the South the calling of a slave-trader was always hateful, odious, even among slave-holders themselves."[42] These examples offer comparable evidence that condemnation of slave traders does not mean condemnation of the institution or ideology of slavery itself. The author of 1 Timothy exploited a stereotype of ancient slave traders, one that the non-Christian world shared with the Christian. Rather than being a text proving that early Christians condemned slavery, the passage actually reinforces cultural stereotypes present in the ideology of ancient slavery and in the ancient Christian

congregation that received this letter. The household duty code of 1 Tim
6:1-2 makes an abolitionist reading even more unlikely.

The charge that opponents were like *andrapodistai* meant that their
speech was untrustworthy, their treatment of people exploitative, their
association to be with the sexually immoral, and their deeds unlawful. Yet if this is all that is intended by *andrapodistai*, the term is merely
redundant. Why, then, did the author of 1 Timothy include it? One possible reason for the term's inclusion is assonance. It is, after all, in a list
that contains eight alpha-words, and perhaps the author simply needed
another one for acoustic effect. Ancient rhetoricians knew well the power
of assonance, alliteration, and rhyme, and there is no reason to doubt
that the author of 1 Timothy was aware of sounds as phenomena of persuasion. But was the choice of *andrapodistai*, not some other alpha-word,
arbitrary or intentional? If intentional, does it then express additional
information about the opponents that the other words in the vice list do
not convey?

The kidnapping of fellow citizens may provide a clue. This is a unique
aspect of the Greek and Roman semantic field of slave dealer, a feature
not paralleled in American slavery; the distinctive and easily visible racial
component in American slavery rendered the kidnapping issue largely
moot. The issue of unlawful deprivation of freedom is also not paralleled
by the other terms of vituperation surrounding 1 Tim 1:10: murdering,
killing father and mother, doing sexually immoral acts, lying, perjuring. While *andrapodistai* shares the criminality expressed especially in
the literary subgroup of its neighboring terms ("fornicators" [*pornoi*],
"sexual exploiters" [*arsenokoitai*], "liars" [*pseustai*], "perjurers" [*epiorkoi*]),
kidnapping is nonetheless a unique charge.

As a unique vituperative term, *slave dealers* in 1 Tim 1:10 can be used
to infer something about how the author of 1 Timothy wants to portray the identity and behavior of the opponents. From the perspective of
early Christian sectarian groups, such as that being defended in 1 Timothy, a perceived heretical separation from the in-group could be an apt
analogy to the charge of kidnapping by slave dealers. The language of
vituperation functions as self-definition. The false teachers act as *andrapodistai* by their "deviation" (1:6) from the proper Christian *oikonomia*
(1:4). The sin is not merely wrong belief, as if the error of the heretics
were primarily in the area of their individual epistemology. Rather, the
language of 1 Tim 1:9-10 points in a more collective direction: toward
familial violation, with terms such as patricide, matricide, and sexual

immorality. These are not descriptive of wrong belief, but are related to some of the greatest crimes in the Greek and Roman world, violating the sanctity of the family. The sinners "swerve" and "turn out of course" from their proper place in the holy household, recruit members by deceptive teaching and depart to another household, which helps explain the emphasis of household language throughout the letter. The opponents kidnap fellow Christians to an alien group through illegitimate use of "the law" (1:8). The vituperation questions the *auctoritas* of the opponents to rule anything legitimately.

The term *andrapodistai* in 1 Tim 1:10 is unique in one other important way. It does not occur in any other New Testament vice list and, surprisingly, it rarely appears in the extant Greek and Roman virtue/vice catalogs.[43] The Greek and Roman catalogs that stand closest to the one in 1 Timothy are those occurring in a discussion of either health or the law.[44] Concerning the law, one comparative passage comes from another source, the epistles of Heraclitus, in the context of Ephesus—interestingly, the same city of 1 Timothy (1:3). The author writes, "You think another man's wealth your own; you consider others' wives your own. You enslave free people (*andrapodizete*); you eat the living. You transgress the laws; you enact illegalities; you perform by force everything that you cannot do by nature."[45] First Timothy stands close to Heraclitus's discussion of the law, because 1 Tim 1:9-10 is not a list of classical *vices* (e.g., the "Seven Deadly Sins" of pride, covetousness, lust, envy, gluttony, anger, and sloth) but of heinous *crimes* against the law (sacrilege, murder, patricide, matricide, and so forth). Gluttony and sloth, for example, may be personality defects but not criminal acts punishable under the law; sacrilege and murder are of an entirely different order.

In this way, it may be misleading to identify 1 Tim 1:9-10 as a "*vice* catalog" in the sense that it corresponds to the classical literary genre of that name. In fact, the structure of the catalog in 1 Timothy does not follow the Greek tradition of four cardinal vices that stand as the opposite of the cardinal virtues. In contrast to the Greek tradition, 1 Timothy makes no effort to base the vices on a theory of virtues or of the individual human psyche. Nor are the vices coordinated as derivative from a foundational group of four, as in the Greek and Roman catalogs. Rather, the list in 1 Timothy seems in form more like the "Two Ways" type of catalog found in Second Temple Jewish literature, which I examined in the preceding chapter in connection with the so-called Apostolic *Haustafeln*.[46] The author of 1 Timothy sees his opponents going down the path of destruction, and in process taking down the whole household of God.

In any event, the kidnapping nuance of *andrapodistai* carries a unique meaning that is not a repetition of the other crimes described in 1 Tim 1:9-10. Critical examination of the stereotype within this topos allows some inference about the author's characterization of his opponents. He saw the leaders of the heretical group (or groups) functioning as "slave dealers" (criminals fundamentally without *auctoritas*) who steal family members from their rightful parents and household, and who sell them to an alien group marked by corruption.

In the next chapter I turn to the ordinary household slave as an instigator of Christian family corruption, the "domestic enemy" par excellence. As in the above investigations, I shall argue that the reference is *literary*—characterization and stereotype associated with particular topoi—dependent on Roman thinking about *auctoritas*.

6

THE DOMESTIC ENEMY

Household Slaves in Early Christian Apologies
and Accounts of Martyrdom

Did the apologies and accounts of martyrdom of second- and third-century Christianity subvert the Greek and Roman family? In the case of gender, several studies have found that, indeed, the stories of women martyrs did subvert the patriarchy of the Roman household ideal.[1] The subversion of traditional gender roles is often presented as evidence of early Christianity's challenge to *all* structures and ideologies of power and hierarchy, including slavery. This chapter evaluates these claims about slaves in the early Christian household after the New Testament.

The presence of slaves in the household made the ancient family an inherent place of danger. Early Christian apologies and martyrdom stories sounded the warning that the household slave was either a "faithful companion" or a "domestic betrayer." Either way, by saying that only one kind of person in the household (sc. the slave) could be the source of familial ruin, the discourses of apology and martyrdom sought to contain the anxiety that danger could reside in family members of blood kinship. The explanation offered a partial solution for the problem of persecution. Slaves faithful to the last provided at least a thread of moral continuity in the family,[2] and those exposed as domestic enemies acquitted Christian kin of vice. But are these stories additional examples of literary artifice, as with the other slave references examined in previous chapters? I argue that the moral polarities of the "faithful slave" and the "domestic enemy" are, in fact, literary—complementary stock figures, which early Christian writers

used because they were rhetorically advantageous; they do not necessarily describe actual persons or events.[3]

Although the literary nature of the evidence may be too fictional to
give specific data about the historical martyrs, the general household
situations that martyr stories (and apologies) represent can nonetheless help to reconstruct slavery in ancient life generally.[4] The maxim of
the slave as domestic enemy expressed common sense, the content of
thinking circulating widely in the ancient Mediterranean. Couched in
clear warfare imagery of Rome's military culture, the maxim warned
that "You have as many enemies as you have slaves" (e.g., Seneca, *Epistulae morales* 47.5), and it pictured every slave as a potential instigator
of family betrayal and sedition, an "obvious" situation because of the
full integration of slaves into the actualities of ancient family life. The
maxim was also reversible; its flip side celebrated the "faithful slave,"
who accepted the master's authority and point of view so fully as to
endure torture and to give all, even life itself, to save the master. The
moral polarities of the domestic enemy and the faithful companion
reinforced ancient ideologies of masculinity: betrayal by one's own
domestics questioned the legitimacy (*potestas* and *auctoritas*) of the
male householder's right to dominate others, both inside and outside
the home. In short, it unmade the man (the *vir*).[5] Ancient Christian
authors recognized this need to construct Roman manhood in the literary descriptions of householders. They also appreciated the value of
exploiting the reversibility of the various slave exempla according to
which best suited the rhetorical goals of the moment, a known historiographic technique, as I note below.

The first section below examines the domestic enemy maxim and
its origins in material culture by surveying the physical environment
of the ancient house and the integration of slaves in ancient work, religion, and family relations. The second explores the maxim's function
in early Christian apologies. The third section investigates the stories
about slaves in martyrdom accounts in light of the moral exemplum
of domestic slave fidelity. I investigate the apologies and accounts of
martyrdom in order to evaluate the degree to which Christian tales
of slaves, especially in martyrdom, subverted Roman ideologies of the
family. Against a standard consensus in early Christian studies, I argue
that such slave tales did not entirely overthrow the hierarchy of the
Roman family.

The Slave as Domestic Enemy:
A Case of "Mastercide"

In 61 C.E. Pedanius Secundus, the emperor's deputy at Rome (*praefectus urbi*) was murdered at home by his own slave. The details on why are unclear: either the domestic expected to be freed at a previously agreed price, or the slave and master were competitors for the affection of the same slave lover. The particular motivation did not concern the Roman Senate. After some debate and despite protests from the populace about the innocents, the Senate ordered, in accordance with ancient custom, the immediate execution of *all* slaves "residing under the same roof" (*sub eodem tecto mansitaverat*), in this case four hundred lives, no matter how loyal or high-ranking, as an example to others of how Rome would respond to a mastercide.[6] Accepting such a high number as historical is difficult, given the archaeological evidence for resident domestic space in even the largest extant houses uncovered at Rome. But the murdered master was *urban prefect*, the magistrate placed in charge of, among other things, public slaves (slaves owned by the state) employed in the Roman aqueducts, baths, and other public works throughout the city.[7] When we consider all the public slaves of the urban wards, four hundred as the number of slaves "residing under the same roof" of the prefect's "house" becomes more intelligible. Yet the use of a high number does stylize monetary valuations into decupled multiples of forty and of powers of ten, perhaps indicating merely a large amount of slaves and so an example of literary artifice and not social reality.[8]

In any case, any murder of a master by his or her slaves warranted public execution of the condemned. At the games, some emperors even elevated the ritual execution of mastercides to the level of performance art, a theater of mimes. With the construction of the Roman Colosseum (*Amphitheatrum flavium*), pantomimes were replaced with actual criminals, and the execution was staged for real. The condemned would be forced to play that "guilty wretch who had plunged a sword" into his master's throat. The slave was hung (for real) "on no sham cross" and gave "his naked flesh to a Calcedonian boar." "His lacerated limb lived on, dripping gore, and his whole body no longer looked like a body." Thus he "met with the punishment he deserved" and suffered a double penalty of crucifixion and being condemned to face the beasts.[9] The condemned was a commodity whose ritual execution was more remarkable as spectacle (*spectaculum*) than as punishment. The visual display celebrated in "real theater" was a powerful mechanism of social control.[10] The public execution of mastercides was a spectacle that had to be swift and brutal, because Romans imagined that such slaves, if not made examples of, would inspire slave rebellion, even open warfare, in the household, city, and state; the legacy of Spartacus died hard. Mastercides reinforced the proverb that the slave was *the* domestic enemy.

The domestic enemy proverb originated in its material culture, the close physical environment of the Roman household. That home arranged slaves pervasively, in every aspect of domestic responsibility, which gave rise to exempla of slave plots and sedition. In such domestic integration, the material conditions of slaves varied greatly, depending upon the slave's specific job or function and the master's resources and general care to provide.[11]

Wealthy slave owners managed numerous domestics in a hierarchy of slave ranks and multifarious jobs under a *vilicus*, as discussed in chapter 4. Many slaves even owned other slaves (*servus vicarius*) as part of their *peculium* (property technically belonging to the master but in practice to the slave for his or her daily needs); elite slaves thus belonged to slave-owning orders in Roman imperial society.[12] Given the hierarchy and specialization of domestic duties, we should best understand the housing of slaves as dynamic, in different circulation patterns depending on the time of day, rather than in any particular physical room. Slaves could be found all over the house, as their duties demanded. They rarely had permanent beds but slept in the hallways, on the roof, or wherever else space was available, such as in narrow storage rooms (*cellae, cellulae*). The circulation pattern renders so-called slave quarters in the archaeology of the Roman house difficult to identify. In this way, the housing situation for slaves in antiquity was different from that in the American South, which typically segregated slaves in separate slave quarters outside the master's manor, not under the same roof as the owner.[13]

Slave jobs had extraordinary specialization. There were bath attendants, masseurs, hairdressers, barbers, announcers of guests, waiters, tasters, choristers, child minders (*paedagogi*), secretaries, business managers (*procuratores*), physicians, and cooks.[14] As cooks and servers, slaves figured prominently at Roman banquets (*convivia*), surrounding the dinning area. Pliny the Elder refers to waiters standing like "legions" (*mancipiorum legiones*) protecting "our food and drink" but also pilfering for themselves (*Naturalis historia* 33.26). On the topic of "the crowd of standing slaves" at meals, Seneca condemns the customary practice of making them wait stationary "all night long," hungry, silent, and in trembling fear of punishment (*Epistulae morales* 47.3). The character Trimalichio, written by Petronius, gives each guest his own table "so these filthy slaves won't make us so hot by crowding past us" (*Satyrica* 34).[15] Since early Christian worship revolved around ritual meals (the Eucharist and the *agapē*), the teeming slave waiters at Roman *convivia* are noteworthy. Some scholars suggest a model for the early Christian house church that relies heavily on Roman peristyle villas, such as those found at Pompeii and Herculaneum, which housed such lavish Roman *convivia*.[16] Tenement apartment buildings (*insulae*), another probable setting for Christian congregations and their ritual meals, also had specialized and full integration of slaves into each activity of domestic life. In this regard, Tacitus emphasizes the Roman exact hierarchy of slave jobs in the household by a contrast to the situation in barbarian Germania. He writes:

> Their . . . slaves are not organized in our fashion: that is, by an exact definition of services throughout a household. Each freedman remains master of his own house and home: the master requires a certain quantity of grain or cattle or clothing from the slave, as if from a tenant farmer. The slave so far is subservient; but the rest—the services of the household—is discharged by the master's wife and children. (*Germania* 25.1–2; Hutton and Warmington, LCL)

Tacitus deemed slave quarters absolutely separate from the owner's residence odd indeed.[17] Unlike barbarians, the Romans integrated slave jobs into the close quarters and hierarchy of their own household structure.[18]

The religious life of Roman slaves, whether in peristyle houses or tenement flats, required participation in the daily ritual of the household cult, which centered on the protective idols (*Lares*) that represented the ancestral spirit (*genius*) of the estate owner (*pater familias*). During one pagan rite in January (the *Compitalia*), the family hung male and female dolls for each free member of the house (*domus*), but woolen balls for each slave. While the ritual integrated slaves as house members, the representation nonetheless also subordinated them as dehumanized, genderless balls. The interplay of gender and status distinctions also was part of religious festivals for the benefit of slaves, the *Saturnalia* in December and the slaves' holiday on 13 August (*servorum dies festus*). Both celebrations "recognized the permeability of the boundary between master and slave status in the household, but only as the exception that confirmed that boundary."[19] The inclusivity of ancient Mediterranean polytheism as an open religious system allowed ritual diversity in the Roman household, but only to a certain point. Slaves did their own (often unnoticed) private worship alongside that of the master and his or her position in civic life or voluntary associations (such as *collegia*).[20] Slaves brought alien religious observance even into Christian homes, where (unlike pagan homes) it was not supposed to be, according to the theology of many patristic authors. Tertullian, for example, reports the case of a Christian householder who went on a journey and whose slaves took advantage of the master's absence to garland his front gate in celebration of their (formerly inconspicuous) regular pagan rites for the season, evidence for the open religious system of paganism being tenacious even in the (ideally closed) ancient Christian household. Tertullian uses the episode to exhort the strict discipline required to police idolatry in the family, especially among the (often unnoticed) family slaves.[21]

In contrast, Roman jurists, magistrates, and other aristocratic pagan thinkers expressed little need to weed out such garden-variety slave *superstitio*, until it endangered the "ancestral tradition" (*mos maiorum*) of the family cult and "piety" (*pietas*), "public prayer" (*vota publica*), and "divine providence" (*providentia*) of the Roman state.[22] The jurist Vivianus considered a daft slave, who "from time to time" joined "religious fanatics" and their "ecstatic utterances," a weirdo, to be sure, but nonetheless a chattel with "minor mental defects" only. Likewise, the loony slave, who once "indulged in Bacchanalian revels around shrines" and danced wildly like a Bacchic maenad uttering oracular "responses," was considered no more defective merchandise than a slave who once had a high fever. Even persistence "in that bad habit" of cavorting around occult shrines and uttering glossolalia meant (for Vivianus and jurists who respected his opinions) a slave gone a bit mental but not having the physical defect of disease that would lower his or her market value. Vivianus understood slave curiosity for strange rites to be irrational experimentation, harmless and puerile, and not a legal-economic liability for the owner.[23]

However, masters' tolerance of infantile superstition had limits. Prime concern was *superstitio* that subverted family and state, which was believed to have caused in part the bloodiest slave revolts in Roman history. The rebel leader of the First Sicilian Slave War (ca. 136–132 B.C.E.) was a slave named Eunus with deep devotion to the Anatolian mysteries of the Great Mother and the Syrian Goddess (Atargatis/Astarte). Roman sources brand Eunus a religious fraud, a wizard who gained supporters by breathing fire sparks through a walnut.[24] Roman fears pointed also to the Thracian gladiator Spartacus and especially his prophetess wife, who was believed to have been a maenad initiated into mysteries of Dionysus.[25] Masters' anxiety over their slaves engaging in antifamily *superstitio* persisted long after the major slave wars of the late Republic, because slaves—being fundamental outsiders—continued to live, labor, worship, and die within negotiated domestic space.

To deal with this anxiety, some ancient moralists condemned cruelty to slaves, as I noted in chapter 4 on the prohibition of harsh commands being linked to exhortations about justice and the ideology of (male) anger control. Posidonius, for example, blamed the arrogant abuse of a single master, Damophilus of Enna (among whose agricultural slaves revolt first broke out) for the First Sicilian Slave War, on the logic that the "public transcript" (we would say) of slaves proved that they would never revolt on their own without cause: "The slaves were coming to be treated worse and worse, and were correspondingly more and more alienated from their owners" (*apud* Diodorus Siculus 34/2.26).[26] Additionally, the Stoic moralist Seneca condemned the condition of many households that gave rise to the domestic enemy proverb in the first place. He writes that

> wretched slaves aren't even allowed to move their lips in order to speak. Every sound is suppressed by the threat of a beating; and not even unintentional noises like coughing, sneezing or hiccups are exempted from chastisement. If the silence is disturbed by any sounds, it must be atoned for by a dire punishment. Throughout the night they stand there hungry and silent. That's how it comes about that those who aren't allowed to talk in the presence of their master will tell tales about him behind his back. But those slaves who are allowed to talk not just in their master's presence, but actually with the master, were ready to offer their neck on his behalf, and to turn aside onto their own head danger that was threatening him: they talked when they served dinner, but kept quiet when they were being tortured. Thus there is the proverb (*proverbium*) which originates from the same arrogant attitude, that we have as many enemies as we have slaves. (*Epistulae morales* 47.3–5; Gummere, LCL)

Seneca bemoans abuse of slaves by masters as unmanly behavior and a sign of fallen morality: the domestic enemy proverb is not timeless gnomic truth but recent, bad coinage reflecting inferior mastery on the part of contemporary slave owners.[27] Yet the proverb persisted in Roman cultural understanding despite Seneca's condemnation. As late as the fifth century, an author like Macrobius still repeated Seneca's reproof, with explicit reference to the proverb (and quoting Seneca nearly verbatim):

What do you suppose was the origin of that oft-quoted and arrogant proverb which says that in every slave we possess we have an enemy? They are not natural enemies, but we make them our enemies by the inordinate pride, insolence, and cruelty that we show toward them, when luxurious living makes us so prone to anger that to be crossed in anything leads to an outburst of violent rage. . . . That is why these slaves who may not speak before their master speak of him behind his back. (*Saturnalia* 1.11.13–15)[28]

Ancient grammarians also commented on the proverb and its etiology: *quot hostis tot servi* ("We have as many slaves as we have enemies," because war captives were enslaved).[29] And early Jewish writers incorporated the proverb into their own exempla tradition, which closely followed Roman models.[30]

Other Roman authors echoed Seneca's concern, but without explicit mention of the maxim. Juvenal, for example, assumed the criminality of slaves to be obvious and satirized the difficulty of the aristocrat elite trying to keep secrets, precisely because slaves were self-contradictory creatures: the oxymoron of the insider within. He writes:

Do you suppose that a rich man has any secrets? . . . Let him shut the windows and close every chink with curtains; let him fasten the doors, remove the light, turn everyone out of the house, and permit no one to sleep near—yet the tavern-keeper close by will know before dawn what he was doing at the second rooster crow; he will hear also all the tales invented by the pastry-chef (*libarius*), by the chief cook (*archimagirus*) and the carvers (*carptores*). For what defamation (*crimen*) will they hesitate to concoct against their master when a slander will avenge them for their whippings. . . . There are many reasons for right living; but chief of all is this, that you need pay no attention to the talk of your slaves. For the tongue is the worst part of a bad slave. (*Satirae* 9.103–121; Ramsay, LCL)

This maxim recurs in Pseudo-Lucian: "For slaves know all that goes on [in the household], whether good or bad" (*As.* 5). As with the Stoics Posidonius and Seneca, the call for humane treatment of slaves (analogous to animal-rights activism today) was motivated by a concern to help the abuser—and especially the *dignitas* that arrogance degrades in the master.[31] This evidence does not support some ancient "social-justice" activist program (Stoic or otherwise) to abolish slavery as an institution or an ideology.

At no period in Roman history was concern for masters higher than during the civil wars that destroyed the late Republic. Appian narrates examples of domestic slave betrayal even before the application of torture, to stress the shock of its regularity and abundance. But the "faithful slave," that rare hero, holds the narrative spotlight as a moral exemplum of slave loyalty (*fides servorum*) even to death, protecting the life of the master, a monumental spectacle testifying to imitation of the master's self.[32] Livy also uses this topos: "Men's fears were many and various; above all the rest stood out dread of their slaves. Everybody suspected that he had an enemy in his own household, whom it was not safe to trust" (3.16.3). In his panegyric on Trajan, Pliny the Younger praises the emperor as good in contrast to the bad Domitian: "For no longer are our slaves the emperor's particular friends. . . . You have freed us from the fear of an accuser within our own households" (*Panegyricus* 42.3). Additional (and redundant) episodes appear in the handbook of illustrative examples "Of the Fidelity of Slaves," by Valerius Maximus (6.8.1–7).

Classical historiography, then, set such moral exempla against a historical backdrop of the past to teach that instability and disorder found in former periods confirmed the clear and present danger of current violence in the family to the state.[33] The greatest such danger to the family was slave eyewitness (or autopsy), a didactic theme of Roman historiography that early Christian apologies and martyrdom accounts borrowed.[34]

Vision and Authority:
Slave Autopsy in Early Christian Apology

In his *Legatio pro Christianis*, addressed to the Roman emperors Marcus Aurelius and Commodus, Athenagoras defends Christian ritual practice as harmless by, among other things, appeal to the autopsy of household slaves owned by Christians.[35] To dismiss the charge that the Eucharist involves cannibalism, Athenagoras argues that "Furthermore, we have slaves, some many, some few, and it is impossible to escape their observation. Yet not one of them has ever told such monstrous lies about us."[36] Although Athenagoras refers exclusively to the charge of cannibalism, he seems to assert also that slaves never have otherwise betrayed their Christian masters. Few scholars have commented on this passage, except to note that it is "interesting" because other apologists like Tertullian (*Ad nationes* 1.7.15) and Justin Martyr (*Apologia ii* 12.4) indicate the contrary (that household slaves have betrayed their Christian owners to Roman authorities at every opportunity). Reading the apologies as social description (even literal transcripts of actual trial hearings), some modern scholars attempt to solve the problem of this contradiction geographically, by conjecturing that the experience of

Justin in Rome and of Tertullian in Carthage was different from that of Athenagoras in Athens.[37]

What patristic scholars overlook is that these slave episodes are *apologetic* and *literary*, corresponding to stock moral exempla. Roman literary and rhetorical topoi (as opposed to actual events) were the sources of these Christian tales. Christian apologists recycled Roman ("pagan") exempla of household slaves into their own moral tales, exploiting the moral polarity's power to neutralize the value of slave autopsy. Key to this interpretation is to read early Christian apology as *discourse* rather than *transcript*.[38]

In his apology, Athenagoras describes the vulnerability of the family to slave autopsy. He explains that it is "impossible to escape" the observation of "our domestic slaves" (*Leg.* 35.3). His argument depends upon the use of maxims about slaves familiar from wider classical culture, presented as common sense ignored at one's peril.[39] No behavior at home escaped the slave's gaze. If unlawful atrocities did actually take place in the Christian household, slaves would have seen it and rushed by their very nature as domestic enemies to inform against the family. Yet, because there was nothing unlawful for them to spy, slaves had nothing to tell, convincing "proof" (in Athenagoras's mind) why domestics have never informed against their Christian masters. Yet Athenagoras does not say the alternative explanation for reticence to inform Romans authorities, the possibility of slave loyalty to the family even to death. He presents a veritable argument from silence. Athenagoras's fallacy reveals the reversibility and moral polarity of the domestic enemy saying. While authenticating slave autopsy, the maxim also discredits such witness as a lie.

Doing Athenagoras one better, Tertullian exploits this legal paradox in his early apologetic work *Ad nationes*. Through diatribe with an imaginary pagan interlocutor, he explains:

> If they [sc. the Christians] themselves are not the betrayers, it follows that it must be strangers. Now how could strangers get intimate knowledge, since all mysteries [sc. mystery religions of Isis, Eleusis, Mithras, and the like]—even those lawful—keep away strangers, unless the unlawful mysteries are not so careful? Could it not be rather than strangers are capable of showering accusations to such a degree as to invent?
>
> But, you may say, the curiosity of household slaves (*domesticorum curiositas*) has obtained such knowledge though peepholes and crevices.
>
> So what of domestics betraying their secrets to you? Why shouldn't they, when they are all betrayers?
>
> Indeed they are, and isn't it more likely that such betrayal should occur when atrocities like these are in question, when a righteous indignation

destroys the trust within the household? When it can no longer contain what horrifies the mind, and what the eye shutters at?

If this were true, the wonder is that who, with such impatient justice, leapt forth to turn informant did not likewise eagerly desire to show proof, and that the one who heard did not care to see for himself, since no doubt the reward is the same for the informant who offers proof and for the hearer who convinces himself of the credibility of the testimony.[40]

If Christian assemblies were as secret as reputed, Tertullian argues, then it is unlikely that the atrocities alleged to them would be known publicly. Outsiders, then, likely know nothing about them and so must have invented the grisly tales to accuse Christians falsely. To the apologist, the only other possibility to explain the puzzle of how outsiders got alleged "insider" information could have been that the (always untrustworthy) rumor and gossip began by household slaves whom Christians owned. But, Tertullian asks rhetorically, what master ever took seriously the puerile tattle of slaves? The diction is striking: slaves are "impatient" (*impatientiae*) and "leap forth" (*prosilire*) to turn informant; they "eagerly desire" (*gestire*) to show proof. Such language alludes to the dramatic stock figure of the "running slave" (*servus currens*) examined in chapter 3, above. In Tertullian's diatribe, the device functions to deflate the allegation of Christian atrocities by slave testimony, since running slaves by their own silly antics invariably confuse the news they are so eager to report. Either outright concoction by pagan prosecutors or slave gossip (always suspect) has led to the rumor. Again, Tertullian's diction is key. He indicates *curiositas* to be the source of rumor, an undignified vice of lower sorts in Greek and Roman cultural understandings.[41]

Tertullian follows a standard philosophical distinction. Plutarch, for example, condemned curiosity as a "disease" that "infects" with "slavish envy and desire," his target being the vulgar officiousness which earlier Greek comedy satirized, especially in Aristophanes. The moralist contrasts *good* interest in proper intellectual subjects, like natural science, and *bad* "curiosity" (Latin *curiositas*; Greek *polypragmosynē* [better translated "officiousness" or "meddlesomeness"]) into things deemed attractive merely because they are hidden (*Moralia* 515b–523b). The theme recurs in *The Golden Ass*, by Apuleius, an older contemporary of Tertullian and a fellow African, with the asinine downfall of Lucius because of his *curiositas* for the occult. In this narrative context, the *curiosi* are spies, gossipmongers, and skulking informers, the peeping Toms of the ancient world—and who listens to peeping Toms?[42] By explicit reference to the servile vice of *curiositas*, Tertullian encourages stereotyping of domestic slaves to let prejudice convict, testifying to his need for and implication in ancient slaveholder ideology.

In a later work, *Apologeticus*, Tertullian changes his mind (but not his slave ideology) and accepts (rather than blames) betrayal on the unavoidable consequence of simply being a Christian: "We are daily besieged, we are daily betrayed; oftentimes in the midst of our meetings and gatherings, we are surprised by assault."[43] Tertullian finds solace in the classical proverb (from a play of Terence) that truth brings forth hate.[44] Tertullian explains: "Truth and hatred came into existence together. As soon as the former appeared, the latter began its enmity. It has as many foes as there are outsiders, particularly among Jews because of their jealousy, among soldiers because of their blackmailing, and even among the very slaves of our own household because of their corrupt nature."[45]

Using the Roman maxim about slaves to "think with," Tertullian guides his theology toward "plain sense" in secular culture and finds a hermeneutical key to read Scripture. He claims that "our domestics" have caused persecution "through whose agency the betrayal has been appointed,"[46] alluding to a gnomic saying of Jesus on the conditions of discipleship: "And one's foes will be members of one's own household" (Matt 10:36).[47] Moreover, Tertullian laments the "desperation and excessive malice" in "the most abandoned slaves" who "do not even hesitate to slay their masters. For it is written in my Gospel that 'Satan entered into Judas.'"[48] Tertullian cites the Judas story of gospel betrayal as the hermeneutical key that neutralizes the shock of household slave betrayal, using the pagan maxim of the slave as domestic enemy to "think with."

This finding clarifies our initial interpretative puzzle of why the testimony of Athenagoras (slaves never betray their Christian owners) contradicts that of Tertullian and Justin (slaves routinely betray, even more so under torture). Justin, in particular, writes that the authorities "dragged to torture also our domestic slaves (*oiketas tōn hēmeterōn*), either children or women, and by dreadful torments forced them to admit those incredible actions."[49] Why two different stories? The answer lies in the flexibility of the domestic enemy maxim to cut both ways, according to the needs of the particular writer. Athenagoras can claim that the *lack* of slave betrayal proves Christian innocence because "obviously" slaves would betray their masters at the slightest chance. Yet, with identical appeal to a hermeneutics of "plain sense," Justin and Tertullian can assert the same Christian innocence based on the *abundance* of slave betrayal. Rather than being evidence of different geographic or historical circumstances, the conflicting reports of slave behavior in the early Christian household reflect proverbial thinking about slaves in stock types. The patristic arguments are reversible because the maxim is reversible.

Torture and Truth:
The Slave Body as Spectacle in Early Christian Martyrdom

Having examined early Christian apologies, I now move to the use of the maxim in martyrdom narratives. Martyrdom was quite literally spectacle (*spectaculum*). As such, it participated in the wider cultural use of *spectaculum* in rhetorical and historiographic traditions. Spectacles were of two different kinds in Roman imperial society. One was superficial entertainment—the shows (*ludens*) of the circus and the arena—a hollow image pointing away from the location of real power. The visual corollary was a higher form of spectacle, the ocular display in national monument fashion of the "realities" of power (*imperium*) for public awe and emulation.[50]

In contrast to what Tertullian and Justin say, few martyrdom accounts show slaves turning in their masters. But slaves in martyrdom stories nonetheless display both kinds of spectacle, because "the slave" was a reversible moral construct. When the slave is the *instigator* of persecution by betraying the master under torture, the spectacle is reduced to an image empty of meaning and truth, opposed to the "realities" of divine power. The loyal slave in contrast functions as a monument of faith, "spectacle" of real, divine *imperium* for the other characters and the reader to emulate. Martyrdom stories contain spectacles in this latter, meaningful sense, the goal being transcendence of literature itself as a secondhand reflection of reality, enabling the reader to do real autopsy (or *deiknymena*) of God.[51]

For example, the *Martyrdom of Polycarp* has the bishop flee into the countryside, changing farm hideouts to avoid capture, only to have one of his own domestics under torture betray his whereabouts. By a gospel theme seen previously in Tertullian, the author tries to neutralize the reader's shock with the hermeneutics of the domestic enemy proverb. The narrator explains: "When they did not find him, they arrested two young slaves, and one of them confessed under torture. For it was indeed impossible for [Polycarp] to remain hidden, since those who betrayed him were of his own house, and the police captain who had been allotted the very name, being called Herod, hastened to bring him to the arena that he might fulfill his appointed lot by becoming a partaker of Christ, while they who betrayed him should undergo the same punishment as Judas."[52] The comparison with Judas may appear to be exaggeration but becomes intelligible in light of the absolute loyalty owed the master in Roman slaveholder ideology.[53] As I noted in chapter 1 on the slave self, the particularly Roman moral value of mastery (*auctoritas*) required achievement, in a series of specific, concrete events, not just of the slave's obedience to individual commands but also of the slave's acceptance of the master's viewpoint so fully as to anticipate the master's wishes and to become an extension of the master's self.[54]

The torture of Polycarp's domestic slave to obtain truth requires further contextualization. In their juridical examinations, the Greeks and Romans "marked the body of the slave as a privileged site for the production of truth through torture."[55] The term in Greek for this process is *basanos* (touchstone), the flinty slate used to test the purity of silver and gold by the streak that it left on the stone when scraped against the metal. In the logic of ancient slaveholding ideology, "the tortured slave has no choice but to 'break' into a truth that she or he contains but does not possess. Defined by torture, the slave cannot witness freely: the slave must give witness when coerced."[56] This touchstone theory of torture and truth marked the slave body as a site of meaning to be excavated by flogging, burning, and racking.[57] The Roman whip used for such purposes had metal pieces attached to its thongs and was meant to make deep, cutting wounds: the victim was either hung up, with feet weighted down, or stood with arms tied to a beam across the shoulders. Burning called for boiling pitch, hot metal plates, and flaming torches applied directly to the skin. Racking by the "little horse" (*eculeus*) or "lyre strings" (*fidiculae*) meant tearing the body limb from limb. Slave owners weary of the effort could hire the services of professional torturers. To be sure, scenes of extreme torture form an important part of the literary artifice of the martyrdom account. But an inscription from the city of Puteoli (the *Lex Lucerina*), which offers professional flogging and/or crucifixion of slaves for a flat fee, shows extreme torture also to be a social reality and not just a literary trope.[58]

Questioning slaves by the use of torture was both routine and required under the criminal law of Rome (and Athens).[59] Because the slave was considered naturally criminous, the slave's truth could only be obtained through her or his body. Although the Roman jurists debated among themselves the merits of slave testimony given under torture—wouldn't the victim admit to anything to stop the pain? (Quintilian, *Institutio oratoria* 5.4.1; *Digesta* 48.18.1.23–24)—torture nonetheless was considered the best means to question a slave, because that ideology understood only violence: the need to "break" a slave's inherent nature to lie.[60] The *Martyrdom of Polycarp* confirms the truth excavated from the slave body, for the tortured domestic correctly led the police chief to Polycarp's hideout.

The *Letter of the Churches of Vienne and Lyons* provides another test case for the moral polarity of slave character, and one of the most revealing.[61] The account, written by Christians who managed to escape the massacre in the amphitheater at Lyons (177 c.e., ancient Lugdunum), possibly by Irenaeus himself,[62] appears in a fragment quoted by Eusebius (*Historia ecclesiastica* 5.1–3). The *Letter* reports:

> The arrests continued, and every day the finest (*hoi axioi*) were taken to fill up the number of the martyrs. The result was that they collected all the most zealous Christians of the two communities and those on whom everything depended. Arrested too were some of our pagan slaves (*ethnikoi tines oiketai*), for the governor had publicly ordered a full-scale investigation of all Christians. Thus the slaves, ensnared by Satan and terrified of the tortures they saw the faithful suffering, at the soldiers' instigation falsely accused the Christians of Thyestean feasts and Oedipean intercourse, and many other things that it should be sinful for us even to think of or even speak about or even to believe that such things could ever happen among people.[63]

The spectacle terrorizes the pagan slaves into betrayal without torture for their "testimony." The author contrasts the pagan slaves' fake autopsy (vacuous spectacle) with the authentic autopsy of fidelity in the martyrs (meaningful spectacle). Because the touchstone of torture was never applied to the servile betrayers, their testimony is blind before the realities of God's power.[64]

No monument of faith stood taller than the slave martyr Blandina.[65]

> All the wrath of the mob, the prefect, and the soldiers fell with overwhelming force on . . . Blandina, through whom Christ proved that the things people regard cheap, ugly, and contemptuous are deemed worthy of glory before God, by reason of her love for him which was not merely vaunted in appearance (*mē en eidei kauchōmenēn*) but demonstrated in achievement (*en dynamei deiknymenēn*). All of us were in terror; and Blandina's human master (*tēs sarkinēs despoinēs*), who was herself among the martyrs in the conflict (*agōnistria*), was in agony lest because of her bodily weakness she [sc. Blandina] would not be able to make a bold confession of her faith.[66]

Blandina's human master agonized over not the pain of torture but the fear of her slave's lack of will to profess Christ. But, in sharp contrast to the pagan servile betrayers, Blandina supplies in the touchstone of torture unexpected proof of genuineness. In a physiognomic reversal, the sight (*eidos*) of Blandina's slave body—cheap, ugly, and contemptuous—turns out, in the end, to be the most beautiful and prized spectacle of divine power (*dynamis*), the real "autopsy" and direct sighting of God.[67]

This irony extends to her very name (from the Latin *blandus*: "cozening," "insidious," "insincere"). Torture proves Blandina to be the moral reversal of her name, which better labels the cozening betrayers *not* being tortured. Her name is an etymological pun heightening the dramatic surprise. This use of names, to (mis)lead the reader to associate qualities of character in a certain episode, only to develop the contrary as the story progresses, was a popular device of suspense and surprise in ancient novels. The literary phenomenon reflects ancient philosophical speculation on the origin and nature of language—whether etymology was meaning, and whether *name* and *essence* bear a necessary and internal relation to each other.[68] Blandina is not bland; Biblis is not a fragile strip of *biblis* (Egyptian papyrus); Pothinus has a pressing desire (*potheinos*) for martyrdom, as does Martyrus; Sanctus is blessed (*sanctus*) for he says to his tormentors nothing but the declaration of his faith; or (in another martyrdom) Perpetua does not enjoy a long-lasting life; the slave Felicitas does not have good fortune, and so on. From this insight, the system of name giving in Christian martyrdom stories suggests an irony familiar from Greek and Roman novels.

The *Letter* continues:

> Yet Blandina was filled with such power that even those who were taking turns to torture (*basanizontas*) her in every way from dawn to dusk were weary and exhausted. They themselves admitted that they were beaten, that there was nothing further they could do to her, and they were surprised (*thaumazein*) that she was still breathing, for her entire body was broken and torn. They testified (*martyrein*) that even one kind (*eidos*) of torture was enough to release her soul, let alone the many they applied with such intensity. Instead this blessed woman like a noble (*gennaios*) athlete got renewed strength with her confession of faith: her admission, "I am a Christian; we do nothing to be ashamed of," brought her refreshment, rest, and insensibility to her present pain.[69]

The graphic blood and gore heighten the irony of a "faithful slave" by contrasting Blandina's reaction to torture with that of the pagan slaves to nontorture. The details make the scene dramatic, clear, and immediate, enabling the very experience of reading (or auditing) itself to be an act of autopsy. The reader witnesses further, as Blandina is led out with others

> into the amphitheater to be exposed to the beasts and to give a public spectacle (*theama*) of the pagans' inhumanity, for a day of gladiatorial games was expressly arranged for our sake. . . . Though their spirits endured much throughout the long contest, they were in the end sacrificed, after being made all the day long a spectacle to the world (*theama genomenoi tō kosmō*) to replace the varied entertainment of the gladiatorial combat. Blandina was hung on a post and exposed as bait for the wild animals that were let loose on her. She seemed to hang there in the form of a cross, and by her fervent prayer she aroused intense enthusiasm in those who were undergoing their ordeal, for in their torment with their physical eyes (*dia tou blepesthai*) they saw in the person of their sister him who was crucified for them, that she might convince all who believe in him that all who suffer for Christ's glory (*doxēs*) will have eternal fellowship in the living God.[70]

The reader's autoptic gaze into the text penetrates into the narrative world to see what the onlookers in the narrative do. Hung on a cross, Blandina is a spectacle of the crucified Jesus Christ:

> But none of the animals had touched her, and so she was taken down from the post and brought back to the jail to be kept for another ordeal: and thus for her victory in further contests (*agōna*) she would make irreversible the condemnation of the crooked serpent [Isa 27:1], and tiny (*mikra*), weak (*asthenēs*), and insignificant (*eukataphronētos*) as she was, she would give inspiration to her brothers, for she had put on Christ [cf. Rom 13:14; Gal 3:27], that mighty (*megan*) and invincible athlete, and had overcome the adversary in many contests, and through her conflict had won the crown of immortality [cf. 1 Pet 5:4; Jas 1:12].[71]

Torture "straightens" the Blandina figure from a dishonored slave body into a monument of honor (*timē*) and nobility (*eugeneia*), uplifting the freeborn martyrs, including her mistress.[72]

Such fidelity and endurance by an unlikely hero resembles the moral exemplum of the "faithful slave" in Roman literature. The freedwoman Epicharis, for example, did not betray members of the Pisonian conspiracy:

> In the meantime, Nero recollected that Epicharis was in custody on the information of Volusius Proculus; and, assuming that female flesh and blood must be unequal to the pain, he ordered her to be racked. But neither the lash nor fire, nor yet the anger of the torturers, who redoubled their efforts rather than be braved by a woman, broke down her denial of the allegations. Thus the first day of torment had been defied. On the next, as she was being dragged back

in a chair to a repetition of the agony—her dislocated limbs were unable to support her—she fastened the breast-band (which she had stripped from her bosom) in a sort of noose to the canopy of the chair, thrust her neck into it, and, throwing the weight of her body into the effort, squeezed out such feeble breath as remained to her. An emancipated slave and a woman, by shielding, under this dire coercion, men, unconnected with her and all but unknown, she had set an example which shone the brighter at a time when persons free-born and male, Roman knights and senators, untouched by torture, were betraying each his nearest and his dearest.[73]

My using this story as a parallel does not argue that the author of the *Letter of the Churches of Vienne and Lyons* necessarily read Tacitus (though that is likely). Rather, I claim that Epicharis illustrates a stock figure and the content of thinking widely diffuse in Roman literary imagination, in which early Christian martyrdom stories also participated, and even promoted.

Conclusion

Recent scholarship has drawn important attention to martyrdom as a discourse that questioned ancient ideologies of the family. Martyrdom, writes Judith Perkins, "projects a subversion of the contemporary hier-archy through the power acquired by suffering."[74] Focusing on gender, scholars point to women martyrs who rejected their traditional place in the family. As significant as this recovery of Christianity's challenge to Roman hierarchies is, at its extreme this approach suggests that the "blood of the martyrs" overthrew the entire oppressive ideology of the ancient family and state.[75] The slave Blandina, for example, does display the reversal of normal domestic hierarchies in dramatic and forceful spectacle. Yet her loyalty to her mistress also reinforces ancient ideol-ogies of slavery and the particularly Roman moral value of *auctoritas*, which made the story believable and "true" to an ancient audience. The system of name giving suggests that Blandina is a fiction serving the author's faith and not a historical person. Even if historical, the effort by scholars to recover nonhegemonic voices, though laudable, has not suf-ficiently emphasized martyrology as the official—and so not the whole—story, the "public transcript" that the practice of domination socially constructed.[76]

Stories about slaves are admittedly not prevalent in accounts of mar-tyrdoms but tend to favor the faithful-slave trope. In contrast to what Tertullian and Justin say, the few martyr accounts involving slaves rarely show domestic betrayal, except by pagans owned by Christians. Although it may not be surprising to discover early Christian apologies defending traditional Roman family values, to find these themes even in the few instances of slave martyrs is unexpected in light of the recent scholarly attention on the hierarchical reversal implied in martyrdom as subversive discourse. Early Christian martyrdom may indeed contest the prevailing ideology of the family in the case of gender as scholars like Perkins and others have shown, but not entirely in the case of slavery. Elements of that ideology do appear, especially the stereotypical moral polarities of the slave as domestic enemy and faithful companion. In the case of slavery, therefore, early Christian discourse participated in the very ideology of the Roman family that it was trying to subvert.

7

THE USE OF THE NEW TESTAMENT
IN THE AMERICAN SLAVE CONTROVERSY

A Case History in the Hermeneutical Tension
between Biblical Criticism and Christian Moral Debate

In the previous chapters I examined a representative sampling of early Christian texts on slaves in their ancient contexts. I now investigate how modern ideology affects historical interpretation, offering several hermeneutical observations for the book as a whole. The assumptions that guide the study of slavery in early Christianity come out of a long tradition of studying the Bible and classical antiquity with modern problems in mind. Perhaps the best example of this practice is the use of the New Testament in the nineteenth-century American slave controversy, an important case history in the tension between biblical criticism and Christian moral debate on which the previous chapters have touched.

The history of U.S. biblical exegesis on the slavery question illumines a fundamental paradox in American religious culture. The relationship between the moral imperative of antislavery and the evolution of biblical criticism resulted in a major paradigm shift away from literalism.[1] This moral imperative fostered an interpretative approach that found conscience to be a more reliable guide to Christian morality than biblical authority. Yet the political imperative of proslavery nourished a biblicism that long antedated the proslavery argumentation and remains prevalent in American moral preaching. The nineteenth-century desire to resolve this paradox led to important innovations in American interpretations of the Bible.

A variety of cultural forces shaped the nineteenth-century intellectual environment that produced professional biblical studies in American higher education. Deists had already introduced European sources for

historical-critical methods that exposed what they took to be Scripture's
textual errancy; to them, the Bible was internally inconsistent as well
as intrinsically unbelievable in places.[2] The Unitarians of New England
were developing a technique of studying the Bible that included careful comparison of all texts relevant to a particular doctrine, linguistic
analysis of obscure words in their original Hebrew or Greek, and the
elucidation of unclear passages by paraphrases.[3] The natural sciences
raised questions about biblical literalism: geologist Charles Lyell's controversial *Principles of Geology* (1830–1833) attacked biblicists as incom-
petent on the age of the earth; organic chemistry appeared to degrade
the biblically affirmed spiritual dignity of life into mere chemicals; and
zoologists took renewed interest in polygenism, the ethnographic theory
that the white and black human races sprang from distinct geographic
origins and thereby constituted separate species, in direct contradiction to the creation account of Adam and Eve in Genesis.[4] In addition,
American literary studies, undergoing professionalization, was moving
toward a critical hermeneutics (influential on biblical studies) that not
only aimed at recovery of the author's intended meaning as a norm for
validating conflicting readings of a text, but also aimed to complete and
develop what the author had only sketched and suggested—a task that
inevitably carried the critic beyond the author's intention into a hermeneutics of moral intuition.[5]

Scholars have neglected, however, another significant ingredient in
this cultural mix. The antislavery and abolitionist interpretations of the
New Testament during the American slave controversy also pushed biblical exegetes toward a critical hermeneutics, preparing the way in the
United States for the eventual reception of German higher criticism.
When biblical studies emerged as a professional academic discipline in
U.S. colleges, seminaries, and divinity schools, it thus had more than
one precedent.[6] Educated Americans were already accustomed to a more
sophisticated kind of biblical criticism if they had followed the literature
of antislavery and abolitionism.

Antislavery/Abolitionist Theology and Exegesis

Antislavery and abolitionist crusaders ransacked Scripture for texts condemning slavery, but the New Testament proved a particularly thorny
place for them to look. Two primary problems demanded detailed exe-

getical solution: first, the disturbing silence of Jesus Christ on slavery; and second, the perhaps more disturbing outspokenness of the apostle Paul. To be sure, abolitionists themselves frankly admitted, Jesus never once denounced slavery as a sin in so many words, not even in his most important ethical speech, the Sermon on the Mount (Matt 5:1—7:29). But this silence proved nothing, in their view, since Jesus also never condemned sodomy, polygamy, infanticide, idolatry, or blasphemy, each of which was clearly a sin.[7] Jesus therefore, it was reasoned, did not have to repeat prohibitions that the abolitionists saw outlawed in other passages of Scripture.

A second solution to the problematic silence of Jesus was historical and semantic. Making use of a Golden Age historiography, antislavery and abolitionist writers claimed that Jesus never spoke of slaves because his land, ancient Palestine, contained none. Only after the ministry of Jesus did pagan slaves, brought by the Romans, arrive in Palestine. The Jews of Jesus' era, presumably the only inhabitants of Roman Judea, did not own slaves, because they obeyed the Mosaic laws against Hebrews owning Hebrews as permanent chattels (Exod 21:2-6; Deut 15:12-18; Lev 25:39-54) and especially the prohibition of kidnapping (Exod 21:16). Yet, the New Testament records Jesus meeting so-called slaves, and so interpreters advanced a semantic thesis to reinforce their historical one. The "slaves" (Greek *douloi*) mentioned in the Gospels were, in fact, nothing more than voluntary hired servants, young apprentices, or employees. The moderate antislavery Presbyterian minister Albert Barnes tried to make just such a case from biblical criticism,[8] but his revivalist efforts to reach the intelligentsia appealed only to a limited audience and to standards of authority alien to traditional churches.[9]

Most clergy favored an anti-intellectual argument, straightforward and simple, which insisted on a hermeneutics of "plain sense." The "learned and pious" translators of the King James Version "never once, in the whole Bible," gave the word *doulos* the meaning "slave," but "servant." "*If they were slaves, the translators* of our Bible *would have called them so.*"[10] This literalism about, and semantic subterfuge of, the biblical text in English came from an orthodox attempt to protect antislavery and abolitionism from infidelity charges. It was also a response, albeit weak, as anti-intellectual arguments generally are, to the critical research of America's leading biblical scholars, such as Moses Stuart (1780–1852) of Andover Theological Seminary,[11] who tried to debunk this "servant" theory as absurd. The antislavery and abolitionist preachers, however, questioned the wisdom of taking "a solemn practical question at first into Greek and Hebrew lexicons, grammars, critics, and commentators, one-half of whose ideas are baked stiff in the oven of German hermeneutics."[12] The best explanation for the silence of Jesus concerning slavery was found in the "plain sense" of the King James term *servant*: Jesus encountered only free servants.

If Jesus talked too little (or not at all) about slavery, Paul talked too much. The hermeneutics of plain sense used to excuse the silence of Jesus also helped to neutralize the harsh sayings of Paul. Authors in this intellectual camp used philological subterfuge of the original Greek to exculpate Paul from positions dangerous and hostile to their own. The main target was Paul's Letter to Philemon, which (as I noted in the introduction) refers to a "servant" named Onesimus whom Paul returns to a householder named Philemon, presumably the master; proslavery authors called this letter the Pauline Mandate for federal slave law, and so it commanded large attention. Antislavery and abolitionist authors tried to force exegetical control over this letter because it was potentially the most dangerous book in the entire Bible. The danger of defeat from damning proslavery exegesis outweighed the danger of infidelity from philology and the German biblical criticism. Antislavery and abolitionist intellectuals argued that the Onesimus mentioned in the letter was not a slave but a free apprentice, employee, or even actual brother of Philemon.[13] Because Albert Barnes championed this idea that Onesimus was not a slave,[14] proslavery exegetes later dubbed it the Barnes Hypothesis.[15] The Barnes Hypothesis used semantic subterfuge to assert the Golden Age approach to history. With the congressional passage of the Fugitive Slave Law (a provision of the Compromise of 1850), which required local and state authorities to comply with federal extradition procedures for returning runaway slaves to their owners, the need for such subterfuge became acute. It helped dispute the claims of proslavery that Philemon mandated federal slave law.[16]

Racism also helped. Denouncing the proslavery work of John Henry Hopkins, Episcopal bishop of Vermont, the Philadelphia clergyman Daniel Goodwin pointed out an unexamined conclusion of its curious logic. If Jesus Christ and his apostles condoned any form of slavery at all, the form would be *white* slavery. He writes:

> If the New Testament approved and sanctioned slavery, as a legalized system, it approved and sanctioned Roman slavery. Hebrew slavery no longer existed to be either sanctioned or abrogated. Now the system of Roman slavery was per-

haps the most outrageously cruel and inhuman that ever existed. More over, it was slavery of *whites*. Can a Christian believe that Christ and his apostles approved and sanctioned such slavery as that?[17]

This reductio ad absurdum disproof with rhetorical questioning—if you say that Jesus approved slavery, then aren't you forced to abandon its racial justification?—reveals the racism present in some abolitionist arguments: surely Jesus Christ agreed with American beliefs that white people should not be enslaved. The ideology reinforced Golden Age history and semantic subterfuge that Jesus had never met slaves.

Even with racist ideology legitimating the hypothesis that Judea contained no slaves, clergy as early as the mid-1840s began to find the Golden Age view of history problematic. The more the antislavery and abolitionist preachers enlisted German historical criticism in the service of their theology, the more unpersuasive their exegesis appeared even to their fellow antislavery and abolitionist clergymen. "The evidence that there were both slaves and masters in the churches founded and directed by the apostles," pleads the moderate Congregationalist Leonard Bacon, "cannot be gotten rid of without resorting to methods of interpretation which will get rid of anything."[18]

National crises of the 1840s and 1850s influenced this transformation in abolitionist biblical interpretation: the 1840 schism in the original national abolitionist organization, the American Anti-Slavery Society, after the failure of the opponents of Garrisonianism to capture its control; the sectional schisms in the Methodist, Baptist, and Presbyterian churches in the 1840s and 1850s; and the clerical outrage over federal proslavery actions like the Fugitive Slave Law and the Kansas-Nebraska Act. In response to the clerical outrage, Moses Stuart, the most famous biblical scholar in America at the time, published his *Conscience and the Constitution* (1850), an exhortation to the nation to obey the Fugitive Slave Law, which exposed previous abolitionist exegesis as uneducated in biblical criticism.[19] In the face of such a seemingly unimpeachable academic authority as Stuart, the Barnes Hypothesis gave way for some as being untenable. Jesus Christ, many abolitionists began to concede, *did* come into contact with slavery but *did not* condemn it expressly. With the loss of semantic subterfuge and Golden Age history, the silence of Jesus was problematic once again.

To solve this problem, a new generation of abolitionists adopted a different hermeneutical strategy, the search for immutable principles in the New Testament. The exact opposite of the earlier plain-sense approach, the hermeneutics of immutable principles claims that biblical interpretation must look beyond the flat reading of the text. It aims to discern in Protestant fashion the kernel of universal truth lying beneath the superficial meaning of individual passages. This hermeneutics disfavors interpretation of isolated texts and subordinates all reading to the discernment of that kernel of immutable principles, the core teaching of Jesus.

A crucial turning point in the antislavery argument was the move away from literalism in the 1840s and 1850s. Antislavery Christianity was forced away from close readings of the text into a less literal reading of the Bible by the moral imperative of the struggle against slavery. The first step in this move was to find a kernel in the gospel and to make that kernel control biblical interpretation. That kernel was found to be Jesus' so-called Golden Rule, "Do unto others as you would have them do unto you" (Matt 7:12 and Luke 6:31). This egalitarian reciprocity ethic became the interpretative key to unlock the meaning of Jesus' silence on slavery. As I describe below, harmonization to this core Jesus teaching could then neutralize harsh sayings by Paul in his household duty codes. Otherwise, New Testament ethics would appear to have multiple and conflicting rules, an unthinkable proposition in nineteenth-century America.[20] Charismatic abolitionist ministers such as George Cheever (who, with his younger brother Henry, helped organize the new, interdenominational Church Anti-Slavery Society in 1859), Theodore Dwight Weld, and William Hosmer argued that Jesus planted this kernel of egalitarianism knowing its slow, covert growth would eventually destroy slavery.[21]

The hermeneutics of an immutable principle, therefore, was combined with another interpretative approach, the hermeneutics of the seed growing secretly.[22] This second approach believed that Jesus and the apostles planted the original seed of the gospel in the New Testament, expecting it to grow in secret throughout church history until its flowering in the present, nineteenth-century abolitionist Christianity. The hermeneutics of the seed growing secretly viewed history as moving toward universal human progress, the exact opposite of the Golden Age approach. Its combination with the immutable-kernel theory brought, and even forced, the desired unity onto Scripture. Jesus' love ethic annulled the previous Old Testament slave laws, neutralizing their power as texts proving the moral legitimacy of slavery. The seed-growing-secretly theory interpreted slavery, like polygamy and divorce, to have been part of the previous Hebrew "dispensation" whose divine sanction ended with the advent of Jesus and the Christian "dispensation." Important to this theology were beliefs in the periodization of biblical revelation, the evolution of doctrine, and universal human progress—in essence, Whig history (the forward march of progress), a major strand of nineteenth-century thought.[23] As the Methodist abolitionist William Hosmer writes, "The Old Testament is not, in all respects, a standard of morals for the present day. The New Testament has revised the ethical code of the Old, and several things, once allowed, are now prohibited. . . . Hence, it does not by any means follow, as a necessary consequence, that the recognition of slavery, by Moses, gives it a place among the institutions of Christianity." This kind of biblical periodization reinforced the seed-growing-secretly theory: "The New Testament was not given, like the Mosaic law, to one people, but to the whole race; not for one period, but for all time."[24] Old Testament slave laws, which contradicted the Golden Rule of Christ, were neutralized as antiquarian and so irrelevant to the contemporary debate over the moral legitimacy of slavery.

The hermeneutics of the seed growing secretly provided ready explanations not only for the Old Testament slave laws but also for the proslavery character of Christianity before the modern era. In typical Protestant fashion, this hermeneutics contended that Christian abolitionism, although a recent development, was superior to proslavery religions, because it displayed the full-bloomed fruits of a divine kernel that Jesus Christ had planted in the primitive church. History was understood to move forward, toward universal human progress and perfectibility, not backward in decline and moral decay, as the Golden Age view of history had claimed. Jesus, the hermeneutics discovered, in fact was not silent about slavery. Although he met literal masters and literal slaves, Jesus did not intend to perpetuate the institution but worked secretly toward its gradual destruction. True Christianity, through "fair application" of the Golden Rule and related immutable principles such as charity and love of neighbor, is a Christianity against slavery.[25] So even if *servant* did in fact mean *slave*, a concession clergy schooled in classical philology had to make, then the New Testament and the Bible generally could still be read as an antislavery document.

While the hermeneutical combination of (1) the immutable kernel and (2) the seed growing secretly allowed for contradiction between the Old and New Testaments as part of God's plan of gradual human progress, it nonetheless could not accept any contradiction within the New Testament as such, between Jesus' teachings and Paul's ethics. The apparently harsh slave rules in Paul's household duty codes must be found somehow to cohere with the Golden Rule, but Pauline commands like "Slaves, obey your earthly masters with fear and trembling" (Eph 6:5) proved such coherence difficult on a flat reading. Since the defect cannot lie in Paul, the holy apostle of Jesus Christ, the abolitionists reasoned, it must be in the interpreter who reads flatly: the lack of coherence itself must be a sign against the flat reading of the New Testament. The incongruity signals the need for the hermeneutics of the seed growing secretly, argued preachers like Cheever, Weld, Hosmer, and other evangelical abolitionists. The slave who obeys his master cannot be Christian, because slavery denies Christian duties of marriage (Eph 5:23; 1 Cor 11:3), of fatherhood (Eph 6:4), of children (Eph 6:1-2; Col 3:20), and of believers generally to worship God.[26] A flat reading of these texts finds contradiction in two ways: (1) against the immutable principles of egalitarianism, the kernel of the gospel; and (2) against Paul's own principle of evangelism, bringing new converts to the Christian faith. Because he established a slave code impossible for a baptized slave to obey, Paul must be signaling that he was secretly against slavery. A slaveholder could not be Christian either, since the enforcement of the household duty codes would remove Christianity from the slave, making the master an anti-evangelist. With the hermeneutics of the seed growing secretly, the Pauline slave codes were found to neutralize themselves.

Abolitionists in this camp had great interest in Col 4:1. As I noted in chapter 4, the verse reads in part, "Masters give unto your servants that which is just and equal." To abolitionists the key terms, *just* and *equal,* revealed that Paul understood slaves to have natural rights; since chattel slavery means absolute denial of rights and justice, Paul implicitly condemned the institution. By this verse, it was argued, Paul sowed the secret seeds that later bloomed as the Enlightenment philosophy championing inalienable human rights, a cornerstone of antislavery and abolitionist theology.[27] A nineteenth-century inaccurate historical belief reinforced the seed-growing-secretly hermeneutics. The belief was that the immutable freedom principles of Christianity (and Roman Stoicism, in lesser degree) had caused the decline and fall of slavery in the ancient world. Although recent research has proven this belief erroneous—slavery never died out in late antiquity but in fact continued into the medieval period—belief in this theory was unquestioned not only among American intellectual clergy but also in the European academic circles, which pressed for the end of slavery in French and British colonies.[28] Because Col 4:1 cohered with the Golden Rule, it must be the privileged text that exercises hermeneutical control over the interpretation of other, more difficult Pauline passages. Paul's voice was made to harmonize with that of Jesus, and the New Testament was thus found to be without contradiction. When abolitionists looked at Paul via the two hermeneutical lenses of (1) immutable principles and (2) the seed growing secretly, they saw a reflection of themselves.

This solution, however, only begs the larger question of why Paul (or Jesus, for that matter) did not condemn slavery *openly*. Why did he and Jesus sow a *secret* seed? Early antislavery found expediency to be the best explanation. According to this view, Paul did not openly condemn slavery because he feared that such open condemnation would incite slave rebellion and a subsequent Roman military crackdown (or "servile war") that would threaten the public safety of Christians. As a Roman citizen, the apostle realized that to denounce slavery was tantamount to denouncing the entire Roman Empire itself. Such a confrontation, it was believed, would have led Rome to march against nascent Christianity for inciting slave rebellion, a war on the order of that against the famous gladiator rebel Spartacus. In this hypothetical servile war, Rome would have killed Christianity before its flowering. To avoid bloodshed, Paul chose the wisdom of expediency, urging believers to obey governmental powers (Romans 13). The leading spokesman for this view was William Ellery Channing (1780–1842), Professor of Theology at Harvard Divinity School and a Unitarian Christian.[29]

Later abolitionist writers, however, found this antislavery solution unacceptable and rejected the hermeneutics of the seed growing secretly.[30] They claimed that the seed grew *openly*: Paul was not afraid to condemn slavery and does so in two overlooked passages, 1 Cor 7:21 and 1 Tim 1:10. The verse of 1 Cor 7:21 was and is a puzzle that begins on a grammatical level.[31] It reads in the King James Version, "Art thou called *being* a servant? care not for it: but if thou mayest be made free, use *it* rather."[32] The antecedent of *it* is ambiguous, leaving the reader to ask, Use *what*? Did Paul mean to use *being a servant*? Or did he mean the opposite, *becoming free*? For the abolitionist, the solution was clear: Paul urged slaves to seek freedom; "That is to say, If you are a slave and the cars of the underground railroad come along, jump on and get your freedom if you can."[33] By conflating manumission with escape, abolitionists made Paul condemn slavery. They made an even stronger claim of 1 Tim 1:10—"A more tremendous passage against slavery does not exist than this."[34] (For an interpretation of the meaning of this passage in its ancient context, see chapter 5, above.) The sentence in the King James Version reads: "For the whoremongers, for them that defile themselves with mankind, for menstealers, for liars, for perjured persons, and if there be any other thing that is contrary to sound doctrine." Key was the term *menstealers*. The abolitionist George Cheever declared, "Let the Gospel be preached according to Paul's instructions, let the churches apply the discipline of Christ according to sinners in this category, and slavery would be abolished from our land."[35] Cheever made his case from philology, using the new *Greek-English Lexicon* by H. G. Liddell and Robert Scott (first edition, 1843). Paul was found to condemn slavery by calling it the sin of "manstealing."

Despite such attempts, the New Testament—especially Paul—remained a thorn in the flesh of abolitionism. Discouraged by the ineffectiveness of their exegesis, some abolitionists began to suspect that they were wrong about the New Testament and so sought a new hermeneutical strategy. This move is the next crucial step in the turn away from literalism and toward arguments from conscience.

The new strategy was the hermeneutics of moral intuition. With the hermeneutics of moral intuition, even *if* the abolitionists were wrong about the biblical text, they could *still* maintain their cause to be morally right and in accord with the Word of God. To support this claim, they made an emphatic shift away from literalism. This shift was, in part, due to the rationalist, German hermeneutics of the higher criticism that American universities, seminaries, and divinity schools were beginning to teach at the same time as American society was torn over its slavery controversy. The moral norms of the Bible were conditioned by the social arrangements and cultural assumptions of a particular age and people, as the emerging field of critical biblical studies was beginning to show. The biblical authors composed rules and admonitions whose defect lay in their historical conditionedness. It would be "a serious theological mistake to identify as the eternal word of God those elements in their teachings that were simply the common coin of the cultural realm." The better source of inspiration was found to be moral intuition, also known as conscience or "common" sense discernment of "self-evident" moral truths.[36]

The hermeneutics of moral intuition developed from the convergence of two major cultural forces in nineteenth-century America: the new wave of revivalism and evangelicalism (sometimes called the Second Great Awakening) with its emphasis on individual emotions and experiential religious truth, and the moral philosophy of Common Sense Realism with its notion of conscience. Common Sense Realism was an intellectual legacy of the Scottish Enlightenment, highly influential on the evolving American academic discipline of moral philosophy. It argued that humans possess an innate "moral sense," known as conscience, which verified the rationality of moral judgments, a theory first proposed as a correction to John Locke's tabula rasa epistemology and David Hume's radical skepticism.[37] With evangelical religion and moral philosophy combined, the "plain sense" of the Bible became what one's personal experience intuited it to be.

The intuitionist model of biblical interpretation, to be sure, also had the reverse effect of nourishing literalism. The Scottish Enlightenment in America, with its Baconian view of science, advanced a strenuously empiricist approach to all forms of knowledge, a declared desire for objective "fact," and a corresponding distrust of hypotheses, imagination, and even reason itself. Some nineteenth-century clergymen adopted such supreme Baconianism to make a virtual assimilation of laboratory science to orthodox Protestantism in order to protect the literal "plain sense" of the Bible not just from the abolitionist hermeneutics of moral intuition, but also from the mounting dangers in geology, organic chemistry, and the ethnology of polygenism.[38]

An additional danger to proslavery's literalism came from another front: Unitarianism, which espoused an early version of the moral-intuition hermeneutics. William Ellery Channing had argued that humans were endowed with a moral sense, this rational conscience being the Word of God written on the human heart. Direct observation of nature, not the verbal inspiration of Scripture, was considered to be the basis of knowledge, conscience the medium of observation. If, as in observation of the evils of slavery, conscience is found to conflict with certain passages in the Bible, conscience took priority as a more secure access to God's higher law. This moral-intuition hermeneutics had also been advanced by Francis Wayland (1796–1865), president of Brown University. The argument was that individual moral sense, properly cultivated, should control any exegesis of the Bible.[39]

Although admittedly not a representative group, radical abolitionists like William Lloyd Garrison (1805–1879) took this logic to its extreme conclusion. Garrison questioned whether the Bible was even relevant in contemporary debates over abolitionism and other moral issues, such as the Sabbath controversy, the question of woman's suffrage,[40] and the justness of the recent Mexican War (1846–1848). Having broken away from the gradualist and colonization schemes of antislavery, Garrison published, from 1831 to 1865, a national newspaper based in Boston, *The Liberator*, declaring "No Union with Slaveholders" and the immediate, unconditional emancipation of African American slaves without compensation to the masters. Garrison concluded that slavery, like just war and woman's suffrage, "was not a Bible question," since "nothing in regard to controversial matters had ever been settled by the Bible." For example, Garrison was horrified that, during the Mexican War, President Zachary Taylor had used the authority of the Bible and Jesus to justify "giving the Mexicans hell!" Even if there were passages in the Bible that could be interpreted as glorifying war, passages so interpreted were, for Garrison, not the Word of God. As with the biblical justification of war, the biblical justification of slavery was blasphemy. "The God," writes Garrison, "who, in America, is declared to sanction the impious system of slavery—the annihilation of the marriage institution and the sacrifices of all human rights—is my ideal of the devil." In one fell swoop, Garrison rejected the observance of the Sabbath, the authority of clergy, and the inspiration of the Bible. His epigones declared the Bible "a lie and a curse on mankind."[41]

Garrison's political action organization, attracting the likes of Wendell Phillips (1811–1884), Theodore Parker (1810–1860), and Ralph Waldo Emerson (1802–1882), pressed the issue pointedly. At the 1850 annual meeting of the American Anti-Slavery Society in Boston, the Garrisonian Henry C. Wright offered an infamous resolution condemning the Bible of the institutional church: "Resolved, That if the Bible sanctions slavery, and is thus opposed to the self-evident truth that 'all men are created equal, and have an inalienable right to liberty,' the Bible is a self-evident falsehood, and ought to be, and ere long be, regarded as the enemy of Nature and Nature's God, and the progress of the human race in liberty, justice and goodness." Wright attacked Moses Stuart, denounced his *Conscience and the Constitution*, and, as reported in the Southern religious press, called him "the Andover God." The rhetoric confirmed Southern stereotypes of abolitionists as madmen who declared, "Prove to me from the Bible that slavery is to be tolerated, and I will trample your Bible under my feet, as I would the vilest reptile in the face of the earth."[42]

Garrisonian crusaders damned institutional Christianity as collaborating with proslavery. Anticlerical rhetoric soon led to a "come-outer" movement. Radical abolitionists pressed true Christians to "come out" of religious institutions deemed evil rather than risking spiritual contamination by attempting to purify them. A distinction was made between *Christ*ianity, the true religion of Jesus and his apostles, and so-called *Church*ianity, the corrupt, proslavery religion.[43] While a Golden Age history fell out of favor among nineteenth-century Christian intellectuals and scholars, here we see its persistence at the popular level.

The Voices of African Americans

A number of African Americans entered the public argument over slavery. None was more vocal than the abolitionist Frederick Douglass, who was convinced that the Bible, at its core, advanced a gospel of freedom. "I cannot follow," he declared, "the reasonings of those who attempt to defend slavery in the name of divinity, nor in the name of the Bible. But one thing seems to me clear, that if the thing cannot be defended in the name of humanity it is not likely to gain much for its defense in the name of God." Douglass tried to dissuade white abolitionists from the position of Garrisonian radicals to abandon biblical arguments because of the relative success of proslavery exegesis. "It is no evidence," Douglass proclaimed, "that the Bible is a bad book, because those who profess to believe the Bible are bad. The slaveholders of the South, and many of their wicked allies at the North, claim the Bible for slavery; shall we, therefore, fling the Bible away as a pro-slavery book? It would be as reasonable to do so as it would be to fling away the Constitution."[44]

Douglass, along with other black abolitionists, also fought to curtail enforcement of the Fugitive Slave Law of 1850.[45] He denied the law any biblical or constitutional basis and prayed for the day when "Doctors of Divinity shall find a better use for the Bible than in using it to prop up slavery, and a better employment for their time and talents than in finding analogies between Paul's Epistle to Philemon and the slave-catching bill of Millard Fillmore." Douglass lectured on his analogy between biblical interpretation and constitutional interpretation to audiences worldwide:

> The constitution is pro-slavery, because men have interpreted it to be proslavery, and practice upon it as if it were pro-slavery. The very same thing, sir, might be said of the Bible itself; for in the United States men have interpreted the Bible against liberty. They have declared that Paul's epistle to *Philemon* is a full proof for the enactment of that hell-black Fugitive Slave Bill which has desolated my people for the last ten years in that country. They have declared

that the Bible sanctions slavery. What do we do in such a case? What do you do when you are told by the slaveholders of America that the Bible sanctions slavery? Do you go and throw your Bible into the fire? Do you sing out, "No Union with the Bible!"? Do you declare that a thing is bad because it has been misused, abused, and made a bad use of? Do you throw it away on that account? No! You press it to your bosom all the more closely; you read it all the more diligently; and prove from its pages that it is on the side of liberty—and not on the side of slavery.[46]

Frederick Douglass's abolitionist theology grew out of his personal experience with slavery and, specifically, of his former master's demand for slave illiteracy. Master Hugh Auld had prevented young Frederick from learning to read the Bible. Auld had shouted, "If you give a nigger an inch, he will take an ell. Learning will spoil the best nigger in the world. If he learns to read the Bible it will forever unfit him to be slave." In his autobiography, Douglass called Master Hugh's tirade "the first decidedly anti-slavery lecture to which it had been my lot to listen."[47] Later, when he eventually learned to read, he found the Golden Rule—understood through egalitarianism and not through love patriarchalism—to be the hermeneutical key to the Bible's interpretation. Preaching on the "law of love . . . glowing on every page of the New Testament," Douglass exhorted that, if you claim freedom for yourself, you must grant it to your neighbor. The emancipation of slaves became for Douglass *the* moral imperative of nineteenth-century Protestant Christian piety and humanism.[48] This piety places Douglass in the tradition of white abolitionists who also shunned the Garrisonians and their denial of the authority of Scripture on the slavery question.

Not all African Americans, however, stood in this tradition of accepting the whole Bible as authoritative. Discouraged and frustrated, many blacks searched for an effective response to both the Fugitive Slave Law and the Dred Scott decision. In Massachusetts, New Bedford African Americans registered their protest at a June 1858 meeting of the Third Christian Church. The assembly unanimously adopted a series of resolutions, submitted by local black leader Lloyd H. Brooks, that included the following: "*Resolved,* That we neither recognize nor respect any laws for slavery, whether from Moses, Paul, or Taney. We spurn and trample them all under our feet as in violation of the laws of God and the rights of men."[49]

Some African Americans took steps even more defiant. White Presbyterian minister Charles Colcock Jones, a leading advocate of the mission to the slaves and an early historian of their religious instruction, once recalled a religious mutiny by slaves to a sermon he gave before a slave congregation in 1833:

> I was preaching to a large congregation on the *Epistle to Philemon*: and when I insisted upon fidelity and obedience as Christian virtues in servants and upon the authority of Paul, condemned the practice of *running away*, one half of my audience deliberately rose up and walked off with themselves, and those that remained looked any thing but satisfied, either with the preacher or his doctrine. After dismission, there was no small stir among them; some solemnly declared "that there was no such epistle in the Bible"; others, "that they did not care if they ever heard me preach again!" . . . There were some too, who had strong objections against me as a Preacher, because I was a *master*, and said "his people have to work as well as we."[50]

Like Jones, Albert Barnes had cited this episode in his larger argument that Onesimus was not a slave—even the simple minds of illiterate slaves could see that obvious fact, he argued.[51] The episode above shows that African Americans had their own hermeneutics of suspicion and an oral canon of Christian Scripture that competed with the white folks' Bible. Knowledge of biblical stories came from music, not books. It was in the slave spirituals, above all, that enslaved African Americans conjured the biblical characters, themes, and lessons into figures participating in their own lives. Blacks argued that their experiential Christianity was more authentic than the "Bible Christianity" of their white masters.[52]

These slaves developed a hermeneutics of typology, strongly displayed in the Moses and Exodus figuration but with New Testament imagery as well. Paul's words in Phil 2:6-8, of Jesus taking the form of a slave, were transformative for blacks and led to black Christian performances of the imitation of Christ as the archetypal "Suffering Servant." A tombstone (dating sometime after 1812) is illustrative. Erected by the members of the African Baptist church in Savannah, Georgia, the tombstone states that the deceased, Andrew Bryan, the first pastor, had been "imprisoned for the Gospel without ceremony and . . . severely whipped" but told his white tormentors that "he rejoiced not only to be whipped, but . . . was willing to suffer death for the cause of Christ."[53]

Many slaves found power in the New Testament book of Revelation.[54] Interpreted through the hermeneutics of typology, slaves conjured the Lamb of the Apocalypse into an abolitionist Warrior Jesus. The apocalyptic language, especially of Rev 6:15-16 and 19:11-13, invigorated hope for divine wrath and retribution. The Jesus of whom the slaves sang was "King Jesus," a terrifying figure seated on a milk-white horse with

sword and shield in hand. This figuration of Christ in black eschatology would not be the result of social programs, such as political action
or legal reform, but of catastrophe. The "black jeremiad" (coined from
the biblical term *Jeremiah*) warned of ethnic violence and slave insurrection. Such language prompted some of the bloodiest slave revolts in
U.S. history. Denmark Vesey, the leader of a slave revolt in Charleston,
South Carolina (1822), read his Bible, found slavery to be wrong, and
used scriptural passages to win supporters. His co-conspirator, "Gullah"
Jack Pritchard, was a Methodist preacher as well as a "conjure doctor,"
a practitioner in African shamanism. The 1831 revolt in Southampton
County, Virginia, was led by Nat Turner, who, like Vesey before him, was
a compelling Bible seer-prophet.[55] The hermeneutics of typology that
"conjured apocalypse" provided a powerful strategy for African Americans to transform the New Testament into a text calling for the holy war
against slavery.

Proslavery Theology and Exegesis

While radical abolitionism and slave insurrection, on one side of the
moral debate, pressed disunion with slaveholders and the shattering of
traditional understandings of biblical and clerical authority, radical proslavery, on the other, denounced both come-outerism and abolitionism
as infidelity. Proslavery itself, as a discourse, was relatively new in American culture. During the decades preceding the Revolutionary War, the
American colonies saw nearly no white opposition to slavery; what little
there was came from a handful of Quaker emancipationists.[56] Consequently, there was no need for apologetics. The paucity of early American
proslavery literature resulted from a lack of need to defend an institution
that nearly all European settlers took for granted.[57] However, with the
radicalization of antislavery and abolitionism after 1835 (William Lloyd
Garrison's campaigns), proslavery literature increased dramatically. The
proslavery argument from the New Testament arose in response to antislavery and abolitionist claims.

The first claim that proslavery challenged concerned the term *servant*.
It meant *slave*. Proslavery writers upheld this simple and straightforward
claim by the hermeneutics of "plain sense," which charged antislavery
with semantic obfuscation. By strict interpretation of the literal text,
proslavery biblicists made appeal to the flat reading of both the Bible
and scriptural authority, reinforced by nineteenth-century American

millenarianism, Princeton theology, and Scottish Common Sense theories of knowledge.[58] "We . . . believe the Bible to be the Word of God, and to mean just what it says." To claim that *servant* means free servant, hired laborer, apprentice, or employee "disregards the plainest principles of language" and denies that the Bible "is the word of God." The Bible must be interpreted "according to its plain and palpable meaning, and as understood by all mankind for three thousand years [*sic*] before [our] time." One justification for the hermeneutics of plain sense was the alleged fact that the "Scriptures have been purposely written by plain men, so that plain men may understand them." All the "volumes of commentaries and expositions" have really served only "to perplex the truth," and "the accumulation of learned rubbish has made it difficult to discover the simplest matters" like slavery.[59] This hermeneutics consequently led to a distrust of books and libraries generally: the prodigious number of commentary volumes lining the shelves implied that the Scriptures must be dark and difficult to fathom, an impossibility for biblicists.[60]

Ironically, this anti-intellectual hermeneutics of plain sense was confirmed by scholarship on the original languages of the Bible. A dilettante interest in the findings of German biblical criticism and classical philology was common, albeit selective and cautionary.[61] Proslavery authors announced to the general public the consensus of America's first biblical scholars, such as Moses Stuart, who (although personally antislavery but not an immediate abolitionist)[62] had demonstrated the fallacy of the "servant" hypothesis. For proslavery interpreters maintaining plenary verbal inspiration, the problem lay not in the Bible itself but in the English text, the King James translation of the Greek *doulos* as *servant* being the specific source of the trouble. "Our English version itself . . . has a tendency to lead to an inadequate conception of the idea [of slavery] conveyed by the original."[63] The antislavery and abolitionist "servant" hypothesis, a product of the hermeneutics of semantic subterfuge, was clearly wrong even on a scholarly level. "Hence, after trying in vain the whole apparatus of exegetical torture, they have—with, I believe, much unanimity—set all philology and history at defiance, and absolutely deny that the original words mean slave."[64] In the service of proslavery, the hermeneutics of historical criticism helped defeat the antislavery hermeneutics of semantic subterfuge.

Not only was the "servant" hypothesis bad scholarship, proslavery charged, but it was also bad Christian faith:

> You [abolitionists] attempt to avert the otherwise irresistible conclusion, that slavery was thus ordained by God, by declaring that the word "slave" is not . . . found in the Bible. And I have seen many learned dissertations on this point from abolitionist pens. It is well known that both the Hebrew and Greek words translated "servant" in the Scriptures, mean also, and most usually "slave." The use of one word, instead of another, was a mere matter of taste with the translators of the Bible. . . . You endeavor to hang an argument of immortal consequence upon the wretched subterfuge, that the precise word "slave" is not to be found in the *translation* of the Bible. As if the translators were canonical expounders of the Holy Scriptures, and *their words*, not *God's meaning*, must be regarded as his revelation.
>
> It is vain to look to Christ and his Apostles to justify such blasphemous perversions of the word of God.[65]

The hermeneutics of historical criticism helped proslavery to show that reliance on the literal meaning of the word of a translator rather than on the original term of the biblical author was wrong and nothing short of infidelity. The hermeneutics of historical criticism reinforced the hermeneutics of plain sense. *Servant* means *slave*. Semantic obfuscation cannot change the rules of classical philology.

Armed with the hermeneutics of plain sense and a literalism so pure that it rejected the English translation in favor of "original" texts, proslavery clergy moved quickly to discredit the Barnes hypothesis that Onesimus was not a slave. This hypothesis was a clear philological absurdity and religious perversion of the revealed and plain Word of God. Proslavery writers labeled Barnes a "fanatic" and compared him to Satan quoting Scripture. They easily destroyed Barnes's exegetical arguments constructed with the hermeneutics of semantic subterfuge, for the arguments rested only on the single, flimsy contention that *servant* (*doulos* in ancient Greek) means *slave*.[66] "You get nothing," writes the Reverend Fred A. Ross, pastor of the Presbyterian Church in Huntsville, Alabama, "by torturing the English Version. People understand English. Nay, you get little by applying the rack to the Hebrew and Greek." "It will do no good," writes fellow Old School Presbyterian Charles Hodge, "under a paroxysm of benevolence, to attempt to tear the Bible to pieces, or to extort by violent exegesis, a meaning foreign to its obvious sense."[67] To focus on the slave Onesimus rather the master Philemon was to miss the importance of the Pauline Mandate. Paul admitted a great slaveholder into the church. The hermeneutics both of historical criticism and of plain sense showed this fact.

After this exegetical conquest, proslavery marched to attack another flank of the Barnes Hypothesis, the historical claim that Jesus never met slaves. The Gospel story of the Centurion's Servant (Luke 7:1-10; Matt 8:5-13) was a popular weapon in this exegetical holy war over competing claims of religious fidelity. The story afforded an instance where Jesus recognized and applauded a Roman soldier as a good and faithful master. "Surely remarkable" was the fact that the gospel figure "who exhibited the greatest faith . . . was a slaveholder." Importantly, Jesus praised the centurion's use of commands to order military and domestic subordinates (Luke 7:8-9; Matt 8:9-10). The plain sense of this language means that military hierarchy and other forms of patriarchy ought to order human relations, especially between master and slave. The Savior restored the sick slave to health "without desiring his master to free him, or uttering a word in censure of their relation to each other." The silence of Jesus on emancipation proved his support of slavery. Indeed, throughout the entire Bible, God "has singled out the greatest slaveholders of that age, as the object of special favor."[68] The proslavery hermeneutics of plain sense, armed with selective use of the findings of historical criticism (e.g., that slavery existed in Roman Palestine), challenged the antislavery and abolitionist hermeneutics of immutable kernel and the seed growing secretly. The actual "immutable principle" was not liberal love egalitarianism but conservative love patriarchalism.

With their hermeneutics of plain sense, proslavery writers drew on a constellation of related passages to build their case.[69] Not only did Jesus and his apostles welcome slaveholders into the church as model believers, but Jesus also used slaves as characters in his parables to instruct duty and obligation.[70] Proslavery added to this literary evidence the historical evidence, from Edward Gibbon's *Decline and Fall of the Roman Empire* (1776–1788) and others, that significant slave populations existed throughout the entire Roman Empire, including Palestine.[71]

Proslavery aimed its attack next at abolitionist interpretations of the Golden Rule, which the abolitionists based on the hermeneutical combination of immutable kernel and the seed growing secretly. Countering the claim that Jesus preached a kernel of love egalitarianism, proslavery reminded Christian abolitionists that the New Testament, as the inspired Word of God, could not be divided against itself. The hermeneutical key must be to "interpret the Scriptures so that one passage or part will not contradict another."[72] To be sure, many abolitionists agreed with this interpretative rule and had applied it themselves to read freedom, egalitarianism, and natural rights into the Pauline household duty codes.

Proslavery, then, faced the same challenge as abolitionism: to find coherence between the teachings of Jesus and the ethics of Paul.

The proslavery solution was to interpret Jesus' Golden Rule as love patriarchalism. The hermeneutics of plain sense argues against competing hermeneutics of the (1) Golden Age, (2) immutable principles, or (3) the seed growing secretly. The tradition did not miscarry, according to proslavery. There was direct continuation between the love patriarchalism of Jesus' Golden Rule teaching and the love patriarchalism of Paul's household duty codes and southern American slave laws, which operated not to end slavery but to curb its abuse by individual masters.

This solution points to the threat that abolitionism posed to northern proslavery conservatives—its antihierarchical tone. The crucial issue here lies in the interpretation of two nineteenth-century principles: egalitarianism and patriarchalism as basic yet opposing ways of understanding Jesus and Paul. What proslavery ideologues were looking for was continuity, as opposed to the Whig historiography of progress. This opposition reveals a fundamental tension in Southern political culture between the centrality and imperative of hierarchy (among the planter upper-class culture of large slaveholders along the Atlantic and Gulf coasts and the Mississippi River) and a fierce attachment to Jacksonian democracy among yeoman farmers (who owned few slaves) and the white poor (who owned none). The Southern middle and lower classes were religious, but evangelical and egalitarian: their proslavery argument was based on equality (every white man should be able to own a slave) and property.[73] The move to patriarchalism as the hermeneutical key to reading Jesus and Paul, therefore, belongs to a wider move to assault Jacksonian democracy and to defend hierarchy as a political system. Studying the different approaches to biblical exegesis on the slavery question, then, provides another perspective on the antihierarchical polemic that plunged America into civil war.

As the political stakes rose, the preaching against antislavery and abolitionist hermeneutics became more vehement: "The fanatics who find it impossible to explain away these cases of the direct sanction of slavery, and who seek in vain for a line or word which discourages or condemns that institution, seize, in their despair, upon the golden rule . . . and so pervert it as to make it condemn what our Saviour and his apostles directly sanctioned." Proslavery writers pointed out an absurdity in the abolitionist logic of social equality taken to its extreme. The rule, interpreted as love egalitarianism, leads to social anarchy. It must abolish all hierarchy itself—parent over child, master over apprentice, tutor over pupil, judge over convict, jailer over thief—rendering society "a chaotic and jarring mass of wretchedness and crime."[74] Jesus Christ did not preach love egalitarianism but love patriarchalism. The rule affirmed that men in authority should do to subordinates as they would expect to be treated were they the subordinates. "The father," for example, "should do unto his child as he would, if a child, and informed of his own interest, wish his father to do unto him." Likewise, the master should treat his slave as if the master, imagining himself a slave and aware of his own good, would like to be treated. Paul repeated this rule when he commands, "Masters give unto your servants that which is just and equal" (Col 4:1). "Just and equal" means love patriarchalism. Paul, as Jesus before him, attacked not slavery but its abuse by unjust, cruel masters.[75] The hermeneutics of plain sense scored another victory.

Proslavery pursued the victory of exegetical control over the New Testament with two powerful allies in nineteenth-century American political discourse: racism and conservative republicanism. Both of these ideologies reinforced love patriarchalism. The ideology of racism argued that slavery rescued Africans from cruel paganism and savagery. In an extension of the "white man's burden" argument, proslavery contended that the institution was good for African American slaves. "We claim for the institution of Southern slavery, that it has done more for the religious, social and physical condition of the African race, than has ever been done. . . . In less than two centuries, three millions of them now living—to say nothing of the dead—have been brought into a state of . . . Christianity." The African Negro, before slavery, had been "worshipping the Devil."[76] Christian racism argued that slavery was to be part of God's plan for African salvation.

This racist argument joined forces with the nineteenth-century backlash against the liberalizing tendencies of the revolutionary era. Although Thomas Jefferson served as president from 1801 to 1809, as early as the Federalist reaction of the 1780s a small but growing number of conservatives had begun to reject anything that smacked of being French or Jeffersonian. Interestingly, "northern conservatives, not southerners, were the first Americans to revive the defense of slavery in public, polemical writings following the American Revolution." The abolitionist, claimed Virginia Baptist pastor Thornton Stringfellow, should "throw away his Bible as Mr. Jefferson did his. . . . Never disgrace the Bible by making Mr. Jefferson its expounder. . . . How can any man, who believes in the Bible,

admit for a moment that all are born free and equal?" Such anti-Jefferso-
nianism is evident in an 1849 Southern newspaper editorial arguing for
the extension of slavery into the territory acquired by the Treaty of Gua-
dalupe Hidalgo (2 February 1848):

> We think it unfortunate, however, that Mr. Jefferson, doubtless without due
> exercise of his peculiar powers of ratiocination, issued the nonsensical and
> perfectly inexplicable dogma of universality of liberty, and general equaliza-
> tion of human rights; which has been seized hold of not merely by abolitionists
> but by many political and religious reformers, who under the misconception
> of the principles of rational freedom, are really destroying, instead of estab-
> lishing the foundation of right government.[77]

The text requiring Christian obedience to "right government" was
Romans 13, in which Paul exhorts every person to be subject to governing
authorities. Proslavery apologists combined Romans 13 and the Golden
Rule to argue love patriarchalism: the reciprocal love ethic applied only
within a given social structure, which every citizen must uphold. With its
ideology of love patriarchalism, conservative republicanism gave political sanction to proslavery exegesis and theology. Conservative politics
joined proslavery religion in challenging the hermeneutics of immutable
principles, a misguided Jeffersonian belief in natural right and human
liberty. Jesus never preached this utopian nonsense, claimed proslavery religion. Historical criticism appeared to prove proslavery correct,
because slavery was not only present in Roman Palestine but also clearly
patriarchal in nature.

The proslavery crusade to battle infidelity inspired further attacks
against antislavery and abolitionist hermeneutics. The expediency
hypothesis, built on the hermeneutics of the seed growing secretly, took
fatal hits. The hypothesis that either Jesus or Paul held back on their
alleged condemnation of slavery for reasons of expediency—fearing a
Christian slave uprising and Roman military response that would have
destroyed the early church—was held to be a historical implausibility
and scandalous blasphemy. The so-called servile-war hypothesis was infidelity because it betrayed "limited ideas of God's providence and a disre-
gard for the plain letter and meaning of his word."[78] Such views forgot not
only God's protection of the church but also the power of the Holy Spirit
to direct historical events. The hypothesis assumed God to be absent or
even nonexistent—sheer atheism. The hypothesis was denounced also
as historically implausible. It painted a perverse portrait of Christ and

his Apostle Paul, both of whom in fact were not timid men. Jesus boldly exposed the hypocrisy of the Jewish rulers, though he knew that he would be crucified for his truthfulness. Paul was unyielding in his assault on the idolatry of Greece and Rome, an institution more fundamental to pagan society than slavery and so an attack far more seditious. Neither Jesus nor Paul ever feared the wrath of authorities, military or judicial, and each willingly accepted imprisonment and execution for his beliefs.

The supposition, therefore, that either Jesus or Paul refrained from condemning the alleged sin of slavery because he feared it might offend public opinion and threaten his personal safety (or that of the future church) was to call each a coward or worse. As the South Carolina pro-slavery clergyman Richard Fuller stated with scathing irony, Paul "'satisfies himself' while millions on all sides are sinking into hell through this crime—he 'satisfies himself' with spreading principles which would slowly work a cure! Craven and faithless herald! and after this, with what face can he say 'I have kept back nothing' [Acts 20:20]!" With post–Civil War racism and resentment of the abolition of slavery, Robert Lewis Dabney, the Presbyterian minister who served as aide-de-camp to Confederate General Thomas J. "Stonewall" Jackson, added, "This hypothesis represents that Saviour who claimed omniscience, as adopting a policy which was as futile as dishonest. He forbore the utterance of any express testimony against the sin of slaveholding, say they [sc. the abolitionists], leaving the church to find it out by deduction from general principles of equity. But in point of fact, the church never began to make such deductions until near the close of the 18th century."[79] The hermeneutics of the seed growing secretly was held as untenable, as the hermeneutics of plain sense showed.

Proslavery theology also used the hermeneutics of plain sense to counter antislavery and abolitionist claims, based on 1 Cor 7:21; Gal 3:28; and 1 Tim 1:10, that Paul was an emancipationist. These passages were being misread, plain and simple. First Corinthians 7:21 told slaves not to worry about their status and to remain slaves even if presented with offers of liberty.[80] Even if the passage could be read in the alternative way, "take freedom," the meaning remained proslavery. Slaves could accept freedom only if it were offered legally under slave law, through master-sanctioned manumission.[81] The ideology of racism reinforced the hermeneutics of plain sense. This alternative reading ("take freedom") worked only when master and slave were of the same color. Since (unlike white Roman freedmen) black American freedmen could never attain citizenship or social equality with whites, Paul's words ("take freedom") could not apply to Negroes.[82] In the end, then, it did not matter which reading ("use slavery" or "take freedom") was correct. Paul had said "Art thou called being a servant? Care not for it," yet abolitionists did care for it and so disobeyed the word of God.

Galatians 3:28 must be interpreted "in a spiritual sense"; it was metaphoric, not literal. As proof, proslavery authors reminded their audience that Paul, while saying "neither male nor female," did not destroy literal gender differences in actual life: women were still told to obey their husbands.[83] The reference in 1 Tim 1:10 addressed slave traders, not slaveholders generally. If abolitionist exegesis were correct, then Abraham and other slaveholding Old Testament patriarchs mentioned in the New Testament as models of faith would have been great sinners, an absurdity to "plain sense" believers. Southerners themselves acknowledged slave traders to be immoral lowlifes with reputations for dishonesty.[84] Slavery itself was "manholding," an acceptable Christian activity, whereas illegal slave trading was "manstealing." Proslavery, then, turned the tables on abolitionists. Those whom 1 Tim 1:10 denounces as sinners were "menstealers," none other than the abolitionists who kidnapped or otherwise stole Southern slaves from their rightful owners.[85] The proslavery, plain sense of all these sacred texts had remained undisturbed throughout their history of interpretation until "abolitionism set its cloven foot upon the Bible."[86] The hermeneutics of plain sense took priority in proslavery argumentation to attack the infidel antislavery and abolitionist hermeneutics of (1) semantic subterfuge, (2) immutable principles, (3) the Golden Age historical view, and (4) the seed growing secretly.

Paul himself provided an example of how to deal with the infidelity of abolitionism, because he apparently encountered ancient abolitionists in his own ministry, claimed proslavery. First Timothy 6:1-5 provided the evidence. After commanding slaves to obey even non-Christian masters, Paul warned that, "If any man teaches otherwise," such a teacher perverted godliness. Just as Paul condemned men like this as having corrupt minds and being destitute of the truth, so must Christians today condemn the infidelity of modern abolitionists.[87] This passage proved to proslavery adherents that abolitionism was incompatible with Christian orthodoxy. Abolitionism was ancient and came from the devil. Since the face of infidelity had not changed since New Testament times, there was no Golden Age.

The greatest threat to orthodoxy, however, was something more sinister: the fifth and final hermeneutics of moral intuition. The abolitionists called believers to follow the authority of personal conscience rather than the plenary inspired authority of the Bible. That hermeneutics was un-Christian because it attacked biblical authority. The appeal to conscience over the Bible made Scripture defective as a system of morality.[88]

Proslavery aimed its hermeneutical and exegetical weapons at Francis Wayland and his college textbook on moral science.[89] Proslavery apologists accused Wayland of inculcating in American students a hatred toward slavery. After this brainwashing, proslavery charged, Wayland then informed students that they possess "a 'distinct mental faculty'—distinct from judgment—that teaches those who cultivate it, infallibly, all that is right and wrong; that this conscience, or moral sense, is more to be relied on than the Bible—than the ancient inspirations of God!" as if, said one critic, "man possesses a faculty of *clairvoyance*." The truth was, argued proslavery, that so-called moral conscience was a human product of education and, thus, fallible. Anti-intellectualism encouraged this proslavery argument. Wayland's hermeneutics of moral intuition (that God's Word must be discerned through personal conscience) clashed with the hermeneutics of plain sense (that God's Word was obvious even to those without the benefit of the moral cultivation that education brought). After all, "Most men live without reflection." Unlike conscience, the Bible can be read "with all simplicity of mind."[90] The Bible was divine, plain, and infallible, whereas conscience was decried as human, erring, and requiring education.[91] One only needed to observe different people to see that each had a different moral sense. How could conscience be reliable when it generated multiple and conflicting moral voices?

The anti-intellectualism of literalism combined with xenophobia toward France, which, in 1848, had abolished slavery in its colonies.[92] Abolitionism was idolatry. "Ye have," charged one proslavery adherent, "like the French infidels, made *reason* your goddess, and are exalting her above the Bible; and, in your unitarianism and neology and all modes of infidelity, ye are rejecting and crucifying the Son of God." To make the Bible conform to human notions of right and wrong was to repeat the blasphemy of France, "an attempt to know the divine attributes and character in *some other way* than through the divine word."[93] Reliance upon conscience made the Word of God subordinate to the teaching of the human heart. The debate over the intuitive power of conscience was part of a wider clash in American culture between the eighteenth-century liberal, pro-French rationalism of the revolutionary era and the anti-intellectualism, anti-French xenophobia of nineteenth-century conservatism. Xenophobia was also directed toward England, which, in 1838, abolished slavery in its colonies, and toward Germany and its biblical "higher criticism," which denied the plenary inspiration of Scripture and so could be used in the name of proslavery only with extreme caution.[94] The theological hermeneutics of plain sense joined the rising tide of conservative politics that would lead to the secession of the Southern slave states from the Union and the subsequent Civil War.

The proslavery argument illustrates the complicated relationship between the historical-critical interpretation of the Bible and contemporary debate over moral issues. Proslavery charged that abolitionists used the new higher criticism to distort scriptural plain sense. The proslavery clergyman John Henry Hopkins, Episcopal bishop of Vermont, bemoaned:

> Even the commentators who have written since the abolition excitement in England, and who show, here and there, its powerful influence, do not intimate the slightest wish to wrest the true meaning of those [biblical] texts. *That* seems to have been the task of a still later period, and is one of the newest inventions of Biblical interpretation which threaten the welfare of the Church and of the country. For I can imagine no transgression more odious in the sight of God, and more sure to forfeit His blessing, than the willful determination to distort His revealed Word, and *make it speak, not as it truly is*, but as men, in their insane pride of superior philanthropy, fancy that *it ought to be*.[95]

A misguided sense of philanthropy—so it was thought—had replaced the Bible as the standard of truth.

In one of the most revealing passages in proslavery literature, Bishop Hopkins argued this point. Hopkins himself was racked by a moral unease about slavery's goodness; nonetheless, he remained convinced that the hermeneutics of plain sense was the key to divine truth. He yielded his own conscience to biblical authority:

> With entire correctness, therefore, your letter refers the question to the only infallible criterion—the Word of God. If it were a matter to be determined by personal sympathies, tastes, or feelings, I should be as ready as any man to condemn the institution of slavery, for all my prejudices of education, habit, and social position stand entirely opposed to it. But as a Christian, I am solemnly warned not to be "wise in my own conceit" [Rom 12:16], and not to "lean to my own understanding" [Prov 2:5]. As a Christian, I am compelled to

submit my weak and erring intellect to the authority of the Almighty. For then only can I be safe in my conclusions, when I know that they are in accordance with the will of Him, before whose tribunal I must render a strict account in the last great day.[96]

This passage illustrates the conflict that anti-intellectualism caused. Torn between the rational humanity of conscience and the irrational orthodoxy of literalism, Bishop Hopkins felt compelled by the hermeneutics of plain sense to support an institution he intuited to be evil. His personal dislike of slavery that conflicted with the plain sense of the Bible convinced him that moral taste was relative and so unreliable. Proslavery's biblicism was so extreme as to render rational judgment in debate over moral issues a form of religious infidelity.

Conclusion

Antislavery exegesis constituted an early form of biblical criticism. It was one of many cultural forces, such as deism, Unitarianism, controversies over geology and other natural sciences, and the hermeneutical turns of literary criticism, that promoted more critical readings of the biblical text. The interplay of all these forces prepared the way in the United States for the eventual reception of German higher criticism.

Because of its moral imperative against the pure evil of human chattel bondage, antislavery and abolitionist Christianity was forced away from biblicism into a less literal reading of Scripture. The first step in this move was the development of a hermeneutics of immutable principles, which advanced an egalitarian reading of Jesus' Golden Rule (as the kernel of the New Testament) over against its patriarchal reading by proslavery. This view was combined with Whig theories of human progress in history to form a hermeneutics of the seed growing secretly. Yet, a growing doubt about using egalitarianism to interpret the Pauline household duty codes led radical abolitionists, especially Garrisonians (admittedly not a representative group), to the second step—the total abandonment of biblical authority in favor of secular arguments from conscience.

Some African American abolitionists, such as Frederick Douglass, did not want to go that far and worked with white clergymen to save a biblical understanding of Christianity. These abolitionists were more representative because of their eagerness to build popular support. However, other African Americans such as Denmark Vesey and Nat Turner rejected white Christianity altogether and took the third step, that of violence. They employed a hermeneutics of biblical typology and the visions of apocalyptic eschatology.

The political imperative of proslavery, in contrast, fostered a move toward literalism emboldened by the findings of biblical criticism that the New Testament writers did not condemn slavery (as abolitionists would wish) but instead expressed views similar to those in the wider Greco-Roman slave culture. Biblical scholars argued that the New Testament contained passages that did not merely recommend subjection by slaves to their masters. Those passages signaled acceptance of an organic model of civilization for which such subjection was essential.[97] Most embarrassing for today's readers of the Bible, the proslavery spokesmen were holding the more defensible position from the perspective of historical criticism.[98]

This study, then, carries implication beyond its case history of slavery. The opposing values of literalism and moral intuition remain at odds in American religious culture, shaping contemporary debates over race relations, military conflict, capital punishment, poverty, abortion, full emancipation of women, and lesbian and gay rights. Ready answers to these moral questions all too often fall short of persuasive power because they merely repeat truth claims found in the nineteenth-century battle over slavery and the Bible. Biblical criticism is seldom able to settle contemporary moral debate, but contemporary moral debate can and does shape broad and influential trends in biblical criticism.

EPILOGUE

In Atlanta, Georgia, on 20 June 1995, America's largest Protestant denomination—one founded largely in defense of slavery—repented of its historic roots. Twenty thousand delegates of the Southern Baptist Convention gathered in the Georgia Dome, an indoor sports arena, for the denomination's annual meeting and overwhelmingly approved a resolution to repudiate its past stand on slavery and the Bible, with an official apology to African Americans.[1] As they introduced a modification of church teaching, the messengers, as Southern Baptist delegates are called, asserted that the Bible has always taught the principles that they were approving. The "Resolution on Racial Reconciliation," timed for its maximum symbolic value of coinciding with the denomination's 150th anniversary, contains a curious mix of the hermeneutics of the seed growing secretly, immutable principles, and "plain sense," which illustrates the fundamental paradox in American religious culture described in the preceding chapter.

On the one hand, the resolution appeals to the timeless truth of "what the Bible says" as a foundation for Christian moral arguments. The resolution cites a handful of biblical passages, thirteen in all, mainly stacked one upon another in the concluding two paragraphs on the need "to commit ourselves to be doers of the Word." But only two Scriptures bear the burden of the claim that the Bible condemns slavery. The first is Gen 1:27, interpreted by the method of paraphrase to teach that "every human life is sacred and is of equal and immeasurable worth, made in God's image, regardless of race or ethnicity." The second is Gal 3:28, which is quoted with a slight alteration to the text (and no commentary) to demonstrate "with respect to salvation through Christ" that "there is neither Jew nor Greek, there is neither slave nor free, there is neither male nor female, for (we) are all one in Christ Jesus." The message is clear: God planted the seeds of his Word about antislavery and abolitionism in both the New and the Old Testaments, plain for all to see, and even in the Garden of Eden. Like "answers" on other moral questions such as abortion, homosexuality, and the ordination of women as church pastors, the staunchly conservative powers that be in the Southern Baptist Convention find the ancient Scriptures to correspond precisely to their own modern morality of "family values," which they assert to be universal and inerrant moral truths by the hermeneutics of "plain sense."

On the other hand, the resolution repents of the sad fact that this obvious biblical truth was not plain sense to the Southern Baptist Convention in nearly all of its history as a denomination. "Many of our Southern Baptist forbears," the resolution grieves, "defended the right to own slaves, and either participated in, supported, or acquiesced" in the American institution of legal slavery. Condemning racism as the legacy of American legal slavery and a "deplorable sin," the resolution faults Southern Baptists who more recently "failed, in many cases, to support, and in some cases opposed, legitimate initiatives to secure the civil rights" of African Americans. Furthermore, the resolution focuses its specific condemnation on *American* slavery for its "particularly inhumane nature." Slavery in the ancient worlds of Abraham, Moses, David, Jesus, and Paul receives no comment. An implicit assumption may be that ancient slavery was not as sinful as modern slavery, for there is no apology for the practices of biblical slaveholders, or for slavery *in itself* as a sin (only racism is called sinful). Also conspicuously absent in the document are references to Jesus' parables on slaves, the Pauline household duty codes, the Old Testament slave laws, and all the other Scriptures that proslavery Baptists have traditionally used to justify enslavement of and racism toward African Americans. The plain sense is not so plain after all.

In sum, the method of interpretation is a bare listing of selected passages (what professional biblical studies would criticize as *proof texting*), whose relevance is more asserted than proved, without regard for literary or historical context and without attention to other, more difficult passages that might challenge what is being asserted. The resolution aims to read the Scriptures by the rule that they contain a single and consistent moral teaching—the hermeneutics of immutable principles. Presenting itself as a literal interpretation of Scripture, the resolution in actuality constantly shifts its hermeneutics from plain sense to immutable principles, the seed growing secretly, and even to moral intuition. It switches the rules of interpretation capriciously like players changing the rules of a game to ensure the score of their goal. In this way, the Bible is made to say what it is supposed to say on slavery.

The hypocrisy of the logic, however noble the aims, became even more blatant three years later, in June 1998, when the Southern Baptist Convention passed another motion, this time on women. Among the most prominent statements on the family in the 1990s, the approved motion amended a section on the topic "The Family" in *The Baptist Faith and Message*, the denomination's basic theological statement of beliefs. The amendment relies on the anti-intellectualism of the hermeneutics of "plain sense" and on a core group of biblical texts, the Pauline household duty codes. Conveniently ignored in the previous resolution on slavery, the household codes are used here to declare that a wife should "submit herself graciously to the servant leadership of her husband." The amendment quotes (selected) Scriptures as authoritative, without explicit acknowledgment of the agency and contingency of the interpreter. Ephesians 5:22-33, for example, forms a major part of the citation apparatus, because its comparison of the husband-wife relationship to that of Christ ruling the church suits the modern patriarchy. The motion to amend was extraordinary. *Faith and Message* had only been amended once before in its history, in 1963 when a section on higher education was added. A triumph for conservative leadership of the Convention, the declaration belongs to the gradual shift of the denomination to the right since fundamentalists came to power in 1979. Leaders and delegates who supported their views hailed the amendment as a great Christian denomination's return to its historic roots in the traditional family and its moral values.[2] That those historic roots also included the other traditional moral value of slavery was nowhere mentioned. This amendment on women, which explicitly affirms the inerrant and timeless truth of the household duty codes, contradicts the resolution on slavery, which implicitly denies their moral relevance today. The contradiction exposes the specious argument present in the amendment.

I mention the Southern Baptist Convention not to single it out but to point to a wider trend in American religious culture of which it is representative. Liberal positions that claim Paul's letters or the Gospels to be fundamentally subversive of slavery and other Roman moral values are equally problematic, as I note many times in this book. Liberal theologians and scholars are also at fault for perpetuating favorably disposed opinions about the New Testament that are just as specious.

Doubtless some of my readers will always believe in appealing solely to the Scriptures to settle Christian moral debate. Although I do not entertain delusions of convincing everyone, I do hope that I have demonstrated that such a view fails to comprehend the complexity of either moral reasoning or biblical interpretation. Appeals to "what the Bible says" do not promote knowledge but merely attempt to end inquiry altogether. On the level of exegesis, one goal of this study has been to argue that any critical interpretation of the New Testament must start by situating the early Christian writings in their literary, social, and moral context of the early Roman Empire. I find that most slaves in the New Testament and early Christian literature are *literary* products, drawn from classic stock scenarios that reflected the conventional Roman value of *auctoritas*. In terms of ideology, the New Testament writings participate and are implicated in the ancient prejudice and stereotyping that functioned to dehumanize slaves and to make masters better masters. Given this finding, shouldn't we challenge Christian moral debate to move beyond the specious biblicism of "traditional family values," and create a better moral vision?

ABBREVIATIONS

The citation of ancient authors follows *The SBL Handbook of Style: For Ancient Near Eastern, Biblical, and Early Christian Studies* (ed. Patrick H. Alexander et al.; Peabody, Mass.: Hendrickson Publishers, 1999).

AB   Anchor Bible
ABD   *Anchor Bible Dictionary*, ed. David Noel Freedman, 6 vols.; New York, 1992
ACW   Ancient Christian Writers
AGJU   Arbeiten zur Geschichte des antiken Judentums und des Urchristentums
AJP   *American Journal of Philology*
ANF   *Ante-Nicene Fathers: The Writings of the Fathers Down to* A.D. *325*, ed. Alexander Roberts and James Donaldson, 1885; reprint, Peabody, Mass., 1994
ANRW   *Aufstieg und Niedergang der römischen Welt*, ed. H. Temporini and W. Haase; Berlin, 1972–
ATLA   American Theological Library Association
BDAG   Bauer, Walter, William F. Arndt, and F. W. Gingrich, *A Greek-English Lexicon of the New Testament and Other Early Christian Literature*, 3d ed., rev. and ed. Frederick W. Danker; Chicago, 2000
BBB   Bonner biblische Beiträge
B.C.E.   Before the Common Era (equivalent to B.C.)
BETL   Bibliotheca ephemeridum theologicarum lovaniensium
BGU   *Aegyptische Urkunden aus den Königlichen* (later *Staatlichen*) *Museen zu Berlin, Griechische Urkunden*; Berlin, 1895–
BHT   Beiträge zur historischen Theologie
Bib   *Biblica*
BibInt   *Biblical Interpretation*
BibInt   Biblical Interpretation monograph series

BJRL	*Bulletin of the John Rylands University Library of Manchester*
BZ	*Biblische Zeitschrift*
BZNW	Beihefte zur Zeitschrift für die neutestamentliche Wissenschaft
CBQ	*Catholic Biblical Quarterly*
CCSL	Corpus Christianorum, Series Latina
C.E.	Common Era (equivalent to A.D.)
CGTC	Cambridge Greek Testament Commentary
CJ	*Classical Journal*
CNT	Commentaire du Nouveau Testament
CP	*Classical Philology*
CPJ	*Corpus Papyrorum Judaicorum,* ed. V. Tcherikover, 3 vols.; Cambridge, 1957–64
CQ	*Classical Quarterly*
CRINT	Compendia rerum iudaicarum ad Novum Testamentum
Ebib	Études bibliques
EKKNT	Evangelisch-katholischer Kommentar zum Neuen Testament
EvQ	*Evangelical Quarterly*
FC	Fathers of the Church
GR	*Greece and Rome*
HDR	Harvard Dissertations in Religion
HNT	Handbuch zum Neuen Testament
HNTC	Harper's New Testament Commentaries
HSCP	*Harvard Studies in Classical Philology*
HTR	*Harvard Theological Review*
HTS	Harvard Theological Studies
HUT	Hermeneutische Untersuchungen zur Theologie
ICC	International Critical Commentary
JBL	*Journal of Biblical Literature*
JdI	*Jahrbuch des deutschen archäologischen Instituts*
JECS	*Journal of Early Christian Studies*
JHI	*Journal of the History of Ideas*
JÖAI	*Jahreshefte des Österreichischen Archäologischen Instituts*
JRS	*Journal of Roman Studies*
JRT	*Journal of Religious Thought*
JSJ	*Journal for the Study of Judaism in the Persian, Hellenistic, and Roman Periods*
JSNT	*Journal for the Study of the New Testament*
JSNTSup	Journal for the Study of the New Testament Supplement Series
JSOT	Journal for the Study of the Old Testament Press
JTS	*Journal of Theological Studies*
KEK	Kritisch-exegetischer Kommentar über das Neue Testament (Meyer-Kommentar)

Kühn	Kühn, Carolus Gottlob, ed., *Claudii Galeni opera omnia*, 20 vols.; Leipzig, 1821–33
L&S	Lewis, Charlton T., and Charles Short, *A Latin Dictionary*; Oxford, 1879, reprint, 1975
LCL	Loeb Classical Library
LSJ	Liddell, H. G., R. Scott, and H. S. Jones, *A Greek-English Lexicon*, 9th ed. with revised supplement; Oxford, 1996
LXX	Septuagint Bible (ed. Rahlfs)
MBPF	Münchener Beiträge zur Papyrusforschungen und antiken Rechtsgeschichte
NewDocs	*New Documents Illustrating Early Christianity*, ed. G. H. R. Horsley and S. Llewelyn; North Ryde, N.S.W. (Australia), 1981–
NICNT	New International Commentary on the New Testament
NIGTC	The New International Greek Testament Commentary
NIV	New International Version
NovT	*Novum Testamentum*
NovTSup	Novum Testamentum Supplements
NTAbh	Neutestamentliche Abhandlungen
NTApoc	*New Testament Apocrypha*, rev. ed., ed. Wilhelm Schneemelcher, trans. R. McL. Wilson, 2 vols.; Louisville, 1991–92
NTG	New Testament Guides
NTS	*New Testament Studies*
OCD	*Oxford Classical Dictionary*, 3d ed., ed. Simon Hornblower and Antony Spawforth; Oxford, 1996
OECT	Oxford Early Christian Texts
OTP	*Old Testament Pseudepigrapha*, ed. J. H. Charlesworth, 2 vols.; New York, 1983
PG	*Patrologia Graeca* (= *Patrologiae cursus completus: Series graeca*), ed. J.-P. Migne, 162 vols.; Paris, 1857–86
PHI	*Packard Humanities Institute* electronic database of Latin works
P. Mich.	*Michigan Papyri*; vol. 5: *Papyri from Tebtunis*, Part II, ed. E. M. Husselman, A. E. R. Boak, and W. F. Edgerton; Ann Arbor, 1944
P. Oxy.	*The Oxyrhynchus Papyri*, ed. B. P. Grenfell, A. S. Hunt et al., London, 1898–
RAr	*Revue archéologique*
RB	*Revue biblique*
RHE	*Revue d'histoire ecclésiastique*
SANT	Studien zum Alten und Neuen Testament
SBL	Society of Biblical Literature
SBLCP	Society of Biblical Literature Centennial Publications
SBLDS	Society of Biblical Literature Dissertation Series
SBLMS	Society of Biblical Literature Mongraph Series

SBLSBS   Society of Biblical Literature Sources for Biblical Study
SBLSP   *Society of Biblical Literature Seminar Papers*
SBLWAW Society of Biblical Literature Writings of the Ancient World
SC   Sources chrétiennes
SCHNT   Studia ad Corpus Hellenisticum Novi Testamenti
SNTSMS   Society for New Testament Studies Monograph Series
SP   Sacra Pagina
StPatr   *Studia Patristica*
Str-B   Strack, H. L., and P. Billerbeck, eds. *Kommentar zum Neuen Testament aus Talmud und Midrash*, 6 vols.; Munich, 1922–61
SVTP   Studia in Veteris Testamenti Pseudepigrapha
TAPA   *Transactions of the American Philological Association*
TB   Theologische Bücherei
THKNT   Theologischer Handkommentar zum Neuen Testament
TLG   *Thesaurus Linguae Graecae* electronic database of Greek works
TS   *Theological Studies*
TZ   *Theologische Zeitschrift*
UNT   Untersuchungen zum Neuen Testament
VC   *Vigiliae Christianae*
VCSup   Vigiliae Christianae Supplements
WBC   Word Biblical Commentary
WUNT   Wissenschaftliche Untersuchungen zum Neuen Testament
ZNW   *Zeitschrift für die neutestamentliche Wissenschaft und die Kunde der älteren Kirche*
ZPE   *Zeitschrift für Papyrologie und Epigraphik*

NOTES

Introduction:
Imagining Slaves

1. Dale B. Martin, "*Arsenokoitēs* and *Malakos*: Meanings and Consequences," in *Biblical Ethics and Homosexuality: Listening to Scripture* (ed. Robert L. Brawley; Louisville: Westminster John Knox, 1996), 130–31.

2. Troels Engberg-Pedersen, *Paul and the Stoics* (Louisville: Westminster John Knox, 2000), ix; and Wayne A. Meeks, "The Christian Proteus," in idem, *The Writings of St. Paul* (New York: W. W. Norton, 1972), 439. See also Peter Novak, *That Noble Dream: The "Objectivity Question" and the American Historical Profession* (Cambridge: Cambridge University Press, 1988), 1–17; and Elizabeth A. Clark, *History, Theory, Text: Historians and the Linguistic Turn* (Cambridge, Mass.: Harvard University Press, 2004), who suggests how to attend to theoretical considerations in early Christian studies.

3. Wayne A. Meeks, "Judaism, Hellenism, and the Birth of Christianity," in *Paul beyond the Judaism/Hellenism Divide* (ed. Troels Engberg-Pedersen, Louisville: Westminster John Knox, 2001), 21; idem, "Why Study the New Testament," *NTS* 51 (2005): 155–70; and Dale B. Martin, *The Corinthian Body* (New Haven: Yale University Press, 1995), xiii–xiv.

4. Readers can find surveys of ancient slavery and the New Testament in previous works: J. Albert Harrill, "Paul and Slavery," in *Paul in the Greco-Roman World* (ed. J. Paul Sampley; Harrisburg, Pa.: Trinity Press International, 2003), 575–607; and idem, *The Manumission of Slaves in Early Christianity* (Tübingen: Mohr [Siebeck], 1995), 11–56.

5. Karl Galinsky, *Augustan Culture: An Interpretive Introduction* (Princeton, N.J.: Princeton University Press, 1996), 10–41; and Kathleen McCarthy,

Slaves, Masters, and the Art of Authority in Plautine Comedy (Princeton, N.J.: Princeton University Press, 2000), 22–25.

6. Martin, *Corinthian Body*, xiii, xiv–xv; James C. Scott, *Domination and the Arts of Resistance: Hidden Transcripts* (New Haven: Yale University Press, 1990), 45–69; and Peter L. Berger and Thomas Luckmann, *The Social Construction of Reality: A Treatise in the Sociology of Knowledge* (Garden City, N.Y.: Doubleday, 1966).

7. Martin, *Corinthian Body*, xiv, emphasis in original.

8. On the retelling of exempla as the main vehicle by which Romans traditionally perpetuated their moral and religious values, rather than through systematic philosophy or sacred texts, see Richard P. Saller, *Patriarchy, Property and Death in the Roman Family* (Cambridge: Cambridge University Press, 1994), 109.

9. I agree with the consensus of most New Testament scholars who take Colossians, Ephesians, and the Pastoral Epistles to be pseudepigraphy, written by followers after Paul's death, and that the author of Ephesians used Colossians as a source. The findings of chapters 4 and 5 are independent of and do not depend on these conclusions, however.

10. Here and in subsequent chapters, I use the term *pater familias* in its ancient meaning of "estate owner"; see Richard P. Saller, "Pater Familias, Mater Familias, and the Gendered Semantics of the Roman Household," *CP* 94 (1999): 182–97.

11. I situate my use of social history, cast in the language of current debates in New Testament studies, in Harrill, *Manumission of Slaves*, 4–5.

12. Pace John M. G. Barclay, "Paul, Philemon, and the Dilemma of Christian Slave-Ownership," *NTS* 37 (1991): 161–86.

13. One of the better but nonetheless problematic attempts to solve the exegetical difficulties by the method of story creation is Norman R. Petersen, *Rediscovering Paul: Philemon and the Sociology of Paul's Narrative World* (Philadelphia: Fortress Press, 1985).

14. Among the more insightful studies that rightfully criticizes scholars for turning hypothesis into "fact" is Brook W. R. Pearson, "Assumptions in the Criticism and Translation of Philemon," in *Translating the Bible: Problems and Prospects* (ed. Stanley E. Porter and Richard S. Hess; Sheffield: Sheffield Academic Press, 1999), 253–80.

15. For an overview of the exegetical issues, see S. Scott Bartchy, "Philemon, Epistle to," *ABD*, 5:305–10.

16. On maroon gangs, see Keith R. Bradley, *Slavery and Rebellion in the Roman World, 140 B.C.–70 B.C.* (Bloomington: Indiana University Press, 1989), 4–11, 38–41, 54, 111, 123–24. On the ancient stereotyping of runaways as robbers and murderers, see Fridolf Kudlien, "Zur sozialen Situation des flüchtigen Sklaven in der Antike," *Hermes* 116 (1988): 232–52.

17. We do not know the location of Paul's imprisonment. It could be either Rome, Ephesus, or Caesarea in Palestine, but I find Ephesus the most plausible city; see Joseph A. Fitzmyer, *The Letter to Philemon: A New Translation with Introduction and Commentary* (New York: Doubleday, 2000), 9–11.

18. Eduard Lohse, *Colossians and Philemon: A Commentary on the Epistles to the Colossians and to Philemon* (Philadelphia: Fortress Press, 1971), 196–97.

19. Paul, furthermore, imbues his letter with kinship imagery, something lacking in Pliny's letter; Chris Frilingos, "'For my Child, Onesimus': Paul and Domestic Power in Philemon," *JBL* 119 (2000): 92.

20. Peter Lampe, "Keine 'Sklavenflucht' des Onesimus," *ZNW* 76 (1985): 135–37; idem, "Der Brief an Philemon," in *Die Briefe an die Philipper, Thessalonicher und an Philemon* (ed. Nikolaus Walter, Eckart Reinmuth, and Peter Lampe; Göttingen: Vandenhoeck & Ruprecht, 1998), 206–7. The juridical clarification of *servus fugitivus* was noted previously by W. W. Buckland, *The Roman Law of Slavery: The Condition of the Slave in Private Law from Augustus to Justinian* (1908; repr., New York: AMS Press, 1969), 268.

21. Jean-François Collange, *L'épître de Saint Paul à Philémon* (Geneva: Labor et Fides, 1987), 18 n. 12; Hermann Binder, *Der Brief des Paulus an Philemon* (Berlin: Evangelische Verlagsanstalt, 1990), 34–35; Brian M. Rapske, "The Prisoner Paul in the Eyes of Onesimus," *NTS* 37 (1991): 195–203; Bartchy, "Philemon," 307–8; John G. Nordling, "Onesimus Fugitivus. A Defense of the Runway Slave Hypothesis in Philemon," *JSNT* 41 (1991): 97–119; James D. G. Dunn, *The Epistles to the Colossians and to Philemon: A Commentary on the Greek Text* (Grand Rapids, Mich.: Eerdmans; Carlisle: Paternoster, 1996), 304; Allen Dwight Callahan, "Paul's Epistle to Philemon: Toward an Alternative *Argumentum*," *HTR* 86 (1993): 357–76; idem, *Embassy of Onesimus: The Letter of Paul to Philemon* (Valley Forge, Pa.: Trinity Press International, 1997), 6; Hans Hübner, *An Philemon. An die Kolosser. An die Epheser* (Tübingen: Mohr [Siebeck], 1997), 34; and Fitzmyer, *Philemon*, 17–23.

22. Lampe, "Keine 'Sklavenflucht,'" 137. A better argument could be made from Greek fictional letters; see C. D. N. Costa, ed., *Greek Fictional Letters* (New York: Oxford University Press, 2001), 65–67, for a "comic" letter by the Sophist Aristaenetus (third century C.E., probably used in declamation) on the case of a slave running to a friend for intercession.

23. Aulus Ofilius was a jurist of equestrian rank closely connected with Julius Caesar; Bruce W. Frier, *The Rise of the Roman Jurists: Studies in Cicero's pro Caecina* (Princeton, N.J.: Princeton University Press, 1985), 265.

24. Barry Nicholas, *An Introduction to Roman Law* (1962; repr., Oxford: Clarendon Press, 1982), 42–43.

25. J. A. Crook, *Legal Advocacy in the Roman World* (Ithaca, N.Y.: Cornell University Press, 1995), 16; see the larger discussion on pp. 1–29, 37–46.

26. Richard A. Bauman, *Lawyers in Roman Republican Politics: A Study of*

the Roman Jurists in Their Political Setting, 316–82 B.C. (Munich: C. H. Beck, 1983), 1–4.

27. Bauman, *Lawyers*, 2.

28. Peter Garnsey and Richard P. Saller, *The Roman Empire: Economy, Society and Culture* (Berkeley and Los Angeles: University of California Press, 1987), 21–40; Crook, *Law and Life*, 282; Nicholas, *Introduction to Roman Law*, 209; Fergus Miller, "The World of the Golden Ass," *JRS* 71 (1981): 63–75. Cf. Hartmut Galsterer, "Roman Law in the Provinces: Some Problems of Transmission," in *L'impero romano e le strutture economiche e sociali delle province* (ed. Michael H. Crawford; Como, Italy: New Press, 1986), 13–27.

29. E.g., Craig S. Wansink, *Chained in Christ: The Experience and Rhetoric of Paul's Imprisonments* (Sheffield: Sheffield Academic Press, 1996), 179–99.

30. See Fitzmyer, *Philemon*, 20–23.

31. Sara C. Winter, "Paul's Letter to Philemon," *NTS* 33 (1987): 1–15.

32. Wansink, *Chained in Christ*, 188–89.

33. Brian Rapske, *The Book of Acts and Paul in Roman Custody*; vol. 3 of *The Book of Acts in Its First-Century Setting* (ed. Bruce W. Winter; Grand Rapids, Mich.: Eerdmans; Carlisle: Paternoster Press, 1994), 195–225.

34. Harrill, *Manumission of Slaves*, 35; and Fitzmyer, *Philemon*, 13.

35. On the second alternative, see Peter Arzt-Grabner, "Onesimus erro: Zur Vorgeschichte des Philemonbriefs," *ZNW* 95 (2004): 131–43.

36. Wansink, *Chained in Christ*, 189–90.

37. *BGU* 1.37; Adolf Deissmann, *Light from the Ancient East: The New Testament Illustrated by Recently Discovered Texts of the Graeco-Roman World* (rev. ed.; 1927; repr., Peabody, Mass.: Hendrickson, 1995), 170. For commentary, see W. Hersey Davis, *Greek Papyri of the First Century* (New York: Harper and Bros., 1933), 57–59; Petersen, *Rediscovering Paul*, 44–53, 78–81; Peter Arzt, "Brauchbare Sklaven: Ausgewählte Papyrustexte zum Philemonbrief," *Protokolle zur Bibel* 1 (1992): 44–55; and Peter Arzt-Grabner, *Philemon* (Göttingen: Vandenhoeck & Ruprecht, 2003), 98–99, 210, 216.

38. David E. Garland, *Colossians and Philemon* (Grand Rapids, Mich.: Zondervan, 1988), 337.

39. Wansink, *Chained in Christ*, 183–88; Clarice J. Martin, "The Rhetorical Function of Commercial Language in Paul's Letter to Philemon (Verse 18)," in *Persuasive Artistry: Studies in New Testament Rhetoric in Honor of George A. Kennedy* (ed. Duane F. Watson; Sheffield: Sheffield Academic Press, 1991), 321–37.

40. See Frilingos, "'For My Child, Onesimus,'" 99.

41. The argument that the letter is a manumission request, perhaps "among friends" (known in Roman private law as *manumissio inter amicos* and *per epistulam*), does not depend on Onesimus being a runaway and is

a separate issue to consider. Interestingly, similar affective language does appear in a letter to Cicero by his brother Quintus expressing joy at Cicero's recent decision to manumit Tiro (Cicero's faithful secretary): "preferring us to have him as a friend rather than a slave" (*Epistulae ad familiares* 16.6); see Keith R. Bradley, *Slavery and Society at Rome* (Cambridge: Cambridge University Press, 1994), 1; and Harrill, *Manumission of Slaves*, 2–3, 54. But the claim that Paul is clearly making a manumission request is risky.

42. Frilingos, "'For My Child, Onesimus,'" 102–3.

43. How "to use" a slave properly was an ancient philosophical topos; see Dio Chrysostom, *Orationes* 10.2–22; and Epictetus, *Diatribai* 1.19.22–23 (Arzt-Grabner, *Philemon*, 234 n. 203).

44. This paragraph summarizes the evidence in Arzt-Grabner, *Philemon*, 66–70, 190–263. The best examples of apprentice contracts are *P. Mich.* 5.346; *P. Oxy.* 2.275; 41.2971 and 2977. See also Allan Chester Johnson, *Roman Egypt to the Reign of Diocletian*; vol. 2 of *An Economic Survey of Ancient Rome* (ed. Tenney Frank; Baltimore: Johns Hopkins University Press, 1936), 388–94; Ethel H. Brester, "A Weaver of Oxyrhynchus: Sketch of a Humble Life in Roman Egypt," *TAPA* 58 (1937): 132–54; John Rea, "A Student's Letter to his Father: P.Oxy. XVIII 2190 Revised," *ZPE* 99 (1993): 75–88; W. L. Westermann, "Apprentice Contracts and the Apprentice System in Roman Egypt," *CP* 9 (1914): 295–315; and Jean A. Straus, "L'esclavage dans l'Égypte romaine," *ANRW* 2.10.1 (1988): 841–911.

45. For example, the so-called formula "I command," cited in Arzt-Grabner, *Philemon*, 66.

46. My hypothesis builds on what I see are the implications of Arzt-Grabner, *Philemon*, although he himself does not go in this direction.

47. While not stated explicitly, professional transformation of a slave from "useless" to "useful" was the aim of apprenticeship.

1. The Slave Self: Paul and the Discursive "I"

1. Stanley K. Stowers, *A Rereading of Romans: Justice, Jews, and Gentiles* (New Haven: Yale University Press, 1994), 1–4, 258–59; J. Louis Martyn, "A Formula for Communal Discord as a Clue to the Nature of Pastoral Guidance," in *Putting Body and Soul Together: Essays in Honor of Robin Scroggs* (ed. Virginia Wiles, Alexandra Brown, and Graydon F. Snyder; Valley Forge, Pa.: Trinity Press International, 1997), 207; Eugene TeSelle, "Exploring the Inner Conflict: Augustine's Sermons on Romans 7 and 8," in *Engaging Augustine on Romans: Self, Context, and Theology in Interpretation* (ed. Daniel Patte and Eugene TeSelle; Harrisburg, Pa.: Trinity Press International, 2002), 111–46;

Phillip Cary, *Augustine's Invention of the Inner Self: The Legacy of a Christian Platonist* (New York: Oxford University Press, 2000); and Paula Fredriksen, "Paul and Augustine: Conversion Narratives, Orthodox Traditions, and the Redemptive Self," *JTS*, n.s. 37 (1986): 3–34.

2. For example, Gerd Theissen, *Psychological Aspects of Pauline Theology* (Philadelphia: Fortress Press, 1987), 177–265, in spite of admitting that the *egō* is discursive and a rhetorical device.

3. Wayne A. Meeks, *The First Urban Christians: The Social World of the Apostle Paul* (2d ed.; New Haven: Yale University Press, 2003), 186; the fundamental article is Krister Stendahl, "The Apostle Paul and the Introspective Conscience of the West," in idem, *Paul among Jews and Gentiles and Other Essays* (Philadelphia: Fortress Press, 1976), 78–96.

4. The literature is extensive, and commentaries sometimes claim that the identity of the *egō* remains an open question: whether personal for Paul, typical for all human beings (as Adam's voice), or fictive as a rhetorical figure. However, most scholarship today agrees that the *egō* cannot be the personal voice of Paul's *preconversion* experience. (I understand that Paul himself does not use the language of conversion but that of *calling* [as of a prophet] in Gal 1:15, his autobiography.) A minority view claims that Paul speaks at least partly autobiographically, out of his personal *post*conversion experience; see James Dunn, "Rom. 7,14–25 in the Theology of Paul," *TZ* 31 (1975): 257–73; idem, *Romans 1–8* (Dallas: Word Books, 1988), 382–83. A good survey of the exegetical issues and history of research for the nonspecialist is Jan Lambrecht, *The Wretched "I" and Its Liberation: Paul in Romans 7 and 8* (Louvain: Peeters, 1992), 29–91. Cf. Austin Busch, "The Figure of Eve in Romans 7:5-25," *BibInt* 12 (2004): 1–36.

5. First proposed in 1929 by Werner Georg Kümmel and reprinted as *Römer 7 und das Bild des Menschen im Neuen Testament: Zwei Studien* (Munich: C. Kaiser, 1974), 1–160. Stanley K. Stowers, "Romans 7.7-25 as a Speech-in-Character (*prosōpopoiia*)," in *Paul in His Hellenistic Context* (ed. Troels Engberg-Pedersen; Edinburgh: T. & T. Clark, 1994), 180–202; idem, *Rereading Romans*, 264–73.

6. This paragraph and the next follows the excellent discussion in Stowers, *Rereading Romans*, 16–21 (and idem, "Speech-in-Character," 180–91), with further literature cited there.

7. Sources: George A. Kennedy, *Progymnasmata: Greek Textbooks of Prose Composition and Rhetoric* (Atlanta: SBL, 2003), 47–49, 115–17, 164–66, 213–17.

8. The slave's stock type, like that of the others on the speech-in-character list, is informed by comic figures in the ancient theater. Aelius Theon, *Progymnasmata* 8 (115–18); Michel Patillon with Giancarlo Bolognesi, eds., *Aelius Théon: Progymnasmata* (Paris: Les Belles Lettres, 1997), 70–71. See also James R. Butts, "The Progymnasmata of Theon: A New Text with Trans-

lation and Commentary" (Ph.D. diss., The Claremont Graduate School, 1986), 445–64; Kennedy, *Progymnasmata*, 48 and 214 (slave speech-in-character); and W. Martin Bloomer, "Schooling in Persona: Imagination and Subordination in Roman Education," *Classical Antiquity* 16 (1997): 57–78.

9. For a persuasive reply to objections, see Stanley K. Stowers, "Apostrophe, *Prosōpopoiia* and Paul's Rhetorical Education," in *Early Christianity and Classical Culture: Comparative Studies in Honor of Abraham J. Malherbe* (ed. John T. Fitzgerald, Thomas H. Olbricht, and L. Michael White; Leiden: Brill, 2003), 351–69.

10. Hans Dieter Betz, "The Concept of the 'Inner Human Being' (*ho esō anthrōpos*) in the Anthropology of Paul," *NTS* 46 (2000): 315–41; and Theo K. Heckel, *Der Innere Mensch: Die paulinische Verarbeitung eines platonischen Motivs* (Tübingen: Mohr [Siebeck] 1993), 153–97 (see Stanley K. Stowers, review of *Innere Mensch*, by Heckel, *JBL* 114 [1995]: 342–44).

11. Betz, "Concept of the 'Inner Human Being,'" 334.

12. Aristotle, *Politics* 1.1252a–56a; *Nicomachean Ethics* 8.1161b; Eugene Garver, "Aristotle's Natural Slaves: Incomplete *Praxeis* and Incomplete Human Beings," *Journal of the History of Philosophy* 32 (1994): 173–95. See also P. A. Brunt, "Aristotle and Slavery," in idem, *Studies in Greek History and Thought* (Oxford: Clarendon, 1993), 343–88; and Nicholas D. Smith, "Aristotle's Theory of Natural Slavery," in *A Companion to Aristotle's Politics* (ed. David Keyt and Fred D. Miller Jr.; Oxford: Blackwell, 1990), 142–55.

13. Page duBois, *Slaves and Other Objects* (Chicago: University of Chicago Press, 2003), 189–205.

14. Keith Hopkins, "Novel Evidence for Roman Slavery," *Past and Present* 138 (1993): 23; Keith R. Bradley, "Animalizing the Slave: The Truth of Fiction," *JRS* 90 (2000): 110–11; and Jennifer A. Glancy, *Slavery in Early Christianity* (New York: Oxford University Press, 2002), 3–38.

15. For Gentiles as the exclusive "encoded readers" of Romans, see Stowers, *Rereading Romans*, 21–22, 287–89 and passim. For the classical Greek ideology on slavery, see the literature on Aristotle cited above, and Peter Hunt, *Slaves, Warfare, and Ideology in the Greek Historians* (Cambridge: Cambridge University Press, 1998), 19–25 and passim; and Vincent J. Rosivach, "Enslaving *Barbaroi* and the Athenian Ideology of Slavery," *Historia* 48 (1999): 129–57.

16. In contrast to Platonism and its dualistic metaphysics and anthropology, Stoicism had a monistic metaphysics and anthropology that understands the self as a unity; see Brad Inwood, "Hierocles: Theory and Argument in the Second Century A.D.," *Oxford Studies in Ancient Philosophy* 2 (1984): 163, 176–77.

17. C. E. Manning, "Stoicism and Slavery in the Roman Empire," *ANRW* 2.36.3 (1989): 1518–43; and Brent D. Shaw, "The Divine Economy: Stoicism as Ideology," *Latomus* 44 (1985): 16–54.

18. Justinian, *Institutiones* 1.3.2; *Digesta* 1.5.4.1; W. W. Buckland, *The Roman Law of Slavery: The Conditions of the Slave in Private Law from Augustus to Justinian* (New York: AMS Press, 1969), 1. Translations of the *Digesta* are from *The Digest of Justinian* (4 vols.; ed. Theodor Mommsen with Paul Krueger; trans. Alan Watson; Philadelphia: University of Pennsylvania Press, 1985), altered when not sufficiently literal for my purposes. On the mode of citation of Roman legal sources, see J. A. C. Thomas, *Textbook of Roman Law* (Amsterdam: North-Holland Publishing Co., 1976), xv.

19. Jesper Carlsen, *Vilici and Roman Estate Managers until A.D. 284* (Rome: Bretschneider, 1995).

20. Kathleen McCarthy, *Slaves, Masters, and the Art of Authority in Plautine Comedy* (Princeton, N.J.: Princeton University Press, 2000), 24 n. 39; Alan Watson, *Roman Slave Law* (Baltimore: Johns Hopkins University Press, 1987), 102–14; Barry Nicholas, *An Introduction to Roman Law* (3d ed.; Oxford: Clarendon, 1962), 201–4.

21. Jeffrey Stuart Rusten, "Aesop," *OCD*, 29; Lawrence M. Wills, "The Depiction of Slavery in the Ancient Novel," in *Slavery in Text and Interpretation* (ed. Allen D. Callahan et al.; Semeia 83/84; Atlanta: Scholars Press, 1998), 124–25.

22. Lloyd W. Daly, *Aesop without Morals: The Famous Fables, and a Life of Aesop* (New York: Thomas Yoseloff, 1961), 54–53; Hopkins, "Novel Evidence," 18–21; and William Fitzgerald, *Slavery and the Roman Literary Imagination* (Cambridge: Cambridge University Press, 2000), 27.

23. J. E. Lendon, *Empire of Honour: The Art of Government in the Roman World* (Oxford: Clarendon, 1997), 61, 129–30, 275.

24. The Greek version of the *Res Gestae* renders *potestas* as *exousia* (power) and *auctoritas* as *axiōma* (authority), the latter Greek word also a common translation for Latin *dignitas*; P. A. Brunt and J. M. Moore, *Res Gestae Divi Augusti: The Achievements of the Divine Augustus* (New York: Oxford University Press, 1967), 49; J. P. V. D. Balsdon, "Auctoritas, Dignitas, Otium," *CQ* 10 (1960): 44.

25. Karl Galinsky, *Augustan Culture: An Interpretive Introduction* (Princeton, N.J.: Princeton University Press, 1996), 10–41 passim; and Andrew Feldherr, *Spectacle and Society in Livy's History* (Berkeley and Los Angeles: University of California Press, 1998), 6–7, 13–14 and passim.

26. In this context belongs the use of the gladiator's oath (*auctoramentum gladiatorum*) as a literary topos of *auctoritas*: Seneca, *Epistulae morales* 37.1–2; Petronius, *Satyrica* 117; cf. Plautus, *Mostellaria* 780; Carlin A. Barton, *The Sorrows of the Ancient Romans: The Gladiator and the Monster* (Princeton, N.J.: Princeton University Press, 1993), 14–15, 21.

27. McCarthy, *Slaves*, 21–24. As we shall see in chapter 3, the comic complement of the *servus frugi* ("good" or "useful" slave) is the *servus callidus*

("trickster" or "clever" slave), subjective agency out of control. See John Wright, *Dancing in Chains: The Stylistic Unity of the Comoedia Palliata* (Rome: American Academy in Rome, 1974), 161.

28. Epictetus, *Diatribai* 4.7.32; Seneca, *De Beneficiis* 3.20; *Ad Marciam de consolatione* 24.5; see A. A. Long, "Representation and the Self in Stoicism," in *Companions to Ancient Thought*, vol. 2: *Psychology* (ed. Stephen Everson; Cambridge: Cambridge University Press, 1991), 102–20; and Fitzgerald, *Slavery*, 91.

29. Troels Engberg-Pedersen, "Stoic Philosophy and the Concept of the Person," in *The Person and the Human Mind: Issues in Ancient and Modern Philosophy* (ed. Christopher Gill; Oxford: Clarendon, 1990), 122.

30. Cicero, *Pro Caecina* 51–52 (trans. McCarthy, *Slaves*, 23 n. 36).

31. The original version of the parable is lost and comes from the hypothetical Sayings Source (known as Q). Biblical scholars make this determination because the parable appears only in Matthew ("Parable of the Talents," 25:14–30) and Luke ("Parable of the Pounds," 19:12–27), two early Christian sources without a known literary relationship. I do not argue that Q originated from Rome; the parable is illustrative only as a general example of Gentile Christianity in non-Pauline circles.

32. Roman masters, weary of the effort, often hired the services of professional torturers; see Moses I. Finley, *Ancient Slavery and Modern Ideology* (enlarged ed.; ed. Brent D. Shaw; Princeton, N.J.: Markus Wiener, 1998), 163; Keith R. Bradley, *Slaves and Masters in the Roman Empire: A Study in Social Control* (1984; repr., New York: Oxford University Press, 1987), 118–23; and Richard Saller, "The Family and Society," in *Epigraphic Evidence: Ancient History from Inscriptions* (ed. John Bodel; London: Routledge, 2001), 111. For "righteous" punishment as a theme in Matthew's slave parables, see Glancy, *Slavery*, 112–22. Compared with Matthew's account, Luke's version portrays less violence in regard to the slave: the Lukan master, though angry, gives the slave no more than a stern talking to (Luke 19:23). Decreasing the level of violence that Jesus condones is typical of Luke's redaction of Q and Mark, advancing Luke's theme of apologetics.

33. See McCarthy, *Slaves*, 26–28, 71–73 and passim; with Keith R. Bradley, *Slavery and Society at Rome* (Cambridge: Cambridge University Press, 1994), 122–25.

34. For helpful analysis using modern sociological categories of power and authority, see John Howard Schütz, *Paul and the Anatomy of Apostolic Authority* (Cambridge: Cambridge University Press, 1975), 12–13, 204–5, 224–25 and passim.

35. Stowers, *Rereading Romans*, 124; cf. Bernard Frischer, *The Sculpted Word: Epicureanism and Philosophical Recruitment in Ancient Greece* (Berkeley and Los Angeles: University of California Press, 1982), 277.

36. Helpful in my analysis is M. M. Bakhtin, *The Dialogic Imagination* (ed. Michael Holquist; Austin: University of Texas Press, 1981), 12; and McCarthy, *Slaves*, 6.

37. Claude Lévi-Strauss, *Totemism* (Boston: Beacon Press, 1963), 89 (in reference to animals); and Elizabeth A. Castelli, "Romans," in *Searching the Scriptures*; vol. 2: *A Feminist Commentary* (ed. Elisabeth Schüssler Fiorenza; New York: Crossroad, 1994), 294–95 (in reference to women).

38. Stowers, *Rereading Romans*, 34, 42–43, 108–9, 260, 273–79. On "God-fearers," see Shaye J. D. Cohen, *The Beginnings of Jewishness: Boundaries, Varieties, Uncertainties* (Berkeley and Los Angeles: University of California Press, 1999), 168–74; and Judith Lieu, *Neither Jew nor Greek? Constructing Early Christianity* (Edinburgh: T. & T. Clark, 2002), 31–68.

39. On this monologue, see Christopher Gill, *Personality in Greek Epic, Tragedy, and Philosophy: The Self in Dialogue* (Oxford: Clarendon, 1996), 216–26. On the topos of the slave representing the acrastic self in Roman literary imagination, see Fitzgerald, *Slavery*, 22–23. In an influential article, Hildebrecht Hommel ("Das 7. Kapitel des Römerbriefs in Lichte antiker Überlieferung," in idem, *Sebasmata: Studien zur antiken Religionsgeschichte und zum frühen Christentum* [WUNT 32; Tübingen: Mohr (Siebeck), 1984], 141–67) notes the classical parallels but persists the theological reading that the "I" voices the universal human condition under sin. The universal anthropology of both a "Jewish" and "Greek" background to the passage is posited by Jean-Noël Aletti, "Rm 7.7-25 encore une fois: Enjeux et propositions," *NTS* 48 (2002): 358–76. See also Hermann Lichtenberger, *Das Ich Adams und das Ich der Menschheit: Studien zur Menschenbild in Römer 7* (Tübingen: Mohr [Siebeck], 2004).

40. For Stowers (*Rereading Romans*, 180, 257, 271), the slave language is "only a metaphor" (like, "The ship mastered the storm") and simply a shorthand expression for "being overrun by one's passions." According to Engberg-Pedersen (*Paul and the Stoics* [Louisville: Westminster John Knox, 2000], 234–37, 291–92), the slave language has little relation to Paul's central message; Paul distances himself from the metaphor and even "apologizes" for using it. An exception is S. R. Llewelyn, "Slaves and Masters," *NewDocs* 6 (1992): 52–53.

41. The exegetical debate on the "faith of Christ" question has too long a history to repeat here. See Stowers, *Rereading Romans*, 194–26, and literature cited there; see also Jouette M. Bassler, review of *Rereading Romans*, by Stowers, *JBL* 115 (1996): 365–68.

42. Cf. 2 Cor 4:16-18; Margaret E. Thrall, *A Critical and Exegetical Commentary on the Second Epistle to the Corinthians* (2 vols.; Edinburgh: T. & T. Clark, 1994–2004), 1:347–56. The different context of the usage in 2 Corinthians 4 should not override or otherwise control interpretation for Romans 7.

43. David E. Fredrickson, "Paul, Hardships, and Suffering," in *Paul in the*

Greco-Roman World: A Handbook (ed. J. Paul Sampley; Harrisburg, Pa. Trinity Press International, 2003), 189–90.

44. Leander E. Keck, "The Absent Good: The Significance of Rom 7:18a," in *Text und Geschichte: Facetten theologischen Arbeitens aus dem Freundes- und Schüler-kreis Dieter Lührmann zum 60. Geburtstag* (ed. Stefan Maser and Egbert Schlarb; Marburg: Elwert, 1999), 68–69. On the Roman literary image of the slave as the "limbs" and "members" of the master's body, see Fitzgerald, *Slavery*, 49.

45. Paul W. Meyer, "The Worm at the Core of the Apple: Exegetical Reflections on Romans 7," in *The Conversation Continues: Studies in Paul and John in Honor of J. Louis Martin* (ed. Robert R. Fortna and Beverly R. Gaventa; Nashville: Abingdon, 1990), 78–79; Martyn, "Formula for Communal Discord," 209–10; Betz, "Concept of the 'Inner Human Being,'" 338–40; Keck, "Absent Good," 70; and Dale B. Martin, *The Corinthian Body* (New Haven: Yale University Press, 1995), 123–28.

46. On the apocalyptic drama and eschatological tension, see Keck, "Absent Good," 74–75; cf. Dunn, *Romans*, 396, 406–11. Otto Michel (*Der Brief an die Römer* [5th ed.; Göttingen: Vandenhoeck & Ruprecht, 1978], 230) connects the "sold under" language in Paul to LXX usage as a term for debt bondage.

47. See Tonio Hölscher, "Images of War in Greece and Rome: Between Military Practice, Public Memory, and Cultural Symbolism," *JRS* 93 (2003): 5–8; and Edgar Krentz, "Paul, Games, and the Military," in Sampley, *Paul in the Greco-Roman World*, 347–55. For Jewish admiration of Roman military virtues and conquest by "planning and patience," see 1 Macc 8:1-16; and Josephus, *J.W.* 2.577–582; 3.70–109 (oddly, these digressions constitute the best extant account of the Roman army in the first century C.E., and it comes from a *Jewish* author).

48. E.g., Valerius Maximus 6.8.1–7. To Valerius, such faithfulness was not just an instance of *fides*, but of *benevolentia* and *pietas* as well; see Bradley, *Slaves and Masters*, 36. On this topos in early Christianity, see chapter 6, below. On the related Stoic theme of attaching one's "self" (*autos*) in total directedness toward the divine as a "servant of Zeus" (*tou Dios diakonos*), see Epictetus, *Diatr.* 3.4.20; 3.24.65; 4.1.98–102; 4.1.131; 4.12.11–12 (cf. 4.1.175–176; Seneca, *Ep.* 61.3). On *diakonos* as a term designating a slave, see John N. Collins, *Diakonia: Re-interpreting the Ancient Sources* (New York: Oxford University Press, 1990), 92–93, 96–98, 150–53, 247–48.

49. Engberg-Pedersen, *Paul and the Stoics*, 225–46 and passim. Engberg-Pedersen confuses his otherwise clear and excellent analysis by his assumption that the fearful slave (acting like an automaton) is the representation for all "obedient slaves" in classical antiquity.

50. Orlando Patterson, *Slavery and Social Death: A Comparative Study* (Cambridge, Mass.: Harvard University Press, 1982), 35–76 passim; and J. Albert

Harrill, *The Manumission of Slaves in Early Christianity* (Tübingen: Mohr [Sie-beck], 1995), 1, 15–17, 32.

51. Paul's advice in Rom 13:1-7 presupposes Christians sharing in the special relationship of Jewish communities to Roman rule. Paul reuses a traditional piece of Jewish paraenesis that was formed in the Greek syna-gogue, to address *auctoritas* directly: Jewish rights under Roman rule come with mutual obligations on the part of subordinates; see Wayne A. Meeks, "Corinthian Christians as Artificial Aliens," in *Paul beyond the Judaism/Hel-lenism Divide* (ed. Troels Engberg-Pedersen; Louisville: Westminster John Knox, 2001), 137; idem, *First Urban Christians*, 208 n. 192, and literature cited there.

52. Paul defines "Gentiles" as "captives" of their appetites, over against Jewish freedom from such captivity; see Stowers, *Rereading Paul*, 273–76 and passim.

53. See James C. Scott, *Domination and the Arts of Resistance: Hidden Tran-scripts* (New Haven: Yale University Press, 1990), 2-4, 79 and passim.

54. I integrate the "social death" definition of a slave by Patterson (*Slav-ery*, 13 and passim) into my exegesis here. Cf. Paul's use of kinship language to describe the "orphaned" experience of the Jewish proselyte; Abraham J. Malherbe, *The Letters to the Thessalonians* (New York: Doubleday, 2000), 104, 110, 120.

55. Pace Gary W. Burnett, *Paul and the Salvation of the Individual* (Leiden: Brill, 2001), 173–214, whose reading of Rom 7:7-25 is, by the author's own admission, straightforward and simple.

56. E.g., Wolfgang Waldstein, "Zum Menschsein von Sklaven," in *Fünfzig Jahre Forschungen zur antiken Sklaverei an der Mainzer Akademie, 1950–2000: Miscellanea zum Jubiläum* (ed. Heinz Bellen and Heinz Heinen; Stuttgart: Franz Steiner, 2001), 31–49. On the fallacy of "discovering" human rights and humanity in slavery from juridical definitions of the slave as a legal per-sonality, see Patterson, *Slavery*, 22–23.

57. Amélie Oksenberg Rorty, "Persons and *Personae*," in *The Person and the Human Mind: Issues in Ancient and Modern Philosophy* (ed. Christopher Gill; Oxford: Clarendon, 1990), 1–36; Christopher Gill, "The Character–Person-ality Distinction," in *Characterization and Individuality in Greek Literature* (ed. Christopher Pelling; Oxford: Clarendon, 1990), 2; Gill, *Personality in Greek Epic*, 2; and Luther H. Martin, "The Anti-individualistic Ideology of Helle-nistic Culture," *Numen* 41 (1994): 124. Greeks and Romans expressed the *grammatical* meaning of "self" by the use of third-person reflective pronouns (*autos* and *ipse*). This is not in itself evidence that a Foucauldian "technology of the self" existed for classical antiquity. The latter pronoun in Latin was also a common poetic expression for "the master," making the slave a met-onym for the master's self; see Fitzgerald, *Slavery*, 18–22.

58. See Harrill, *Manumission of Slaves*, 18–20; cf. A. A. Long, *Epictetus: A Stoic and Socratic Guide to Life* (Oxford: Clarendon, 2002), 11–12.

59. *The Golden Ass* of Apuleius provides a further example of a Roman author using the "public transcript" of ancient slavery to invent a slave self, who is initially alienated from his true master (the goddess Isis); see discussion in Bradley, "Animalizing the Slave"; and Fitzgerald, *Slavery*, 94–95.

2. The Slave Body: Physiognomics and Invective against Paul

1. Hans Dieter Betz draws attention to the rhetoric of this accusation in *Der Apostel Paulus und die sokratische Tradition: Eine exegetische Untersuchung zu seiner "Apologie" 2 Korinther 10–13* (Tübingen: Mohr [Siebeck], 1972), 44–69.

2. On reading *phēsin* as plural, see Victor Paul Furnish, *II Corinthians* (New York: Doubleday, 1984), 468; but cf. C. K. Barrett, *A Commentary on the Second Epistle to the Corinthians* (New York: Harper and Row, 1973), 260–61. My argument, however, does not depend on the grammatical issue of whether an individual or a group made this invective against Paul.

3. See Timothy B. Savage, *Power through Weakness: Paul's Understanding of the Christian Ministry in 2 Corinthians* (Cambridge: Cambridge University Press, 1996), 64–65; Ralph P. Martin, *2 Corinthians* (Waco, Tex.: Word Books, 1986), 311–14; Furnish, *II Corinthians*, 478–79.

4. Hans Windisch, *Der zweite Korintherbrief* (Göttingen: Vandenhoeck & Ruprecht, 1924), 293; see also Jacob Jervell, "Der schwache Charismatiker," in *Rechtfertigung: Festschrift für Ernst Käsemann zum 70. Geburtstag* (ed. Johannes Friedrich, Wolfgang Pöhlmann, and Peter Stuhlmacher; Tübingen: Mohr [Siebeck]; Göttingen: Vandenhoeck & Ruprecht, 1976), 191–94.

5. *The Acts of Paul and Thecla* 3 (*Acta Apostolorum Apocrypha* [ed. R. A. Lipsius and M. Bonnet; 2 pts. in 3 vols.; 1898; repr., Darmstadt: Wissenschaftliche Buchgesellschaft, 1959], 1:237); trans. in *NTApoc* 2:239. More recent scholarship has shown the portrait to contain not negative but positive physiognomic features; Robert M. Grant, "The Description of Paul in the Acts of Paul and Thecla," *VC* 36 (1982): 1–4; Abraham J. Malherbe, "A Physical Description of Paul," in idem, *Paul and the Popular Philosophers* (Minneapolis: Fortress Press, 1989), 165–70.

6. Alfred Plummer, *A Critical and Exegetical Commentary on the Second Epistle of St. Paul to the Corinthians* (New York: Charles Scribner's Sons, 1915), 282–83; Rudolf Bultmann, *The Second Letter to the Corinthians* (Minneapolis: Augsburg, 1985), 190.

7. Walter Schmithals, *Gnosticism in Corinth: An Investigation of the Letters to the Corinthians* (Nashville: Abingdon, 1971), 106, 176–77; Gerd Lüdemann, *Opposition to Paul in Jewish Christianity* (Minneapolis: Fortress Press, 1989), 83–86.

8. Ronald F. Hock, *The Social Context of Paul's Ministry: Tentmaking and Apostleship* (Philadelphia: Fortress Press, 1980), 59–60.

9. Betz, *Apostel Paulus*.

10. Peter Marshall, *Enmity in Corinth: Social Conventions in Paul's Relations with the Corinthians* (Tübingen: Mohr [Siebeck], 1987), 317–40 (while not denying the medical theory); idem, "Invective: Paul and His Enemies in Corinth," in *Perspectives on Language and Text: Essays and Poems in Honor of Francis I. Andersen's Sixtieth Birthday* (ed. Edgar W. Conrad and Edward G. Newing; Winona Lake, Ind.: Eisenbrauns, 1987), 359–73; and Christopher Forbes, "Comparison, Self-Praise and Irony: Paul's Boasting and the Conventions of Hellenistic Rhetoric," *NTS* 32 (1986): 1–30. See also David Alan Black, *Paul, Apostle of Weakness: Astheneia and Its Cognates in the Pauline Literature* (New York: Peter Lang, 1984), 135–38; and Philip E. Hughes, *Paul's Second Epistle to the Corinthians* (Grand Rapids, Mich.: Eerdmans, 1962), 361–63.

11. See Abraham J. Malherbe, "Antisthenes and Odysseus, and Paul at War," in idem, *Paul and the Popular Philosophers*, 91–119.

12. Maud W. Gleason, *Making Men: Sophists and Self-Representation in Ancient Rome* (Princeton, N.J.: Princeton University Press, 1995), xxviii.

13. Tamsyn S. Barton, *Power and Knowledge: Astrology, Physiognomics, and Medicine under the Roman Empire* (Ann Arbor: University of Michigan Press, 1994), 95–131; Gleason, *Making Men*, 55–81; Maria Michela Sassi, *The Science of Man in Ancient Greece* (Chicago: University of Chicago Press, 2001); Mario Vegetti, *Il coltello e lo stilo: Animali, schiavi, barbari e donne alle origini della razionalita scientifica* (3d ed.; Milan: Il saggiatore, 1996); and Voula Tsouna, "Doubts about Other Minds and the Science of Physiognomics," *CQ* 48 (1998): 175–86. The standard work remains Elizabeth C. Evans, *Physiognomics in the Ancient World* (Philadelphia: American Philosophical Society, 1969), yet not all scholars have been convinced that the physiognomic handbooks had as much influence on ancient literature as Evans assigns them; see Phillip DeLacy, review of *Physiognomics*, by Evans, *AJP* 92 (1971): 508–10.

14. E.g., J. D. Beazley, *Attic Red-Figure Vase-Painters* (2d ed.; 3 vols.; Oxford: Clarendon, 1963), 1:246 (Berlin inv. 4560). Beginning in the second half of the sixth century B.C.E., the representation of slaves in Attic pottery became clearly distinguishable iconographically from freeborns; see Nikolaus Himmelmann, *Archäologisches zum Problem der griechischen Sklaverei* (Mainz: Akademie der Wissenschaften und der Literatur, 1971), 5–46. This change in the iconography of slaves reflected a similar change in the Athenian ideology of slavery toward viewing slaves as essentially inferior; see Vincent J. Rosivach, "Enslaving *Barbaroi* and the Athenian Ideology of Slavery," *Historia* 48 (1999): 129–57.

15. François Lissarrague, "The Sexual Life of Satyrs," in *Before Sexuality: The Construction of the Erotic Experience in the Ancient Greek World* (ed. David

M. Halperin, John J. Winkler, and Froma I. Zeitlin; Princeton, N.J.: Princeton University Press, 1990), 56–57; Claude Bérard, "Pénalité et religion à Athènes: Un témoignage de l'imagerie," *RAr*, 7th ser., 25 (1982): 144–46.

16. H. C. Baldry, *The Unity of Mankind in Greek Thought* (Cambridge: Cambridge University Press, 1965), 14–15, 97–98; and Ruth Scodel, "The Removal of the Arms, the Recognition with Laertes, and Narrative Tension in the *Odyssey*," *CP* 93 (1998): 12–13. For physiognomic principles in Homer generally, see Evans, *Physiognomics*, 58–62; and Donald Lateiner, *Sardonic Smile: Nonverbal Behavior in Homeric Epic* (Ann Arbor: University of Michigan Press, 1995).

17. Aristotle, *Nicomachean Ethics* 8.1161b 5; *Eudemian Ethics* 7.1241b20–25; *Politics* 1.1254a20; 1.1259b20–25. Rosivach, "Enslaving *Barbaroi*," 144–48; Peter Garnsey, *Ideas of Slavery from Aristotle to Augustine* (Cambridge: Cambridge University Press, 1996), 107–27; and literature cited in chapter 1, note 12.

18. Aristotle, *De partibus animalium* 2.653a30; 2.656a13–14; 4.686a25. Trevor J. Saunders, *Politics: Books I and II/Aristotle* (Oxford: Clarendon, 1995), 78. On Aristotle's use of physiognomics, see Evans, *Physiognomics*, 22–24; Giovanni Manetti, *Theories of the Sign in Classical Antiquity* (Bloomington: Indiana University Press, 1993), 84–91; G. E. R. Lloyd, *Science, Folklore and Ideology: Studies in the Life Sciences in Ancient Greece* (Cambridge: Cambridge University Press, 1983), 22–26; and Page duBois, *Slaves and Other Objects* (Chicago: University of Chicago Press, 2003), 189–205.

19. Giuseppe Cambiano, "Aristotle and the Anonymous Opponents of Slavery," in *Classical Slavery* (ed. M. I. Finley; London: Frank Cass, 1987), 21–41; Ekaterini Synodinou, "On the Concept of Slavery in Euripides" (Ph.D. diss., University of Cincinnati, 1974).

20. Joseph Vogt, *Ancient Slavery and the Ideal of Man* (Cambridge, Mass.: Harvard University Press, 1975), 21.

21. See Plutarch, *Antonius* 84.2–3; a fact of slave life that moral philosophers often condemned, e.g., Seneca, *Epistulae morales* 47; and Philo of Alexandria: "Let so-called masters therefore cease from imposing upon their slaves severe and scarcely endurable orders, which break down their bodies by violent usage and force the soul to collapse before the body" (*De specialibus legibus* 2.90). On the construction of the slave body by the whip, see Richard P. Saller, *Patriarchy, Property and Death in the Roman Household* (Cambridge: Cambridge University Press, 1994), 133–53.

22. Kendrick Grobel, "*Sōma* as 'Self, Person' in the Septuagint," in *Neutestamentliche Studien für Rudolf Bultmann* (ed. Walther Eltester; Berlin: Alfred Töpelmann, 1954), 55–56. See also Dominic Montserrat, "Experiencing the Male Body in Roman Egypt," in *When Men Were Men: Masculinity, Power and Identity in Classical Antiquity* (ed. Lin Foxhall and John Salmon; London:

Routledge, 1998), 153; Amy Richlin, "Cicero's Head," in *Constructions of the Classical Body* (ed. James I. Porter; Ann Arbor: University of Michigan Press, 1999), 193–94; and Jennifer A. Glancy, *Slavery in Early Christianity* (New York: Oxford University Press, 2002).

23. The principal extant treatises are Ps.-Aristotle, *Physiognomonica*, in the LCL volume by W. S. Hett (*Aristotle: Minor Works* [Cambridge, Mass.: Harvard University Press, 1936], 83–137); M. Antonius Polemo, *De physiognomonia*, known only in an Arabic version, which is edited and translated into Latin by Richard Foerster (*Scriptores physiognomonici Graeci et Latini* [2 vols.; 1893; repr., Stuttgart and Leipzig: Teubner, 1994], 1:98–294); an epitome in Greek of Polemo's work by the Sophist Adamantius (fourth century C.E.) in Foerster (*Scriptores* 1:295–431); and a fourth-century anonymous work, *Physiognomonica anonymi*, available in the edition of Jacques André (*Traité de physiognomonie: Anonyme latin* [Paris: Les Belles Lettres, 1981]), with a useful introduction (pp. 7–39).

24. Barton, *Power and Knowledge*, 101.

25. Ibid.

26. Ibid., 213 n. 115; Gleason, *Making Men*, 35–36; and Matthew Leigh, *Comedy and the Rise of Rome* (New York: Oxford University Press, 2004), 92.

27. Polemo, epitome by Adamantius, in Foerster, *Scriptores*, 1:314.

28. Polemo, *De physiognomonia* 7 (Foerster, *Scriptores*, 1:204); Barton, *Power and Knowledge*, 213 n. 115. The last phrase, *servorum mores*, is the editor's Latin translation of the Arabic *akhlāq al-ʿabīd* (I thank Warren Schultz for translating the Arabic text for me).

29. For the use of physiognomics, by Polemo and other authors, in rhetorical invective to attack an enemy's manhood, see Gleason, *Making Men*, 21–54; and Barton, *Power and Knowledge*, 111–15.

30. *Physiognomonica anonymi* 24 (André, *Traité*, 71, 102) (= Foerster, *Scriptores*, 2:38–39, 88–89).

31. *Physiognomonica anonymi* 51 (André, *Traité*, 91) (= Foerster, *Scriptores*, 2:70–71).

32. Barton, *Power and Knowledge*, 120; Rosivach, "Enslaving *Barbaroi*," 156.

33. Sassi, *Science of Man*, 55–59; Evans, *Physiognomics*, 33–39; T. B. L. Webster, *Greek Theatre Production* (2d ed.; London Methuen, 1970), 82–85; and Robert Carl, *Die Masken der neueren attischen Komödie* (Halle: M. Niemeyer, 1911), 58–60. The influence of physiognomics on dramatic slave masks was first suggested by Richard Foerster, *Die Physiognomik der Griechen* (Kiel: Schmidt and Klaunig, 1884), 13–16.

34. See the criticism in DeLacy, review of *Physiognomics*, by Evans, 508.

35. W. Beare, *The Roman Stage: A Short History of Latin Drama in the Time of the Republic* (3d ed.; London: Methuen, 1964), 190, although arguing that

the phrase may mean "in human guise" only, as opposed to appearing in divine form.

36. W. Beare, "Slave Costume in New Comedy," *CQ* 43 (1949): 30.

37. Pollux, *Onon.* 4.150; trans. in Eric Csapo and William J. Slater, *The Context of Ancient Drama* (Ann Arbor: University of Michigan Press, 1995), 401. For commentary, based on Ps.-Aristotle's *Physiognomonica* and the other handbooks, see David Wiles, "Greek Theatre and the Legitimation of Slavery," in *Slavery and Other Forms of Unfree Labour* (ed. Léonie J. Archer; London: Routledge, 1998), 60–64; Bear, *Roman Stage*, 186; Arthur Pickard-Cambridge, *The Dramatic Festivals of Athens* (2d ed., rev. John Gould and D. M. Lewis; Oxford: Clarendon, 1968), 266–67; and Gisela Krien, "Der Ausdruck der antiken Theatermasken nach Angaben im Polluxkatalog und in der pseudoaristotelischen 'Physiognomik,'" *JÖAI* 42 (1955): 84–117. For the use of the mask in ancient comedy generally, see David Wiles, *The Masks of Menander: Sign and Meaning in Greek and Roman Performance* (Cambridge: Cambridge University Press, 1991), 129–87.

38. See Elizabeth C. Evans, "Physiognomics in the Roman Empire," *CJ* 45 (1949–50): 278–79; William S. Anderson, "Anger in Juvenal and Seneca," *University of California Publications in Classical Philology* 19.3 (1964): 160–65; Susanna Morton Braund and Paula James, "*Quasi Homo*: Distortion and Contortion in Seneca's *Apocolocyntosis*," *Arethusa* 31 (1998): 288–91; Donald Lateiner, "Blushes and Pallor in Ancient Fictions," *Helios* 25 (1998): 163–89; and William V. Harris, *Restraining Rage: The Ideology of Anger Control in Classical Antiquity* (Cambridge, Mass.: Harvard University Press, 2001). Seneca's description of the angry man whose "hair bristles and stands on end" (*De ira* 1.1.4) makes intelligible also the preponderance of "wavy hair" in the slave masks; see T. B. L. Webster, "Leading Slaves in New Comedy: 300 B.C.– 300 A.D.," *JdI* 76 (1961): 100–110.

39. Dominic Montserrat, *Sex and Society in Graeco-Roman Egypt* (London: Kegan Paul International, 1996), 56; idem, "Experiencing the Male Body," 158.

40. Montserrat, *Sex and Society*, 56.

41. Montserrat, "Experiencing the Male Body," 153–59. Traditions in Roman law and Stoic ethics also declared a shared humanity between slave and free. As I noted in chapter 1, the Roman jurists held that slavery was an institution of the law of nations (*ius gentium*) by which, contrary to nature (*contra naturam*), a person is subjected to the power (*dominium*) of another. The Stoic Seneca exhorted masters to see their slaves as essentially the same as them, being accidents of fortune, not products of nature (*Ep.* 47). In ancient society these cultural beliefs competed with rival ones confident in the natural, physiognomic inferiority of the slave body. Yet it was a disturbing proposition for many upper-order Romans that their slaves had potentially the same

bodies as freeborns. The Roman Senate once debated the merits of requiring slaves to wear uniforms to distinguish their bodies from the free population in the city. The bill failed to pass because senators became more disturbed when they realized that slave uniforms would enable slaves to count their number and to better organize revolt (Seneca, *De clementia* 1.24.1).

42. Cf. Garnsey, *Ideas of Slavery*, 157–72, who argues that Philo employed the Aristotelian theory of natural slavery as well as Stoic ideas refuting it.

43. Unless otherwise noted, the references here and throughout this chapter are collected from Evans, *Physiognomics*, 89–93 (Appendixes A–E), in conjunction with keyword searching in the electronic databases of classical literature (*TLG* and *PHI*).

44. Judith Perkins, *The Suffering Self: Pain and Narrative Representation in the Early Christian Era* (London: Routledge, 1995), 53–54.

45. John Briscoe, *A Commentary on Livy: Books XXXIV–XXXVII* (Oxford: Clarendon, 1981), 214.

46. Barton, *Power and Knowledge*, 113. For *In Pisonem* as invective, see R. G. M. Nisbet, *M. Tulli Ciceronis, In L. Calpurnium Pisonem oratio* (Oxford: Clarendon, 1961), 192–97.

47. Joseph J. Hughes, "Piso's Eyebrows," *Mnemosyne* 45 (1992): 236, responding to D. M. MacDowell, "Piso's Face," *Classical Review*, n.s. 14 (1964): 9–10. See also Joseph J. Hughes, "Invective and Comedic Allusion: Cicero, *In Pisonem*, Fragment 9 (Nisbet)," *Latomus* 57 (1998): 570–77.

48. Hughes, "Piso's Eyebrows," 235.

49. Paul MacKendrick, *The Speeches of Cicero: Context, Law, Rhetoric* (London: Duckworth, 1995), 343. Cf. Epictetus's critique of foolish, unkempt youths behaving like animals without "the grooming that befits a man" (*Diatribai* 4.11.10–18).

50. Cf. Seneca, "An *atrium* full of smoke-stained masks does not make one noble" (*Ep.* 44.5). For the cultural significance of *imagines* in the Roman household and in Latin rhetoric, see Harriet I. Flower, *Ancestor Masks and Aristocratic Power in Roman Culture* (Oxford: Clarendon, 1996), 16–31, 150–51, 186–87, 220–21.

51. Severin Koster, *Die Invektive in der griechischen und römischen Literatur* (Meisenheim am Glan: Anton Hain, 1980), 226–27; and Wilhelm Süss, *Ethos: Studien zur älteren griechischen Rhetorik* (Leipzig and Berlin: Teubner, 1910), 259. Ann Vasaly, *Representations: Images of the World in Ciceronian Oratory* (Berkeley and Los Angeles: University of California Press, 1993), 131–55. For arguments that the Roman Empire knew racial prejudice based on skin color, see G. W. Bowersock, *Roman Arabia* (Cambridge. Mass.: Harvard University Press, 1983), 124 n. 4; Orlando Patterson, *Slavery and Social Death: A Comparative Study* (Cambridge, Mass.: Harvard University Press, 1982), 177–78; and now, Benjamin Isaac, *The Invention of Racism in Classical Antiquity*

(Princeton, N.J.: Princeton University Press, 2004). For more nuance, see the excellent study by David M. Goldenberg, *The Curse of Ham: Race and Slavery in Early Judaism, Christianity, and Islam* (Princeton, N.J.: Princeton University Press, 2003), esp. 95–112, 183–200. Cf. the comic dialogue of characters on the run considering the merits of either dyeing their bodies black to pass as Ethiopian slaves or chalking their faces pale white to pass as Gallic slaves (Petronius, *Satyrica* 102).

52. Marshall, *Enmity in Corinth*, 77; Ps-Aristotle, *Physiognomonica* 6.812a10–15.

53. Marshall, *Enmity in Corinth*, 76. Phillip DeLacy, "Cicero's Invective against Piso," *TAPA* 72 (1941): 49–58, argues that Cicero's attack on Piso as an Epicurean is derived from the anti-Epicurean polemic current in the philosophical literature of Cicero's time.

54. Marshall, "Invective: Paul and His Enemies in Corinth," 362.

55. Ibid.

56. Ibid., 53.

57. Anthony Corbeill, *Controlling Laughter: Political Humor in the Late Roman Republic* (Princeton, N.J.: Princeton University Press, 1996), 19.

58. Cf. the comments of Epictetus on the runaway slave who has a body that quakes and panics easily, becoming "instantly all in a flutter and upset" at the mere mention of the word *master* (*Diatr.* 1.29.59–60).

59. Cicero, *Rab. Post.* 20; Quintus Curtius Rufus, *Historiarum Alexandri* 6.11.4.

60. Marshall, *Enmity in Corinth*, 156.

61. Gleason, *Making Men*, 166.

62. Fritz Graf, "Gestures and Conventions: The Gestures of Roman Actors and Orators," in *A Cultural History of Gesture* (ed. Jan Bremmer; Ithaca, N.Y.: Cornell University Press, 1991), 45, 49–50; Corbeill, *Controlling Laughter*, 99–127; Erik Gunderson, "Discovering the Body in Roman Oratory," in *Parchments of Gender: Deciphering the Bodies of Antiquity* (ed. Maria Wyke; Oxford: Clarendon, 1998), 169–89; Joy Connolly, "Mastering Corruption: Constructions of Identity in Roman Oratory," in *Women and Slaves in Greco-Roman Culture: Differential Equations* (ed. Sheila Murnaghan and Sandra R. Joshel; London: Routledge, 1998), 130–51; and Peter Bing, "The Unruly Tongue: Philitas of Cos as Scholar and Poet," *CP* 98 (2003): 338–39.

63. Marshall, *Enmity in Corinth*, 75.

64. Ibid.

65. Susan Treggiari, *Roman Freedmen during the Late Republic* (Oxford: Clarendon, 1969), 69–75; Wolfgang Waldstein, *Operae Libertorum: Untersuchungen zur Dienstpflicht freigelassener Sklaven* (Stuttgart: Franz Steiner, 1986); and Thomas E. J. Wiedemann, "Duties of Freedmen," *Classical Review*, n.s. 38 (1988): 331–33.

66. Marshall, *Enmity in Corinth*, 74.

67. Ibid., 73–78.

68. Cynthia Damon, *The Mask of the Parasite: A Pathology of Roman Patronage* (Ann Arbor: University of Michigan Press, 1997), 32.

69. Furnish, *II Corinthians*, 479.

70. On Socrates' satyr-like appearance, see Evans, *Physiognomics*, 20–21. The reference from Cicero catches him in a contradiction between his philosophical writings and his judicial oratory (e.g., his calculated invective against Piso). In another work, however, Cicero does modify the story to give physiognomics more credibility: Socrates rescues Zopyrus by admitting the character defects as his natural propensities, but ones that philosophy overcame (*Tusculanae disputationes* 4.80–81).

71. Barton, *Power and Knowledge*, 213 n. 115; and Keith R. Bradley, *Slavery and Society at Rome* (Cambridge: Cambridge University Press, 1994), 142–43. Other references above found in Leofranc Holford-Strevens, "Aulus Gellius: The Non-Visual Portraitist," in *Portraits: Biographical Representation in the Greek and Latin Literature of the Roman Empire* (ed. M. J. Edwards and Simon Swain; Oxford: Clarendon, 1997), 96. See also Pliny, *Epistulae* 1.21.2.

72. See Jennifer Larson, "Paul's Masculinity," *JBL* 123 (2004): 99–135.

73. Jennifer A. Glancy, "Boasting of Beatings (2 Corinthians 11:23-25)," *JBL* 123 (2004): 99–135.

74. Betz, *Apostel Paulus*, passim.

75. Ibid., 44–57.

76. On the strong military language, see Edgar Krentz, "Paul, Games, and the Military," in *Paul in the Greco-Roman World: A Handbook* (ed. J. Paul Sampley: Harrisburg, Pa.: Trinity Press International, 2003), 354.

77. Betz, *Apostel Paulus*, 14–19.

78. Ibid., 44–57.

79. Ibid., 68; summarized in Malherbe, "Antisthenes and Odysseus," 113.

80. Laurence L. Welborn, "The Runaway Paul," *HTR* 92 (1999): 122–59, building on a suggestion by Windisch, *Zweite Korintherbrief,* 316. See also Calvin J. Roetzel, *Paul: The Man and the Myth* (Columbia: University of South Carolina Press, 1998; Minneapolis: Fortress Press, 1999), 58. Betz argues, instead, that Paul received the model of the fool's speech from popular philosophy (*Apostel Paulus*, 80).

81. Malherbe, "Antisthenes and Odysseus," 91–119.

82. Ibid., 99–100; trans. of Antisthenes in H. D. Rankin, *Anthisthenes Sokratikos* (Amsterdam: Adolf M. Hakkert, 1986), 169. On the trickster aspect of the Odyssean masquerade, see Lateiner, *Sardonic Smile,* 182–83.

83. Rankin, *Anthisthenes,* 170.

84. Malherbe, "Antisthenes and Odysseus," 111, 118.

85. On Paul as a reader and misreader of texts, see Richard B. Hays, *Echoes*

of Scripture in the Letters of Paul (New Haven: Yale University Press, 1989), 1–33, 77–83.

86. Pace Glancy, "Boasting of Beatings," 129 n. 113. Cf. the use of slaves as spies in Roman siege warfare against strongholds; N. J. E. Austin and N. B. Rankov, *Exploratio: Military and Political Intelligence in the Roman World from the Second Punic War to the Battle of Adrianople* (London: Routledge, 1995), 70. See also the trickster-enforcer theme discussed in Maud W. Gleason, "Mutilated Messengers: Body Language in Josephus," in *Being Greek under Rome: Cultural Identity, the Second Sophistic and the Development of Empire* (ed. Simon Goldhill; Cambridge: Cambridge University Press, 2001), esp. 59–63.

3. The Comedy of Slavery in Story and Parable

1. Kathleen McCarthy, *Slaves, Masters, and the Art of Authority in Plautine Comedy* (Princeton, N.J.: Princeton University Press, 2000), 5.

2. W. M. Ramsay, "Rhoda the Slave-Girl," in idem, *The Bearing of Recent Discovery on the Trustworthiness of the New Testament* (London: Hodder and Stoughton, 1920), 209–21; E. Jacquier, *Les Actes des Apôtres* (2d ed.; Paris: Gabalda, 1926), 367.

3. Jacob Jervell, *Die Apostelgeschichte* (Göttingen: Vandenhoeck & Ruprecht, 1998), 337–39; C. K. Barrett, *A Critical and Exegetical Commentary on the Acts of the Apostles* (2 vols.; Edinburgh: T. & T. Clark, 1994), 1:584; F. F. Bruce, *The Acts of the Apostles* (3d ed.; Grand Rapids, Mich.: Eerdmans, 1990), 286; Susan R. Garrett, "Exodus from Bondage: Luke 9:31 and Acts 12:1-24," *CBQ* 52 (1990): 670; Gerd Lüdemann, *Early Christianity according to the Traditions in Acts: A Commentary* (Minneapolis: Fortress Press, 1989), 143–44; Ernst Haenchen, *The Acts of the Apostles: A Commentary* (Philadelphia: Westminster, 1971), 391.

4. See Haenchen, *Acts*, 385; and Barrett doubts that extraordinary suspense is present in Acts 12:16: "This is a very modern reading of the situation and it is unlikely that it ever occurred to Luke's mind or the mind of his readers" (Barrett, *Acts*, 1:586).

5. Ivoni Richter Reimer, *Women in the Acts of the Apostles: A Feminist Liberation Perspective* (Minneapolis: Fortress Press, 1995), 242; and Ben Witherington III, *Women in the Earliest Churches* (Cambridge: Cambridge University Press, 1988), 147.

6. Richard I. Pervo, *Profit with Delight: The Literary Genre of the Acts of the Apostles* (Philadelphia: Fortress Press, 1987), 62–63.

7. The literature is extensive, and concentrated on the question whether the Roman device has Greek origins (which now is no longer doubted), the

dramatic function of the slave, and the problem of stage production. The best surveys are Eric G. Csapo, "A Case Study in the Use of Theatre Iconography as Evidence for Ancient Acting," *Antike Kunst* 36 (1993): 41–58, and the standard study of George E. Duckworth, "The Dramatic Function of the *Servus Currens* in Roman Comedy," in *Classical Studies Presented to Edward Capps on His Seventieth Birthday* (Princeton, N.J.: Princeton University Press, 1936), 93–102; and idem, *The Nature of Roman Comedy: A Study in Popular Entertainment* (2d ed.; Norman: University of Oklahoma Press, 1994), 106–7. On the Roman fascination with slave characters generally, see Peter P. Spranger, *Historische Untersuchungen zu den Sklavenfiguren des Plautus and Terenz* (2d ed.; Stuttgart: Franz Steiner, 1984).

8. Martha Krieter-Spiro, *Sklaven, Köche und Hetären: Das Dienstpersonal bei Menander* (Stuttgart: Teubner, 1997), 83–85; Eric G. Csapo, "Plautine Elements in the Running-Slave Entrance Monologues?" *CQ* 39 (1989): 148–63; idem, "Is the Threat-Monologue of the *Servus Currens* an Index of Roman Authorship?" *Phoenix* 41 (1987): 399–419; T. Guardì, "I precedenti greci della figura del 'servus currens' della commedia romana," *Pan* 2 (1974): 5–15; and William S. Anderson, "A New Menandrian Prototype for the *Servus Currens* of Roman Comedy," *Phoenix* 24 (1970): 229–36.

9. In addition to the literature cited above, see Richard C. Beacham, *The Roman Theatre and Its Audience* (Cambridge, Mass.: Harvard University Press, 1992), 113–14; Sander M. Goldberg, *Understanding Terence* (Princeton, N.J.: Princeton University Press, 1986), 16–22, 78–79; R. L. Hunter, *The New Comedy of Greece and Rome* (Cambridge: Cambridge University Press, 1985), 80–81; John Wright, *Dancing in Chains: The Stylistic Unity of the Comoedia Palliata* (Rome: American Academy in Rome, 1974), 114–15, 139, 192.

10. Trans. in David Wiles, *The Masks of Menander: Sign and Meaning in Greek and Roman Performance* (Cambridge: Cambridge University Press, 1991), 146.

11. Ibid. Aelius Donatus's commentary identifies *servus currens* as a technical term in comedy (Paul Wessner, ed., *Aeli Donati quod fertur Commentum Terenti* [3 vols.; Leipzig: Teubner, 1902–8], 2:70 and 2:396).

12. J. C. B. Lowe, "Terence, *Adelphoe*: Problems of Dramatic Space and Time," *CQ* 48 (1998): 483–84.

13. Orlando Patterson (*Slavery and Social Death: A Comparative Study* [Cambridge, Mass.: Harvard University Press, 1982], 87, 91–92) offers as an analogy the nineteenth-century American "Sambo" stereotype of African slaves.

14. Elizabeth Rawson, "Freedmen in Roman Comedy," in *Theater and Society in the Classical World* (ed. Ruth Scodel; Ann Arbor: University of Michigan Press, 1993), 217.

15. Csapo, "Case Study," 46–58, who describes and catalogs twenty-four artifacts illustrating the comic running slave.

16. Duckworth, "Dramatic Function," 101.

17. P. G. McC. Brown, "Aeschinus at the Door: Terence *Adelphoe* 632–43 and the Traditions of Graeco-Roman Comedy," in *Papers of the Leeds International Latin Seminar, Eighth Volume 1995: Roman Comedy, Augustan Poetry, Historiography* (ed. R. Brock and A. J. Woodman; Leeds: Cairns, 1995), 71–89, and W. W. Mooney, *The House-Door on the Ancient Stage* (Baltimore: Williams and Wilkins, 1914), 19–41.

18. Timothy J. Moore, *The Theater of Plautus: Playing to the Audience* (Austin: University of Texas Press, 1998), 181–96. Other instances of a Plautine character calling attention to the fact that he is doing the "running slave" routine include *Amphitruo* 984–989; *Epidicus* 194–195 and *Curculio* 280–298.

19. On the humor in the scene, see Pervo, *Profit with Delight,* 63; and Luke Timothy Johnson, *The Acts of the Apostles* (Collegeville, Minn.: Liturgical Press, 1992), 213, 218.

20. McCarthy, *Slaves,* 105 n. 57.

21. In my exegesis above, I follow the four motifs of the *servus currens* scene outlined in Csapo, "Case Study," 42–46: (1) preparation and announcement; (2) monologue; (3) recall and delayed recognition; (4) postponed delivery. That Luke does not include a monologue probably results from the fact that Acts is a genre different from drama and that Luke avoids monologues in his work. What Luke does with the few monologues he has is examined in the section on the parable of the Dishonest Manager, below.

22. On the protatic character, see Duckworth, *Roman Comedy,* 108–9.

23. See Duckworth, "Dramatic Function," 100–101.

24. Csapo, "Case Study," 42.

25. Ibid.

26. See Moore, *Theater of Plautus,* 192.

27. James Malcolm Arlandson, *Women, Class, and Society in Early Christianity: Models from Luke–Acts* (Peabody, Mass.: Hendrickson, 1997), 195–96; Garrett, "Exodus from Bondage," 670–75; Hans Conzelmann, *Acts of the Apostles* (Philadelphia: Fortress Press, 1987), 95; and Walter Radl, "Befreiung aus dem Gefängnis: Die Darstellung eines biblischen Grundthemas in Apg 12," *BZ* 27 (1983): 92.

28. Pervo, *Profit with Delight,* 12–63.

29. Adolf Jülicher, *Die Gleichnisreden Jesu* (1899; repr., Darmstadt: Wissenschaftliche Buchgesellschaft, 1963), 495; François Bovon, *Das Evangelium nach Lukas;* Part III: *Lk 15,1—19,27* (Zurich: Benziger; Neukirchener-Vluyn: Neukirchener, 2001), 70.

30. Horace, *Sat.* 2.7.37–39; idem, *Epistulae* 2.1.169–176; Lucian, *De parasito;* Epictetus, *Diatribai* 1.9.8; Libanius, *Declamationes* 28, 29; Alciphron, *Epistulae;* Athenaeus, *Deipnosophistae* 6.234d–262b; see also 2.47e; 4.134a–135a, 162f,

164f–165b, 173b–c; 10.421d–e. Favoring parasites of uniform characterization from New Comedy, Terence makes Gnatho in *Eunuchus* purely a flatterer, and the eponymous hero of *Phormio* primarily a swindler; in neither is the theme of food important, for example. Plautus, in contrast, crafts the device with wide comic range: some parasites have a minor or mechanical part in a scam (*Bacchides* 573–605; *Asinaria* 912–918; *Miles gloriosus* 10–79; *Persae* 53–80, 90–163, 329–399); others are more extended (Peniculus in *Menaechmi*, Ergasilus in *Captivi*, Gelasimus in the *Stichus*); and still others take on the leading role (*Curculio, Phormio*).

31. See Elizabeth Ivory Tylawsky, *Saturio's Inheritance: The Greek Ancestry of the Roman Comic Parasite* (New York: Peter Lang, 2002); Heinz-Günther Nesselrath, *Lukians Parasitendialog: Untersuchungen und Kommentar* (Berlin: Walter de Gruyter, 1985), 15–70, 92–121; and Gregory W. Dobrov, "*Mageiros Poiētēs*: Language and Character in Antiphanes," in *The Language of Greek Comedy* (ed. Andreas Willi; New York: Oxford University Press, 2002), 169–90.

32. Duckworth, *Roman Comedy*, 180 n. 7, 265–67; Cynthia Damon, *The Mask of the Parasite: A Pathology of Roman Patronage* (Ann Arbor: University of Michigan Press, 1997), 23–101, 105–9; J. C. B. Lowe, "Plautus' Parasites and the Atellana," in *Studien zur vorliterarischen Periode im frühen Rom* (ed. Gregor Vogt-Spira; Tübingen: Gunter Narr, 1989), 161–63; and P. G. McC. Brown, "Parasite," *OCD*, 1112.

33. J. O. Lofberg, "The Sycophant-Parasite," *CP* 15 (1920): 68.

34. Serving two masters (the father and the son) is a motif also in the comedy of the *servus callidus* (Plautus, *Capt.* 717), a further connection between the parable and the wisdom saying in Luke 16:13.

35. See also Plautus, *Curc.* 328–334. The reputation for financial underhandedness, even outright squandering, connects the parasite to the *servus callidus*, which will be discussed below. See Damon, *Mask of the Parasite*, 44; cf. McCarthy, *Slaves*, 202–3.

36. McCarthy, *Slaves*, 136 n. 38. Even Terence, who rejects the superficiality of some elements in the stock professional (*Eun.* 35–41), uses the dramatic technique of the proud "hungry parasite"; see Goldberg, *Understanding Terence*, 15–16.

37. On the iconographic connection between the comic stage parasite and the Greek Cynic philosopher, see Erich Woytek, *T. Maccius Plautus, Persa: Einleitung, Text und Kommentar* (Vienna: Verlag der Österreichischen Akademie der Wissenschaften, 1982), 204–7; and Tylawsky, *Saturio's Inheritance*, 107–23.

38. See the discussion of the parasite Curculio, and his pretentious claims to scruples and officious airs of a noble, in William S. Anderson, *Barbarian Play: Plautus' Roman Comedy* (Toronto: University of Toronto Press, 1993), 73–74.

39. For cultural context, see chapter 2, above, and literature cited there.

40. *Curculio* in Latin means "weevil," the bark beetle parasite. *Peniculus* is Latin for "brush" ("sponge"), able to wipe a table clean of food (Plautus, *Men.* 77–78). *Ergasilus* denotes laziness from the Greek *ergasia* (labor for gain) and may recall the Latin derivative *ergastulum*, the workhouse prison for disobedient slaves. McCarthy, *Slaves*, 183; Damon, *Mask of the Parasite*, 44; and Eleanor Winsor Leach, "Ergasilus and the Ironies of the Captivi," *Classica et Mediaevalia* 30 (1969): 287.

41. On the emphasis on food, see Nesselrath, *Parasitendialog*, 36–39. On the ancient association of slaves and bodies, see Jennifer A. Glancy, *Slavery in Early Christianity* (New York: Oxford University Press, 2002), 10 and passim, who nonetheless refuses to see the Dishonest Manager in light of Roman slave comedy. On the natal alienation and social dishonor in slave naming, see Strabo 7.3.12; Varro, *De lingua Latina* 8.9.21; *P. Oxy.* 9.1205 (= *CPJ* 3.473); Tertullian, *Adversus Marcionem* 1.7.2 (CCSL 1.447–48); Thomas Wiedemann, *Greek and Roman Slavery* (1981; repr., London: Routledge, 1988), 33–34; J. Albert Harrill, *The Manumission of Slaves in Early Christianity* (Tübingen: Mohr [Siebeck], 1995), 173; Patterson, *Slavery and Social Death*, 54–59; and S. Douglas Olson, "Names and Naming in Aristophanic Comedy," *CQ* 42 (1992): 309–12. On the animalization of the slave, see Keith R. Bradley, "Animalizing the Slave: The Truth of Fiction," *JRS* 90 (2000): 110–25, a good case study in how ancient fiction informs the history of Roman slavery.

42. For an additional example, see Plautus, *Men.* 446–465.

43. W. Geoffrey Arnott, "Phornio Parasitus: A Study in Dramatic Methods of Characterization," *GR* 17 (1970): 32–57; Ortha L. Wilner, "The Character Treatment of Inorganic Rôles in Roman Comedy," *CP* 26 (1931): 264–83; and idem, "The Technical Device of Direct Description of Character in Roman Comedy," *CP* 33 (1938): 20–36.

44. Niall W. Slater, *Plautus in Performance: The Theatre of the Mind* (2d ed.; Amsterdam: Harwood Academic Publishers, 2000), 34; Moore, *Theater of Plautus*, 34–35; and McCarthy, *Slaves*, 42 n. 9.

45. Leach, "Ergasilus," 263–96.

46. The connection between the parasite and the comic slave appears to be an original contribution of Plautus and so distinctive to Roman comedy; Eduard Fraenkel, *Plautinisches im Plautus* (Berlin: Weidmannsche Buchhandlung, 1922), 249–50 (= idem, *Elementi plautini in Plauto* [Florence: La Nuova Italia, 1960], 249–50). The connection recurs in Lucian, *The Parasite*, 47. See Spranger, *Historische Untersuchungen*, 108; William Fitzgerald, *Slavery and Roman Literary Imagination* (Cambridge: Cambridge University Press, 2000), 81; Goldberg, *Understanding Terence*, 76, 111 n. 23; and McCarthy, *Slaves*, 38, 48, 108, 110 and passim.

47. The *servus callidus* as a leading character in Plautus: Chrysalus in *Bac-*

chides; Tranio in *Mostellaria*; Pseudolus in *Pseudolus*; Epidicus in *Epidicus*. See also Terence, *Haut.* 886; *Eun.* 1011. Other primary sources cite the comic slave (*servus callidus* and *fallax servus*, as opposed to *servus frugi*, the honest ["useful"] slave) as typical in New Comedy: Quintilian, *Institutio oratoria* 11.3.178; Apuleius, *Florida* 16; Galen, *De naturalibus facultatibus* 1.17 (§67; Brock, LCL); Manilius, *Astronomica* 5.470–476; Ovid, *Amores* 1.15.17–18; Horace, *Sat.* 1.10.40–42 and *Ars poetica* 237–238.

48. L&S, s.v. "*calliditas.*" Wright, *Dancing in Chains*, 105, 161, 156; Philip Whaley Harsh, "The Intriguing Slave in Greek Comedy," *TAPA* 86 (1955): 135–42; Fraenkel, *Plautinisches*, 231–50 (= idem, *Elementi*, 223–41); Duckworth, *Roman Comedy*, 249–53; H. D. Jocelyn, "Chrysalus and the Fall of Troy (Plautus, *Bacchides* 925–978)," *HSCP* 73 (1969): 143 n. 46; Moore, *Theater of Plautus*, 35–42, 93–100, 187–91, 208 n. 27; and McCarthy, *Slaves*, passim.

49. The *servus callidus*, like the *parasitus*, is invariably male, because it served as a device in the Roman construction of manhood. The exceptional *female* comic slave does sometimes appear, looking more like a male character in drag than a representation of women; see Horace, *Sat.* 1.10.40–42; cf. McCarthy, *Slaves*, 105 n. 57; and J. C. B. Lowe, "The *virgo callida* of Plautus' *Persa*," *CQ* 39 (1989): 390–99.

50. Slater, *Plautus*, 67. A rare counterexample: "Here is a fellow who won his freedom, making good by acting bad. Now applaud and go home" (Plautus, *Epid.* 733–734). Yet Epidicus did not request manumission, the dramatic sequence being a Plautine innovative variation on the familiar theme of the slave's Saturnalia; see Erich Segal, *Roman Laughter: The Comedy of Plautus* (Cambridge, Mass.: Harvard University Press, 1968), 164–65.

51. McCarthy, *Slaves*, 127, 160–61. See also Matthew Leigh, *Comedy and the Rise of Rome* (New York: Oxford University Press, 2004), 24–56, who identifies the Second Punic War (particularly, the cunning of Hannibal) as the historical occasion for the introduction of the trickster slave in Plautus.

52. Plautus, *Pseud.* 395–414; *Mil. glor.* 305–312; *Most.* 662; *Epid.* 81–103. This conforms to the techniques in the parasite's monologue examined above. Bernhard Heininger (*Metaphorik, Erzählstruktur und Szenisch-dramatische Gestaltung in den Sondergutgleichnissen bei Lukas* [Münster: Aschendorff, 1991], 169) parallels these clever slave monologues of Plautus directly with Luke 16:3-4, and argues correctly that Luke draws on the dramatic conventions and comic themes.

53. Moore, *Theater of Plautus*, 34–37; Slater, *Plautus*, 49; and Fitzgerald, *Slavery*, 44.

54. Duckworth, *Roman Comedy*, 151–75.

55. Plautus, *Most.* 775–777, 1068; *Bacch.* 925–952; see also *Pseud.* 1243–1246.

56. Jocelyn, "Chrysalus," 135–52; and Duckworth, *Roman Comedy*, 250.

57. Alfred Plummer (*A Critical and Exegetical Commentary on the Gospel according to S. Luke* [5th ed.; Edinburgh: T. & T. Clark, 1922], 384) notes the parallel to Luke 16:8.

58. McCarthy, *Slaves*, 4, 79–80, 194.

59. *Ti poiēsō* is same question of the Rich Farmer (Luke 12:17) and evidence of Lukan redaction; see Philip Sellew, "Interior Monologue as a Narrative Device in the Parables of Luke," *JBL* 111 (1992): 247; and Heininger, *Metaphorik*, 168–70.

60. See Peter Garnsey and Richard Saller, *The Roman Empire: Economy, Society and Culture* (Berkeley and Los Angeles: University of California Press, 1987), 43–46.

61. Proverbial language: Aristophanes, *Aves* 1432; Nan Dunbar, *Aristophanes, Birds: Edited with Introduction and Commentary* (Oxford: Clarendon, 1995), 680; and I. Howard Marshall, *The Gospel of Luke: A Commentary on the Greek Text* (Exeter: Paternoster, 1978), 618. Digging and plowing as menial occupations: Cicero, *De Finibus* 1.3. To be sure, ancient agricultural manuals recommend strong, broad-shouldered, brawny slaves as "better suited" for digging, plowing, and scything in the field (Columella, *De re rustica* 1.9.4; 11.1.8), but such exhortations prescribe a textbook ideal, not social description, suggesting that *vilici* ("bailiffs," see chapter 4) in actuality used farmhands of all types, even those of lesser strength, because anyone could do the manual labor, although not always in the best way.

62. Horace, *Epistulae* 1.17.19–22; Juvenal, *Satirae* 5.9–10; see Mark Morford, "Juvenal's Fifth Satire," *AJP* 98 (1977): 226–39. Philip B. Corbett, *The Scurra* (Edinburgh: Scottish Academic Press, 1986), 7–22.

63. Michael D. Goulder, *Luke: A New Paradigm* (2 vols.; Sheffield: JSOT, 1989), 2:619; Joachim Jeremias, *The Parables of Jesus* (2d ed.; New York: Charles Scribner's Sons, 1972), 181. For the comic narrative convention of preposterously inflated prices, see John J. Winkler, *Auctor and Actor: A Narratological Reading of Apuleius's "The Golden Ass"* (Berkeley and Los Angeles: University of California Press, 1985), 120. For the stylization of monetary valuations, see Walter Scheidel, "Finances, Figures and Fiction," *CQ* 46 (1996): 222–38.

64. My exegesis draws on the insightful analysis of reasoning and inner dialogue in Greek epic by Christopher Gill, *Personality in Greek Epic, Tragedy, and Philosophy: The Self in Dialogue* (Oxford: Clarendon, 1996), 50–58. James Breech (*The Silence of Jesus: The Authentic Voice of the Historical Man* [Philadelphia: Fortress Press, 1983], 106) makes a passing reference noting the sponger theme that comes close to my thesis, but he neither develops this idea nor connects it to comic parasites.

65. Military: Xenophon, *Cyropaedia* 3.3.57; Ps.-Xenophon, *De equitum magistro* 2.3; 8:16; 8.21; Josephus, *Ant.* 19.112; Plutarch, *Moralia* 856b; Poly-

bius 1.14.3; 1.36.2; 1.83.3; 2.44.5; 3.33.8; 4.48.10; 15.4.9; 15.19.8; 36.9.3; Cassius Dio, *Roman History* 38.41.6. Proverbial: Aristophanes, *Av.* 1330; Athenaeus, *Deipn.* 5.181–182; Ps.-Lucian, *Charidemus* 10.16.

66. Aristotle, *Eudemian Ethics* 8.1246b; Michael Woods, *Eudemian Ethics: Books I, II, and VIII/Aristotle* (2d ed.; Oxford: Clarendon, 1992), 159–64; Plutarch, *Mor.* 139a; Dio Chrysostom, *Orationes* 23.7–12; Diogenes Laertius, *Vitae Philosophorum* 5.40; Dionysius of Halicarnassus, *Antiquitates romanae* 2.3.5. On Peripatetic theories of character types, see Bernard Frischer, *The Sculpted Word: Epicureanism and Philosophical Recruitment in Ancient Greece* (Berkeley and Los Angeles: University of California Press, 1982), 264–69. Epicureanism association: Diogenes Laertius, *Vit.* 10.132 and 140 (= Brad Inwood and L. P. Gerson, eds., *The Epicurus Reader: Selected Writings and Testimonia* [Indianapolis: Hackett, 1994], 31–32); Norman Wentworth DeWitt, *Epicurus and His Philosophy* (Minneapolis: University of Minnesota Press, 1954), 192–215; Nesselrath, *Parasitendialog*, 311–25, 473; William Turpin, "The Epicurean Parasite: Horace, Satires 1.1–3," *Ramus* 27 (1998): 127–40.

67. Mary Ann Beavis, "Ancient Slavery as an Interpretive Context for the New Testament Servant Parables with Special Reference to the Unjust Steward (Luke 16:1-8)," *JBL* 111 (1992): 47.

68. Holt Parker, "Crucially Funny or Tranio on the Couch: The *Servus Callidus* and Jokes about Torture," *TAPA* 119 (1989): 233–46; McCarthy, *Slaves*, 109–10; William G. Thalmann, "Versions of Slavery in the *Captivi* of Plautus," *Ramus* 25 (1996): 112–45; Duckworth, *Roman Comedy*, 160–75; Slater, *Plautus*, 11–12; Annalisa Rei, "Villains, Wives, and Slaves in the Comedies of Plautus," in *Women and Slaves in Greco-Roman Culture: Differential Equations* (ed. Sheila Murnaghan and Sandra R. Joshel; London: Routledge, 1998), 104; Moore, *Theater of Plautus*, 35, 187, 209 n. 38. The only extant instance of a *servus callidus* actually being punished is Tyndarus in *Captivi*, who is sent to the mines but then freed, and so does not suffer what the gallows humor promises; Segal, *Roman Laughter*, 154–55.

69. Beavis, "Ancient Slavery," 43–53; at 51, line numbers for *Pseud.* 1237–1249 are missing. On fables and ancient slaves, see Keith R. Bradley, *Slaves and Masters in the Roman Empire: A Study in Social Control* (1984; repr., New York: Oxford University Press, 1987), 151–53; Keith Hopkins, "Novel Evidence for Roman Slavery," *Past and Present* 138 (1993): 10–27; and W. Martin Bloomer, *Latinity and Literary Society at Rome* (Philadelphia: University of Pennsylvania Press, 1997), 73–109. The claim that ancient fables had servile origins is speculative, and that the literature expressed slave protest, political subversion, or abolition doubtful.

70. Heininger, *Metaphorik*, 167–77. Critique: David Landry and Ben May, "Honor Restored: New Light on the Parable of the Prudent Steward (Luke 16:1-8a)," *JBL* 119 (2000): 291; John Nolland, *Luke 9:21—18:34* (Dal-

las: Word Books, 1993), 801; and Christoph Kähler, *Jesu Gleichnisse als Poesie und Therapie: Versuch eines integrativen Zugangs zum kommunikativen Aspekt von Gleichnissen Jesu* (Tübingen: Mohr [Siebeck], 1995), 139.

71. In this thesis, I do not exclude the possibility that the target audience also may have included Jews, since New Comedy belonged also to the literature of Hellenistic Judaism. See Elias J. Bickerman, *The Jews in the Greek Age* (Cambridge, Mass.: Harvard University Press, 1988), 201–36.

72. E.g., 1 Cor 4:10; 2 Cor 11:19. But cf. 1 Cor 10:15; Luke 12:42 (= Matt 24:45); Matt 7:24; Matt 25:2-9; Matt 10:16.

73. L. John Topel, "On the Injustice of the Unjust Steward: Lk 16:1–13," *CBQ* 37 (1975): 219; and Jeremias, *Parables*, 45–48.

74. McCarthy, *Slaves*, 3–34.

75. Ibid., 7–17, 173–75; M. M. Bakhtin, *The Dialogic Imagination: Four Essays* (ed. Michael Holquist; Austin: University of Texas Press, 1981), 12. See also K. J. Dover, *Greek Popular Morality in the Time of Plato and Aristotle* (Berkeley and Los Angeles: University of California Press, 1974), 18–22.

76. McCarthy, *Slaves*, 12–14, 19–34, 211–13; James C. Scott, *Domination and the Arts of Resistance: Hidden Transcripts* (New Haven: Yale University Press, 1990), 2–4, 79; and Thalmann, "Versions of Slavery," 112–45. On *auctoritas*, see esp. chapter 1.

77. McCarthy, *Slaves*, 19–21. Cf. Carlin Barton, *The Sorrows of the Ancient Romans: The Gladiator and the Monster* (Princeton, N.J.: Princeton University Press, 1993), 29–30, on the Roman aristocrat's willingness to identify and assume the role of the gladiator, a figure closely associated with slavery.

78. McCarthy, *Slaves*, 6, 17–21, 25, 29; and Fitzgerald, *Slavery*, 25. Saturnalian overthrow: Segal, *Roman Laughter*, 70–136; and Hopkins, "Novel Evidence," 22, albeit tentatively.

79. This caricature of Solomon aims at Hellenistic rulers and their Judean representatives, such as the Tobiad Joseph, who think mistakenly that the good life ("happiness") and "wisdom" consist in wealth and possessions gained by one's own clever efforts; see Thomas Krüger, *Qoheleth: A Commentary* (Minneapolis: Fortress Press, 2004), 60–74.

80. See Lawrence M. Wills, *The Jew in the Court of the Foreign King* (Minneapolis: Fortress Press, 1990), 1–38.

81. Bickerman, *Jews in the Greek Age*, 157–60, 165, 231–33; idem, *Four Strange Books of the Bible: Jonah, Daniel, Koheleth, Esther* (New York: Schocken, 1967), 158–67.

82. The paired themes of squandering money and of unreconciled household members recur in the parable of the Prodigal Son (Luke 15:11-32), which also ends unresolved: the older brother lingers in anger at the younger and still finds his father's love unfair. On Luke's use of ancient economics here, see J. Albert Harrill, "The Indentured Labor of the Prodigal

Son (Luke 15:15)," *JBL* 115 (1996): 714–17.

83. On the thematic and verbal connections among the parables, see Landry and May, "Honor Restored," 305–8; Bovon, *Lukas*, 71–82; and Joseph Fitzmyer, *The Gospel according to Luke (X–XXIV): Introduction, Translation, Notes* (Garden City, N.Y.: Doubleday, 1985), 1099–110. On the comedy present, see Ronald F. Hock, "Lazarus and Micyllus: Greco-Roman Backgrounds to Luke 16:19-31," *JBL* 106 (1987): 456–58 (discussing Philostratus, *Vitae sophistarum* 481, and Lucian's satire of rich and poor); and J. Duncan M. Derrett, "Dives and Lazarus and the Preceding Sayings," in idem, *Law in the New Testament* (London: Darton, Longman and Todd, 1970), 89. On diptych, see Thomas L. Brodie, "The Unity of Proto-Luke," in *The Unity of Luke–Acts* (ed. J. Verheyden; Leuven: Leuven University Press, 1999), 627–38. Also helpful in my exegesis is McCarthy, *Slaves*, 207.

4. Subordinate to Another:
Elite Slaves in the Agricultural Handbooks and the Household Codes

1. C. F. D. Moule, *The Epistles of Paul the Apostle to the Colossians and to Philemon* (Cambridge: Cambridge University Press, 1958), 127; J. N. Sevenster, *Paul and Seneca* (Leiden: Brill, 1961), 192; Otto Merk, *Handeln aus Glauben: Die Motivierung der paulinischen Ethik* (Marburg: Elwert, 1968), 221–24; Eduard Lohse, *Colossians and Philemon: A Commentary on the Epistles to the Colossians and to Philemon* (Philadelphia: Fortress Press, 1971), 162; John H. Yoder, *The Politics of Jesus* (Grand Rapids, Mich.: Eerdmans, 1972), 170–83; E. Schweizer, "Traditional Ethical Patterns in the Pauline and Post-Pauline Letters and Their Development (Lists of Vices and House-Tables)," in *Text and Interpretation: Studies in the New Testament Presented to Matthew Black* (ed. Ernest Best and R. McL. Wilson; Cambridge: Cambridge University Press, 1979), 203; Ferdinand Hahn, "Die christologische Begründung urchristlicher Paränese," *ZNW* 72 (1981): 94–95; Peter T. O'Brien, *Colossians, Philemon* (Waco, Tex.: Word Books, 1982), 226–30; Andrew Lincoln, "The Household Code and Wisdom Mode of Colossians," *JSNT* 74 (1999): 101–2; Angela Standhartinger, "The Origin and Intention of the Household Code in the Letter to the Colossians," *JSNT* 79 (2000): 129–30; and Allan R. Bevere, *Sharing the Inheritance: Identity and the Moral Life in Colossians* (London: Sheffield Academic Press, 2003), 236–39, 246–48. David L. Balch, "Household Codes," in *Greco-Roman Literature and the New Testament* (ed. David E. Aune; Atlanta: Scholars Press, 1988), 33, is a bit more nuanced.

2. Richard B. Hays, *The Moral Vision of the New Testament: Community, Cross, New Creation* (San Francisco: Harper, 1996), 65.

3. My formulation of the problem follows Orlando Patterson, *Slavery and*

Social Death: A Comparative Study (Cambridge: Mass.: Harvard University Press, 1982), 22–23, who discusses the red herring of declaring a slave a legal person.

4. On the elite slave, see Jesper Carlsen, *Vilici and Roman Estate Managers until A D 284* (Rome: L'Erma di Bretschneider, 1995); and Jean-Jacques Aubert, *Business Managers in Ancient Rome: A Social and Economic Study of Institores, 200 B.C.–A.D. 250* (Leiden: Brill, 1994). Bailiffs were always elite slaves (or freedmen); no instance of a free person referred to as a *vilicus* (Greek *epitropos*) appears in classical literature; Walter Scheidel, "Free-born and Manumitted Bailiffs in the Graeco-Roman World," *CQ* 40 (1990): 591–93.

5. David L. Balch, *Let Wives Be Submissive: The Domestic Code in 1 Peter* (Chico, Calif.: Scholars Press, 1981), 1–59; idem, "Household Codes," *ABD*, 3:318–20; idem, "Household Codes," in Aune, *Greco-Roman Literature*, 25–50. Pace Betsy J. Bauman-Martin, "Woman on the Edge: New Perspectives on Women in the Petrine *Haustafel*," *JBL* 123 (2004): 253–79.

6. Page duBois, *Slaves and Other Objects* (Chicago: University of Chicago Press, 2003), 195–204.

7. See Stanley Rosen, *Plato's "Statesman": The Web of Politics* (New Haven: Yale University Press, 1995), 15.

8. *Neuthetēteon* ("warning"; "reproof"; "instruction"), a term found also in Colossians (1:8; 3:16) and Ephesians (6:4).

9. Aristotle, *Politics* 1.1255b16–37; Peter L. Phillips Simpson, *A Philosophical Commentary on the Politics of Aristotle* (Chapel Hill: University of North Carolina Press, 1998), 44–45, 69–70.

10. Thomas K. Abbott, *A Critical and Exegetical Commentary on the Epistles to the Ephesians and to the Colossians* (New York: Scribner's, 1916), 180; and Ernest Best, *A Critical and Exegetical Commentary on Ephesians* (Edinburgh: T. & T. Clark, 1998), 581. This dramatic theme typically involves freeborn people becoming enslaved in a cruel twist of fate: Seneca, *Thyestes* 607–621; Euripides, *Helena* 267–277; *Hecuba* 59–60, 864–865; *Electra* 1000–1011; Chariton, *De Chaerea et Callirhoe* 2.8; Xenophon of Ephesus, *Ephesiaca* 5.11–12; Achilles Tatius, *Leucippe et Clitophon* 5.17; Apuleius, *The Golden Ass* 8.24; 11.15 and passim; Cassius Dio, *Roman History* 48.2; Athenaeus, *Deipnosophistae* 7.281b.

11. Wayne A. Meeks, "The Polyphonic Ethics of the Apostle Paul," in idem, *In Search of the Early Christians: Selected Essays* (ed. Allen R. Hilton and H. Gregory Snyder; New Haven: Yale University Press, 2002), 196–209.

12. First group: Col 3:22—4:1; Eph 6:5-9; *Barn.* 19.7 (Bart D. Ehrman, *The Apostolic Fathers* [2 vols.; Cambridge, Mass.: Harvard University Press, 2003], 2:78–79); *Did.* 4.10–11 (Ehrman, *Apostolic Fathers,* 1:424–25); *Doctr.* 4.10–11 (SC 248:209), trans. in Edgar J. Goodspeed, *The Apostolic Fathers: An American Translation* (New York: Harper, 1950), 6–7. Second group: 1 Pet 2:18-25; 1 Tim 6:1-2; Tit 2:9-10.

13. An analogous concern about misreading appears in Seneca, *Epistulae morales* 47.

14. Commentators sometimes wonder whether the antecedent of "the wrongdoer" (Col 3:25) is ambiguous, in which case it might refer to masters. But the specific admonition to masters does appear to start with the address in 4:1; Margaret Y. MacDonald, *Colossians and Ephesians* (Collegeville, Minn.: Liturgical Press, 2000), 158. If there is ambiguity in the Colossian clause, Ephesians resolves it.

15. Paul's notable sentence in Rom 2:11 may influence how the author of Ephesians takes over the words from Colossians; C. Leslie Mitton, *The Epistle to the Ephesians: Its Authorship, Origin and Purpose* (Oxford: Clarendon, 1951), 144; cf. Jouette Bassler, *Divine Impartiality: Paul and a Theological Axiom* (Chico, Calif.: Scholars Press, 1982), 121–70, 178–80 (Bassler's claim about "slave unrest" at Colossae is doubtful; see below).

16. Wayne A. Meeks, "'To Walk Worthily of the Lord': Moral Formation in the Pauline School Exemplified by the Letter to Colossians," in *Hermes and Athena: Biblical Exegesis and Philosophical Authority* (ed. Eleonore Stump and Thomas P. Flint; Notre Dame, Ind.: University of Notre Dame Press, 1993), 40; idem, "Responses to Stump," in Stump and Flint, *Hermes and Athena*, 70.

17. Stobaeus, *Ioannis Stobaei Anthologium* (vol. 4; ed. Otto Hense; Berlin: Weidmann, 1958), 660–61; Kenneth Sylvan Guthrie, *The Pythagorean Sourcebook and Library* (Grand Rapids, Mich.: Phanes Press, 1987), 279 (Hierocles incorrectly identified as a fifth-century Pythagorean); Balch, *Let Wives*, 3. On this "golden rule," see Seneca, *Ep.* 47.11; William Fitzgerald, *Slavery and the Roman Literary Imagination* (Cambridge: Cambridge University Press, 2000), 70; cf. Isocrates, *Ad Demonicum* 14 (on parents and children).

18. As an ancient moral virtue of slaves, *eunoia* is often coupled with *pistis* in the topos of the "faithful slave"; Lucian, *Bis accusatus* 16; BDAG, 409. The will of a certain Akousilaos (*P. Oxy.* 3.494) stipulates the testamentary manumission of a group of slaves "because of their *eunoia* and *philostorgia* (affection)" they showed the master; Thomas Wiedemann, *Greek and Roman Slavery* (1981; repr., London: Routledge, 1988), 101; Andrew T. Lincoln, *Ephesians* (Dallas: Word Books, 1982), 422.

19. See Shadi Bartsch, *The Mirror of the Self: Sexuality, Self-Knowledge, and the Gaze in the Early Roman Empire* (Chicago: University of Chicago Press, 2006, in press). Cf. Stanley E. Hoffer, *The Anxieties of Pliny the Younger* (Atlanta: Scholars Press, 1999), 45–59.

20. Cf. duBois, *Slaves*, 82–100. Cf. also the suggestion by Jennifer A. Glancy that 1 Thess 4:3–8 could encompass sexual access to slaves as household "vessels": *Slavery in Early Christianity* (New York: Oxford University Press, 2002), 62. While intriguing, the exegesis does not convince; see J. Albert Harrill, review of *Slavery in Early Christianity*, by Glancy, *CBQ* 64 (2002): 758–59.

21. See Christopher A. Faraone, "The Agonistic Context of Early Greek Binding Spells," in *Magika Hiera: Ancient Greek Magic and Religion* (ed. Faraone; New York: Oxford University Press, 1991), 14–15. For a good survey of this material, see John G. Gager, *Curse Tablets and Binding Spells from the Ancient World* (New York: Oxford University Press, 1992). Cf. James D. G. Dunn, *The Epistles to the Colossians and to Philemon: A Commentary on the Greek Text* (Grand Rapids, Mich.: Eerdmans; Carlisle: Paternoster, 1996), 255–56.

22. Lincoln, *Ephesians*, 420.

23. Mitton, *Ephesians*, 70–71; and Lincoln, *Ephesians*, 422–23.

24. "The inheritance" is a Colossian metaphor of salvation that Ephesians develops elsewhere (Eph 1:14; 1:18; 5:5), but not to mean salvation. According to Ephesians, a Christian has "salvation" already at baptism (Eph 2:5).

25. The *Doctrina Apostolorum*, possibly the least familiar to modern readers, survives in two medieval manuscripts that go back to a single archetype. Although previous commentary considered the *Doctrina* to be simply a Latin translation of the *Didache*, minor agreements between *Doctrina* and *Barnabas* against the *Didache* prove it to be a Latin translation of a Greek original that as a version must be independent of *Didache*; Jean-Paul Audet, "Literary and Doctrinal Affinities of the 'Manual of Discipline,'" in *The Didache in Modern Research* (ed. Jonathan Draper; Leiden: Brill, 1996), 135. Huub van de Sandt and David Flusser, *The Didache: Its Jewish Sources and Its Place in Early Judaism and Christianity* (Assen: Van Gorcum; Minneapolis: Fortress Press, 2002), 61–63, 113–20.

26. Ehrman, "Epistle of Barnabas," in idem, *The Apostolic Fathers*, 2:3–11; and Jay Curry Treat, "Barnabas, Epistle to," *ABD*, 1:611–14. For detailed discussion of authorship, date, provenance, and literary form, see James Carleton Paget, *The Epistle of Barnabas: Outlook and Background* (Tübingen: Mohr [Siebeck], 1994), 3–42.

27. See the comments in Paget, *Epistle*, 45 (but with reservations about rejecting the epistolary genre altogether).

28. Virginia Burrus, "Hierarchicalization and Genderization of Leadership in the Writings of Irenaeus," *StPatr* 21 (1989): 43–45; and David Brakke, "Canon Formation and Social Conflict in Fourth-Century Egypt: Athanasius of Alexandria's Thirty-ninth *Festal Letter*," *HTR* 87 (1994): 407.

29. The so-called *teknon*-sayings, see *Did.* 3.1–6; Kurt Niederwimmer, *The Didache: A Commentary* (Minneapolis: Fortress Press, 1998), 94–96.

30. The author's favorite method of instruction: *Barn.* 7.5; 7.10–11; 8.1–6; 9.6; 10.11–12; 11.10; 12.3; 12.8; 16.9.

31. Niederwimmer, *Didache*, 1–3; Robert A. Kraft, "Didache," *ABD*, 2:197–98; and Everett Ferguson, "Didache," in *Encyclopedia of Early Christianity* (ed. Ferguson; 2d ed.; New York: Garland, 1998), 328–29. For the relationship of the *Didache* and the *Doctrina Apostolorum* among other ancient church

orders, see Paul F. Bradshaw, *The Search for the Origins of Christian Worship: Sources and Methods for the Study of Early Liturgy* (New York: Oxford University Press, 1992), 80–110.

32. Only one manuscript of the *Doctrina* (Monacensis lat. 6264, eleventh century) preserves the *duae viae*; van de Sandt and Flusser, *Didache*, 61.

33. Joseph Schlecht, *Doctrina XII Apostolorum: Die Apostellehre in der Liturgie der Katholischen Kirche* (Freiburg: Herder, 1901), 68; and van de Sandt and Flusser, *Didache*, 62 n. 23.

34. Jonathan Draper, "Torah and Troublesome Apostles in the *Didache* Community," in idem, *Didache in Modern Research*, 340–63; Clayton N. Jefford, *The Sayings of Jesus in the Teaching of the Twelve Apostles* (Leiden: Brill, 1989); but cf. Bentley Layton, "The Sources, Date, and Transmission of *Didache* 1.3b–2.1," *HTR* 61 (1968): 343–83.

35. Armitage Robinson, "The Epistle of Barnabas and the Didache," *JTS* 35 (1934): 134–38; James Muilenburg, *The Literary Relations of the Epistle of Barnabas and the Teaching of the Twelve Apostles* (Ph.D. diss., Yale University; published in Marburg, 1929), 120–21; cf. F. E. Vokes, "Life and Order in an Early Church: The Didache," *ANRW* 2.27.1 (1992): 219.

36. An excellent analysis of the Jewish "Two Ways" Manual is van de Sandt and Flusser, *Didache*, 112–90. See also L. W. Barnard, "The 'Epistle of Barnabas' and Its Contemporary Setting," *ANRW* 2.27.1 (1992): 190–203; Sebastian Brock, "The Two Ways and the Palestinian Targum," in *A Tribute to Geza Vermes: Essays on Jewish and Christian Literature and History* (ed. Philip R. Davies and Richard T. White; Sheffield: JSOT, 1990), 138–52; and M. Jack Suggs, "The Christian Two Ways Traditions: Its Antiquity, Form, and Function," in *Studies in the New Testament and Early Christian Literature: Essays in Honor of Allen P. Wikgren* (ed. David E. Aune; Leiden: Brill, 1972), 60–74. The extant Jewish Two Ways parallels (1 QS 3.13–4.26; *T. Ash.* 1.3–9; *Gen. Rab.* 21.5; *Deut. Rab.* 4.3; *Sifre Deut.* 53; *b. Ber.* 28b; *Pirke R. El.* 15; *2 En.* 30.15; *Sib Or.* 8.399) do not mention slaves or masters.

37. The best synoptic study is John S. Kloppenborg, "The Transformation of Moral Exhortation in *Didache* 1–5," in *The Didache in Context: Essays on Its Text, History and Transmission* (ed. Clayton N. Jefford; Leiden: Brill, 1995), 88–109. See also Niederwimmer, *Didache*, 30–41; and Goodspeed, *Apostolic Fathers*, 285–309.

38. The term is *hyperechō*, which is found also in the New Testament (1 Pet 2:13; Rom 13:1) and in Roman imperial society generally (see BADG, s.v.; LSJ, s.v.).

39. The *Doctrina* adds fear "toward the master," which makes avoidance of abusive speech more immediately in the interest of slaveholders.

40. Plutarch, *Moralia* 463e–464b; William V. Harris, *Restraining Rage: The Ideology of Anger Control in Classical Antiquity* (Cambridge, Mass.: Har-

vard University Press, 2001), 4, 105–25, 317–36; and Miriam Griffin, *Seneca: A Philosopher in Politics* (Oxford: Clarendon, 1976), 256–85. In Roman culture, Stoic absolutism competed with a rival approach to the passions, the Aristotelian, which viewed anger as a valid response provided that the situation justified it ethically; see Christopher Gill, "Introduction II: The Emotions in Greco-Roman Philosophy," in *The Passions in Roman Thought and Literature* (ed. Susanna Morton Braund and Christopher Gill; Cambridge: Cambridge University Press, 1997), 5–15. On *auctoritas*, see chapter 1, above.

41. LXX Job 10:1; LXX Ps 9:28; LXX Isa 28:28; 37:29; Sir 4:6; 7:11; Wis 8:16; 3 Macc 4:4; cf. LXX Ps 16:4; Rom 3:14; and Dunn, *Epistles*, 249.

42. On Torahization of the Two Ways, see Kloppenborg, "Transformation," 99–102.

43. The original *anthrōpos* who is an image (*eikōn*) of God (Gen 1:26-27); see Ferdinand R. Prostmeier, *Der Barnabasbrief* (Göttingen: Vandenhoeck & Ruprecht, 1999), 547 n. 60. By the use of *typos*, rather than *eikōn*, the early Christian authors may have wanted to avoid words implying equality. Masters are "stamped" (like a coin) with the Lord's authority and "stand in" for him, but they are not and do not equal the Lord.

44. See Table 1 (page 89): *Barn.* 19.7; *Did.* 4.10. *Doctr.* 4.10 changes "God" (*theos*) to "the Lord" (*kyrios*).

45. Ehrman, *Apostolic Fathers*, 2.454–55; Carolyn Osiek, *The Shepherd of Hermas* (Minneapolis: Fortress Press, 1999), 243.

46. See Clive Skidmore, *Practical Ethics for Roman Gentlemen: The Work of Valerius Maximus* (Exeter: University of Exeter Press, 1996), 88; and Keith R. Bradley, *Slaves and Masters in the Roman Empire* (1984; repr., New York: Oxford University Press, 1987), 36.

47. Cf. L. W. Countryman, "Patrons and Officers in Club and Church," in *SBLSP* 11 (ed. Paul J. Achtemeier; Missoula, Mont.: The Society, 1977), 139; Elisabeth Schüssler Fiorenza, *In Memory of Her: A Feminist Theological Reconstruction of Christian Origins* (New York: Crossroad, 1987), 245–70, 285–315, although I doubt her picture of Christian origins in a "discipleship of coequals"; J. Albert Harrill, *The Manumission of Slaves in Early Christianity* (Tübingen: Mohr [Siebeck], 1995), 191; Balch, *Let Wives*, 81–21; Clayton N. Jefford, "Household Codes and Conflict in the Early Church," *StPatr* 31 (1997): 121–27; and Suggs, "Christian Two Ways," 73.

48. A rare exception is Marlis Gielen, *Tradition und Theologie neutestamentlicher Haustafelethik: Ein Beitrag zur Frage einer christlichen Auseinandersetzung mit gesellschaftlichen Normen* (Frankfurt: Hain, 1990), 160–68.

49. Manfred Fuhrmann, *Das systematische Lehrbuch: Ein Beitrag zur Geschichte der Wissenschaften in der Antike* (Göttingen: Vandenhoeck & Ruprecht, 1960), 122–44; George A. Kennedy, *The Art of Persuasion in Greece* (Princeton, N.J.:

Princeton University Press, 1963), 54–62; and William V. Harris, *Ancient Literacy* (Cambridge, Mass.: Harvard University Press, 1989), 81–82.

50. William H. Stahl, *Roman Science: Origins, Development, and Influence to the Later Middle Ages* (Madison: University of Wisconsin Press, 1962), 15–28. Greek handbooks were called *technai, eisagōgē, hyphēgēsis, encheiridion, hypomnēmata*; Latin *artes, commentarii, institutiones*.

51. Kenneth D. White, "Roman Agricultural Writers I: Varro and His Predecessors," *ANRW* 1.4 (1973): 467; and Marco Formisano, *Tecnica e scrittura: Le letterature tecnico-scientifiche nello spazio letterario tardolatino* (Rome: Carocci, 2001), 125–61. A closely related genre is the *epitome* used in a formal setting such as a school or philosophical circle; see Hans Dieter Betz, *The Sermon on the Mount: A Commentary on the Sermon on the Mount, Including the Sermon on the Plain (Matthew 5:3—7:27 and Luke 6:20-49)* (Minneapolis: Fortress Press, 1995), 76–79.

52. William Hansen, *Anthology of Greek Popular Literature* (Bloomington: Indiana University Press, 1998), xi–xvii. See also Thorsten Fögen, "Metasprachliche Reflexionen antiker Autoren zu den Charakteristika von Fachtexten und Fachsprachen, in *Antike Fachschriftsteller: Literarischer Diskurs und sozialer Kontext* (ed. Marietta Horster and Christiane Reitz; Stuttgart: Franz Steiner, 2003), 31–60. Pace Harris, *Ancient Literacy,* 126.

53. Brian Campbell, "Teach Yourself How to Be a General," *JRS* 77 (1987): 18; and Holt N. Parker, "Love's Body Anatomized: The Ancient Erotic Handbooks and the Rhetoric of Sexuality," in *Pornography and Representation in Greece and Rome* (ed. Amy Richlin; New York: Oxford University Press, 1992), 100. Stahl, *Roman Science,* 29–42. Burkhard Meißner, *Die technologische Fachliteratur der Antike: Struktur, Überlieferung und Wirkung technischen Wissens in der Antike* (Berlin: Akademie Verlag, 1999). Ida Mastrorosa, Antonino Zumbo, and Carlo Santini, eds., *Letteratura scientifica e tecnica di Grecia e Roma* (Rome: Carocci, 2002).

54. Stahl, *Roman Science,* 29–42; Fuhrmann, *Lehrbuch,* 144–56; and Albrecht Dihle, "Mündlichkeit und Schriftlichkeit nach dem Aufkommen des Lehrbuches," in *Gattungen wissenschaftlicher Literatur in der Antike* (ed. Wolfgang Kullmann, Jochen Althoff, and Markus Asper; Tübingen: Narr, 1998), 265–77.

55. Parker, "Love's Body Anatomized," 91. In Greek and Latin literature, didactic poetry did not constitute a separate genre, which is one reason why didactic epic and handbook writing went hand in hand. See Roy K. Gibson, *Ars Amatoria Book 3/Ovid: Edited with Introduction and Commentary* (Cambridge: Cambridge University Press, 2003), 9–10; Peter Toohey, *Epic Lessons: An Introduction to Didactic Poetry* (London: Routledge, 1996), 4, 12–13; and Monica Gale, *Myth and Poetry in Lucretius* (Cambridge: Cambridge University Press, 1994), 100–104.

56. Campbell, "Teach Yourself," 13–19.

57. Hansen, *Ancient Greek Popular Literature*, xxii. See also the term *evolving literature* in Robert A. Kraft, *Barnabas and the Didache*, vol. 3 of *The Apostolic Fathers: A New Translation and Commentary* (ed. Robert M. Grant; New York: Thomas Nelson, 1965), 1–3.

58. Stahl, *Roman Science*, 12–13, 52–59, 96; and Pamela O. Long, *Openness, Secrecy, Authorship: Technical Arts and the Culture of Knowledge from Antiquity to the Renaissance* (Baltimore: Johns Hopkins University Press, 2001), 16–45. The authority of anonymity: E. P. Sanders, *The Historical Figure of Jesus* (New York: Penguin, 1993), 66.

59. Roman handbooks: Stahl, *Roman Science*, 43–133; Elizabeth Rawson, *Intellectual Life in the Late Roman Republic* (Baltimore: Johns Hopkins University Press, 1985), 134–40; and Michael von Albrecht, *A History of Roman Literature: From Livius Andronicus to Boethius* (2 vols.; Leiden: Brill, 1996–97), 1:564–82; 2:1239–77, 1468–525. Slave management as a topic of Hellenistic and Roman philosophy: Seneca, *Ep.* 89.10; 94.1; Ps.-Plutarch, *Moralia* 7e; Stobaeus, *"Peri despotōn kai doulōn," Anthologium*, 422–33; Martin Plessner, *Der Oikonomikos des Neupythagoreers "Bryson" und sein Einfluß auf die islamische Wissenschaft* (Heidelberg: Carl Winter, 1928), 228–33; Balch, *Let Wives*, 57; and Carlo Natali, *"Oikonomia* in Hellenistic Political Thought," in *Justice and Generosity: Studies in Hellenistic Social and Political Philosophy. Proceedings of the Sixth Symposium Hellenisticum* (ed. André Laks and Malcolm Schofield; Cambridge: Cambridge University Press, 1995), 95–128.

60. Eckhard Christmann, "Zum Verhältnis von Autor und Leser in der römischen Agrarliteratur: Bücher und Schriften für Herren und Sklaven," in Horster and Reitz, *Antike Fachschriftsteller*, 121–52.

61. Jeremy C. Trevett, "Xenophon (1)," in *OCD*, 1630. Xenophon's dialogue is a handbook in the sense of popular literature defined above, not in the sense of an encyclopedic compendium of theoretical knowledge for specialists; Ischomachus himself makes barbs at such technical manuals for their lack of practicality; Sarah B. Pomeroy, *Xenophon, Oeconomicus: A Social and Historical Commentary* (Oxford: Clarendon, 1994), 323.

62. Cato's alleged hostility or disdain toward Hellenism is more of a modern construct than an ancient fact. His posture toward the Greeks had a didactic aim, to throw Roman values into sharper focus and to fortify a sense of cultural identity. Erich S. Gruen, *Culture and National Identity in Republican Rome* (Ithaca, N.Y.: Cornell University Press, 1992), 52–83, 261–60.

63. Pomeroy, *Xenophon*, 68–73.

64. G. Cyril Armstrong, *Metaphysics: Oeconomica and Magna Moralia/Aristotle* (Cambridge, Mass.: Harvard University Press, 1935), 323–25.

65. Alan E. Astin, *Cato the Censor* (Oxford: Clarendon, 1978), 189–203; John Briscoe and Maria M. Sassi, "Porcius Cato (1), Marcus," *OCD*, 1225.

66. White, "Roman Agricultural Writers," 447–48; Astin, *Cato*, 242–43; and Carlsen, *Vilici*, 17–18, 31, 72, 92, 170.

67. Varro does not always adhere to his rigid outline (in book 1), however. He mixes incompatible subjects, muddles into digression, and strays into etymological tangents; Jens Erik Skydsgaard, *Varro the Scholar: Studies in the First Book of Varro's De Re Rustica* (Copenhagen: Munksgaard, 1968), 90–95.

68. White, "Roman Agricultural Writers," 466–92; and Carlsen, *Vilici*, 17–18.

69. On Varro's research method, see Skydsgaard, *Varro*, 64–116.

70. Peter Garnsey and Richard Saller, *The Roman Empire: Economy, Society and Culture* (Berkeley and Los Angeles: University of California Press, 1987), 66–67.

71. Harrison Boyd Ash, *On Agriculture/Lucius Junius Moderatus Columella* (3 vols.; Cambridge, Mass.: Harvard University Press, 1941), 1:xiii–xviii; Barry Baldwin, "Columella's Sources and How He Used Them," *Latomus* 22 (1963): 785–91; René Martin, "État présent des études sur Columelle," *ANRW* 2.32.3 (1985): 1963–72; Carlsen, *Vilici*, 18–19; and M. Stephen Spurr, "Columella, Lucius Iunius Moderatus," *OCD*, 367.

72. Dale B. Martin, *Slavery as Salvation: The Metaphor of Slavery in Pauline Christianity* (New Haven: Yale University Press, 1990), 51–60, 63–68.

73. Censure against absentee landowners may have been more a moral construct than a social reality in Roman handbooks before Columella.

74. The formal orders (*ordo*, rank) of Rome were a republican system of social categories defined by the state through statutory or customary rules, which Augustus restored, but with sharper definition; see Garnsey and Saller, *Roman Empire*, 112–18.

75. My discussion is schematic; of course, the *ordo mancipiorum* varied according to the individual user and referent slave.

76. See Dennis P. Kehoe, *Investment, Profit, and Tenancy: The Jurists and the Roman Agrarian Economy* (Ann Arbor: University of Michigan Press, 1997), 137–80, who considers the legal evidence together with the literary and the documentary.

77. Aubert, *Business Managers*, 169–200, 322, 415–20, 445–62 (appendix of relevant inscriptions); idem, "Workshop Managers," in *The Inscribed Economy: Production and Distribution in the Roman Empire in Light of "instrumentum domesticum"* (ed. W. V. Harris; Ann Arbor, Mich.: Journal of Roman Archaeology, 1993), 171–81; Carlsen, *Vilici*, 9, 15–16, 27–55, 167; and Astin, *Cato*, 245–47. See also Martin, *Slavery as Salvation*, 15–42 (on the *oikonomos*). A topos in Roman literary imagination, the use of rural areas and frontier, outback lands as an index of the morality in the city of Rome is familiar from ancient historiography (e.g., Tacitus's *Germania*).

78. Plautus, *Casina* 99–103, 117–132, 437–439; Seneca, *De ira* 1.21.2; *Epistu-*

lae morales 89.20; Juvenal, *Satirae* 4.77–80; see also *Digesta* 33.7.12.3; Horace, *Satirae* 2.7.117–118; Cicero, *Paradoxa Stoicorum* 5.36–37. Carlsen, *Vilici*, 76–79. Keith R. Bradley, *Slavery and Society at Rome* (Cambridge: Cambridge University Press, 1994), 72. Rhetorical trope: Cicero, *De republica* 1.61. See also Philo, *De plantatione* 56–58.

79. If a slave steals fruit from an orchard, for example, the slave "shall be whipped with as many strokes as the number of grapes or figs that he has taken" (Plato, *Laws* 8.845a). If a slave steals a small article left behind in the fields, to give another example, the slave may be "scourged with many stripes" by anyone "over thirty years of age" who meets the slave in the act (*Laws* 11.914b).

80. Full context: Plato, *Laws* 6.776b–777a. Glenn R. Morrow, *Plato's Law of Slavery in Its Relation to Greek Law* (Urbana: University of Illinois Press, 1939), 37–46. However, I am not persuaded by Marrow's additional claim that Plato's use of *hybris* means the recognition of a certain kind of "dignity" in the slave. On Plato's view of slavery, see also Gregory Vlastos, "Slavery in Plato's Republic," in *Slavery in Classical Antiquity: Views and Controversies* (ed. M. I. Finley; Cambridge, England: W. Heffer, 1960), 132–49; with duBois, *Slaves*, 165–67.

81. Aristotle, *Nicomachean Ethics* 5.1131b–1132b; 1133a–b; 1134a–1135a; 1137a–1138a; *Politics* 2.1261a–b; *Problemata* 29.952a; F. D. Harvey, "Two Kinds of Equality," *Classica et Mediaevalia* 26 (1965): 101–46; F. Rosen, "The Political Context of Aristotle's Categories of Justice," *Phronesis* 20 (1975): 228–40; and W. von Leyden, *Aristotle on Equality and Justice: His Political Argument* (New York: St. Martin's Press, 1985), 1–64. Roman ethics continued this tradition: Cicero, *De officiis* 1.41; Plutarch, *Moralia* 719b–c; Dio Chrysostom, *Orationes* 17.6–8; Dionysius of Halicarnassus, *Antiquitates romanae* 4.23–24. Additional references in Lohse, *Colossians*, 162; Dunn, *Epistles*, 259–60; and MacDonald, *Colossians and Ephesians*, 159.

82. Richard P. Saller, *Patriarchy, Property and Death in the Roman Family* (Cambridge: Cambridge University Press, 1994), 133–34, 142–43.

83. Varro, *De re rustica* 1.17.4–5; Cato, *De re rustica* 5.1–2; 142.1; Xenophon, *Oeconomicus* 9.13; 13.6–12; 14.1–10; Pomeroy, *Xenophon*, 65–67, 176–81. See also Sallust, *Bellum jugurthinum* 31.11; and Hoffer, *Anxieties of Pliny*, 50–59. Cato expressed the duties of the *vilicus* in terms proposed by comedy; see Matthew Leigh, *Comedy and the Rise of Rome* (New York: Oxford University Press, 2004), 18–19. Incentives and rewards: a share in the farm profits (Xenophon, *Oecomonicus* 9.12); permission to have children (*Oec.* 9.5); more food and praise (13.9; 14.9–10); cf. Ps-Aristotle, *Oeconomica*, 1.1344b15, which includes manumission as a "just and expedient reward" in its system of incentives. In her commentary, Margaret MacDonald (*Colossians*, 164) argues that the exhortation in Col 4:1 for masters to treat slaves

"justly and fairly" would "presumably include the granting of manumission in due course."

84. See Erwin R. Goodenough, "Philo's Exposition of the Law and His *De Vita Mosis*," *HTR* 26 (1933): 109, 117, 124–25. Perhaps God-fearers were the intended audience; on God-fearers, see chapter 1, note 38, above.

85. Philo, *Hypothetica* 7.2–3; 7.14; *De posteritate Caini* 181; *Quod omnis probus liber sit* 148–49; *De specialibus legibus* 2.66–69; 3.137–43; *De virtutibus* 121–26. LXX Prov 11:29; 17:2; 19:10; 27:27; 29:19, 21; Sir 4:30; 7:20; 33:31; cf. LXX Lev 25:43. P. W. van der Horst, *The Sentences of Pseudo-Phocylides: With Introduction and Commentary* (Leiden: Brill, 1978), 255–57. James E. Crouch, *The Origin and Intention of the Colossian Haustafel* (Göttingen: Vandenhoeck & Ruprecht, 1972), 74–101, 116–19. Cf. Catherine Hezser, "The Social Status of Slaves in the Talmud Yerushalmi and in Graeco-Roman Society," in *The Talmud Yerushalmi and Graeco-Roman Culture* (vol. 3; ed. Peter Schäfer; Tübingen: Mohr [Siebeck], 1998), 119–20; and eadem, "The Impact of Household Slaves on the Jewish Family in Roman Palestine," *JSJ* 34 (2003): 390–95.

86. Philo, *Spec.* 1.221; 4.71; *Plant.* 55–56; *De Iosepho* 37–39, 196–200; *De vita Mosis* 1.113; *Prob.* 134.

87. Pace John Byron, *Slavery Metaphors in Early Judaism and Pauline Christianity* (Tübingen: Mohr [Siebeck], 2003), whose totalizing interpretative framework sets up an artificial cultural dichotomy between "Judaism" and "Hellenism."

88. N. Purcell, "Wine and Wealth in Ancient Italy," *JRS* 75 (1985): 5.

89. Cato (*Rust.* 2.5–6) recommends that the landowner leave the *vilicus* with a schedule of duties and tasks to be done, which may refer to a written bill or charter (*lex praepositionis*), a quasi-legal instrument of accountability; Carlsen, *Vilici*, 71; and Aubert, *Business Managers*, 9–14, 184–85. As for postings of "slave rules" in Roman houses, the only attestation (as far as I know) is Petronius, *Satyrica* 28.8. This doorpost sign is "direct address" to slaves (to be sure) but not evidence of social practice; actual Romans would likely have found such decor odd, untoward, and comical. The reference is one of several theatrical elements of surprise in the dinner scene, heightening the eccentricity and bluster of the gauche Trimalchio; see Edward Courtney, *A Companion to Petronius* (New York: Oxford University Press, 2001), 75; and Costas Panayotakis, *Theatrum Arbitri: Theatrical Elements in the Satyrica of Petronius* (Leiden: Brill, 1995), 61.

90. See Meeks, "'To Walk Worthily,'" 40; idem, "Response," 70. Additional examples of the accountability of the *vilicus* before the master: Cicero, *In Verrem* 2.3.119; *Tusculanae disputationes* 4.78; *De republica* 1.59; Seneca, *Controversiae* 6.2; Seneca, *Epistulae morales* 12.1–3; Valerius Maximus 4.1.ext.1; Frontius, *De acquae ductu urbis Romae* 105; 112; Apuleius, *Golden Ass* 8.22; *Apologia* 87; Achilles Tatius, *Leucippe et Clitophon* 5.17; 6.3; Carlsen, *Vilici*, 74–75, 86; Aubert, *Business Managers*, 416–17 n. 10.

91. Exemplum of abusive masters causing slave rebellion: Athenaeus, *Deipnosophistae* 12.542b; Diodorus Siculus 34/35.2.10–12, 26–27, 34–38, 46; see Keith R. Bradley, *Slavery and Rebellion in the Roman World, 140 B.C.–70 B.C.* (Bloomington: Indiana University Press, 1989), 50–51, 62, 98.

92. In this regard, claims by commentators that the early Christian domestic codes espouse a "principle of reciprocity" signaling an ethics of "equality" among the whole congregation are misleading; e.g., Georg Strecker, "Die neutestamentlichen Haustafeln," in *Neues Testament und Ethik für Rudolf Schnackenburg* (ed. Helmut Merlein; Freiburg: Herder, 1989), 349–75; and Angela Standhartinger, *Studien zur Entstehungsgeschichte und Intention des Kolosserbriefs* (Leiden: Brill, 1999), 252–47.

93. On *pietas*, see Saller, *Patriarchy, Property and Death*, 102–32; and Charles King, "The Organization of Roman Religious Beliefs," *Classical Antiquity* 22 (2003): 301–7. Cf. Cato, *De Agricultura* 141, discussed below.

94. Columella, *On Agriculture* 1.8.5–6. Cf. the discussion of *vanus* (empty, foolish) in Aulus Gellius, *Attic Nights* 18.4.5–11.

95. On *religio* and *superstitio*, see the excellent discussion in Mary Beard, John North, and Simon Price, *Religions of Rome*; vol. 1: *A History* (Cambridge: Cambridge University Press, 1998), 214–22. See also Dale B. Martin, *Inventing Superstition: From the Hippocratics to the Christians* (Cambridge, Mass.: Harvard University Press, 2004), 125–35.

96. Referring to the *Compitalia* (an annual festival set by the Roman praetor, part of the official ritual year after the *Saturnalia*), rites to the household divinities of the *Penates* and *Lares* (protecting the boundaries of the master's estate), and annual purification of the farm by the *suovetaurilia* (a "lustral" sacrifice of a pig [*sus*], a ram [*ovis*], and a bull [*taurus*] together).

97. Cato, *Rust.* 5.1–5; cf. Louise Adams Holland, "The Shrine of the *Lares Compitales*," *TAPA* 68 (1937): 438. Cato almost certainly speaks directly to the *vilicus* reader in *De Agricultura* 139 and 141–42; the reference to "Manilius" is only for illustration and does not refer to an actual person; see Hubert Petersmann, "Zu einem altrömischen Opferritual (Cato *de agricultura* c. 141)," *Rheinisches Museum für Philologie* 116 (1973): 229.

98. Purcell, "Wine," 5.

99. Cato, *Rust.* 143.1–2; trans. in Leslie D. Johnston, "The Lares and the Kalends Log," *CP* 34 (1939): 343 n. 4. On the bailiff's wife, see Jesper Carlsen, "The 'vilica' and Roman Estate Management," in *De Agricultura: In Memoriam Pieter Willem De Neeve* (ed. Heleen Sancisi-Weerdenburg et al.; Amsterdam: Gieben, 1993), 197–205; and Rosmarie Günther, "Matrona, *vilica* und *ornatrix*: Frauenarbeit in Rom zwischen Topos and Alltagswirklichkeit," in *Frauenwelten in der Antike: Geschlechterordnung und weibliche Lebenspraxis* (ed. Thomas Späth and Beate Wagner-Hasel; Stuttgart: Metzler, 2000), 350–76.

100. This emphasis likely reflects Cato's experience as Censor, a senior Roman magistrate. On calendars and their function in Roman society, see

Beard, North, Price, *Religions of Rome*, 1:1–8, 25–26. The importance of keeping the calendars: Ovid, *Fasti* 1.667–670, addressing the *vilicus* directly.

101. Astin, *Cato*, 344; White, "Roman Agricultural Writers," 455–56; Carlsen, *Vilici*, 80–85; and Peter F. Dorcey, *The Cult of Silvanus: A Study in Roman Folk Religion* (Leiden: Brill, 1992), 111–12; cf. Bradley, *Slavery and Rebellion*, 76. On the importance of "fear" (*phobos*) for inducing slave obedience, see Holger Thesleff, *The Pythagorean Texts of the Hellenistic Period* (Åbo: Åbo Akademi, 1965), 78, 228 (Zaleucus, at lines 13–14); trans. in Guthrie, *Pythagorean Sourcebook*, 230.

102. Rollin A. Ramsaran, "Paul and Maxims," in *Paul in the Greco-Roman World: A Handbook* (ed. J. Paul Sampley; Harrisburg, Pa.: Trinity Press International, 2003), 431; Alfons Weiser, *Die Knechtsgleichnisse der synoptischen Evangelien* (Munich: Kösel, 1971), 178–225; Richard Bauckham, "Synoptic Parousia Parables and the Apocalypse," *NTS* 23 (1976/77): 165–67; Joseph A. Fitzmyer, *The Gospel according to Luke (X–XXIV): Introduction, Translation, Notes* (Garden City, N.Y.: Doubleday, 1985), 983–93; and Arland J. Hultgren, *The Parables of Jesus: A Commentary* (Grand Rapids, Mich.: Eerdmans, 2000), 157–71.

103. My analysis of "contractual" and "reciprocal" conceptualization of the divine is informed by the excellent discussion in Beard, North, Price, *Religions of Rome*, 1:31–34.

104. E.g., Josephus, *J.W.* 5.27. Shadi Bartsch, *Ideology in Cold Blood: A Reading of Lucan's Civil War* (Cambridge, Mass.: Harvard University Press, 1997), 10–47.

105. The Greek term *diakonos* ranges in meaning from go-between and ambassador to slave attendant; John N. Collins, *Diakonia: Re-interpreting the Ancient Sources* (New York: Oxford University Press, 1990), 77–191. Note the use of the term for governmental authorities in Rom 13:3-4, another instance of the *vilicus* motif.

5. The Vice of the Slave Trader

1. Exod 20:15; 21:6; Deut 5:19; 24:7; Burton Scott Easton, "New Testament Ethical Lists," *JBL* 51 (1932): 7; Neil J. McEleney, "The Vice Lists of the Pastoral Epistles," *CBQ* 36 (1974): 209; Joachim Jeremias and August Strobel, *Die Briefe an Timotheus und Titus; Der Brief an die Hebräer* (12th ed.; Göttingen: Vandenhoeck & Ruprecht, 1981), 14; Jouette M. Bassler, *1 Timothy, 2 Timothy, Titus* (Nashville: Abingdon, 1996), 42. See Martin Dibelius and Hans Conzelmann, *The Pastoral Epistles* (Philadelphia: Fortress Press, 1972), 23.

2. Robert Joseph Karris, "The Function and Sitz im Leben of the Paraenetic Elements in the Pastoral Epistles" (Ph.D. diss., Harvard University,

1971), 65–67; Margaret Davies, *The Pastoral Epistles* (Sheffield: Sheffield Academic Press, 1996), 93; and John T. Fitzgerald, "Virtue/Vice Lists," *ABD*, 6:857–59. For an attempt to find parallels in Roman comedy (Plautus), see Adolf Deissmann, *Light from the Ancient Near East: The New Testament Illustrated by Recently Discovered Texts of the Graeco-Roman World* (rev. ed.; 1927; repr., Peabody, Mass.: Hendrickson, 1995), 317. Deissmann, however, does not discuss the term *andrapodistai*.

3. An exception is John T. Fitzgerald, "The Problem of Perjury in Greek Context: Prolegomena to an Exegesis of Matthew 5:33; 1 Timothy 1:10; and *Didache* 2.3," in *The Social World of the First Christians: Essays in Honor of Wayne A. Meeks* (ed. L. Michael White and O. Larry Yarbrough; Minneapolis: Fortress Press, 1995), 156–77.

4. Scholium to Aristophanes' *Plutus* 5.521; Gottlob Eduard Leo, *Pauli epistola prima ad Timotheum graece: Cum commentario perpetuo* (Leipzig: Ch. G. Kayser, 1837), 10. See also Pollux, *Onomasticon* 3.78: *andrapodistēs* is "one who reduces a freeborn person to slavery or who kidnaps someone else's slave."

5. See Dale B. Martin, "*Arsenokoitēs* and *Malakos*: Meanings and Consequences," in *Biblical Ethics and Homosexuality: Listening to Scripture* (ed. Robert L. Brawley; Louisville: Westminster John Knox, 1996), 119. Pace Henry Alford, *The Greek New Testament* (5th ed.; 4 vols.; Boston and New York: Lee and Shepard, 1872), 3:306–7; and C. Spicq, "Le vocabulaire de l'esclavage dans le Nouveau Testament," *RB* 85 (1978): 201–4.

6. Plato, *Gorgias* 507e; Cicero, *Epistulae ad Atticum* 18.2; Martial 12.63.12; Pliny, *Epistulae* 1.12; Anton J. L. van Hooff, "Ancient Robbers: Reflections behind the Facts," *Ancient Society* 19 (1988): 105–24.

7. Malcolm Heath, *Hermogenes, "On Issues": Strategies of Argument in Later Greek Rhetoric* (Oxford: Clarendon, 1995), 29, 64.

8. *Die Fragmente der griechischen Historiker* (ed. F. Jacoby; 3 vols. in 15; Leiden: Brill, 1923–58), 3:156 and 3:157.

9. Interestingly, later Christian authors exploit the stereotype of the slave trader as dangerous criminal in a different rhetorical context, vituperation against demons. John Chrysostom warns, "Just as slave dealers (*andrapodistai*) show sweets and cakes, dice and other things to small children to entice them and deprive them of their freedom and even of their lives; so also demons, promising to heal the sick limbs of our body, completely destroy the health of the soul" (*Contra Judaeos* 1.7 [*PG* 48.855] = Pseudo-Chrysostom, *Ecloga de adversa Valetudine et Medicis*, homil. 13 [*PG* 63.654]); trans. in Wayne A. Meeks and Robert L. Wilken, *Jews and Christians in Antioch in the First Four Centuries of the Common Era* (Missoula, Mont.: Scholars Press, 1978), 102.

10. Pollux, *Onomasticon* 3.78; Plato, *Laws* 9.879a–b and 12.955a; Demosthenes, *Philippica i* 47 [54]; Glenn R. Morrow, *Plato's Law of Slavery in Its Relation to Greek Law* (Urbana: University of Illinois Press, 1939), 23, 62, 114; and Douglas M. MacDowell, *The Law in Classical Athens* (Ithaca, N.Y.: Cornell University Press, 1978), 148.

11. Strabo 14.5.2; Susan Treggiari, *Roman Freedmen during the Late Republic* (Oxford: Clarendon, 1969), 2–3, 9, 88–89; Brent D. Shaw, "The Bandit," in *The Romans* (ed. Andrea Giardina; Chicago: University of Chicago Press, 1993), 300–341; and David Braund, "Piracy under the Principate and the Ideology of Imperial Eradication," in *War and Society in the Roman World* (ed. John Rich and Graham Shipley; London: Routledge, 1993), 195–212.

12. Full context: Cicero, *Pro lege Manilia* 11.31–12.35; cf. Cicero, *Pro Cluentio* 21–22, 162; E. J. Jonkers, *Social and Economic Commentary on Cicero's "De Imperio Cn. Pompei"* (Leiden: Brill, 1959), 39–41.

13. See *Dig.* 21.1.1.1; 21.2.32.pr.; Barry Nicholas, *An Introduction to Roman Law* (1962; repr., Oxford: Clarendon, 1982), 181–82; J. A. Crook, *Law and Life of Rome, 90 B.C.–A.D. 212* (Ithaca, N.Y.: Cornell University Press, 1967), 181–85. For a discussion of *erro* and *fugitivus*, see the introduction, above.

14. Suetonius, *De Grammaticis* 4.3; Robert A. Kaster, ed., *De Grammaticis et Rhetoribus* (Oxford: Clarendon, 1995), 9 (translation), 98 and 167–68 (commentary).

15. Illegal activity of slave dealers before official magistrates appears not only in legal but also pedagogical contexts. Roman declamation used the topos in rhetorical education; Kaster, *De Grammaticis*, 33; Michael Winterbottom, *The Minor Declamations Ascribed to Quintilian* (Berlin: Walter de Gruyter, 1984), 222–23 (Declamation 340); and S. F. Bonner, *Roman Declamation in the Late Republic and Early Empire* (Liverpool: University Press of Liverpool, 1949), 19.

16. For the social status of the ancient slave trader, see William V. Harris, "Towards a Study of the Roman Slave Trade," in *The Seaborne Commerce of Ancient Rome: Studies in Archaeology and History* (ed. J. H. D'Arms and E. C. Kopff; Rome: American Academy in Rome, 1980), 117–40; Keith R. Bradley, *Slavery and Society at Rome* (Cambridge: Cambridge University Press, 1994), 31–56; idem, *Slaves and Masters in the Roman Empire* (1984; repr., New York: Oxford University Press, 1987), 114–16; idem, "On the Roman Supply and Slave Breeding," in *Classical Slavery* (ed. M. I. Finley; London: Frank Cass, 1987), 42–64; idem, "Social Aspects of the Slave Trade in the Roman World," *Münstersche Beiträge zur antiken Handelsgeschichte* 5 (1986): 49–58; A. Bodor, "The Control of Slaves during the Roman Empire," in *Forms of Control*

and Subordination in Antiquity (ed. Toru Yuge and Masaoki Doi; Tokyo: Society for Studies on Resistance Movements in Antiquity; Leiden: Brill, 1988), 396–409; and Philip de Souza, "Greek Piracy," in *The Greek World* (ed. Anton Powell; London: Routledge, 1995), 179–98.

17. Treggiari, *Roman Freedmen,* 88–89; M. I. Finley, *Aspects of Antiquity: Discoveries and Controversies* (2d ed.; New York: Penguin, 1977), 154–66; and Hervé Duchêne, "Sur la stèle d'Aulus Caprilius Timotheos, Sōmatemporos," *Bulletin de correspondance hellénique* 110 (1986): 513–30.

18. Seneca, *De constantia sapientis* 13.4; Peter P. Spranger, *Historische Untersuchungen zur den Sklavenfiguren des Plautus und Terenz* (2d ed.; Stuttgart: Franz Steiner, 1984), 62; P. V. D. Balsdon, *Romans and Aliens* (Chapel Hill: University of North Carolina Press, 1979), 80. Pace Timothy J. Moore, "*Palliata Togata*: Plautus, *Curculio* 462–86," *AJP* 112 (1991): 353–54.

19. Suetonius, *Augustus Divus* 69.2; Horace, *Epistulae* 2.2.1–19; Balsdon, *Romans and Aliens,* 80.

20. See Rev 18:11-13; Petronius, *Satyrica* 76; Lionel Casson, *The "Periplus Maris Erythraei": Text with Introduction and Commentary* (Princeton, N.J.: Princeton University Press, 1989), 182. See also G. Petzke, *Die Traditionen über Apollonius von Tyana und das Neue Testament* (Leiden: Brill, 1970), 227.

21. Nicholas K. Rauh, *The Sacred Bonds of Commerce: Religion, Economy, and Trade Society at Hellenistic Roman Delos* (Amsterdam: J. C. Gieben, 1993), 135–36. On the social status of ancient merchants generally, see John H. D'Arms, *Commerce and Social Standing in Ancient Rome* (Cambridge, Mass.: Harvard University Press, 1981); Andrea Giardina, "The Merchant," in Giardina, *Romans,* 245–71.

22. Trans. Lloyd W. Daly, *Aesop without Morals: The Famous Fables, and a Life of Aesop* (New York: Thomas Yoseloff, 1961), 40.

23. Ibid., 41.

24. Beert C. Verstraete, "Slavery and the Social Dynamics of Male Homosexual Relations in Ancient Rome," *Journal of Homosexuality* 5 (1980): 227–36. For the formation of social policy on prostitution in the early Empire, see Thomas A. J. McGinn, *Prostitution, Sexuality, and the Law in Ancient Rome* (New York: Oxford University Press, 1998).

25. Galen, *In Hippocratis librum vi epidemaiarum commentarii vi* 29 (Kühn 17b.83); *De methodo medendi* 11.16 (Kühn 10.998–99); and *De dignoscendis pulsibus libri iv* 4.2 (Kühn 8.945–46).

26. Galen, *De usu partium* 1.9 (Kühn 3.24–25); trans. Margaret Tallmadge May, *Galen: On the Usefulness of the Parts of the Body* (2 vols.; Ithaca, N.Y.: Cornell University Press, 1968), 1:79.

27. See Martin, "*Arsenokoitēs*," 118–23; and Bernadette J. Brooten, *Love between Women: Early Christian Responses to Female Homoeroticism* (Chicago: University of Chicago Press, 1996), 260, and literature there cited.

28. Galen, *De alimentorum facultatibus libri iii* 19 (Kühn 6.530); and *In Hippocratis de victu actorum commentaria iv* 17 (Kühn 15.458–59).

29. See Abraham J. Malherbe, "Medical Imagery in the Pastoral Epistles," in idem, *Paul and the Popular Philosophers* (Philadelphia: Fortress Press, 1989), 121–36.

30. Geneva Misener, "Iconistic Portraits," *CP* 19 (1924): 112–13; and Elizabeth C. Evans, *Physiognomics in the Ancient World* (Philadelphia: American Philosophical Society, 1969), 36–37. On slave physiognomics, see chapter 2, above.

31. Trans. emended from George Rawlinson, *The Persian Wars* (New York: Random House, 1942), 636–37.

32. Robert J. Penella, *The Letters of Apollonius of Tyana: A Critical Text with Prolegomena, Translation and Commentary* (Leiden: Brill, 1979), 72–73. The letters are doubtfully authentic.

33. See Carlin A. Barton, *The Sorrows of the Ancient Romans: The Gladiator and the Monster* (Princeton, N.J.: Princeton University Press, 1993), 85–86.

34. Only the *barbaroi* sell their own people into slavery, so "kidnappers" (*andrapodistai*) and "dealers of slaves" (*andrapodōn kapēloi*) prowl mostly among barbaric realms outside Hellas for their merchandise (Philostratus, *Vita Apollonii* 8.7.12).

35. Exod 21:16 (LXX Exod 21:17): "Whoever kidnaps [LXX: *kleptein*] a person [LXX limits to 'sons of Israel'], whether that person has been sold or is still held in possession, shall be put to death"; Deut 24:7: "If someone is caught kidnapping [LXX: *kleptein*] another Israelite, enslaving or selling the Israelite, then that kidnapper [LXX: *kleptēs*] shall die. So shall you purge that kidnapper from your midst."

36. Another Jewish source, the *Testament of Joseph*, also exploits the stereotype that slave traders are kidnappers with untrustworthy speech: "Pentephris . . . ordered the trader to come, and said to him, 'What is this I hear about you, that you steal persons from the land of Canaan and sell them as slaves?' The trader fell at his feet and besought him saying, 'I pray you, my lord, I do not know what you are saying.' Pentephris said to him, 'Where is this Hebrew from then?' And he said, 'The Ishmaelites left him with me until they return.' But he did not believe the trader and ordered that he be stripped and beaten" (*T. Jos.* 13:1–5, trans. in *OTP*, 1:822).

37. Brooten, *Love between Women*, 115–41, although with a different topic under study. See also Tamsyn S. Barton, *Power and Knowledge: Astrology, Phys-*

iognomics, and Medicine under the Roman Empire (Ann Arbor: University of Michigan Press, 1994).

38. *Anthologiae*, appendix 1.150–52; David Pingree, ed., *Vettii Valentis Antiocheni anthologiarum libri novem* (Leipzig: B. G. Teubner, 1986), 382 ("concerning Mars"); and Ehrhard Kamlah, *Die Form der katalogischen Paränese im Neuen Testament* (Tübingen: Mohr [Siebeck], 1964), 137–39.

39. The "poster" interpretation: Dibelius and Conzelmann, *Pastoral Epistles*, 23; and Lewis R. Donelson, *Pseudepigraphy and Ethical Argument in the Pastoral Epistles* (Tübingen: Mohr [Siebeck], 1986), 174–76.

40. Condemnation of the Roman slave trade, not ancient slavery itself: Walter Lock, *A Critical and Exegetical Commentary on the Pastoral Epistles* (New York: Charles Scribner's Sons, 1924), 12; and A. T. Hanson, *The Pastoral Epistles: Commentary on the First and Second Letters to Timothy and the Letter to Titus* (Grand Rapids, Mich.: Eerdmans, 1982), 59. Condemnation of slavery itself: William Barclay, *The Letters to Timothy, Titus and Philemon* (Philadelphia: Westminster, 1960), 45.

41. Nehemiah Adams, *South-Side View of Slavery; or, Three Months at the South, in 1854* (Boston: T. R. Marvin and B. B. Mussey, 1854), 77; and Michael Tadman, *Speculators and Slaves: Masters, Traders, and Slaves in the Old South* (Madison: University of Wisconsin Press, 1989), 182.

42. Frederic Bancroft, *Slave Trading in the Old South* (1931; repr., New York: Frederick Ungar, 1959), 366; and Finley, *Aspects of Antiquity*, 154.

43. I rely on the studies by R. Hauser, "Lasterkatalog," *Historisches Wörterbuch der Philosophie*, (12 vols. to date; ed. Joachim Ritter et al.; Basel: Schwabe, 1971–), vol. 5 (1980): 37–39; Easton, "New Testament Ethical Lists"; F. Varo, "El lexico del pecado en la Epistola de San Pablo a los Romanos," *Scripta Theologica (Navarra)* 21 (1989): 99–116; Kamlah, *Form der katalogischen Paränese*; and Siegfried Wibbing, *Die Tugend- und Lasterkataloge im Neuen Testament und ihre Traditionsgeschichte unter besonderer Berücksichtigung der Qumran-Texte* (Berlin: Töpelmann, 1959). For a list of the extant Greek and Roman vice catalogs, see Fitzgerald, "Virtue/Vice Lists," 875.

44. Concerning health: e.g., Cicero, *Tusculanae disputationes* 4.11.26–27; Horace, *Ep.* 1.1.33; Plutarch, *Moralia* 468b–c. None of these, however, contains *andrapodistai*. Concerning the law, see the passages discussed above, esp. Pollux, *Onomasticon* 6.151 (although not technically a "vice" catalog, but a list of criminals) and the astrological vice lists.

45. Heraclitus, *Epistulae* 7; Harold W. Attridge, *First-Century Cynicism in the Epistles of Heraclitus* (Missoula, Mont.: Scholars Press, 1976), 75.

46. E.g., 1QS 4:3–14, but not reflecting the eschatology or dualistic anthropology of Qumran. See the literature cited in chapter 4, above.

6. The Domestic Enemy:
Household Slaves in Early Christian Apologies
and Accounts of Martyrdom

1. Judith B. Perkins, *The Suffering Self: Pain and Narrative Representation in the Early Christian Era* (London: Routledge, 1995), 113; and Kate Cooper, "The Voice of the Victim: Gender, Representation and Early Christian Martyrdom," *BJRL* 80.3 (1998), 149.

2. Cf. G. Maslakov, "Valerius Maximus and Roman Historiography: A Study of the *exempla* Tradition," *ANRW* 2.32.1 (1984): 451.

3. For martyrdom as a discourse rather than a "thing," see Daniel Boyarin, *Dying for God: Martyrdom and the Making of Christianity and Judaism* (Stanford: Stanford University Press, 1999), 94; Tessa Rajak, "Dying for the Law: The Martyr's Portrait in Jewish-Greek Literature," in *Portraits: Biographical Representation in the Greek and Latin Literature of the Roman Empire* (ed. M. J. Edwards and Simon Swain; Oxford: Clarendon, 1997), 40; Elizabeth A. Castelli, "Visions and Voyeurism: Holy Women and the Politics of Sight in Early Christianity," *Protocol of the Colloquy of the Center for Hermeneutical Studies*, n.s. 2 (1995): 12; and Perkins, *Suffering Self*, 104–23. The literature on martyrdom is extensive but concentrated mostly on the criminal charges and possible relation to actual court proceedings. Older scholarship assumed these accounts to be contemporary or accurate trial records (*commentarii*). The best survey is Timothy D. Barnes, "Pre-Decian *Acta Martyrum*," *JTS* 19 (1968): 509–31 (with idem, "Legislation against the Christians," *JRS* 58 [1968]: 32–50).

4. This approach follows Hippolyte Delehaye, *Les passions des martyrs et les genres littéraires* (2d ed.; Brussels: Société des Bollandistes, 1966).

5. For *auctoritas*, see chapter 1, above; for manhood, see chapter 2. Richard Alston, "Arms and the Man: Soldiers, Masculinity and Power in Republican and Imperial Rome," in *When Men Were Men: Masculinity, Power and Identity in Classical Antiquity* (ed. Lin Foxhall and John Salmon; London: Routledge, 1998), 215.

6. Tacitus, *Annales* 14.42–45; Richard P. Saller, "Slavery and the Roman Family," in *Classical Slavery* (ed. M. I. Finley; London: Frank Cass, 1987), 65–66. For similar cases of murder, see Pliny, *Epistulae* 3.14 and 8.14.12; Stanley E. Hoffer, *The Anxieties of Pliny the Younger* (Atlanta: Scholars Press, 1999), 45–54.

7. I owe this insight to Andrew Wallace-Hadrill, who responded to my work during an oral presentation. The exact scope of the urban prefect's jurisdiction at this period is unclear, especially since the other city magistrate, the

urban praetor, presided over major civic events, such as the games, which would have employed numerous public slaves. The standard work on public slaves is Walter Eder, *Servitus Publica* (Wiesbaden: Franz Steiner, 1980).

8. Walter Scheidel, "Finances, Figures and Fiction," *CQ* 46 (1996): 237 n. 34.

9. Martial, *Spectacula* 7.8–10; Ramsay MacMullen, "Judicial Savagery in the Roman Empire," in idem, *Changes in the Roman Empire: Essays in the Ordinary* (Princeton, N.J.: Princeton University Press, 1990), 205; see also Richard C. Beacham, *The Roman Theatre and Its Audience* (Cambridge, Mass.: Harvard University Press, 1992), 136.

10. Cf. K. M. Coleman, "Fatal Charades: Roman Executions Staged as Mythological Enactments," *JRS* 80 (1990): 63; and Andrew Feldherr, *Spectacle and Society in Livy's History* (Berkeley and Los Angeles: University of California Press, 1998), 4–50.

11. Keith R. Bradley, *Slavery and Society at Rome* (Cambridge: Cambridge University Press, 1994), 89.

12. Ibid., 2–3.

13. Simon P. Ellis, *Roman Housing* (London: Duckworth, 2000), 158–59, 166–70; Bradley, *Slavery and Society*, 84; and Michele George, "*Servus* and *Domus*: The Slave in the Roman House," in *Domestic Space in the Roman World: Pompeii and Beyond* (ed. Ray Laurence and Andrew Wallace-Hadrill; Portsmouth, R.I.: Journal of Roman Archaeology, 1997), 15–24. An exception is the description by Pliny, *Epistulae* 2.17.9, whose luxury villa was large enough for dedicated slave rooms; for commentary, see Hoffer, *Anxieties of Pliny*, 29–44.

14. Jérôme Carcopino, *Daily Life in Ancient Rome: The People and the City at the Height of the Empire* (New Haven: Yale University Press, 1968), 70–71; and Bradley, *Slavery and Society*, 61–65. Cf. Andrew Garland, "Cicero's *Familia Urbana*," *GR* 39 (1992): 163–72.

15. John H. D'Arms, "Slaves at Roman Convivia," in *Dining in a Classical Context* (ed. William J. Slater; Ann Arbor: University of Michigan Press, 1991), 179–80.

16. Carolyn Osiek and David L. Balch, *Families in the New Testament World: Households and House Churches* (Louisville: Westminster John Knox, 1997).

17. Bradley, *Slavery and Society*, 84.

18. The roles of slaves in Jewish households of Roman Palestine conformed to this Roman pattern; see Catherine Hezser, "The Impact of Household Slaves on the Jewish Family in Roman Palestine," *JSJ* 34 (2003): 402–11.

19. Richard P. Saller, "Symbols of Gender and Status Hierarchies in the

Roman Household," in *Women and Slaves in Greco-Roman Culture: Differential Equations* (ed. Sheila Murnaghan and Sandra R. Joshel; London: Routledge, 1998), 90.

20. Jan Theo Bakker, *Living and Working with the Gods: Studies of Evidence for Private Religion and its Material Environment in the City of Ostia (100–500 AD)* (Amsterdam: J. C. Gieben, 1994), 42–43, 194; the standard work on slave religion is Franz Bömer, *Untersuchungen über die Religion der Sklaven in Griechenland und Rom* (3 vols.; 2d ed.; Wiesbaden and Stuttgart: Franz Steiner, 1982, 1960, 1990).

21. Tertullian, *De idololatria* 15.7–8 (CCSL 2.1116); Robin Lane Fox, *Pagans and Christians* (New York: Alfred A. Knopf, 1987), 296; and J. Albert Harrill, "The Metaphor of Slavery in the Writings of Tertullian," *StPatr* 41 (2006, in press).

22. On pagan piety, see Robert L. Wilken, *The Christians as the Romans Saw Them* (New Haven: Yale University Press, 1984), 48–67.

23. *Digesta* 21.1.9–10; Ramsay MacMullen, *Enemies of the Roman Order: Treason, Unrest, and Alienation in the Empire* (Cambridge, Mass: Harvard University Press, 1996), 332 n. 26.

24. Keith R. Bradley, *Slavery and Rebellion in the Roman World, 140 B.C.–70 B.C.* (Bloomington: Indiana University Press, 1989), 55–56. Note also the slandering of the Bacchanalia by the claim that a *Graecus ignobilis* first introduced the cult to Italy, and the repeated discrediting of Catiline and his conspiracy with the taint of servile association; Keith R. Bradley, "Slaves and the Conspiracy of Catiline," *CP* 73 (1978): 330; and J. Albert Harrill, *The Manumission of Slaves in Early Christianity* (Tübingen: Mohr [Siebeck], 1995), 149 n. 91.

25. Bradley, *Slavery and Rebellion*, 92–93; see Tacitus, *Annales* 15.46. Whether the wife of Spartacus was actually a maenad is an open historical question; it may be a construct of the Roman ideology of *superstitio*, an attempt to discredit her by association with irrational fanaticism.

26. For an excellent critique of the reliance on the "public transcript" to explain the causes of slave resistance and revolt, see James C. Scott, *Domination and the Arts of Resistance: Hidden Transcripts* (New Haven: Yale University Press, 1990), 70–107.

27. This belongs to Seneca's wider critique of proverbs generally, and his exhortation for moral progress beyond dependency on gnomic compilations learned in school exercises (*Epistulae morales* 33.5–9); Abraham J. Malherbe, *Moral Exhortation: A Greco-Roman Sourcebook* (Philadelphia: Westminster, 1986), 118–20.

28. Trans. in Percival V. Davies, *Macrobius: The Saturnalia* (New York: Columbia University Press, 1969), 76. On the fifth-century date for Macrobius, see Alan Cameron, "The Date and Identity of Macrobius," *JRS* 56 (1966): 35–38. Cicero also employs the "enemy within" topos, in his speech against Catiline: "If my slaves feared me," Cicero declares, "as much as all your countrymen fear you, I would think that I should get out of my house" (*In Catilinam* 1.17). The proverb endured well beyond antiquity; see the fourteenth-century Italian humanist Petrarch, *De remediis utriusque Fortunae* 1.33 (Conrad H. Rawski, *Petrarch's Remedies for Fortune Fair and Foul* [5 vols.; Bloomington: Indiana University Press, 1991], 1:101–3); and Iris Origo, "The Domestic Enemy: The Eastern Slaves in Tuscany in the Fourteenth and Fifteenth Centuries," *Speculum* 30 (1955): 321–66, on slaves in medieval Tuscany; and Cissie Fairchilds, *Domestic Enemies: Servants and Their Masters in Old Regime France* (Baltimore: Johns Hopkins University Press, 1984), on servants in Old Regime France.

29. Sinnius Capito 17 (Gino Funaioli, ed., *Grammaticae Romanae fragmenta collegit; Volumen prius* [Leipzig: Teubner, 1907], 463; Wallace M. Lindsay, ed., *Sexti Pompei Festi: De verborum significatu quae supersunt cum Pauli epitome* [Bibliotheca scriptorum Graecorum et Romanorum Teubneriana; 1913; repr., Hildesheim: Georg Olms, 1965], 314).

30. Hezser, "Impact of Household Slaves," 390–401.

31. William S. Anderson, "Anger in Juvenal and Seneca," *University of California Publications in Classical Philology* 19.3 (1964): 160–65.

32. Appian, *Bella civilia* 4.4.22–23; 4.4.26; 4.4.28–29; 4.6.39; 4.10.81; 4.12.94–95. On the "faithful slave" topos, see Holt Parker, "Loyal Slaves and Loyal Wives: The Crisis of the Outsider-within and Roman *exemplum* Literature," in Murnaghan and Joshel, *Women and Slaves*, 152–73; and Joseph Vogt, "The Faithful Slave," in idem, *Ancient Slavery and the Ideal of Man* (Cambridge, Mass.: Harvard University Press, 1975), 129–45.

33. Maslakov, "Valerius Maximus," 451.

34. Influential on my analysis is the excellent work of spectacle and autopsy by Feldherr, *Spectacle and Society*, 5 and passim.

35. On autopsy (eyewitness) as a historiographic technique of validation in ancient narrative, see Polybius 12.27; Josephus, *J.W.* 3 and 22; Luke 1:1; John Marincola, *Authority and Tradition in Ancient Historiography* (Cambridge: Cambridge University Press, 1997), 63–86; John Buckler, "Plutarch and Autopsy," *ANRW* 2.33.6 (1992): 4788–830; and Llewelyn Morgan, "The Autopsy of C. Asinius Pollio," *JRS* 90 (2000): 51–69.

36. Athenagoras, *Legatio pro Christianis* 35.3 (SC 379:202 = William R.

Schoedel, ed., *Athenagoras: Legatio and De Resurrectione* [Oxford: Clarendon, 1972], 82–83). On the charge of cannibalism and ritual murder (so-called Thyestean banquets), see Stephen Benko, *Pagan Rome and the Early Christians* (Bloomington: Indiana University Press, 1984), 54–78; Wilken, *Christians as the Romans*, 17; and Andrew McGowan, "Eating People: Accusations of Cannibalism against Christians in the Second Century," *JECS* 2 (1994): 413–42.

37. Leslie W. Barnard, trans., *St. Justin Martyr: The First and Second Apologies* (New York: Paulist Press, 1997), 195 n. 64; and Lawrence Jones, "A Case Study in 'Gnosticism': Religious Responses to Slavery in the Second Century C.E." (Ph.D. diss., Columbia University, 1988), 139–40.

38. My thesis builds upon Boyarin, *Dying for God*, 95, on martyrdom as a "discourse" rather than a "thing."

39. Athenagoras uses proverbs to carry his argument in other places, such as *Leg.* 34.3 (Schoedel, *Athenagoras*, 81–83) concerning harlots. On classical proverbs influencing the thinking of other early Christian authors, such as Irenaeus, see Robert M. Grant, *After the New Testament* (Philadelphia: Fortress Press, 1967), 168; on the rhetorical use of proverbs and maxims in classical culture, see George Kennedy, *The Art of Persuasion in Greece* (Princeton, N.J.: Princeton University Press, 1963), 5, 99, 101, 108, 270, 278, 289; Jan Fredrik Kindstrand, "The Greek Concept of Proverbs," *Eranos* 76 (1978): 71–85; Walter T. Wilson, *Love without Pretense: Romans 12.9-21 and Hellenistic-Jewish Wisdom Literature* (Tübingen: Mohr [Siebeck], 1991), 9–39; and Rollin A. Ramsaran, "Paul and Maxims," in *Paul in the Greco-Roman World: A Handbook* (ed. J. Paul Sampley: Harrisburg, Pa.: Trinity Press International, 2003), 429–56.

40. Tertullian, *Ad nationes* 1.7.14–17 (CCSL 1.19); Ernest Evans, "Tertullian *Ad Nationes*," *VC* 9 (1955): 38; André Schneider, "Notes critiques sur Tertullian, *Ad Nationes* I," *Museum Helveticum* 19 (1962): 181. Pliny and Tacitus served as literary sources for *Ad nationes*, informing Tertullian's mocking denunciation of torture to extract information; see A. R. Birley, "Persecutors and Martyrs in Tertullian's Africa," in *The Later Roman Empire Today: Papers Given in Honour of Professor John Mann* (ed. D. F. Clark, M. M. Roxan, and J. J. Wilkes; London: Institute of Archaeology, 1993), 41–42. The passage recurs in Tertullian's *Apology* (on the literary relationship between *Ad nationes* and *Apologeticus*, see Timothy D. Barnes, *Tertullian: A Historical and Literary Study* [2d ed.; Oxford: Clarendon, 1985], 49, 104–6), but with domestics edited out and the diatribe redacted into a more focused apostrophe discrediting rumor generally, rather than slave autopsy per se (*Apologeticus* 7.6–7 [CCSL

1.99]). Perhaps, in the end, Tertullian did not find what he wrote previously in *Ad nationes* convincing. Interestingly for our study of a maxim, Tertullian cites another classical proverb, about the fast flight of rumor's falsehood (*Apol.* 7.8).

41. See P. G. Walsh, "The Rights and Wrongs of Curiosity (Plutarch to Augustine)," *GR* 35 (1988): 73–85; J. L. Penwill, "Slavish Pleasures and Profitless Curiosity: Fall and Redemption in Apuleius' Metamorphoses," *Ramus* 4 (1975): 49–82; and Joseph G. DeFilippo, "*Curiositas* and the Platonism of Apuleius' *Golden Ass*," *AJP* 111 (1990): 471–92.

42. Walsh, "Rights and Wrongs," 74–81; William Fitzgerald, *Slavery and the Roman Literary Imagination* (Cambridge: Cambridge University Press, 2000), 104–5; and Carlin A. Barton, *The Sorrows of the Ancient Romans: The Gladiator and the Monster* (Princeton, N.J.: Princeton University Press, 1993), 88–89.

43. Tertullian, *Apol.* 7.4 (CCSL 1.99).

44. Terence, *Andria* 68. The proverb is not identified as such by Tertullian.

45. Tertullian, *Apol.* 7.3 (CCSL 1.98–99). My translation disagrees with that in the FC, "because of human nature" (Rudolph Arbesmann, Emily Joseph Daly, and Edwin A. Quain, trans., *Tertullian: Apologetical Works; and Minucius Felix: Octavius* [Washington, D.C.: Catholic University of America Press, 1950], 26)—which has the passage express the later, Augustinian doctrine of "original sin." Tertullian asserts betrayal to result from the vice specific to slaves by virtue of the domestic enemy maxim (*Tot hostes eius quot extrani . . . ex natura etiam ipsi domestici nostri*), not some "universal sin" in all humans (including Tertullian) arising from Adam's fall.

46. Tertullian, *Scorpiace* 10.11 (CCSL 2.1089).

47. Cf. Édouard Massaux, *The Influence of the Gospel of Saint Matthew on Christian Literature before Saint Irenaeus*; vol. 2: *The Later Christian Writings* (Macon, Ga.: Mercer University Press, 1992), 48–49, although commenting on *Martyrdom of Polycarp* 6.1, not Tertullian. On Matt 10:36, its relation to the Q Sayings Source, and its allusion to Micah 7:6, see Christoph Heil, "Die Rezeption von Micha 7,6 LXX in Q und Lukas," *ZNW* 88 (1997): 218–22.

48. Tertullian, *Adversus Marcionem* 5.6.7 (CCSL 1.680).

49. Justin, *Apologia ii* 12.4 (Edgar J. Goodspeed, *Die ältesten Apologeten: Texte mit kurzen Einleitungen* [Göttingen: Vandenhoeck & Ruprecht, 1914], 87).

50. Feldherr, *Spectacle and Society*, 6–7, 13–14; and David Potter, "Martyrdom as Spectacle," in *Theater and Society in the Classical World* (ed. Ruth Scode; Ann Arbor: University of Michigan Press, 1993), 53–88.

51. I apply to martyrdom the discussion in Feldherr, *Spectacle*, 8, 100 and passim.

52. *Martyrdom of Polycarp* 6.1–2 (Herbert Musurillo, trans., *The Acts of the Christian Martyrs* [Oxford: Clarendon, 1972], 6–7); parallel in Eusebius, *Historia ecclesiastica* 4.15.11–12. Hans Campenhausen ("Bearbeitungen und Interpolationen des Polykarpmartyriums," in idem, *Aus der Frühzeit des Christentums: Studien zur Kirchengeschichte des ersten und zweiten Jahrhunderts* [Tübingen: Mohr (Siebeck), 1963], 261–63) argues that the section about the magistrate named Herod and the allusion to Judas (*Martyrdom of Polycarp* 6:2–7.1a) are interpolations (in part simply because Eusebius omits it), a hypothesis not persuasive to recent commentary; Gerd Buschmann, *Das Martyrium des Polycarp* (Göttingen: Vandenhoeck & Ruprecht, 1998), 140–60; idem, *Martyrium Polycarpi: Eine formkritische Studie: Ein Beitrag zur Frage nach der Entstehung der Gattung Märtyrerakte* (Berlin: Walter de Gruyter, 1994), 48–53, 178–82; Boudewijn Dehandschutter, "The Martyrium Polycarpi: A Century of Research," *ANRW* 2.27.1 (1993): 493–97; idem, *Martyrium Polycarpi: Een literair-kritische studie* (Leuven: Leuven University Press, 1979), 140–55, 225; and Leslie W. Barnard, "In Defence of Pseudo-Pionius' Account of Saint Polycarp's Martyrdom," in *Kyriakon: Festschrift Johannes Quasten* (2 vols.; Münster: Aschendorff, 1970), 1:193–97.

53. Judith M. Lieu, *Image and Reality: The Jews in the World of the Christians in the Second Century* (Edinburgh: T. & T. Clark, 1996), 88.

54. Kathleen McCarthy, *Slaves, Masters, and the Art of Authority in Plautine Comedy* (Princeton, N.J.: Princeton University Press, 2000), 22–23.

55. Virginia Burrus, "Torture and Travail: Producing the Christian Martyr," in *A Feminist Companion to Patristic Literature* (ed. Amy-Jill Levine; London: Continuum, 2006, in press).

56. Ibid.

57. Burrus, "Torture and Travail"; Cooper, "Voice of the Victim," 152–53; Page duBois, *Torture and Truth* (London: Routledge, 1991), 35–38, 47–68.

58. Bradley, *Slavery and Society*, 166–67; John Bodel, "Graveyards and Groves: A Study of the *Lex Lucerina*," *American Journal of Ancient History* 11 (1986): 73; and literature cited in chaper 1, note 32.

59. Michael Gagarin, "The Torture of Slaves in Athenian Law," *CP* 91 (1996): 1–18; duBois, *Torture*, 63–74; P. A. Brunt, "Evidence Given under Torture in the Principate," *Zeitschrift der Savigny-Stiftung für Rechtsgeschichte (romanistische Abteilung)* 97 (1980): 256–65; Olivia Robinson, "Slaves and the Criminal Law," *Zeitschrift der Savigny-Stiftung für Rechtsgeschichte (romanistische Abteilung)* 98 (1981): 213–54; and Peter Garnsey, *Social Status and Legal Privilege in the Roman Empire* (Oxford: Clarendon, 1970), 213–16.

60. Garnsey, *Social Status*, 215; duBois, *Torture*, 36, 66–68; and Alan Wat-

son, "Roman Slave Law and Romanist Ideology," *Phoenix* 37 (1983): 58–59.

61. For literary and historical background, see Frederick W. Weidmann, "The Martyrs of Lyons," in *Religions of Late Antiquity in Practice* (ed. Richard Valantasis; Princeton, N.J.: Princeton University Press, 2000), 398–412; see also the older but disappointing analysis in William H. C. Frend, *Martyrdom and Persecution in the Early Church: A Study of the Conflict from the Maccabees to Donatus* (Oxford: Basil Blackwell, 1965), 1–21; and Jean Colin, *L'empire des Antonins et les martyrs gaulois de 177* (Bonn: Rudolf Habelt, 1964).

62. Pierre Nautin, *Lettres et écrivains chrétiens des IIe et IIIe siècles* (Paris: Cerf, 1961), 54–61; for source and redaction issues, see Winrich A. Löhr, "Der Brief der Gemeinden von Lyon und Vienne (Eusebius, *h.e.* V, 1–2 (4))," in *Oecumenica et Patristica: Festschrift für Wilhelm Schneemelcher zum 75. Geburtstag* (ed. Damaskinos Papandreou, Wolfgang A. Bienert, and Knut Schäferdiek; Stuttgart: W. Kohlhammer, 1989), 135–49.

63. *Letter of the Churches of Vienne and Lyons* 1.13–14 (Musurillo, *Acts*, 64–67 = Eusebius, *Hist. eccl.* 5.1.13.14). Thyestean feasts (cannibalism) and Oedipean intercourse (incest) are stock accusations of Roman *superstitio*.

64. Cf. Irenaeus, Fr. 13 (*ANF*, 1:570), and the testimony of the slave Christian *ministrae* in Pliny, *Epistulae* 10.96 (although a pagan author admittedly unsympathetic to Christian discourse). Emperor worship restricted *minister* to slaves and *magister* to freedmen (Bakker, *Living and Working*, 204), perhaps a useful distinction for contextualizing what Pliny understands when he writes that these slave women were Christian *ministrae*. J. Albert Harrill, "Servile Functionaries or Priestly Leaders? Roman Domestic Religion, Narrative Intertextuality, and Pliny's Reference to Slave Christian *Ministrae* (Ep. 10,96,8)," *ZNW* 97 (2006, in press).

65. Because of its adherence to flat reading, patristic scholarship on Blandina and other slave martyrs is disappointing: Garth Thomas, "La condition sociale de l'église de Lyon en 177," in *Les martyrs de Lyon (177): Lyon 20–23 septembre 1977* (ed. Jean Rougé and Robert Turcan; Paris: Centre national de la recheche scientifique, 1978), 93–106; William H. C. Frend, "Blandina and Perpetua: Two Early Christian Martyrs," in Rougé and Turcan, *Martyrs de Lyon*, 167–75; and Marie-Louise Guillaumin, "'Une Jeune Fille qui s'appelait Blandine': Aux origines d'une tradition hagiographique," in *Epektasis: Mélanges patristiques offerts au Cardinal Jean Daniélou* (ed. Jacques Fontaine and Charles Kannengiesser; Paris: Beauchesne, 1972), 93–98.

66. *Letter of the Churches of Vienne and Lyons* 1.17–18 (Musurillo, *Acts*, 66–67 = Eusebius, *Hist. eccl.* 5.1.17–18). The phrase *en dynamei deiknymenēn* might be an allusion to the *deiknymena* in ancient mystery religions; cf. Marvin W. Meyer,

The Ancient Mysteries: A Sourcebook of Sacred Texts (1987; repr., Philadelphia: University of Pennsylvania Press, 1999), 11; and Lane Fox, *Pagans*, 143, 160.

67. For doubts about physiognomy in classical antiquity, see chapter 2. Brent D. Shaw, "Body/Power/Identity: Passions of the Martyrs," *JECS* 4 (1996): 308–9; Perkins, *Suffering Self*, 113–14.

68. Blanche Brotherton, "The Introduction of Characters by Name in the *Metamorphoses* of Apuleius," *CP* 29 (1934): 36–52; Alexander Scobie, *Aspects of the Ancient Romance and Its Heritage: Essays on Apuleius, Petronius, and the Greek Romances* (Meisenheim am Glan: Anton Hain, 1969), 58–64; Gerald N. Sandy, "Serviles Voluptates in Apuleius' Metamorphoses," *Phoenix* 28 (1974): 243; R. De Smet, "The Erotic Adventure of Lucius and Photis in Apuleius' *Metamorphoses*," *Latomus* 46 (1987): 618–19; and Arthur J. Droge, *Homer or Moses? Early Christian Interpretations of the History of Culture* (Tübingen: Mohr [Siebeck], 1989), 104–8. Cf. Paul's pun on *Onesimus* as the name of a formerly "useless" slave (Phlm 11).

69. *Letter of the Churches of Vienne and Lyons* 1.18–19 (Musurillo, *Acts*, 66–67 = Eusebius, *Hist. eccl.* 5.1.18–19).

70. *Letter of the Churches of Vienne and Lyons* 1.37–42 (Musurillo, *Acts*, 72–75 = Eusebius, *Hist. eccl.* 5.1.37–42); Elizabeth A. Goodine and Matthew W. Mitchell, "The Persuasiveness of a Woman: The Mistranslation and Misinterpretation of Eusebius' *Historia Ecclesiastica* 5.1.41," *JECS* 13 (2005): 1–9.

71. *Letter of the Churches of Vienne and Lyons* 1.42 (Musurillo, *Acts*, 74–75 = Eusebius, *Hist. eccl.* 5.1.42).

72. Stuart G. Hall, "Women among the Early Martyrs," in *Martyrs and Martyrologies* (ed. Diana Wood; London: Blackwell, 1993), 14–15; and Jan Willem van Henten, "The Martyrs as Heroes of the Christian People: Some Remarks on the Continuity between Jewish and Christian Martyrology, with Pagan Analogies," in *Martyrium in Multidisciplinary Perspective: Memorial Louis Reekmans* (ed. M. Lamberigts and P. van Deun; Leuven: Leuven University Press, 1995), 317, pointing to the parallel of the ignoble-becomes-noble theme in the Macabbean martyrs (2 Macc 7:20-41). See also Carin A. Barton, "Savage Miracles: The Redemption of Lost Honor in Roman Society and the Sacrament of the Gladiator and the Martyr," *Representations* 45 (1994): 54.

73. Tacitus, *Annales* 15.57 (Jackson, LCL). The moral exemplum of Epicharis appears also in Polyaenus, *Strategemata* 8.62 (trans. Peter Krentz and Everett L. Wheeler, *Stratagems of War/Polyaenus* [2 vols.; Chicago: Ares, 1994], 2:841). Note the "noble death" theme.

74. Perkins, *Suffering Self*, 113. See also Cooper, "Voice of the Victim," 149.

75. Cées Mertens, "Les premiers martyrs et leurs rêves: Cohésion de

l'histoire et des rêves dans quelques 'Passions' latines de l'Afrique du nord," *RHE* 81 (1986): 15; rightly criticized by Judith B. Perkins, "The *Passion of Perpetua*: A Narrative of Empowerment," *Latomus* 53 (1994): 846 n. 29.

76. See Scott, *Domination*, 1–16 and passim.

7. The Use of the New Testament in the American Slave Controversy: A Case History in the Hermeneutical Tension between Biblical Criticism and Christian Moral Debate

1. See David Brion Davis, *The Problem of Slavery in the Age of Revolution, 1770–1823* (Ithaca, N.Y.: Cornell University Press, 1975), 523–56; and Jerry Dean Campbell, "Biblical Criticism in America, 1858–1892: The Emergence of the Biblical Critic" (Ph.D. diss., University of Denver, 1982), 29–66.

2. See Kerry S. Walters, *The American Deists: Voices of Reason and Dissent in the Early Republic* (Lawrence: University Press of Kansas, 1992), 29–31; and idem, *Rational Infidels: The American Deists* (Durango, Colo.: Longwood Academic, 1992), 294.

3. See Conrad Wright, *The Beginnings of Unitarianism in America* (Boston: Beacon Press, 1955), 77.

4. See Theodore Dwight Bozeman, *Protestants in an Age of Science: The Baconian Ideal and Antebellum American Religious Thought* (Chapel Hill: University of North Carolina Press, 1977), 95–96; Herbert Hovenkamp, *Science and Religion in America, 1800–1860* (Philadelphia: University of Pennsylvania Press, 1978), 57–78; James Turner, *Without God, without Creed: The Origins of Unbelief in America* (Baltimore: Johns Hopkins University Press, 1985), 143–50; and James R. Moore, "Geologists and Interpreters of Genesis in the Nineteenth Century," in *God and Nature: Historical Essays on the Encounter between Christianity and Science* (ed. David C. Lindberg and Ronald L. Numbers; Berkeley and Los Angeles: University of California Press, 1986), 322–50.

5. See M. D. Walhout, "The Hermeneutical Turn in American Critical Theory, 1830–1860," *JHI* 57 (1996): 683–703.

6. On the emergence of American biblical studies, see Jerry Wayne Brown, *The Rise of Biblical Criticism in America, 1800–1870: The New England Scholars* (Middletown, Conn.: Wesleyan University Press, 1969). For its precedents, see William Baird, *History of New Testament Research*; vol. 1: *From Deism to Tübingen* (Minneapolis: Fortress Press, 1992). The Society of Biblical Literature and Exegesis was founded in 1880 and is one of the oldest learned societies in the United States.

7. See George B. Cheever, *The Guilt of Slavery and the Crime of Slavehold-ing: Demonstrated from the Hebrew and Greek Scriptures* (Boston: John P. Jewett, 1860), 332–40. This work was the most scholarly attempt to argue abolition-ism from biblical exegesis.

8. See Albert Barnes, *An Inquiry into the Scriptural Views of Slavery* (Phila-delphia: Perkins and Purves, 1846), 242–49; see also Charles Elliott, *Sinful-ness of American Slavery* (2 vols.; Cincinnati: L. Swormstedt and J. H. Power, 1851), 2:337; and idem, *The Bible and Slavery* (Cincinnati: L. Swormstedt and A. Poe, 1857), 34, 281–82.

9. See Richard Hofstadter, *Anti-intellectualism in American Life* (New York: Vintage Books, 1963), 91; and Bertram Wyatt-Brown, *Lewis Tappan and the Evangelical War against Slavery* (Cleveland: Press of Case Western Reserve University, 1969), 317. See also Daryl Fisher-Ogden, "Albert Barnes (1798–1870)," in *Dictionary of Heresy Trials in American Christianity* (ed. George H. Shriver; Westport, Conn.: Greenwood Press, 1997), 11–20, although the charges of Old School Presbyterians that condemned Barnes twice for her-esy concerned his preaching and publication of New School evangelical theology on original sin, atonement, justification, and other doctrines unre-lated to his views on slavery.

10. J. Blanchard and N. L. Rice, *A Debate on Slavery Held in the City of Cin-cinnati, on the First, Second, Third, and Sixth Days of October, 1845, upon the Ques-tion: Is Slave-Holding in Itself Sinful, and the Relation between Master and Slave, a Sinful Relation?* (Cincinnati: Wm. H. Moore, 1846), 336, emphasis in origi-nal.

11. For background, see G. Whit Hutchison, "The Bible and Slavery, a Test of Ethical Method: Biblical Interpretation, Social Ethics, and the Herme-neutics of Race in America, 1830–1861" (Ph.D. diss., Union Theological Seminary, New York, 1996), 153–228; Robert Bruce Mullen, "Biblical Critics and the Battle over Slavery," *Journal of Presbyterian History* 61 (1983): 210–26; J. Earl Thompson Jr., "Abolitionism and Theological Education at Andover," *New England Quarterly* 47 (1974): 238–61; John H. Giltner, "Moses Stuart and the Slavery Controversy: A Study in the Failure of Moderation," *JRT* 18 (1961): 27–39; and idem, *Moses Stuart: The Father of Biblical Science in America* (Atlanta: Scholars Press, 1988), 123–30.

12. Blanchard and Rice, *Debate on Slavery*, 228; see also 229, 240, 327, 340, 360, 419.

13. See Augustus Baldwin Longstreet, *Letters on the Epistle of Paul to Phile-mon* (Charleston, S.C.: B. Jenkins, 1845), 14; G. Bourne, *A Condensed Anti-Slavery Bible Argument* (New York: S. W. Benedict, 1845; repr., in *Essays and*

Pamphlets on Antislavery [Westport, Conn.: Negro Universities Press, 1970]), 82–83; and Caroline L. Shanks, "The Biblical Anti-Slavery Argument of the Decade 1830–1840," *Journal of Negro History* 16 (1931): 148–49. See also Allen Dwight Callahan, *Embassy of Onesimus: The Letter of Paul to Philemon* (Valley Forge, Pa.: Trinity Press International, 1997), 11–12, although without awareness of the contemporary debate over the "servant" translation or of the ideology that affects the interpretation; see J. Albert Harrill, review of *Embassy of Onesimus*, by Callahan, *CBQ* 60 (1998): 757–59; and Joseph A. Fitzmyer, *The Letter to Philemon: A New Translation and Commentary* (New York: Doubleday, 2000), 19–20.

14. Barnes, *Inquiry*, 318–31; see also Hutchison, "The Bible and Slavery," 140–50.

15. See Fred A. Ross, *Slavery Ordained of God* (Philadelphia: J. B. Lippincott, 1857), 176–79; and Robert Lewis Dabney, *A Defence of Virginia* (New York: E. J. Hale and Son, 1867), 182–85.

16. See Laura L. Mitchell, "'Matters of Justice between Man and Man': Northern Divines, the Bible, and the Fugitive Slave Act of 1850," in *Religion and the Antebellum Debate over Slavery* (ed. John R. McKivigan and Mitchell Snay; Athens: University of Georgia Press, 1998), 134–65.

17. Daniel R. Goodwin, *Southern Slavery in Its Present Aspects: Containing a Reply to a Late Work of the Bishop of Vermont on Slavery* (Philadelphia: J. B. Lippincott, 1864), 116, emphasis in original.

18. Leonard Bacon, *Slavery Discussed in Occasional Essays* (1846; repr., Miami, Fla.: Mnemosyne Publishing, 1969), 180. On Bacon's role in antislavery, see John R. McKivigan, *The War against Proslavery Religion: Abolitionism and the Northern Churches, 1830–1865* (Ithaca, N.Y.: Cornell University Press, 1984), 122, 153, 176, 190; and Hugh Davis, "Leonard Bacon, the Congregational Church, and Slavery, 1845–1861," in McKivigan and Snay, *Religion and the Antebellum Debate*, 221–45. See also Barnes, *Inquiry*, 258.

19. See Mitchell, "'Matters of Justice,'" 139–49; and Victor B. Howard, *Conscience and Slavery: The Evangelistic Calvinist Domestic Missions, 1837–1861* (Kent, Ohio: Kent State University Press, 1990), 89–99.

20. An important finding of twentieth-century historical criticism is that the New Testament does contain multiple voices, with different theologies and ethics. See, e.g., Wayne A. Meeks, "The Polyphonic Ethics of the Apostle Paul," in idem, *In Search of the Early Christians* (ed. Allen R. Hilton and H. Gregory Snyder; New Haven: Yale University Press, 2002), 196–209.

21. See Willard M. Swartley, *Slavery, Sabbath, War, and Women: Case Issues in Biblical Interpretation* (Scottdale, Pa., and Waterloo, Ont.: Herald Press,

1983), 43–46, 61, although without tracing the historical development of the abolitionist argument. On the Cheevers, Weld, and Hosmer, see McKivigan, *War against Proslavery*, 137–41, 171.

22. I owe the formation of these hermeneutical strategies to Wayne A. Meeks, "The 'Haustafeln' and American Slavery: A Hermeneutical Challenge," in *Theology and Ethics in Paul and His Interpreters: Essays in Honor of Victor Paul Furnish* (ed. Eugene H. Lovering Jr. and Jerry L. Sumney; Nashville: Abingdon, 1996), 245–52.

23. See H. Butterfield, *The Whig Interpretation of History* (1931; repr., London: G. Bell and Sons, 1965); and Peter Novick, *That Noble Dream: The "Objectivity Question" and the American Historical Profession* (Cambridge: Cambridge University Press, 1988), 13 and passim on the ideological factors involved in how one thinks about history.

24. William Hosmer, *Slavery and the Church* (Auburn, Me.: William J. Moses, 1853), 44–45; Richard Fuller and Francis Wayland, *Domestic Slavery Considered as a Scriptural Institution* (New York: Lewis Colby, 1845), 78.

25. See Barnes, *Inquiry*, 376; Elliott, *Bible and Slavery*, 284; William E. Channing, *Slavery* (Boston: James Munroe, 1835), 8–9; Fuller and Wayland, *Domestic Slavery*, 77–94; Francis Wayland, *Elements of Moral Science* (1841; repr., New York: Sheldon, 1877), 221–28; *The Letters of William Lloyd Garrison*, vol. 3: *No Union with Slave-Holders: 1841–1849* (ed. Walter M. Merrill; Cambridge. Mass.: The Belknap Press of Harvard University Press, 1973), 485.

26. An idea present as early as Barnes, *Inquiry*, 346–55.

27. See Cheever, *Guilt of Slavery*, 411–13.

28. See Moses I. Finley, *Ancient Slavery and Modern Ideology* (enl. edition; ed. Brent D. Shaw; Princeton, N.J.: Markus Wiener, 1998), 80–85, 95, 100–101, 110, 123, 132, 195–96. The influential work arguing that Christianity ended slavery was Henri Wallon, *Histoire de l'esclavage dans l'antiquité* (3 vols., 2d ed.; Paris: Hachette, 1879), which elevated this moral-spiritual idea to the level of dogma. Wallon's work proved useful to American abolitionists.

29. Channing, *Slavery*, 111; Channing was a gradualist who, although antislavery, opposed abolitionism. See also Wayland, *Elements*, 223–25; Wayland and Fuller, *Domestic Slavery*, 63–76; and Barnes, *Inquiry*, 283–304.

30. See Cheever, *Guilt of Slavery*, 340, who criticizes Barnes for overlooking 1 Tim 1:10.

31. For a history of scholarship and possible exegetical solution, see J. Albert Harrill, *The Manumission of Slaves in Early Christianity* (Tübingen: Mohr [Siebeck], 1995), 66–128; Will Deming, "A Diatribe Pattern in 1 Cor 7:21-22: A New Perspective on Paul's Directions to Slaves," *NovT* 37 (1995):

130–37; and idem, "Paul and Indifferent Things," in *Paul in the Greco-Roman World: A Handbook* (ed. J. Paul Sampley; Harrisburg, Pa.: Trinity Press International, 2003), 392–94.

32. Emphasis in original. The use of italic identifies a word inserted by the translators, which is not in the original Greek; see American Bible Society, Committee on Versions, *Report on the History and Recent Collation of the English Versions of the Bible: Presented by the Committee on Versions to the Board of Managers of the American Bible Society* (New York: American Bible Society's Press, 1851), 24.

33. W. G. Brownlow and A. Pryne, *Ought American Slavery to be Perpetuated? A Debate* (Philadelphia: J. B. Lippincott, 1858), 131 (see also 211); and La Roy Sunderland, *The Testimony of God against Slavery* (1835; repr., St. Clair Shores, Mich.: Scholarly Press, 1970), 86; Elliott, *Sinfulness of American Slavery*, 1:104; 2:295; Elliott, *Bible and Slavery*, 287.

34. Cheever, *Guilt of Slavery*, 416.

35. Ibid.

36. Meeks, "'Haustafeln' and American Slavery," 245; James Brewer Stewart, "Abolitionists, the Bible, and the Challenge of Slavery," in *The Bible and Social Reform* (ed. Ernest R. Sandeen; Philadelphia: Fortress Press; Chico, Calif.: Scholars Press, 1982), 51. Influential was also the Scottish school of Common Sense Realism. See George M. Marsden, "Everyone One's Own Interpreter? The Bible, Science, and Authority in Mid-Nineteenth-Century America," in *The Bible in America: Essays in Cultural History* (ed. Nathan O. Hatch and Mark A. Noll; New York: Oxford University Press, 1982), 79–100.

37. Douglas Sloan, *The Scottish Enlightenment and the American College Ideal* (New York: Teachers College, Columbia University, 1971); Henry F. May, *The Enlightenment in America* (New York: Oxford University Press, 1976); Richard B. Sher, *Church and University in the Scottish Enlightenment: The Moderate Literati of Edinburgh* (Princeton, N.J.: Princeton University Press, 1985); Richard B. Sher and Jeffrey R. Smitten, eds., *Scotland and America in the Age of Enlightenment* (Princeton, N.J.: Princeton University Press, 1990); and Robert P. Forbes, "Slavery and the Evangelical Enlightenment," in McKivigan and Snay, *Religion and the Antebellum Debate*, 68–106. The American Transcendentalists held similar views. See Richard A. Grusin, *Transcendentalist Hermeneutics: Institutional Authority and the Higher Criticism of the Bible* (Durham, N.C.: Duke University Press, 1991).

38. See Bozeman, *Protestants in an Age of Science*, 132–59; and Hovenkamp, *Science and Religion*, 57–78.

39. See Daniel Walker Howe, *The Unitarian Conscience: Harvard Moral Philosophy, 1805–1861* (Cambridge, Mass.: Harvard University Press, 1970), 270–305; Wayland, *Elements*, 57–69; and William Sumner Jenkins, *Proslavery Thought in the Old South* (Chapel Hill: University of North Carolina Press, 1935), 234. Wayland's work was the "moral science" textbook used in many colleges, something Southerners lamented. See James A. Sloan, *The Great Question Answered; or, Is Slavery a Sin in Itself?* (Memphis, Tenn.: Hutton, Gallaway, 1857), 140. Although holding antislavery views (such as amelioration of slave conditions toward gradual emancipation), Wayland was no abolitionist. He banned discussion of slavery in Brown University classes, and his 1838 tract, *The Limitations of Human Responsibility*, condemned abolitionists and particularly the Garrisonian immediatists for their lack of sensitivity to the burdens of Christian slaveholders. See Deborah Bingham Van Broekhoven, "Suffering with Slaveholders: The Limits of Francis Wayland's Antislavery Witness," in McKivigan and Snay, *Religion and the Antebellum Debate*, 196–220.

40. J. Philip Wogaman, *Christian Ethics: A Historical Introduction* (Louisville: Westminster John Knox, 1993), 180–90.

41. Garrison, *Letters*, vol. 6: *To Rouse the Slumbering Land: 1868–1879* (ed. Walter M. Merrill and Louis Ruchames; Cambridge, Mass.: The Belknap Press of Harvard University Press, 1981), 145; Garrison, *Letters*, vol. 4: *From Disunionism to the Brink of War: 1850–1860* (ed. Louis Ruchames; Cambridge, Mass.: The Belknap Press of Harvard University Press, 1975), 25, 75; Stewart, "Abolitionists," 51, quoting Henry C. Wright. On Garrison's view that Bible passages glorifying war are not the Word of God, see Mitchell Snay, *Gospel of Disunion: Religion and Separatism in the Antebellum South* (Cambridge: Cambridge University Press, 1993), 64. For the Mexican War's influence on antislavery campaigns, see Howard, *Conscience and Slavery*, 73–88. See also Henry Mayer, *All on Fire: William Lloyd Garrison and the Abolition of Slavery* (New York: St. Martin's Press, 1998), 300–329.

42. *The Liberator*, 31 May 1850 (see also *The Liberator*, 7 June 1850, and 14 June 1850); *The Liberator*, 28 June 1850, and 2 August 1850; George Howe, "The Raid of John Brown and the Progress of Abolition," *Southern Presbyterian Review* 12 (January 1860): 797; W. T. Hamilton, *Duties of Masters and Slaves Respectively; or, Domestic Servitude as Sanctioned by the Bible* (Mobile, Ala.: F. H. Brooks, 1845), 8.

43. McKivigan, *War against Proslavery*, 66 (see also 93–110), 184.

44. Frederick Douglass, Speech in Boston, Massachusetts, 8 February 1855, in *The Frederick Douglass Papers, Series One: Speeches, Debates, and Inter-*

views, vol. 3: *1855–1863* (ed. John W. Blassingame; New Haven: Yale University Press, 1985), 6; Frederick Douglass, Speech in New York, New York, 3 August 1857, in *Frederick Douglass Papers*, 182. Garrison did just what Douglass proposed, when he flung the Constitution into a fire at a public meeting in 1854. See Lewis Perry, *Radical Abolitionism: Anarchy and the Government of God in Antislavery Thought* (Ithaca, N.Y.: Cornell University Press, 1973), 189.

45. See Lewis Hayden, Testimony at the Massachusetts State House, Boston, 13 February 1855, in *The Black Abolitionist Papers* (ed. C. Peter Ripley; Chapel Hill: University of North Carolina Press, 1985), 4:266–69; Jermain Wesley Loguen, Letter to Frederick Douglass, March 1855, in Ripley, *Black Abolitionist Papers*, 4:270–73.

46. Frederick Douglass, Speech in New York, New York, 12 May 1859, in Blassingame, *Frederick Douglass Papers*, 258; Frederick Douglass, Speech in Glasgow, Scotland, 26 March 1860, in Blassingame, *Frederick Douglass Papers*, 363. Douglass satirizes the Garrisonian slogan, "No Union with Slaveholders." See also Blassingame, *Frederick Douglass Papers*, 559, where Douglass mocks the proslavery claim that Philemon supports the Fugitive Slave Law.

47. Frederick Douglass, *Life and Times of Frederick Douglass*, rev. ed. of *My Bondage and My Freedom* (1892; repr., New York: Collier Books, 1962), 78–79.

48. See Frederick Douglass, Speech in Halifax, England, 7 December 1859, in Blassingame, *Frederick Douglass Papers*, 283–85; Frederick Douglass, Speech in Rochester, New York, 16 June 1861, in Blassingame, *Frederick Douglass Papers*, 440–41; and Waldo E. Martin Jr., *The Mind of Frederick Douglass* (Chapel Hill: University of North Carolina Press, 1984), 48–49.

49. Resolutions by Lloyd H. Brooks delivered at the Third Christian Church, New Bedford, Massachusetts, 16 June 1858, in Ripley, *Black Abolitionist Papers*, 4:392.

50. Association for the Religious Instruction of the Negroes in Liberty County, Georgia, *Tenth Annual Report of the Association for the Religious Instruction of the Negroes in Liberty County, Georgia* (Savannah, Ga.: The Association, 1845), 24–25, emphasis in original; Albert J. Raboteau, *Slave Religion: The "Invisible Institution" in the Antebellum South* (New York: Oxford University Press, 1978), 294–95.

51. Barnes, *Inquiry*, 319n. See also Callahan, *Embassy of Onesimus*, 1–2; Milton C. Sernett, *Black Religion and American Evangelicalism: White Protestants, Plantation Missions, and the Flowering of Negro Christianity, 1787–1865*

(Metuchen, N.J.: Scarecrow Press and ATLA, 1975), 77; and Clarice J. Martin, "The *Haustafeln* (Household Codes) in African American Biblical Interpretation: 'Free Slaves' and 'Subordinate Women,'" in *Stony the Road We Trod* (ed. Cain Hope Felder; Minneapolis: Fortress Press, 1991), 216–17.

52. See Raboteau, *Slave Religion*, 242–43, 250–51; and Hutchison, "The Bible and Slavery," 276–341.

53. Theophus H. Smith, *Conjuring Culture: Biblical Formations of Black America* (New York: Oxford University Press, 1994), 207.

54. Ibid., 222–48.

55. Raboteau, *Slave Religion*, 163–64; Smith, *Conjuring Culture*, 159–60; Gerald W. Mullin, *Flight and Rebellion: Slave Resistance in Eighteenth-Century Virginia* (New York: Oxford University Press, 1972), 160; and Margaret Washington, "The Meanings of Scripture in Gullah Concepts of Liberation and Group Identity," in *African Americans and the Bible: Sacred Texts and Social Textures* (ed. Vincent L. Wimbush; New York: Continuum, 2000), 321–41. For the contrast with Frederick Douglass, see James H. Cook, "Fighting with Breath, not Blows: Frederick Douglass and Antislavery Violence," in *Antislavery Violence: Sectional, Racial, and Cultural Conflict in Antebellum America* (ed. John R. McKivigan and Stanley Harrold; Knoxville: University of Tennessee Press, 1999), 128–63.

56. See Lester B. Scherer, *Slavery and the Churches in Early America, 1619–1819* (Grand Rapids, Mich.: Eerdmans, 1975), 39–43, 69–74, 129–32. There were a few other isolated white voices speaking out against slavery, some Presbyterian and Baptist, others Methodist, but not many (see ibid., 132–41).

57. Larry E. Tise, *Proslavery: A History of the Defense of Slavery in America, 1701–1840* (Athens: University of Georgia Press, 1987), 16, 116–20, 308–22; John Patrick Daly, *When Slavery Was Called Freedom: Evangelicalism, Proslavery, and the Causes of the Civil War* (Lexington: University Press of Kentucky, 2002), 30–72; and Jean R. Soderlund, *Quakers and Slavery: A Divided Spirit* (Princeton, N.J.: Princeton University Press, 1985).

58. See Ernest R. Sandeen, *The Roots of Fundamentalism: British and American Millenarianism, 1800–1930* (Chicago: University of Chicago Press, 1970), esp. 103–31; Mark A. Noll, "The Bible and Slavery," in *Religion and the American Civil War* (ed. Randall M. Miller, Harry S. Stout, and Charles Reagan Wilson; New York: Oxford University Press, 1998), 43–73; and Christopher H. Owen, "'To Keep the Way Open for Methodism': Georgia Wesleyan Neutrality toward Slavery, 1844–1861," in McKivigan and Snay, *Religion and the Antebellum Debate*, 114–15.

59. Iveson L. Brookes, *A Defence of the South against the Incroachments of the North* (Hamburg, S.C.: Republican Office, 1850), 32 (see also William C. Buck, *The Slavery Question* [Louisville: Harney, Hughes and Hughes, 1849], 4, 9); Blanchard and Rice, *Debate on Slavery*, 291 (see also Hamilton, *Duties of Masters and Slaves*, 6); James H. Hammond, "Letters on Slavery," in *The Pro-Slavery Argument* (1852; repr., New York: Negro Universities Press, 1968), 108; Fuller and Wayland, *Domestic Slavery*, 169, 185.

60. See Fuller and Wayland, *Domestic Slavery*, 186; see also Hofstadter, *Anti-intellectualism*, 125 n. 5.

61. Forbes, "Slavery and the Evangelical Enlightenment," 92–93.

62. On Stuart's anti-abolitionism, see Mitchell, "'Matters of Justice,'" 139–49.

63. John Fletcher, *Studies on Slavery, in Easy Lessons* (Natchez, Miss.: Jackson Warner, 1852), 163, 506–85, criticism directed at the "servant" hypothesis of Albert Barnes. See also Ross, *Slavery*, 59; Thornton Stringfellow, *Scriptural and Statistical Views in Favor of Slavery* (Richmond, Va.: J. W. Randolf, 1856), 52; [William Henry Drayton], *The South Vindicated from the Treason and Fanaticism of the Northern Abolitionists* (Philadelphia: H. Manly, 1836), 94; George D. Armstrong, *The Christian Doctrine of Slavery* (New York: Charles Scribner, 1857), 18–21; John Henry Hopkins, *Bible View of Slavery* (New York: Society for the Diffusion of Political Knowledge, 1863), 1; Sloan, *Great Question*, 204–6; William Graham, *The Contrast, or the Bible and Abolitionism: An Exegetical Argument* (Cincinnati: Daily Cincinnati Atlas, 1844), 23–26; and Philip Schaff, *Slavery and the Bible: A Tract for the Times* (Chambersburg, Pa.: M. Kieffer, 1861), 20–21.

64. Fuller and Wayland, *Domestic Slavery*, 167.

65. Hammond, "Letters on Slavery," 106–7, emphasis in original.

66. See Albert T. Bledsoe, "Liberty and Slavery," in *Cotton Is King, and Pro-Slavery Arguments* (ed. E. N. Elliott; 1860; repr., New York: Negro Universities Press, 1969), 359–74; Thomas Meredith, *Christianity and Slavery* (Boston: Gould, Kendall, and Lincoln, 1847), 45–51; Ross, *Slavery Ordained*, 176–85; and Longstreet, *Letters*, 8–47.

67. Ross, *Slavery Ordained*, 97 (he adds: "Many of your most pious men, soundest scholars, have been led to the study of the Bible more faithfully in the light of the times. And they are reading it more and more in harmony with the views which have been reached by the highest Southern minds" [97–99]); Charles Hodge, *Essays and Reviews: Selected from the Princeton Review* (New York: Robert Carter and Bros., 1857), 481.

68. N. L. Rice, *Lectures on Slavery; Delivered in the North Presbyterian Church,*

Chicago (Chicago: Church, Goodman and Cushing, 1860), 18; [Drayton], *South Vindicated*, 95 (see also Fletcher, *Studies*, 116–17; Dabney, *Defence*, 153–54; and Meredith, *Christianity and Slavery*, 16); Stringfellow, *Scriptural and Statistical Views*, 23. Stringfellow's proslavery tract became one of the most influential in the late antebellum period. See Beth Barton Schweiger, "The Restructuring of Southern Religion: Slavery, Denominations, and the Clerical Profession in Virginia," in McKivigan and Snay, *Religion and the Antebellum Debate*, 300–301.

69. Including Old Testament passages; see Stephen R. Haynes, *Noah's Curse: The Biblical Justification of American Slavery* (New York: Oxford University Press, 2002), 65–160.

70. See Brookes, *Defence*, 2–3.

71. See Stringfellow, *Scriptural and Statistical Views*, 42–43; and Sloan, *Great Question*, 176–78.

72. Sloan, *Great Question*, 152. See also Fuller and Wayland, *Domestic Slavery*, 172; and J. K. Paulding, *Slavery in the United States* (New York: Harper and Bros., 1836), 20–29.

73. James Oakes, *The Ruling Race: A History of American Slaveholders* (New York: Vintage Books, 1983), 52–67, 145–47.

74. [Drayton], *The South Vindicated*, 95, 98. See also Armstrong, *Christian Doctrine*, 114–16; Samuel B. How, *Slaveholding Not Sinful: Slavery, the Punishment of Man's Sin; Its Remedy, the Gospel of Christ* (New Brunswick, N.J.: John Terhune, 1856), 39–41; John Henry Hopkins, *The Scriptural, Ecclesiastical, and Historical View of Slavery* (New York: W. I. Pooley, 1864), 240–43; and Jenkins, *Proslavery Thought*, 223–27.

75. [Drayton], *The South Vindicated*, 99; Hamilton, *Duties of Masters and Slaves*, 14–17.

76. William H. Barnwell, *Views upon the Present Crisis: A Discourse Delivered in St. Peter's Church, Charleston* (Charleston, S.C.: Letter-Press of E. C. Councell, 1850), 14; N. S. Wheaton, *A Discourse on St. Paul's Epistle to Philemon* (Hartford, Conn.: Case, Tiffany, 1851), 23.

77. Tise, *Proslavery*, 229; Stringfellow, *Scriptural and Statistical Views*, 75 (see also Ross, *Slavery Ordained*, 97; and Blanchard and Rice, *Debate on Slavery*, 44; on conservative republicanism as the center of proslavery ideology, see Tise, *Proslavery*, 204–60); Brookes, *Defence*, 30, the editorial reprinted in pamphlet form (see also Dabney, *Defence*, 188).

78. Jesse B. Ferguson, *Address on the History, Authority and Influence of Slavery* (Nashville: J. T. S. Fall, 1850), 4.

79. Fuller and Wayland, *Domestic Slavery*, 6; Dabney, *Defence*, 203. See also Edward R. Crowther, "'Religion Has Something . . . to Do with Politics': Southern Evangelicals and the North, 1845–1860," in McKivigan and Snay, *Religion and the Antebellum Debate*, 332–33; Sloan, *Great Question*, 166–75; and Brookes, *Defence*, 28–29.

80. See Graham, *Contrast*, 41; Fuller and Wayland, *Domestic Slavery*, 189–90 (on the authority of John Chrysostom's interpretation); Rice, *Lectures*, 34, 56; Hopkins, *Scriptural, Ecclesiastical, and Historical View*, 100, 161, 168 (important evidence for the use of scholarly commentaries in the nineteenth-century debate over slavery), 211; Bledsoe, *Liberty and Slavery*, 375–78; and John Saillant, "Origins of African American Biblical Hermeneutics in Eighteenth-Century Black Opposition to the Slave Trade and Slavery," in Wimbush, *African Americans and the Bible*, 240–41.

81. See Schaff, *Slavery*, 25–26, with knowledge of the patristic exegetical history on the crux. See also Thomas Smyth, gen. ed., *The Christian Doctrine of Human Rights and of Slavery: In Two Articles, from the Southern Presbyterian Review for March, 1849* (Columbia, S.C.: I. C. Morgan, 1849), 6; Moses Stuart, *Conscience and the Constitution* (1850; repr., New York: Negro Universities Press, 1969), 52–56; Blanchard and Rice, *Debate on Slavery*, 157, 218; and J. L. Dagg, *The Elements of Moral Science* (New York: Sheldon, 1861), 349.

82. See Dabney, *Defence*, 160–61.

83. See Sloan, *Great Question*, 209. Part of the condemnation included criticism of abolitionism joining forces with the women's suffrage movement, which unsexed the female gender. See Bledsoe, *Liberty and Slavery*, 379; and Hammond, "Letters on Slavery," 174n. For an interpretation of Gal 3:28 in its ancient context, see J. Albert Harrill, "Paul and Slavery," in Sampley, *Paul in the Greco-Roman World*, 593–98.

84. See Frederic Bancroft, *Slave Trading in the Old South* (1931; repr., New York: Frederick Ungar, 1959), 365–81; and Michael Tadman, *Speculators and Slaves: Masters, Traders, and Slaves in the Old South* (Madison: University of Wisconsin Press, 1989), 179–210. Interestingly, an analogous contempt is found in ancient slavery, as I noted in chapter 5.

85. See Bledsoe, *Liberty and Slavery*, 358; Sloan, *Great Question*, 211–14; Ross, *Slavery Ordained*, 140–59; and Fletcher, *Studies on Slavery*, 570–72.

86. Bledsoe, *Liberty and Slavery*, 377.

87. See James Shannon, *An Address Delivered before the Pro-Slavery Convention of the State of Missouri* (St. Louis: Republican Book and Job Office, 1855),

14; Hopkins, *Bible View of Slavery*, 5; George D. Armstrong, *Politics and the Pulpit: A Discourse Preached in the Presbyterian Church, Norfolk, Va.* (Norfolk: J. D. Ghiselin Jr., 1856), 35–36; Dabney, *Defence*, 185–92; and Stringfellow, *Scriptural and Statistical Views*, 48–49.

88. See Jenkins, *Proslavery Thought*, 233–34.

89. On the public debate over Wayland's textbook, see Van Broekhoven, "Suffering with Slaveholders."

90. Fletcher, *Studies*, 15, 17 (emphasis in original), 19.

91. Ibid., 20; Bledsoe, *Liberty and Slavery*, 375–76; Stuart, *Conscience*, 61–62; Fuller and Wayland, *Domestic Slavery*, 140; and Graham, *Contrast*, 39–41.

92. Slavery had been abolished in the French territories previously, in 1794, by the French National Convention, but the law was repealed by Napoleon in 1802. See Lawrence C. Jennings, *French Anti-Slavery: The Movement for the Abolition of Slavery in France, 1802–1848* (Cambridge: Cambridge University Press, 2000).

93. Ross, *Slavery Ordained*, 77 (emphasis in original), 86 (emphasis in original).

94. Jenkins, *Proslavery Thought*, 236; and William H. Ruffner, *Lectures on the Evidences of Christianity* (New York: Robert Carter and Bros., 1853), 297. Yet, the major source of xenophobia was perhaps the heavy rate of immigration in this period.

95. Hopkins, *Scriptural, Ecclesiastical, and Historical View*, 219–20, emphasis in original.

96. Hopkins, *Bible View*, 118; see also 132.

97. See Meeks, "'Haustafeln' and American Slavery," 245; Kevin Giles, "The Biblical Argument for Slavery: Can the Bible Mislead? A Case Study in Hermeneutics," *EvQ* 66 (1994): 3–17; and Haynes, *Noah's Curse*, 187, 201–2.

98. Meeks, "'Haustafeln' and American Slavery," 233.

Epilogue

1. "Baptist Group Votes to Repent Stand on Slaves," *New York Times*, 21 June 1995. "Resolution on Racial Reconciliation on the 150th Anniversary of The Southern Baptist Convention: June 1995," retrieved 24 May 2005, from the official Web site of the Southern Baptist Convention, http://www.sbc.net/resolutions/amResolution.asp?ID=899.

2. "Southern Baptists Declare Wife Should 'Submit' to Her Husband," *New York Times*, 10 June 1998. "The Baptist Faith and Message," retrieved

24 May 2005, from the official Web site of the Southern Baptist Convention, http://www.sbc.net/bfm/bfm2000.asp.

WORKS CITED

Abbott, Thomas K. *A Critical and Exegetical Commentary on the Epistles to the Ephesians and to the Colossians.* ICC 36. New York: Scribner's, 1916.

Adams, Nehemiah. *South-Side View of Slavery; or, Three Months at the South, in 1854.* Boston: T. R. Marvin and B. B. Mussey, 1854.

Albrecht, Michael von. *A History of Roman Literature: From Livius Andronicus to Boethius.* 2 vols. Mnemosyne Suppl. 165. Leiden: Brill, 1996–97.

Aletti, Jean-Noël. "Rm 7.7-25 encore une fois: Enjeux et propositions." *NTS* 48 (2002): 358–76.

Alford, Henry. *The Greek New Testament.* 5th ed. 4 vols. Boston and New York: Lee and Shepard, 1872.

Alston, Richard. "Arms and the Man: Soldiers, Masculinity and Power in Republican and Imperial Rome." Pages 205–23 in Foxhall and Salmon, *When Men Were Men.*

American Bible Society, Committee on Versions. *Report on the History and Recent Collation of the English Versions of the Bible: Presented by the Committee on Versions to the Board of Managers of the American Bible Society.* New York: American Bible Society's Press, 1851.

Anderson, William S. "Anger in Juvenal and Seneca." *University of California Publications in Classical Philology* 19.3 (1964): 127–96.

———. *Barbarian Play: Plautus' Roman Comedy.* Robson Classical Lectures. Toronto: University of Toronto Press, 1993.

———. "A New Menandrian Prototype for the *Servus Currens* of Roman Comedy." *Phoenix* 24 (1970): 229–36.

André, Jacques. *Traité de physiognomonie: Anonyme latin.* Collection des universités de France. Paris: Les Belles Lettres, 1981.

Arbesmann, Rudolph, Emily Joseph Daly, and Edwin A. Quain, trans. *Tertul-*

lian: Apologetical Works; and Minucius Felix: Octavius. FC 10. Washington, D.C.: Catholic University of America Press, 1950.

Arlandson, James Malcolm. *Women, Class, and Society in Early Christianity: Models from Luke–Acts.* Peabody, Mass.: Hendrickson, 1997.

Armstrong, A. H. *Enneads/Plotinus.* 7 vols. LCL. Cambridge, Mass.: Harvard University Press, 1984–90.

Armstrong, G. Cyril. *Metaphysics, Oeconomica and Magna Moralia/Aristotle.* LCL. Cambridge, Mass.: Harvard University Press, 1935.

Armstrong, George D. *The Christian Doctrine of Slavery.* New York: Charles Scribner, 1857.

———. *Politics and the Pulpit: A Discourse Preached in the Presbyterian Church, Norfolk, Va.* Norfolk: J. D. Ghiselin Jr., 1856.

Arnott, W. Geoffrey. "Phornio Parasitus: A Study in Dramatic Methods of Characterization." *GR* 17 (1970): 32–57.

Arzt, Peter. "Brauchbare Sklaven: Ausgewählte Papyrustexte zum Philemon-brief." *Protokolle zur Bibel* 1 (1992): 44–55.

Arzt-Grabner, Peter. "Onesimus erro: Zur Vorgeschichte des Philemon-briefs." *ZNW* 95 (2004): 131–43.

———. *Philemon.* Papyrologische Kommentare zum Neuen Testament 1. Göttingen: Vandenhoeck & Ruprecht, 2003.

Ash, Harrison Boyd. *On Agriculture/Lucius Junius Moderatus Columella.* 3 vols. LCL. Cambridge, Mass.: Harvard University Press, 1941.

Association for the Religious Instruction of the Negroes in Liberty County, Georgia. *Tenth Annual Report of the Association for the Religious Instruction of the Negroes in Liberty County, Georgia.* Savannah: The Association, 1845.

Astin, Alan E. *Cato the Censor.* Oxford: Clarendon, 1978.

Attridge, Harold W. *First-Century Cynicism in the Epistles of Heraclitus.* HTS 29. Missoula, Mont.: Scholars Press, 1976.

Aubert, Jean-Jacques. *Business Managers in Ancient Rome: A Social and Economic Study of Institores, 200 B.C.–A.D. 250.* Columbia Studies in the Classical Tradition 21. Leiden: Brill, 1994.

———. "Workshop Managers." Pages 171–81 in *The Inscribed Economy: Production and Distribution in the Roman Empire in Light of "instrumentum domesticum."* Edited by W. V. Harris. Journal of Roman Archaeology Suppl. 6. Ann Arbor, Mich.: Journal of Roman Archaeology, 1993.

Audet, Jean-Paul. "Literary and Doctrinal Affinities of the 'Manual of Discipline.'" Pages 129–47 in Draper, *Didache in Modern Research.*

Austin, N. J. E., and N. B. Rankov. *Exploratio: Military and Political Intelligence in the Roman World from the Second Punic War to the Battle of Adrianople.* London: Routledge, 1995.

Bacon, Leonard. *Slavery Discussed in Occasional Essays.* 1846. Reprint, Miami, Fla.: Mnemosyne Publishing, 1969.

Baird, William. *History of New Testament Research.* Vol. 1: *From Deism to Tübingen.* Minneapolis: Fortress Press, 1992.

Bakhtin, M. M. *The Dialogic Imagination: Four Essays.* Edited and translated by Michael Holquist. Slavic Series 1. Austin: University of Texas Press, 1981.

Bakker, Jan Theo. *Living and Working with the Gods: Studies of Evidence for Private Religion and Its Material Environment in the City of Ostia (100–500 AD).* Dutch Monographs on Ancient History and Archaeology 12. Amsterdam: J. C. Gieben, 1994.

Balch, David L. "Household Codes." *ABD,* 3:318–20.

———. "Household Codes." Pages 25–50 in *Greco-Roman Literature and the New Testament.* Edited by David E. Aune. SBLSBS 21. Atlanta: Scholars Press, 1988.

———. *Let Wives Be Submissive: The Domestic Code in 1 Peter.* SBLMS 26. Chico, Calif.: Scholars Press, 1981.

Baldry, H. C. *The Unity of Mankind in Greek Thought.* Cambridge: Cambridge University Press, 1965.

Baldwin, Barry. "Columella's Sources and How He Used Them." *Latomus* 22 (1963): 785–91.

Balsdon, J. P. V. D. "Auctoritas, Dignitas, Otium." *CQ* 10 (1960): 43–50.

———. *Romans and Aliens.* Chapel Hill: University of North Carolina Press, 1979.

Bancroft, Frederic. *Slave Trading in the Old South.* 1931. Reprint, New York: Frederick Ungar, 1959.

Barclay, John M. G. "Paul, Philemon, and the Dilemma of Christian Slave-Ownership." *NTS* 37 (1991): 161–86.

Barclay, William. *The Letters to Timothy, Titus and Philemon.* Philadelphia: Westminster, 1960.

Barnard, Leslie W. "The 'Epistle of Barnabas' and Its Contemporary Setting." *ANRW* 2.27.1 (1992): 159–207.

———. "In Defence of Pseudo-Pionius' Account of Saint Polycarp's Martyrdom." Pages 192–204 in *Kyriakon: Festschrift Johannes Quasten.* Vol. 1. Münster: Aschendorff, 1970.

———, trans. *St. Justin Martyr: The First and Second Apologies.* ACW 56. New York: Paulist Press, 1997.

Barnes, Albert. *An Inquiry into the Scriptural Views of Slavery.* Philadelphia: Perkins and Purves, 1846.

Barnes, Timothy D. "Legislation against the Christians." *JRS* 58 (1968): 32–50.

———. "Pre-Decian Acta Martyrum." *JTS* 19 (1968): 509–31.

———. *Tertullian: A Historical and Literary Study.* 2d ed. Oxford: Clarendon, 1985.

Barnwell, William H. *Views upon the Present Crisis: A Discourse Delivered in St. Peter's Church, Charleston.* Charleston, S.C.: Letter-Press of E. C. Councell, 1850.

Barrett, C. K. *A Commentary on the Second Epistle to the Corinthians.* HNTC. New York: Harper and Row, 1973.

———. *A Critical and Exegetical Commentary on the Acts of the Apostles.* ICC. 2 vols. Edinburgh: T. & T. Clark, 1994.

Bartchy, S. Scott. "Philemon, Epistle to." *ABD,* 5:305–10.

Barton, Carlin A. "Savage Miracles: The Redemption of Lost Honor in Roman Society and the Sacrament of the Gladiator and the Martyr." *Representations* 45 (1994): 41–71.

———. *The Sorrows of the Ancient Romans: The Gladiator and the Monster.* Princeton, N.J.: Princeton University Press, 1993.

Barton, Tamsyn S. *Power and Knowledge: Astrology, Physiognomics, and Medicine under the Roman Empire.* The Body, in Theory: Histories of Cultural Materialism. Ann Arbor: University of Michigan Press, 1994.

Bartsch, Shadi. *Ideology in Cold Blood: A Reading of Lucan's Civil War.* Cambridge, Mass.: Harvard University Press, 1997.

———. *The Mirror of the Self: Sexuality, Self-Knowledge, and the Gaze in the Early Roman Empire.* Chicago: University of Chicago Press, forthcoming 2006.

Bassler, Jouette M. *Divine Impartiality: Paul and a Theological Axiom.* SBLDS 59. Chico, Calif.: Scholars Press, 1982.

———. *1 Timothy, 2 Timothy, Titus.* Nashville: Abingdon, 1996.

———. Review of *Rereading Romans,* by Stowers. *JBL* 115 (1996): 365–68.

Bauckham, Richard. "Synoptic Parousia Parables and the Apocalypse." *NTS* 23 (1976/77): 162–76.

Bauman, Richard A. *Lawyers in Roman Republican Politics: A Study of the Roman Jurists in Their Political Setting, 316–82 B.C.* MBPF 75. Munich: C. H. Beck, 1983.

Bauman-Martin, Betsy J. "Woman on the Edge: New Perspectives on Women in the Petrine Haustafel." *JBL* 123 (2004): 253–79.

Beacham, Richard C. *The Roman Theatre and Its Audience.* Cambridge, Mass.: Harvard University Press, 1992.

Beard, Mary, John North, and Simon Price. *Religions of Rome.* Vol. 1: *A History.* Cambridge: Cambridge University Press, 1998.

Beare, W. *The Roman Stage: A Short History of Latin Drama in the Time of the Republic.* 3d ed. London: Methuen, 1964.

———. "Slave Costume in New Comedy." *CQ* 43 (1949): 30–31.

Beavis, Mary Ann. "Ancient Slavery as an Interpretive Context for the New Testament Servant Parables with Special Reference to the Unjust Steward (Luke 16:1-8)." *JBL* 111 (1992): 37–54.

Beazley, J. D. *Attic Red-Figure Vase-Painters.* 2d ed. 3 vols. Oxford: Clarendon, 1963.

Benko, Stephen. *Pagan Rome and the Early Christians.* Bloomington: Indiana University Press, 1984.

Bérard, Claude. "Pénalité et religion à Athènes: Un témoignage de l'image-rie." *RAr*, 7th ser., 25 (1982): 137–50.

Berger, Peter L., and Thomas Luckmann. *The Social Construction of Reality: A Treatise in the Sociology of Knowledge.* Garden City, N.Y.: Doubleday, 1966.

Best, Ernest. *A Critical and Exegetical Commentary on Ephesians.* ICC. Edinburgh: T. & T. Clark, 1998.

Betz, Hans Dieter. *Der Apostel Paulus und die sokratische Tradition: Eine exegetische Untersuchung zu seiner "Apologie" 2 Korinther 10–13.* BHT 45. Tübingen: Mohr (Siebeck), 1972.

———. "The Concept of the 'Inner Human Being' (*ho esō anthrōpos*) in the Anthropology of Paul." *NTS* 46 (2000): 315–41.

———. *The Sermon on the Mount: A Commentary on the Sermon on the Mount, Including the Sermon on the Plain (Matthew 5:3—7:27 and Luke 6:20-49).* Edited by Adela Yarbro Collins. Hermeneia. Minneapolis: Fortress Press, 1995.

Bevere, Allan R. *Sharing the Inheritance: Identity and the Moral Life in Colossians.* JSNTSup 226. London: Sheffield Academic Press, 2003.

Bickerman, Elias J. *Four Strange Books of the Bible: Jonah, Daniel, Koheleth, Esther.* New York: Schocken, 1967.

———. *The Jews in the Greek Age.* Cambridge, Mass.: Harvard University Press, 1988.

Binder, Hermann. *Der Brief des Paulus an Philemon.* THKNT 11.2. Berlin: Evangelische Verlagsanstalt, 1990.

Bing, Peter. "The Unruly Tongue: Philitas of Cos as Scholar and Poet." *CP* 98 (2003): 330–48.

Birley, A. R. "Persecutors and Martyrs in Tertullian's Africa." Pages 37–68 in *The Later Roman Empire Today: Papers Given in Honour of Professor John Mann.* Edited by D. F. Clark, M. M. Roxan, and J. J. Wilkes. London: Institute of Archaeology, 1993.

Black, David Alan. *Paul, Apostle of Weakness: Astheneia and Its Cognates in the Pauline Literature.* American University Studies 7.3. New York: Peter Lang, 1984.

Blanchard, J., and N. L. Rice. *A Debate on Slavery Held in the City of Cincinnati, on the First, Second, Third, and Sixth Days of October, 1845, upon the Question: Is Slave-Holding in Itself Sinful, and the Relation between Master and Slave, a Sinful Relation?* Cincinnati: Wm. H. Moore, 1846.

Bledsoe, Albert T. "Liberty and Slavery." Pages 271–458 in *Cotton Is King, and Pro-Slavery Arguments.* Edited by E. N. Elliott. 1860. Reprint, New York: Negro Universities Press, 1969.

Bloomer, W. Martin. *Latinity and Literary Society at Rome.* Philadelphia: University of Pennsylvania Press, 1997.

———. "Schooling in Persona: Imagination and Subordination in Roman Education." *Classical Antiquity* 16 (1997): 57–78.

Bodor, A. "The Control of Slaves during the Roman Empire." Pages 396–409 in *Forms of Control and Subordination in Antiquity*. Edited by Toru Yuge and Masaoki Doi. Tokyo: Society for Studies on Resistance Movements in Antiquity; Leiden: Brill, 1988.

―――. "Graveyards and Groves: A Study of the *Lex Lucerina*." *American Journal of Ancient History* 11 (1986): 1–133.

Bömer, Franz. *Untersuchungen über die Religion der Sklaven in Griechenland und Rom*. 3 pts. 2d ed. Abhandlungen der Akademie der Wissenschaften in Mainz, Geistes- und Sozialwissenschaftliche Klasse. Forschungen zur antiken Sklaverei 14 and 14.3. Revised by Peter Herz. Wiesbaden and Stuttgart: Franz Steiner, 1982, 1960, 1990.

Bonner, S. F. *Roman Declamation in the Late Republic and Early Empire*. Liverpool: University Press of Liverpool, 1949.

Bourne, G. *A Condensed Anti-Slavery Bible Argument*. New York: S. W. Benedict, 1845. Reprinted in *Essays and Pamphlets on Antislavery*. Westport, Conn.: Negro Universities Press, 1970.

Bovon, François. *Das Evangelium nach Lukas*. Vol. 3: *Lk 15,1—19,27*. EKKNT. Zurich: Benziger; Neukirchener-Vluyn: Neukirchener, 2001.

Bowersock, G. W. *Roman Arabia*. Cambridge, Mass.: Harvard University Press, 1983.

Boyarin, Daniel. *Dying for God: Martyrdom and the Making of Christianity and Judaism*. Figurae: Reading Medieval Culture. Stanford: Stanford University Press, 1999.

Bozeman, Theodore Dwight. *Protestants in an Age of Science: The Baconian Ideal and Antebellum American Religious Thought*. Chapel Hill: University of North Carolina Press, 1977.

Bradley, Keith R. "Animalizing the Slave: The Truth of Fiction." *JRS* 90 (2000): 110–25.

―――. "On the Roman Supply and Slave Breeding." Pages 42–64 in Finley, *Classical Slavery*.

―――. *Slavery and Rebellion in the Roman World, 140 B.C.–70 B.C.* Bloomington: Indiana University Press, 1989.

―――. *Slavery and Society at Rome*. Key Themes in Ancient History. Cambridge: Cambridge University Press, 1994.

―――. *Slaves and Masters in the Roman Empire: A Study in Social Control*. 1984. Reprinted with suppl. bibliog. New York: Oxford University Press, 1987.

―――. "Slaves and the Conspiracy of Catiline." *CP* 73 (1978): 329–36.

―――. "Social Aspects of the Slave Trade in the Roman World." *Münstersche Beiträge zur antiken Handelsgeschichte* 5 (1986): 49–58.

Bradshaw, Paul F. *The Search for the Origins of Christian Worship: Sources and Methods for the Study of Early Liturgy*. New York: Oxford University Press, 1992.

Brakke, David. "Canon Formation and Social Conflict in Fourth-Century Egypt: Athanasius of Alexandria's Thirty-ninth *Festal Letter*." *HTR* 87 (1994): 395–419.

Braund, David. "Piracy under the Principate and the Ideology of Imperial Eradication." Pages 195–212 in *War and Society in the Roman World*. Edited by John Rich and Graham Shipley. London: Routledge, 1993.

Braund, Susanna Morton, and Paula James. "*Quasi Homo*: Distortion and Contortion in Seneca's *Apocolocyntosis*." *Arethusa* 31 (1998): 285–311.

Breech, James. *The Silence of Jesus: The Authentic Voice of the Historical Man*. Philadelphia: Fortress Press, 1983.

Brester, Ethel H. "A Weaver of Oxyrhynchus: Sketch of a Humble Life in Roman Egypt." *TAPA* 58 (1937): 132–54.

Briscoe, John. *A Commentary on Livy: Books XXXIV–XXXVII*. Oxford: Clarendon, 1981.

Briscoe, John, and Maria Michela Sassi. "Porcius Cato (1), Marcus." *OCD*, 1224–25.

Brock, Arthur John. *On the Natural Faculties/Galen*. LCL. Cambridge, Mass.: Harvard University Press, 1991.

Brock, Sebastian. "The Two Ways and the Palestinian Targum." Pages 138–52 in *A Tribute to Geza Vermes: Essays on Jewish and Christian Literature and History*. Edited by Philip R. Davies and Richard T. White. JSNTSup 100. Sheffield: JSOT, 1990,

Brodie, Thomas L. "The Unity of Proto-Luke." Pages 627–38 in *The Unity of Luke–Acts*. Edited by J. Verheyden. BETL 142. Leuven: Leuven University Press, 1999.

Brookes, Iveson L. *A Defence of the South against the Incroachments of the North*. Hamburg, S.C.: Republican Office, 1850.

Brooten, Bernadette J. *Love between Women: Early Christian Responses to Female Homoeroticism*. The Chicago Series on Sexuality, History, and Society. Chicago: University of Chicago Press, 1996.

Brotherton, Blanche. "The Introduction of Characters by Name in the *Metamorphoses* of Apuleius." *CP* 29 (1934): 36–52

Brown, Jerry Wayne. *The Rise of Biblical Criticism in America, 1800–1870: The New England Scholars*. Middletown, Conn.: Wesleyan University Press, 1969.

Brown, P. G. McC. "Aeschinus at the Door: Terence Adelphoe 632–43 and the Traditions of Graeco-Roman Comedy." Pages 71–89 in *Papers of the Leeds International Latin Seminar, Eighth Volume 1995: Roman Comedy, Augustan Poetry, Historiography*. Edited by R. Brock and A. J. Woodman. ARCA Classical and Medieval Texts, Papers and Monographs 33. Leeds: Cairns, 1995.

———. "Parasite." *OCD*, 1112.

Brownlow, W. G., and A. Pryne. *Ought American Slavery to Be Perpetuated? A Debate*. Philadelphia: J. B. Lippincott, 1858.

Bruce, F. F. *The Acts of the Apostles*. 3d ed. Grand Rapids, Mich.: Eerdmans, 1990.

Brunt, P. A. "Aristotle and Slavery." Pages 343–88 in idem, *Studies in Greek History and Thought*. Oxford: Clarendon, 1993.

———. "Evidence Given under Torture in the Principate." *Zeitschrift der Savigny-Stiftung für Rechtsgeschichte (romanistische Abteilung)* 97 (1980): 256–65.

Brunt, P. A., and J. M. Moore, eds. *Res Gestae Divi Augusti: The Achievements of the Divine Augustus*. New York: Oxford University Press, 1967.

Buck, William C. *The Slavery Question*. Louisville: Harney, Hughes and Hughes, 1849.

Buckland, W. W. *The Roman Law of Slavery: The Conditions of the Slave in Private Law from Augustus to Justinian*. 1908. Reprint, New York: AMS Press, 1969.

Buckler, John. "Plutarch and Autopsy." *ANRW* 2.33.6 (1992): 4788–830.

Bultmann, Rudolf. *The Second Letter to the Corinthians*. Translated by Roy A. Harrisville. Minneapolis: Augsburg, 1985.

Burnett, Gary W. *Paul and the Salvation of the Individual*. BibInt 57. Leiden: Brill, 2001.

Burrus, Virginia. "Hierarchicalization and Genderization of Leadership in the Writings of Irenaeus." *StPatr* 21 (1989): 42–48.

———. "Torture and Travail: Producing the Christian Martyr." In *A Feminist Companion to Patristic Literature*. Edited by Amy-Jill Levine. London: Continuum, forthcoming.

Bury, R. G. *Laws/Plato*. LCL. Cambridge, Mass.: Harvard University Press, 1984.

Busch, Austin. "The Figure of Eve in Romans 7:5-25." *BibInt* 12 (2004): 1–36.

Buschmann, Gerd. *Das Martyrium des Polycarp*. Kommentar zu den Apostolischen Vätern. Göttingen: Vandenhoeck & Ruprecht, 1998.

———. *Martyrium Polycarpi—Eine formkritische Studie: Ein Beitrag zur Frage nach der Entstehung der Gattung Märtyrerakte*. BZNW 70. Berlin: Walter de Gruyter, 1994.

Butterfield, H. *The Whig Interpretation of History*. 1931. Reprint, London: G. Bell and Sons, 1965.

Butts, James R. "The Progymnasmata of Theon: A New Text with Translation and Commentary." Ph.D. diss., Claremont Graduate School, 1986.

Byron, John. *Slavery Metaphors in Early Judaism and Pauline Christianity*. WUNT 2/162. Tübingen: Mohr (Siebeck), 2003.

Callahan, Allen Dwight. *Embassy of Onesimus: The Letter of Paul to Philemon*. New Testament in Context. Valley Forge, Pa.: Trinity Press International, 1997.

———. "Paul's Epistle to Philemon: Toward an Alternative *Argumentum*." *HTR* 86 (1993): 357–76.

Cambiano, Giuseppe. "Aristotle and the Anonymous Opponents of Slavery." Pages 21–41 in Finley, *Classical Slavery*.

Cameron, Alan. "The Date and Identity of Macrobius." *JRS* 56 (1966): 35–38.

Campbell, Brian. "Teach Yourself How to Be a General." *JRS* 77 (1987): 13–29.

Campbell, Jerry Dean. "Biblical Criticism in America, 1858–1892: The Emergence of the Historical Critic." Ph.D. diss., University of Denver, 1982.

Campenhausen, Hans von. "Bearbeitungen und Interpolationen des Polykarpmartyriums." Pages 197–301 in idem, *Aus der Frühzeit des Christentums: Studien zur Kirchengeschichte des ersten und zweiten Jahrhunderts.* Tübingen: Mohr (Siebeck), 1963.

Carcopino, Jérôme. *Daily Life in Ancient Rome: The People and the City at the Height of the Empire.* Edited and annotated by Henry T. Rowell. Translated by E. O. Lorimer. New Haven: Yale University Press, 1968.

Carl, Robert. *Die Masken der neueren attischen Komödie.* Hallisches Winckelmannsprogramm 25. Halle: M. Niemeyer, 1911.

Carlsen, Jesper. "The 'vilica' and Roman Estate Management." Pages 197–205 in *De Agricultura: In Memoriam Pieter Willem De Neeve.* Edited by Heleen Sancisi-Weerdenburg et al. Dutch Monographs on Ancient History and Archaeology 10. Amsterdam: Gieben, 1993.

———. *Vilici and Roman Estate Managers until AD 284.* Analecta Romana Instituti Danici Supplementum 24. Rome: L'Erma di Bretschneider, 1995.

Cary, Phillip. *Augustine's Invention of the Inner Self: The Legacy of a Christian Platonist.* New York: Oxford University Press, 2000.

Casson, Lionel. *The "Periplus Maris Erythraei": Text with Introduction and Commentary.* Princeton, N.J.: Princeton University Press, 1989.

Castelli, Elizabeth A. "Romans." Pages 272–300 in *Searching the Scriptures.* Vol. 2: *A Feminist Commentary.* Edited by Elisabeth Schüssler Fiorenza. New York: Crossroad, 1994.

———. "Visions and Voyeurism: Holy Women and the Politics of Sight in Early Christianity." *Protocol of the Colloquy of the Center for Hermeneutical Studies,* n.s. 2 (1995): 1–34.

Channing, William E. *Slavery.* Boston: James Munroe, 1835.

Cheever, George B. *The Guilt of Slavery and the Crime of Slaveholding: Demonstrated from the Hebrew and Greek Scriptures.* Boston: John P. Jewett, 1860.

Christmann, Eckhard. "Zum Verhältnis von Autor und Leser in der römischen Agrarliteratur: Bücher und Schriften für Herren und Sklaven." Pages 121–52 in *Antike Fachschriftsteller: Literarischer Diskurs und sozialer Kontext.* Edited by Marietta Horster and Christiane Reitz. Palingensia 80. Stuttgart: Franz Steiner, 2003.

Clark, Elizabeth A. *History, Theory, Text: Historians and the Linguistic Turn.* Cambridge: Mass., Harvard University Press, 2004.

Cohen, Shaye J. D. *The Beginnings of Jewishness: Boundaries, Varieties, Uncertainties.* Berkeley and Los Angeles: University of California Press, 1999.

Coleman, K. M. "Fatal Charades: Roman Executions Staged as Mythological Enactments." *JRS* 80 (1990): 44–73.

Colin, Jean. *L'empire des Antonins et les martyrs gaulois de 177.* Antiquitas, ser. 1. Abhandlungen zur alten Geschichte 10. Bonn: Rudolf Habelt, 1964.

Collange, Jean-François. *L'épître de Saint Paul à Philémon.* CNT 11C. Geneva: Labor et Fides, 1987.

Collins, John N. *Diakonia: Re-interpreting the Ancient Sources.* New York: Oxford University Press, 1990.

Colson, F. H., and G. H. Whitaker. *Works/Philo, of Alexandria.* 12 vols. LCL. Cambridge, Mass.: Harvard University Press, 1966–71.

Connolly, Joy. "Mastering Corruption: Constructions of Identity in Roman Oratory." Pages 130–51 in Murnaghan and Joshel, *Women and Slaves.*

Conzelmann, Hans. *Acts of the Apostles.* Translated by James Limburg, A. Thomas Kraabel, and Donald H. Juel. Edited by Eldon Jay Epp. Hermeneia. Philadelphia: Fortress Press, 1987.

Cook, James H. "Fighting with Breath, not Blows: Frederick Douglass and Antislavery Violence." Pages 128–63 in *Antislavery Violence: Sectional, Racial, and Cultural Conflict in Antebellum America.* Edited by John R. McKivigan and Stanley Harrold. Knoxville: University of Tennessee Press, 1999.

Cooper, Kate. "The Voice of the Victim: Gender, Representation and Early Christian Martyrdom." *BJRL* 80.3 (1998): 147–57.

Corbeill, Anthony. *Controlling Laughter: Political Humor in the Late Roman Republic.* Princeton, N.J.: Princeton University Press, 1996.

Corbett, Philip B. *The Scurra.* Scottish Classical Studies. Edinburgh: Scottish Academic Press, 1986.

Costa, C. D. N., ed. *Greek Fictional Letters.* New York: Oxford University Press, 2001.

Courtney, Edward. *A Companion to Petronius.* New York: Oxford University Press, 2001.

Crook, J. A. *Law and Life of Rome, 90 B.C.–A.D. 212.* Ithaca, N.Y.: Cornell University Press, 1967.

———. *Legal Advocacy in the Roman World.* Ithaca, N.Y.: Cornell University Press, 1995.

Crouch, James E. *The Origin and Intention of the Colossian Haustafel.* FRLANT 109. Göttingen: Vandenhoeck & Ruprecht, 1972.

Crowther, Edward R. "'Religion Has Something . . . to Do with Politics': Southern Evangelicals and the North, 1845–1860." Pages 317–42 in McKivigan and Snay, *Religion and the Antebellum Debate.*

Csapo, Eric G. "A Case Study in the Use of Theatre Iconography as Evidence for Ancient Acting." *Antike Kunst* 36 (1993): 41–58.

———. "Is the Threat-Monologue of the *Servus Currens* an Index of Roman Authorship?" *Phoenix* 41 (1987): 399–419.

———. "Plautine Elements in the Running-Slave Entrance Monologues?" *CQ* 39 (1989): 148–63.

Csapo, Eric G., and William J. Slater. *The Context of Ancient Drama.* Ann Arbor: University of Michigan Press, 1995.

Dabney, Robert Lewis. *A Defence of Virginia.* New York: E. J. Hale and Son, 1867.

Dagg, J. L. *The Elements of Moral Science.* New York: Sheldon, 1861.

Daly, John Patrick. *When Slavery Was Called Freedom: Evangelicalism, Proslavery, and the Causes of the Civil War.* Lexington: University Press of Kentucky, 2002.

Daly, Lloyd W. *Aesop without Morals: The Famous Fables, and a Life of Aesop.* New York: Thomas Yoseloff, 1961.

Damon, Cynthia. *The Mask of the Parasite: A Pathology of Roman Patronage.* Ann Arbor: University of Michigan Press, 1997.

D'Arms, John H. *Commerce and Social Standing in Ancient Rome.* Cambridge, Mass.: Harvard University Press, 1981.

———. "Slaves at Roman Convivia." Pages 171–83 in *Dining in a Classical Context.* Edited by William J. Slater. Ann Arbor: University of Michigan Press, 1991.

Davies, Margaret. *The Pastoral Epistles.* NTG. Sheffield: Sheffield Academic Press, 1996.

Davies, Percival V. *Macrobius: The Saturnalia.* New York: Columbia University Press, 1969.

Davis, David Brion. *The Problem of Slavery in the Age of Revolution, 1770–1823.* Ithaca, N.Y.: Cornell University Press, 1975.

Davis, Hugh. "Leonard Bacon, the Congregational Church, and Slavery, 1845–1861." Pages 221–45 in McKivigan and Snay, *Religion and the Antebellum Debate.*

Davis, W. Hersey. *Greek Papyri of the First Century.* New York: Harper and Bros., 1933.

DeFilippo, Joseph G. "Curiositas and the Platonism of Apuleius' Golden Ass." *AJP* 111 (1990): 471–92.

Dehandschutter, Boudewijn. "The Martyrium Polycarpi: A Century of Research." *ANRW* 2.27.1 (1993): 485–522.

———. *Martyrium Polycarpi: Een literair-kritische studie.* BETL 52. Leuven: Leuven University Press, 1979.

Deissmann, Adolf. *Light from the Ancient East: The New Testament Illustrated by Recently Discovered Texts of the Graeco-Roman World.* Rev. ed. Translated by R. M. Strachan. 1927. Reprint, Peabody, Mass.: Hendrickson, 1995.

DeLacy, Phillip. "Cicero's Invective against Piso." *TAPA* 72 (1941): 49–58.

———. Review of *Physiognomics,* by Evans. *AJP* 92 (1971): 508–10.

Delehaye, Hippolyte. *Les passions des martyrs et les genres littéraires.* 2d ed. Subsidia hagiographica 13B. Brussels: Société des Bollandistes, 1966.

Deming, Will. "A Diatribe Pattern in 1 Cor. 7:21-22: A New Perspective on Paul's Directions to Slaves." *NovT* 37 (1995): 130–37.

———. "Paul and Indifferent Things." Pages 384–403 in Sampley, *Paul in the Greco-Roman World.*

Derrett, J. Duncan M. *Law in the New Testament*. London: Darton, Longman and Todd, 1970.

De Smet, R. "The Erotic Adventure of Lucius and Photis in Apuleius' *Metamorphoses*." *Latomus* 46 (1987): 613–23.

de Souza, Philip. "Greek Piracy." Pages 179–98 in *The Greek World*. Edited by Anton Powell. London: Routledge, 1995.

DeWitt, Norman Wentworth. *Epicurus and His Philosophy*. Minneapolis: University of Minnesota Press, 1954.

Dibelius, Martin, and Hans Conzelmann. *The Pastoral Epistles*. Translated by Philip Buttolph and Adela Yarbro. Edited by Helmut Koester. Hermeneia. Philadelphia: Fortress Press, 1972.

The Digest of Justinian. 4 vols. Latin text edited by Theodor Mommsen with Paul Krueger. Translated by Alan Watson. Philadelphia: University of Pennsylvania Press, 1985.

Dihle, Albrecht. "Mündlichkeit und Schriftlichkeit nach dem Aufkommen des Lehrbuches." Pages 265–77 in *Gattungen wissenschaftlicher Literatur in der Antike*. Edited by Wolfgang Kullmann, Jochen Althoff, and Markus Asper. ScriptOralia 95. Series A: Altertumswissenschaftliche Reihe 22. Tübingen: Narr, 1998.

Dobrov, Gregory W. "*Mageiros Poiētēs*: Language and Character in Antiphanes." Pages 169–90 in *The Language of Greek Comedy*. Edited by Andreas Willi. New York: Oxford University Press, 2002.

Donelson, Lewis R. *Pseudepigraphy and Ethical Argument in the Pastoral Epistles*. HUT 22. Tübingen: Mohr (Siebeck), 1986.

Dorcey, Peter F. *The Cult of Silvanus: A Study in Roman Folk Religion*. Columbia Studies in the Classical Tradition 20. Leiden: Brill, 1992.

Douglass, Frederick. *The Frederick Douglass Papers, Series One: Speeches, Debates, and Interviews*. Vol. 3: *1855–1863*. Edited by John W. Blassingame. New Haven: Yale University Press, 1985.

———. *Life and Times of Frederick Douglass*. Revised edition of *My Bondage and My Freedom*. 1892. Reprint, New York: Collier Books, 1962.

Dover, K. J. *Greek Popular Morality in the Time of Plato and Aristotle*. Berkeley and Los Angeles: University of California Press, 1974.

Draper, Jonathan. "Torah and Troublesome Apostles in the *Didache* Community." Pages 340–63 in idem, *Didache*.

———, ed. *The Didache in Modern Research*. AGJU 37. Leiden: Brill, 1996.

[Drayton, William Henry]. *The South Vindicated from the Treason and Fanaticism of the Northern Abolitionists*. Philadelphia: H. Manly, 1836.

Droge, Arthur J. *Homer or Moses? Early Christian Interpretations of the History of Culture*. HUT 26. Tübingen: Mohr (Siebeck), 1989.

duBois, Page. *Slaves and Other Objects*. Chicago: University of Chicago Press, 2003.

————. *Torture and Truth.* London: Routledge, 1991.

Duckworth, George E. "The Dramatic Function of the *Servus Currens* in Roman Comedy." Pages 93–102 in *Classical Studies Presented to Edward Capps on His Seventieth Birthday.* Princeton, N.J.: Princeton University Press, 1936.

————. *The Nature of Roman Comedy: A Study in Popular Entertainment.* 2d ed. Norman: University of Oklahoma Press, 1994.

Dunbar, Nan. *Aristophanes, Birds: Edited with Introduction and Commentary.* Oxford: Clarendon, 1995.

Dunchêne, Hervé. "Sur la stèle d'Aulus Caprilius Timotheos, Sōmatemporos." *Bulletin de correspondance hellénique* 110 (1986): 513–30.

Dunn, James D. G. *The Epistles to the Colossians and to Philemon: A Commentary on the Greek Text.* NIGTC. Grand Rapids, Mich.: Eerdmans; Carlisle: Paternoster, 1996.

————. "Rom. 7,14-25 in the Theology of Paul." *TZ* 31 (1975): 257–73.

————. *Romans 1–8.* WBC 38A. Dallas: Word Books, 1988.

Easton, Burton Scott. "New Testament Ethical Lists." *JBL* 51 (1932): 1–12.

Eder, Walter. *Servitus Publica.* Forschungen zur antiken Sklaverei 13. Wiesbaden: Franz Steiner, 1980.

Ehrman, Bart D., ed. and trans. *The Apostolic Fathers.* 2 vols. LCL. Cambridge, Mass.: Harvard University Press, 2003.

Elliott, Charles. *The Bible and Slavery.* Cincinnati: L. Swormstedt and A. Poe, 1857.

————. *Sinfulness of American Slavery.* 2 vols. Cincinnati: L. Swormstedt and J. H. Power, 1851.

Ellis, Simon P. *Roman Housing.* London: Duckworth, 2000.

Engberg-Pedersen, Troels. *Paul and the Stoics.* Louisville: Westminster John Knox, 2000.

————. "Stoic Philosophy and the Concept of the Person." Pages 109–35 in Gill, *Person and the Human Mind.*

————, ed. *Paul beyond the Judaism/Hellenism Divide.* Louisville: Westminster John Knox, 2001.

Evans, Elizabeth C. *Physiognomics in the Ancient World.* Transactions of the American Philosophical Society, n.s. 59.5. Philadelphia: American Philosophical Society, 1969.

————. "Physiognomics in the Roman Empire." *CJ* 45 (1949–50): 277–82.

Evans, Ernest. "Tertullian Ad Nationes." *VC* 9 (1955): 37–44.

Fairchilds, Cissie. *Domestic Enemies: Servants and Their Masters in Old Regime France.* Baltimore: Johns Hopkins University Press, 1984.

Faraone, Christopher A. "The Agonistic Context of Early Greek Binding Spells." Pages 3–32 in *Magika Hiera: Ancient Greek Magic and Religion.* Edited by idem. New York: Oxford University Press, 1991.

Feldherr, Andrew. *Spectacle and Society in Livy's History.* Berkeley and Los Angeles: University of California Press, 1998.

Ferguson, Everett. "Didache." Pages 328–29 in *Encyclopedia of Early Christianity.* Edited by idem. 2d ed. New York: Garland, 1998.

Ferguson, Jesse B. *Address on the History, Authority and Influence of Slavery.* Nashville: J. T. S. Fall, 1850.

Finley, Moses I. *Ancient Slavery and Modern Ideology.* Enlarged edition. Edited by Brent D. Shaw. Princeton, N.J.: Markus Wiener, 1998.

————. *Aspects of Antiquity: Discoveries and Controversies.* 2d ed. New York: Penguin, 1977.

————, ed. *Classical Slavery.* Slavery and Abolition special issue 8. London: Frank Cass, 1987.

————, ed. *Slavery in Classical Antiquity: Views and Controversies.* Cambridge: W. Heffer and Sons, 1960.

Fisher-Ogden, Daryl. "Albert Barnes (1798–1870)." Pages 11–20 in *Dictionary of Heresy Trials in American Christianity.* Edited by George H. Shriver. Westport, Conn.: Greenwood Press, 1997.

Fitzgerald, John T. "The Problem of Perjury in Greek Context: Prolegomena to an Exegesis of Matthew 5:33; 1 Timothy 1:10; and *Didache* 2.3." Pages 156–77 in White and Yarbrough, *Social World.*

————. "Virtue/Vice Lists." *ABD,* 6:857–59.

Fitzgerald, William. *Slavery and the Roman Literary Imagination.* Roman Literature and Its Contexts. New York: Cambridge University Press, 2000.

Fitzmyer, Joseph A. *The Gospel according to Luke (X–XXIV).* AB 28A. Garden City, N.Y.: Doubleday, 1985.

————. *The Letter to Philemon.* AB 34C. New York: Doubleday, 2000.

————. "The Story of the Dishonest Manager (Lk 16:1-13)." *TS* 25 (1964): 23–42.

Fletcher, John. *Studies on Slavery, in Easy Lessons.* Natchez, Miss.: Jackson Warner, 1852.

Flower, Harriet I. *Ancestor Masks and Aristocratic Power in Roman Culture.* Oxford: Clarendon, 1996.

Foerster, Richard. *Die Physiognomik der Griechen.* Kiel: Schmidt and Klaunig, 1884.

————. *Scriptores physiognomonici Graeci et Latini.* 2 vols. 1893. Reprint, Stuttgart and Leipzig: Teubner, 1994.

Fögen, Thorsten. "Metasprachliche Reflexionen antiker Autoren zu den Charakteristika von Fachtexten und Fachsprachen." Pages 31–60 in *Antike Fachschriftsteller: Literarischer Diskurs und sozialer Kontext.* Edited by Marietta Horster and Christiane Reitz. Palingensia 80. Stuttgart: Franz Steiner, 2003.

Forbes, Christopher. "Comparison, Self-Praise and Irony: Paul's Boasting and the Conventions of Hellenistic Rhetoric." *NTS* 32 (1986): 1–30.

Forbes, Robert P. "Slavery and the Evangelical Enlightenment." Pages 68–106 in McKivigan and Snay, *Religion and the Antebellum Debate.*

Formisano, Marco. *Tecnica e scrittura: Le letterature tecnico-scientifiche nello spazio letterario tardolatino.* Recerche 95. Rome: Carocci, 2001.

Foxhall, Lin, and John Salmon, eds. *When Men Were Men: Masculinity, Power and Identity in Classical Antiquity.* Leicester-Nottingham Studies in Ancient Society 8. London: Routledge, 1998.

Fraenkel, Eduard. *Elementi plautini in Plauto.* Translated by Franco Munari, with addenda by the author. Pensiero storico 41. Florence: La Nuova Italia, 1960.

———. *Plautinisches im Plautus.* Philologische Untersuchungen 28. Berlin: Weidmannsche Buchhandlung, 1922.

Fredrickson, David E. "Paul, Hardships, and Suffering." Pages 172–97 in Sampley, *Paul in the Greco-Roman World.*

Fredriksen, Paula. "Paul and Augustine: Conversion Narratives, Orthodox Traditions, and the Redemptive Self." *JTS*, n.s. 37 (1986): 3–34.

Frend, William H. C. "Blandina and Perpetua: Two Early Christian Martyrs." Pages 167–75 in Rougé and Turcan, *Martyrs de Lyon.*

———. *Martyrdom and Persecution in the Early Church: A Study of the Conflict from the Maccabees to Donatus.* Oxford: Basil Blackwell, 1965.

Frier, Bruce W. *The Rise of the Roman Jurists: Studies in Cicero's "pro Caecina."* Princeton, N.J.: Princeton University Press, 1985.

Frilingos, Chris. "'For My Child, Onesimus': Paul and Domestic Power in Philemon." *JBL* 119 (2000): 91–104.

Frischer, Bernard. *The Sculpted Word: Epicureanism and Philosophical Recruitment in Ancient Greece.* Berkeley and Los Angeles: University of California Press, 1982.

Fuhrmann, Manfred. *Das systematische Lehrbuch: Ein Beitrag zur Geschichte der Wissenschaften in der Antike.* Göttingen: Vandenhoeck & Ruprecht, 1960.

Fuller, Richard, and Francis Wayland. *Domestic Slavery Considered as a Scriptural Institution.* New York: Lewis Colby, 1845.

Funaioli, Gino, ed. *Grammaticae Romanae fragmenta collegit.* Volumen prius. Bibliotheca scriptorum Graecorum et Romanorum Teubneriana. Leipzig: Teubner, 1907.

Furnish, Victor Paul. *II Corinthians.* AB 32A. New York: Doubleday, 1984.

Gagarin, Michael. "The Torture of Slaves in Athenian Law." *CP* 91 (1996): 1–18.

Gager, John G. *Curse Tablets and Binding Spells from the Ancient World.* New York: Oxford University Press, 1992.

Gale, Monica. *Myth and Poetry in Lucretius.* Cambridge Classical Studies. Cambridge: Cambridge University Press, 1994.

Galinsky, Karl. *Augustan Culture: An Interpretive Introduction.* Princeton, N.J.: Princeton University Press, 1996.

Galsterer, Hartmut. "Roman Law in the Provinces: Some Problems of Transmission." Pages 12–27 in *L'impero romano e le strutture economiche e sociali delle province.* Edited by Michael H. Crawford. British School at Rome. Biblioteca di Athenaeum 4. Como, Italy: New Press, 1986.

Garland, Andrew. "Cicero's *Familia Urbana.*" *GR* 39 (1992): 163–72.

Garland, David E. *Colossians and Philemon.* The NIV Application Commentary. Grand Rapids, Mich.: Zondervan, 1988.

Garnsey, Peter. *Ideas of Slavery from Aristotle to Augustine.* The W. B. Stanford Memorial Lectures. Cambridge: Cambridge University Press, 1996.

———. "Independent Freedmen and the Economy of Roman Italy under the Principate." *Klio* 63 (1981): 359–71.

———. *Social Status and Legal Privilege in the Roman Empire.* Oxford: Clarendon, 1970.

Garnsey, Peter, and Richard Saller. *The Roman Empire: Economy, Society and Culture.* Berkeley and Los Angeles: University of California Press, 1987.

Garrett, Susan R. "Exodus from Bondage: Luke 9:31 and Acts 12:1-24." *CBQ* 52 (1990): 656–80.

Garrison, William Lloyd. *The Letters of William Lloyd Garrison.* Vol. 3: *No Union with Slave-Holders: 1841–1849.* Edited by Walter M. Merrill. Cambridge. Mass.: The Belknap Press of Harvard University Press, 1973.

———. *The Letters of William Lloyd Garrison.* Vol. 4: *From Disunionism to the Brink of War: 1850–1860.* Edited by Louis Ruchames. Cambridge, Mass.: The Belknap Press of Harvard University Press, 1975.

———. *The Letters of William Lloyd Garrison.* Vol. 6: *To Rouse the Slumbering Land: 1868–1879.* Edited by Walter M. Merrill and Louis Ruchames. Cambridge, Mass.: The Belknap Press of Harvard University Press, 1981.

Garver, Eugene. "Aristotle's Natural Slaves: Incomplete Praxeis and Incomplete Human Beings." *Journal of the History of Philosophy* 32 (1994): 173–95.

George, Michele. "Servus and Domus: The Slave in the Roman House." Pages 15–24 in *Domestic Space in the Roman World: Pompeii and Beyond.* Edited by Ray Laurence and Andrew Wallace-Hadrill. Journal of Roman Archaeology Supplement Series 22. Portsmouth, R.I.: Journal of Roman Archaeology, 1997.

Giardina, Andrea. "The Merchant." Pages 245–71 in Giardina, *Romans.*

———, ed. *The Romans.* Translated by Lydia G. Cochrane. Chicago: University of Chicago Press, 1993.

Gibson, Roy K. *Ars Amatoria Book 3/Ovid: Edited with Introduction and Commentary.* Cambridge Classical Texts and Commentaries 40. Cambridge: Cambridge University Press, 2003.

Gielen, Marlis. *Tradition und Theologie neutestamentlicher Haustafelethik: Ein Beitrag zur Frage einer christlichen Auseinandersetzung mit gesellschaftlichen Normen.* BBB 75. Frankfurt: Anton Hain, 1990.

Giles, Kevin. "The Biblical Argument for Slavery: Can the Bible Mislead? A Case Study in Hermeneutics." *EvQ* 66 (1994): 3–17.

Gill, Christopher. "The Character-Personality Distinction." Pages 1–31 in *Characterization and Individuality in Greek Literature.* Edited by Christopher Pelling. Oxford: Clarendon, 1990.

———. "Introduction II: The Emotions in Greco-Roman Philosophy." Pages 5–15 in *The Passions in Roman Thought and Literature.* Edited by Susanna Morton Braund and Christopher Gill. Cambridge: Cambridge University Press, 1997.

———. *Personality in Greek Epic, Tragedy, and Philosophy: The Self in Dialogue.* Oxford: Clarendon, 1996.

———, ed. *The Person and the Human Mind: Issues in Ancient and Modern Philosophy.* Oxford: Clarendon, 1990.

Giltner, John H. *Moses Stuart: The Father of Biblical Science in America.* SBLCP. Atlanta: Scholars Press, 1988.

———. "Moses Stuart and the Slavery Controversy: A Study in the Failure of Moderation." *JRT* 18 (1961): 27–39.

Glancy, Jennifer A. "Boasting of Beatings (2 Corinthians 11:23-25)." *JBL* 123 (2004): 99–135.

———. *Slavery in Early Christianity.* New York: Oxford University Press, 2002.

Gleason, Maud W. *Making Men: Sophists and Self-Representation in Ancient Rome.* Princeton, N.J.: Princeton University Press, 1995.

———. "Mutilated Messengers: Body Language in Josephus." Pages 50–85 in *Being Greek under Rome: Cultural Identity, the Second Sophistic and the Development of Empire.* Edited by Simon Goldhill. Cambridge: Cambridge University Press, 2001.

Goldberg, Sander M. *Understanding Terence.* Princeton, N.J.: Princeton University Press, 1986.

Goldenberg, David M. *The Curse of Ham: Race and Slavery in Early Judaism, Christianity, and Islam.* Princeton, N.J.: Princeton University Press, 2003.

Goodenough, Erwin R. "Philo's Exposition of the Law and His *De Vita Mosis.*" *HTR* 26 (1933): 109–25.

Goodine, Elizabeth A., and Matthew W. Mitchell. "The Persuasiveness of a Woman: The Mistranslation and Misinterpretation of Eusebius' *Historia Ecclesiastica* 5.1.41." *JECS* 13 (2005): 1–19.

Goodspeed, Edgar J. *The Apostolic Fathers: An American Translation.* New York: Harper, 1950.

———, ed. *Die ältesten Apologeten: Texte mit kurzen Einleitungen.* Göttingen: Vandenhoeck & Ruprecht, 1914.

Goodwin, Daniel R. *Southern Slavery in Its Present Aspects: Containing a Reply to a Late Work of the Bishop of Vermont on Slavery.* Philadelphia: J. B. Lippincott, 1864.

Goulder, Michael D. *Luke: A New Paradigm.* 2 vols. JSNTSup 20. Sheffield: JSOT, 1989.

Graf, Fritz. "Gestures and Conventions: The Gestures of Roman Actors and Orators." Pages 36–58 in *A Cultural History of Gesture.* Edited by Jan Bremmer. Ithaca, N.Y.: Cornell University Press, 1991.

Graham, William. *The Contrast, or the Bible and Abolitionism: An Exegetical Argument.* Cincinnati: Daily Cincinnati Atlas, 1844.

Grant, Robert M. *After the New Testament.* Philadelphia: Fortress Press, 1967.

———. "The Description of Paul in the Acts of Paul and Thecla." *VC* 36 (1982): 1–4.

Griffin, Miriam. *Seneca: A Philosopher in Politics.* Oxford: Clarendon, 1976.

Grobel, Kendrick. "*Sōma* as 'Self, Person' in the Septuagint." Pages 52–59 in *Neutestamentliche Studien für Rudolf Bultmann.* Edited by Walther Eltester. BZNW 21. Berlin: Alfred Töpelmann, 1954.

Gruen, Erich S. *Culture and National Identity in Republican Rome.* Ithaca, N.Y.: Cornell University Press, 1992.

Grusin, Richard A. *Transcendentalist Hermeneutics: Institutional Authority and the Higher Criticism of the Bible.* Post-Contemporary Interventions. Durham, N.C.: Duke University Press, 1991.

Guardì, T. "I precedenti greci della figura del 'servus currens' della commedia romana." *Pan* 2 (1974): 5–15.

Guillaumin, Marie-Louise. "'Une Jeune Fille qui s'appelait Blandine': Aux origines d'une tradition hagiographique." Pages 93–98 in *Epektasis: Mélanges patristiques offerts au Cardinal Jean Daniélou.* Edited by Jacques Fontaine and Charles Kannengiesser. Paris: Beauchesne, 1972.

Gummere, Richard M. *Ad Lucilium epistulae morales/Seneca, the Younger.* 3 vols. LCL. Cambridge, Mass.: Harvard University Press, 1971–79.

Gunderson, Erik. "Discovering the Body in Roman Oratory." Pages 169–89 in *Parchments of Gender: Deciphering the Bodies of Antiquity.* Edited by Maria Wyke. Oxford: Clarendon, 1998.

Günther, Rosmarie. "Matrona, vilica und ornatrix: Frauenarbeit in Rom zwischen Topos and Alltagswirklichkeit." Pages 350–76 in *Frauenwelten in der Antike: Geschlechterordnung und weibliche Lebenspraxis.* Edited by Thomas Späth and Beate Wagner-Hasel. Stuttgart: Metzler, 2000.

Guthrie, Kenneth Sylvan, trans. *The Pythagorean Sourcebook and Library.* Grand Rapids, Mich.: Phanes Press, 1987.

Haenchen, Ernst. *The Acts of the Apostles: A Commentary.* Translated by Bernard Noble and Gerald Shinn. Revised by R. McL. Wilson. Philadelphia: Westminster, 1971.

Hahn, Ferdinand. "Die christologische Begründung urchristlicher Paränese." *ZNW* 72 (1981): 88–99.

Hall, Stuart G. "Women among the Early Martyrs." Pages 1–21 in *Martyrs and Martyrologies*. Edited by Diana Wood. London: Blackwell, 1993.

Hamilton, W. T. *Duties of Masters and Slaves Respectively; or, Domestic Servitude as Sanctioned by the Bible*. Mobile, Ala.: F. H. Brooks, 1845.

Hammond, James H. "Hammond's Letters on Slavery." Pages 99–174 in *The Pro-Slavery Argument*. 1852. Reprint, New York: Negro Universities Press, 1968.

Hansen, William. *Anthology of Greek Popular Literature*. Bloomington: Indiana University Press, 1998.

Hanson, A. T. *The Pastoral Epistles: Commentary on the First and Second Letters to Timothy and the Letter to Titus*. Cambridge Bible Commentary: New English Bible. Grand Rapids, Mich.: Eerdmans, 1982.

Harmon, A. M. *Works/Lucian, of Samosata*. 8 vols. LCL. Cambridge, Mass.: Harvard University Press, 1967–79.

Harrill, J. Albert. "The Indentured Labor of the Prodigal Son (Luke 15:15)." *JBL* 115 (1996): 714–17.

———. *The Manumission of Slaves in Early Christianity*. HUT 32. Tübingen: Mohr (Siebeck), 1995.

———. "The Metaphor of Slavery in the Writings of Tertullian." *StPatr* 41 (2006, in press).

———. "Paul and Slavery." Pages 575–607 in Sampley, *Paul in the Greco-Roman World*.

———. Review of *Embassy of Onesimus*, by Callahan. *CBQ* 60 (1998): 757–59.

———. Review of *Slavery in Early Christianity*, by Glancy. *CBQ* 64 (2002): 758–59.

———. "Servile Functionaries or Priestly Leaders? Roman Domestic Religion, Narrative Intertextuality, and Pliny's Reference to Slave Christian *Ministrae* (Ep. 10,96,8)." *ZNW* 97 (2006, in press).

Harris, William V. *Ancient Literacy*. Cambridge, Mass.: Harvard University Press, 1989.

———. *Restraining Rage: The Ideology of Anger Control in Classical Antiquity*. Cambridge, Mass.: Harvard University Press, 2001.

———. "Towards a Study of the Roman Slave Trade." Pages 117–40 in *The Seaborne Commerce of Ancient Rome: Studies in Archaeology and History*. Edited by J. H. D'Arms and E. C. Kopff. Memoirs of the American Academy in Rome 36. Rome: American Academy in Rome, 1980.

Harsh, Philip Whaley. "The Intriguing Slave in Greek Comedy." *TAPA* 86 (1955): 135–42.

Harvey, F. D. "Two Kinds of Equality." *Classica et Mediaevalia* 26 (1965): 101–46.

Hauser, R. "Lasterkatalog." In *Historisches Wörterbuch der Philosophie*. 12 vols. to date. Edited by Joachim Ritter et al. Basel: Schwabe, 1971–. Vol. 5 (1980): 37–39.

Haynes, Stephen R. *Noah's Curse: The Biblical Justification of American Slavery*. New York: Oxford University Press, 2002.

Hays, Richard B. *Echoes of Scripture in the Letters of Paul*. New Haven: Yale University Press, 1989.

———. *The Moral Vision of the New Testament: Community, Cross, New Creation.* San Francisco: HarperSanFransisco, 1996.

Heath, Malcolm. *Hermogenes, "On Issues": Strategies of Argument in Later Greek Rhetoric.* Oxford: Clarendon, 1995.

Heckel, Theo K. *Der Innere Mensch: Die paulinische Verarbeitung eines platonischen Motivs.* WUNT 2/53. Tübingen: Mohr (Siebeck), 1993.

Heil, Christoph. "Die Rezeption von Micha 7,6 LXX in Q und Lukas." *ZNW* 88 (1997): 211–22.

Heininger, Bernhard. *Metaphorik, Erzählstruktur und szenisch-dramatische Gestaltung in den Sondergutgleichnissen bei Lukas.* NTAbh, n.s. 24. Münster: Aschendorff, 1991.

Helmbold, W. C. *Moralia/Plutarch.* Vol. 6. LCL. Cambridge, Mass.: Harvard University Press, 1993.

Henten, Jan Willem van. "The Martyrs as Heroes of the Christian People: Some Remarks on the Continuity between Jewish and Christian Martyrology, with Pagan Analogies." Pages 303–22 in *Martyrium in Multidisciplinary Perspective: Memorial Louis Reekmans.* Edited by M. Lamberigts and P. van Deun. Leuven: Leuven University Press, 1995.

Hett, W. S. *Aristotle: Minor Works.* LCL. Cambridge, Mass.: Harvard University Press, 1936.

Hezser, Catherine. "The Impact of Household Slaves on the Jewish Family in Roman Palestine." *JSJ* 34 (2003): 375–424.

———. "The Social Status of Slaves in the Talmud Yerushalmi and in Graeco-Roman Society." Pages 91–137 in *The Talmud Yerushalmi and Graeco-Roman Culture.* Edited by Peter Schäfer. Vol. 3. Tübingen: Mohr (Siebeck), 1998.

Himmelmann, Nikolaus. *Archäologisches zum Problem der griechischen Sklaverei.* Abhandlungen der Geistes- und Sozialwissenschaftlichen Klasse 1971/13. Mainz: Akademie der Wissenschaften und der Literatur, 1971.

Hock, Ronald F. "Lazarus and Micyllus: Greco-Roman Backgrounds to Luke 16:19-31." *JBL* 106 (1987): 447–63.

———. *The Social Context of Paul's Ministry: Tentmaking and Apostleship.* Philadelphia: Fortress Press, 1980.

Hodge, Charles. *Essays and Reviews: Selected from the Princeton Review.* New York: Robert Carter and Bros., 1857.

Hoffer, Stanley E. *The Anxieties of Pliny the Younger.* American Classical Studies 43. Atlanta: Scholars Press, 1999.

Hofstadter, Richard. *Anti-intellectualism in American Life.* New York: Vintage Books, 1963.

Holford-Strevens, Leofranc. "Aulus Gellius: The Non-Visual Portraitist." Pages 93–116 in *Portraits: Biographical Representation in the Greek and Latin Literature of the Roman Empire.* Edited by M. J. Edwards and Simon Swain. Oxford: Clarendon, 1997.

Holland, Louise Adams. "The Shrine of the Lares Compitales." *TAPA* 68 (1937): 428–41.

Hölscher, Tonio. "Images of War in Greece and Rome: Between Military Practice, Public Memory, and Cultural Symbolism." *JRS* 93 (2003): 1–17.

Hommel, Hildebrecht. "Das 7. Kapitel des Römerbriefs in Lichte antiker Überlieferung." Pages 141–67 in idem, *Sebasmata: Studien zur antiken Religionsgeschichte und zum frühen Christentum.* WUNT 32. Tübingen: Mohr (Siebeck), 1984.

Hooff, Anton J. L. van. "Ancient Robbers: Reflections behind the Facts." *Ancient Society* 19 (1988): 105–24.

Hopkins, John Henry. *Bible View of Slavery.* New York: Society for the Diffusion of Political Knowledge, 1863.

———. *The Scriptural, Ecclesiastical, and Historical View of Slavery.* New York: W. I. Pooley, 1864.

Hopkins, Keith. "Novel Evidence for Roman Slavery." *Past and Present* 138 (1993): 3–27.

Horst, P. W. van der. *The Sentences of Pseudo-Phocylides: With Introduction and Commentary.* SVTP 4. Leiden: Brill 1978.

Hosmer, William. *Slavery and the Church.* Auburn, Me.: William J. Moses, 1853.

Hovenkamp, Herbert. *Science and Religion in America, 1800–1860.* Philadelphia: University of Pennsylvania Press, 1978.

How, Samuel B. *Slaveholding Not Sinful: Slavery, the Punishment of Man's Sin; Its Remedy, the Gospel of Christ.* New Brunswick, N.J.: John Terhune, 1856.

Howard, Victor. *Conscience and Slavery: The Evangelistic Calvinist Domestic Missions, 1837–1861.* Kent, Ohio: Kent State University Press, 1990.

Howe, Daniel Walker. *The Unitarian Conscience: Harvard Moral Philosophy, 1805–1861.* Cambridge, Mass.: Harvard University Press, 1970.

Howe, George. "The Raid of John Brown and the Progress of Abolition." *Southern Presbyterian Review* 12 (January 1860): 784–815.

Hübner, Hans. *An Philemon. An die Kolosser. An die Epheser.* HNT 12. Tübingen: Mohr (Siebeck), 1997.

Hughes, Joseph J. "Invective and Comedic Allusion: Cicero, *In Pisonem,* Fragment 9 (Nisbet)." *Latomus* 57 (1998): 570–77.

———. "Piso's Eyebrows." *Mnemosyne* 45 (1992): 234–37.

Hughes, Philip E. *Paul's Second Epistle to the Corinthians.* NICNT. Grand Rapids, Mich.: Eerdmans, 1962.

Hultgren, Arland J. *The Parables of Jesus: A Commentary.* Grand Rapids, Mich.: Eerdmans, 2000.

Hunt, Peter. *Slaves, Warfare, and Ideology in the Greek Historians.* Cambridge: Cambridge University Press, 1998.

Hunter, R. L. *The New Comedy of Greece and Rome.* Cambridge: Cambridge University Press, 1985.

Hutchison, G. Whit. "The Bible and Slavery, a Test of Ethical Method: Biblical

Interpretation, Social Ethics, and the Hermeneutics of Race in America, 1830–1861." Ph.D. diss., Union Theological Seminary, New York, 1996.

Hutton, M., and E. H. Warmington. *Selections/Tacitus*. LCL. Cambridge, Mass.: Harvard University Press, 1970.

Inwood, Brad. "Hierocles: Theory and Argument in the Second Century AD." *Oxford Studies in Ancient Philosophy* 2 (1984): 151–83.

Inwood, Brad, and L. P. Gerson, eds. *The Epicurus Reader: Selected Writings and Testimonia*. Indianapolis: Hackett, 1994.

Isaac, Benjamin. *The Invention of Racism in Classical Antiquity*. Princeton, N.J.: Princeton University Press, 2004.

Jackson, John. *The Annals/Tacitus*. 3 vols. LCL. Cambridge, Mass.: Harvard University Press, 1992.

Jacoby, F., ed. *Die Fragmente der griechischen Historiker*. 3 vols. in 15. Leiden: Brill, 1923–58.

Jacquier, E. *Les Actes des Apôtres*. EBib. 2d ed. Paris: Gabalda, 1926.

Jefford, Clayton N. "Household Codes and Conflict in the Early Church." *StPatr* 31 (1997): 121–27.

———. *The Sayings of Jesus in the Teaching of the Twelve Apostles*. VCSup 11. Leiden: Brill, 1989.

———, ed. *The Didache in Context: Essays on Its Text, History and Transmission*. NovTSup 77. Leiden: Brill, 1995.

Jenkins, William Sumner. *Proslavery Thought in the Old South*. Chapel Hill: University of North Carolina Press, 1935.

Jennings, Lawrence C. *French Anti-Slavery: The Movement for the Abolition of Slavery in France, 1802–1848*. Cambridge: Cambridge University Press, 2000.

Jeremias, Joachim. *The Parables of Jesus*. Translated by S. H. Hooke. 2d ed. New York: Charles Scribner's Sons, 1972.

Jeremias, Joachim, and August Strobel. *Die Briefe an Timotheus und Titus; Der Brief an die Hebräer*. 12th ed. Göttingen: Vandenhoeck & Ruprecht, 1981.

Jervell, Jacob. *Die Apostelgeschichte*. KEK 3. Göttingen: Vandenhoeck & Ruprecht, 1998.

———. "Der schwache Charismatiker." Pages 185–98 in *Rechtfertigung: Festschrift für Ernst Käsemann zum 70. Geburtstag*. Edited by Johannes Friedrich, Wolfgang Pöhlmann, and Peter Stuhlmacher. Tübingen: Mohr (Siebeck); Göttingen: Vandenhoeck & Ruprecht, 1976.

Jocelyn, H. D. "Chrysalus and the Fall of Troy (Plautus, *Bacchides* 925–978)." *HSCP* 73 (1969): 135–52.

Johnson, Allan Chester. *Roman Egypt to the Reign of Diocletian*. Vol. 2 of *An Economic Survey of Ancient Rome*. Edited by Tenney Frank. Baltimore: Johns Hopkins University Press, 1936.

Johnson, Luke Timothy. *The Acts of the Apostles*. SP 5. Collegeville, Minn.: Liturgical Press, 1992.

Johnston, Leslie D. "The Lares and the Kalends Log." *CP* 34 (1939): 342–56.

Jones, Lawrence P. "A Case Study in 'Gnosticism': Religious Responses to Slavery in the Second Century CE." Ph.D. diss., Columbia University, 1988.

Jonkers, E. J. *Social and Economic Commentary on Cicero's "De Imperio Cn. Pompei."* Social and Economic Commentaries on Classical Texts 1. Leiden: Brill, 1959.

Joshel, Sandra R. *Work, Identity, and Legal Status at Rome: A Study of the Occupational Inscriptions.* Norman: University of Oklahoma Press, 1992.

Jülicher, Adolf. *Die Gleichnisreden Jesu.* 1899. Reprint, 2 vols. in 1. Darmstadt: Wissenschaftliche Buchgesellschaft, 1963.

Kähler, Christoph. *Jesu Gleichnisse als Poesie und Therapie: Versuch eines integrativen Zugangs zum kommunikativen Aspekt von Gleichnissen Jesu.* WUNT 78. Tübingen: Mohr (Siebeck), 1995.

Kamlah, Ehrhard. *Die Form der katalogischen Paränese im Neuen Testament.* Tübingen: Mohr (Siebeck), 1964.

Karris, Robert Joseph. "The Function and Sitz im Leben of the Paraenetic Elements in the Pastoral Epistles." Ph.D. diss., Harvard University, 1971.

Kaster, Robert A., ed. *De Grammaticis et Rhetoribus.* Oxford: Clarendon, 1995.

Keck, Leander E. "The Absent Good: The Significance of Rom 7:18a." Pages 66–75 in *Text und Geschichte: Facetten theologischen Arbeitens aus dem Freundes- und Schülerkreis Dieter Lührmann zum 60. Geburtstag.* Edited by Stefan Maser and Egbert Schlarb. Marburger theologische Studien 50. Marburg: Elwert, 1999.

Kehoe, Dennis P. *Investment, Profit, and Tenancy: The Jurists and the Roman Agrarian Economy.* Ann Arbor: University of Michigan Press, 1997.

Kennedy, George A. *The Art of Persuasion in Greece.* Princeton, N.J.: Princeton University Press, 1963.

———. *Progymnasmata: Greek Textbooks of Prose Composition and Rhetoric.* SBLWAW 10. Atlanta: SBL, 2003.

Kindstrand, Jan Fredrik. "The Greek Concept of Proverbs." *Eranos* 76 (1978): 71–85.

King, Charles. "The Organization of Roman Religious Beliefs." *Classical Antiquity* 22 (2003): 275–312.

Kloppenborg, John S. "The Transformation of Moral Exhortation in *Didache* 1–5." Pages 88–109 in Jefford, *Didache in Context.*

Koster, Severin. *Die Invektive in der griechischen und römischen Literatur.* Beiträge zur klassischen Philologie 99. Meisenheim am Glan: Anton Hain, 1980.

Kraft, Robert A. *Barnabas and the Didache.* Vol. 3 of *The Apostolic Fathers: A New Translation and Commentary.* Edited by Robert M. Grant. New York: Thomas Nelson, 1965.

———. "Didache." *ABD,* 2:197–98.

Krentz, Edgar. "Paul, Games, and the Military." Pages 344–83 in Sampley, *Paul in the Greco-Roman World.*

Krentz, Peter, and Everett L. Wheeler, eds. and trans. *Stratagems of War/Polyaenus*. 2 vols. Chicago: Ares, 1994.

Krien, Gisela. "Der Ausdruck der antiken Theatermasken nach Angaben im Polluxkatalog und in der pseudoaristotelischen 'Physiognomik.'" *JÖAI* 42 (1955): 84–117.

Krieter-Spiro, Martha. *Sklaven, Köche und Hetären: Das Dienstpersonal bei Menander*. Beiträge zur Altertumskunde 93. Stuttgart: Teubner, 1997.

Krüger, Thomas. *Qoheleth: A Commentary*. Translated by O. C. Dean Jr. Edited by Klaus Baltzer. Hermeneia. Minneapolis: Fortress Press, 2004.

Kudlien, Fridolf. "Zur sozialen Situation des flüchtigen Sklaven in der Antike." *Hermes* 116 (1988): 232–52.

Kümmel, Werner Georg. *Römer 7 und die Bekehrung des Paulus*. WUNT 17. Leipzig: Hinrichs, 1929. References are to the reprint in *Römer 7 und das Bild des Menschen im Neuen Testament: Zwei Studien*. TB 53. Munich: C. Kaiser, 1974.

Lamb, W. R. M. *Lysis; Symposium; Gorgias/Plato*. LCL. Cambridge, Mass.: Harvard University Press, 1983.

Lambrecht, Jan. *The Wretched "I" and Its Liberation: Paul in Romans 7 and 8*. Louvain Theological and Pastoral Monographs 14. Louvain: Peeters, 1992.

Lampe, Peter. "Der Brief an Philemon." Pages 203–32 in *Die Briefe an die Philipper, Thessalonicher und an Philemon*. Edited by Nikolaus Walter, Eckart Reinmuth, and Peter Lampe. Das Neue Testament Deutsch 8/2. 18th ed. Göttingen: Vandenhoeck & Ruprecht, 1998.

———. "Keine 'Sklavenflucht' des Onesimus." *ZNW* 76 (1985): 135–37.

Landry David, and Ben May. "Honor Restored: New Light on the Parable of the Prudent Steward (Luke 16:1-8a)." *JBL* 119 (2000): 287–309.

Lane Fox, Robin. *Pagans and Christians*. New York: Alfred A. Knopf, 1987.

Larson, Jennifer. "Paul's Masculinity." *JBL* 123 (2004): 99–135.

Lateiner, Donald. "Blushes and Pallor in Ancient Fictions." *Helios* 25 (1998): 163–89.

———. *Sardonic Smile: Nonverbal Behavior in Homeric Epic*. Ann Arbor: University of Michigan Press, 1995.

Layton, Bentley. "The Sources, Date, and Transmission of *Didache* 1.3b–2.1." *HTR* 61 (1968): 343–83.

Leach, Eleanor Winsor. "Ergasilus and the Ironies of the Captivi." *Classica et Mediaevalia* 30 (1969): 263–96.

Leigh, Matthew. *Comedy and the Rise of Rome*. New York: Oxford University Press, 2004.

Lendon, J. E. *Empire of Honour: The Art of Government in the Roman World*. Oxford: Clarendon, 1997.

Leo, Gottlob Eduard. *Pauli epistola prima ad Timotheum graece: Cum commentario perpetuo*. Leipzig: Ch. G. Kayser, 1837.

Lévi-Strauss, Claude. *Totemism.* Translated by Rodney Needham. Boston: Beacon Press, 1963.

Leyden, W. von. *Aristotle on Equality and Justice: His Political Argument.* New York: St. Martin's Press, 1985.

Lichtenberger, Hermann. *Das Ich Adams und das Ich der Menschheit: Studien zum Menschenbild in Römer 7.* WUNT 164. Tübingen: Mohr (Siebeck), 2004.

Lieu, Judith M. *Image and Reality: The Jews in the World of the Christians in the Second Century.* Edinburgh: T. & T. Clark, 1996.

———. *Neither Jew nor Greek? Constructing Early Christianity.* Edinburgh: T. & T. Clark, 2002.

Lincoln, Andrew T. *Ephesians.* WBC 42. Dallas: Word Books, 1982.

———. "The Household Code and Wisdom Mode of Colossians." *JSNT* 74 (1999): 93–112.

Lindsay, Wallace M., ed. *Sexti Pompei Festi. De verborum significatu quae supersunt cum Pauli epitome.* Bibliotheca scriptorum Graecorum et Romanorum Teubneriana. 1913. Reprint, Hildesheim: Georg Olms, 1965.

Lipsius, R. A., and M. Bonnet. *Acta Apostolorum Apocrypha.* 2 pts. in 3 vols. 1898. Reprint, Darmstadt: Wissenschaftliche Buchgesellschaft, 1959.

Lissarrague, François. "The Sexual Life of Satyrs." Pages 53–81 in *Before Sexuality: The Construction of the Erotic Experience in the Ancient Greek World.* Edited by David M. Halperin, John J. Winkler, and Froma I. Zeitlin. Princeton, N.J.: Princeton University Press, 1990.

Llewelyn, S. R. "Slaves and Masters." *NewDocs* 6 (1992): 48–81.

Lloyd, G. E. R. *Science, Folklore and Ideology: Studies in the Life Sciences in Ancient Greece.* Cambridge: Cambridge University Press, 1983.

Lock, Walter. *A Critical and Exegetical Commentary on the Pastoral Epistles.* New York: Charles Scribner's Sons, 1924.

Lofberg, J. O. "The Sycophant-Parasite." *CP* 15 (1920): 61–72.

Löhr, Winrich A. "Der Brief der Gemeinden von Lyon und Vienne (Eusebius, h.e. V, 1–2 (4))." Pages 135–49 in *Oecumenica et Patristica: Festschrift für Wilhelm Schneemelcher zum 75. Geburtstag.* Edited by Damaskinos Papandreou, Wolfgang A. Bienert, and Knut Schäferdiek. Stuttgart: W. Kohlhammer, 1989.

Lohse, Eduard. *Colossians and Philemon: A Commentary on the Epistles to the Colossians and to Philemon.* Translated by William R. Poehlmann and Robert J. Karris. Edited by Helmut Koester. Hermeneia. Philadelphia: Fortress Press, 1971.

Long, A. A. *Epictetus: A Stoic and Socratic Guide to Life.* Oxford: Clarendon, 2002.

———. "Representation and the Self in Stoicism." Pages 102–20 in *Companions to Ancient Thought.* Vol. 2: *Psychology.* Edited by Stephen Everson. Cambridge: Cambridge University Press, 1991.

Long, Pamela O. *Openness, Secrecy, Authorship: Technical Arts and the Culture of*

Knowledge from Antiquity to the Renaissance. Baltimore: Johns Hopkins University Press, 2001.

Longstreet, Augustus Baldwin. *Letters on the Epistle of Paul to Philemon.* Charleston, S.C.: B. Jenkins, 1845.

Lowe, J. C. B. "Plautus' Parasites and the Atellana." Pages 161–69 in *Studien zur vorliterarischen Periode im frühen Rom.* Edited by Gregor Vogt-Spira. Script-Oralia 12. Tübingen: Gunter Narr, 1989.

———. "Terence, *Adelphoe*: Problems of Dramatic Space and Time." *CQ* 48 (1998): 470–86.

———. "The *Virgo Callida* of Plautus' *Persa.*" *CQ* 39 (1989): 390–99.

Lüdemann, Gerd. *Early Christianity according to the Traditions in Acts: A Commentary.* Translated by John Bowden. Minneapolis: Fortress Press, 1989.

———. *Opposition to Paul in Jewish Christianity.* Translated by M. Eugene Boring. Minneapolis: Fortress Press, 1989.

MacDonald, Margaret Y. *Colossians and Ephesians.* SP 17. Collegeville, Minn.: Liturgical Press, 2000.

MacDowell, Douglas M. *The Law in Classical Athens.* Ithaca, N.Y.: Cornell University Press, 1978.

———. "Piso's Face." *Classical Review,* n.s. 14 (1964): 9–10.

MacKendrick, Paul. *The Speeches of Cicero: Context, Law, Rhetoric.* London: Duckworth, 1995.

MacMullen, Ramsay. *Enemies of the Roman Order: Treason, Unrest, and Alienation in the Empire.* Cambridge, Mass.: Harvard University Press, 1996.

———. "Judicial Savagery in the Roman Empire." Pages 204–17 in idem, *Changes in the Roman Empire: Essays in the Ordinary.* Princeton, N.J.: Princeton University Press, 1990.

Malherbe, Abraham J. *The Letters to the Thessalonians.* AB 32B. New York: Doubleday, 2000.

———. *Moral Exhortation: A Greco-Roman Sourcebook.* Library of Early Christianity. Philadelphia: Westminster, 1986.

———. *Paul and the Popular Philosophers.* Philadelphia: Fortress Press, 1989.

Manetti, Giovanni. *Theories of the Sign in Classical Antiquity.* Translated by Christine Richardson. Advances in Semiotics. Bloomington: Indiana University Press, 1993.

Manning, C. E. "Stoicism and Slavery in the Roman Empire." *ANRW* 2.36.3 (1989): 1518–43.

Marincola, John. *Authority and Tradition in Ancient Historiography.* Cambridge: Cambridge University Press, 1997.

Marsden, George M. "Everyone One's Own Interpreter? The Bible, Science, and Authority in Mid-Nineteenth-Century America." Pages 79–100 in *The Bible in America: Essays in Cultural History.* Edited by Nathan O. Hatch and Mark A. Noll. New York: Oxford University Press, 1982.

Marshall, I. Howard. *The Gospel of Luke: A Commentary on the Greek Text.* NICNT. Exeter: Paternoster, 1978.

Marshall, Peter. *Enmity in Corinth: Social Conventions in Paul's Relations with the Corinthians.* WUNT 2/23. Tübingen: Mohr (Siebeck), 1987.

———. "Invective: Paul and His Enemies in Corinth." Pages 359–73 in *Perspectives on Language and Text: Essays and Poems in Honor of Francis I. Andersen's Sixtieth Birthday.* Edited by Edgar W. Conrad and Edward G. Newing. Winona Lake, Ind.: Eisenbrauns, 1987.

Martin, Clarice J. "The Haustafeln (Household Codes) in African American Biblical Interpretation: 'Free Slaves' and 'Subordinate Women.'" Pages 206–31 in *Stony the Road We Trod.* Edited by Cain Hope Felder. Minneapolis: Fortress Press, 1991.

———. "The Rhetorical Function of Commercial Language in Paul's Letter to Philemon (Verse 18)." Pages 321–37 in *Persuasive Artistry: Studies in New Testament Rhetoric in Honor of George A. Kennedy.* Edited by Duane F. Watson. JSNTSup 50. Sheffield: Sheffield Academic Press, 1991.

Martin, Dale B. "*Arsenokoitēs* and *Malakos*: Meanings and Consequences." Pages 117–36 in *Biblical Ethics and Homosexuality: Listening to Scripture.* Edited by Robert L. Brawley. Louisville: Westminster John Knox, 1996.

———. *The Corinthian Body.* New Haven: Yale University Press, 1995.

———. *Inventing Superstition: From the Hippocratics to the Christians.* Cambridge, Mass.: Harvard University Press, 2004.

———. *Slavery as Salvation: The Metaphor of Slavery in Pauline Christianity.* New Haven: Yale University Press, 1990.

Martin, Luther H. "The Anti-individualistic Ideology of Hellenistic Culture." *Numen* 41 (1994): 117–41.

Martin, Ralph P. *2 Corinthians.* WBC 40. Waco, Tex.: Word Books, 1986.

Martin, René. "État présent des études sur Columelle." *ANRW* 2.32.3 (1985): 1959–79.

Martin, Waldo E., Jr. *The Mind of Frederick Douglass.* Chapel Hill: University of North Carolina Press, 1984.

Martyn, J. Louis. "A Formula for Communal Discord as a Clue to the Nature of Pastoral Guidance." Pages 203–16 in *Putting Body and Soul Together: Essays in Honor of Robin Scroggs.* Edited by Virginia Wiles, Alexandra Brown, and Graydon F. Snyder. Valley Forge, Pa.: Trinity Press International, 1997.

Maslakov, G. "Valerius Maximus and Roman Historiography: A Study of the *exempla* Tradition." *ANRW* 2.32.1 (1984): 437–96.

Massaux, Édouard. *The Influence of the Gospel of Saint Matthew on Christian Literature before Saint Irenaeus.* Vol. 2: *The Later Christian Writings.* New Gospel Studies 5.2. Macon, Ga.: Mercer University Press, 1992.

Mastrorosa, Ida, Antonino Zumbo, and Carlo Santini, eds. *Letteratura scienti-*

fica e tecnica di Grecia e Roma. Studi superiori 401. Lettere classiche. Rome: Carocci, 2002.

May, Henry F. *The Enlightenment in America.* New York: Oxford University Press, 1976.

May, Margaret Tallmadge, trans. *Galen: On the Usefulness of the Parts of the Body.* 2 vols. Ithaca, N.Y.: Cornell University Press, 1968.

Mayer, Henry. *All on Fire: William Lloyd Garrison and the Abolition of Slavery.* New York: St. Martin's, 1998.

McCarthy, Kathleen. "Servitium Amoris: Amor Servitii." Pages 174–92 in Murnaghan and Joshel, *Women and Slaves.*

————. *Slaves, Masters, and the Art of Authority in Plautine Comedy.* Princeton, N.J.: Princeton University Press, 2000.

McEleney, Neil J. "The Vice Lists of the Pastoral Epistles." *CBQ* 36 (1974): 203–19.

McGinn, Thomas A. J. *Prostitution, Sexuality, and the Law in Ancient Rome.* New York: Oxford University Press, 1998.

McGowan, Andrew. "Eating People: Accusations of Cannibalism against Christians in the Second Century." *JECS* 2 (1994): 413–42.

McKivigan, John R. *The War against Proslavery Religion: Abolitionism and the Northern Churches, 1830–1865.* Ithaca, N.Y.: Cornell University Press, 1984.

McKivigan, John R., and Mitchell Snay, eds. *Religion and the Antebellum Debate over Slavery.* Athens: University of Georgia Press, 1998.

Meeks, Wayne A. "The Christian Proteus." Pages 435–44 in idem, *The Writings of St. Paul.* Norton Criticial Editions. New York: W. W. Norton, 1972.

————. "Corinthian Christians as Artificial Aliens." Pages 129–38 in Engberg-Pedersen, *Paul beyond the Judaism/Hellenism Divide.*

————. *The First Urban Christians: The Social World of the Apostle Paul.* 2d ed. New Haven: Yale University Press, 2003.

————. "The 'Haustafeln' and American Slavery: A Hermeneutical Challenge." Pages 232–53 in *Theology and Ethics in Paul and His Interpreters: Essays in Honor of Victor Paul Furnish.* Edited by Eugene H. Lovering Jr. and Jerry L. Sumney. Nashville: Abingdon, 1996.

————. "The Image of the Androgyne: Some Uses of a Symbol in Earliest Christianity." Pages 3–54 in idem, *In Search of the Early Christians.*

————. *In Search of the Early Christians: Selected Essays.* Edited by Allen R. Hilton and H. Gregory Snyder. New Haven: Yale University Press, 2002.

————. "Judaism, Hellenism, and the Birth of Christianity." Pages 16–27 in Engberg-Pedersen, *Paul beyond the Judaism/Hellenism Divide.*

————. "The Polyphonic Ethics of the Apostle Paul." Pages 196–209 in idem, *In Search of the Early Christians.*

———. "Responses to Stump." Pages 71–74 in Stump and Flint, *Hermes and Athena.*

———. "'To Walk Worthily of the Lord': Moral Formation in the Pauline School Exemplified by the Letter to Colossians." Pages 37–58 in Stump and Flint, *Hermes and Athena.*

———. "Why Study the New Testament?" *NTS* 51 (2005): 155–70.

Meeks, Wayne A., and Robert L. Wilken. *Jews and Christians in Antioch in the First Four Centuries of the Common Era.* SBLSBS 13. Missoula, Mont.: Scholars Press, 1978.

Meißner, Burkhard. *Die technologische Fachliteratur der Antike: Struktur, Überlieferung und Wirkung technischen Wissens in der Antike.* Berlin: Akademie Verlag, 1999.

Meredith, Thomas. *Christianity and Slavery.* Boston: Gould, Kendall, and Lincoln, 1847.

Merk, Otto. *Handeln aus Glauben: Die Motivierungen der paulinischen Ethik.* Marburger theologische Studien 5. Marburg: Elwert, 1968.

Mertens, Cées. "Les premiers martyrs et leurs rêves: Cohésion de l'histoire et des rêves dans quelques 'Passions' latines de l'Afrique du nord." *RHE* 81 (1986): 5–46.

Meyer, Marvin W. *The Ancient Mysteries: A Sourcebook of Sacred Texts.* 1987. Reprint, Philadelphia: University of Pennsylvania Press, 1999.

Meyer, Paul W. "The Worm at the Core of the Apple: Exegetical Reflections on Romans 7." Pages 62–84 in *The Conversation Continues: Studies in Paul and John in Honor of J. Louis Martin.* Edited by Robert R. Fortna and Beverly R. Gaventa. Nashville: Abingdon, 1990.

Michel, Otto. *Der Brief an die Römer.* 5th ed. KEK 4. 14th ed. Göttingen: Vandenhoeck & Ruprecht, 1978.

Miller, Fergus. "The World of the Golden Ass." *JRS* 71 (1981): 63–75.

Misener, Geneva. "Iconistic Portraits." *CP* 19 (1924): 97–123.

Mitchell, Laura L. "'Matters of Justice between Man and Man': Northern Divines, the Bible, and the Fugitive Slave Act of 1850." Pages 134–65 in McKivigan and Snay, *Religion and the Antebellum Debate.*

Mitton, C. Leslie. *The Epistle to the Ephesians: Its Authorship, Origin and Purpose.* Oxford: Clarendon, 1951.

Montserrat, Dominic. "Experiencing the Male Body in Roman Egypt." Pages 153–64 in Foxhall and Salmon, *When Men Were Men.*

———. *Sex and Society in Graeco-Roman Egypt.* London: Kegan Paul International, 1996.

Mooney, W. W. *The House-Door on the Ancient Stage.* Baltimore: Williams and Wilkins, 1914.

Moore, James R. "Geologists and Interpreters of Genesis in the Nineteenth

Century." Pages 322–50 in *God and Nature: Historical Essays on the Encounter between Christianity and Science*. Edited by David C. Lindberg and Ronald L. Numbers. Berkeley and Los Angeles: University of California Press, 1986.

Moore, Timothy J. "*Palliata Togata*: Plautus, *Curculio* 462–86." *AJP* 112 (1991): 343–62.

———. *The Theater of Plautus: Playing to the Audience*. Austin: University of Texas Press, 1988.

Morford, Mark. "Juvenal's Fifth Satire." *AJP* 98 (1977): 219–45.

Morgan, Llewelyn. "The Autopsy of C. Asinius Pollio." *JRS* 90 (2000): 51–69.

Morrow, Glenn R. *Plato's Law of Slavery in Its Relation to Greek Law*. Illinois Studies in Language and Literature 25.3. Urbana: University of Illinois Press, 1939.

Moule, C. F. D. *The Epistles of Paul the Apostle to the Colossians and to Philemon*. CGTC. Cambridge: Cambridge University Press, 1958.

Muilenburg, James. *The Literary Relations of the Epistle of Barnabas and the Teaching of the Twelve Apostles*. Ph.D. diss., Yale University. Published in Marburg, 1929.

Mullen, Robert Bruce. "Biblical Critics and the Battle over Slavery." *Journal of Presbyterian History* 61 (1983): 210–26.

Mullin, Gerald W. *Flight and Rebellion: Slave Resistance in Eighteenth-Century Virginia*. New York: Oxford University Press, 1972.

Murnaghan, Sheila, and Sandra R. Joshel, eds. *Women and Slaves in Greco-Roman Culture: Differential Equations*. London: Routledge, 1998.

Musurillo, Herbert, trans. *The Acts of the Christian Martyrs*. OECT. Oxford: Clarendon, 1972.

Natali, Carlo. "*Oikonomia* in Hellenistic Political Thought." Pages 95–128 in *Justice and Generosity: Studies in Hellenistic Social and Political Philosophy. Proceedings of the Sixth Symposium Hellenisticum*. Edited by André Laks and Malcolm Schofield. Cambridge: Cambridge University Press, 1995.

Nautin, Pierre. *Lettres et écrivains chrétiens des IIe et IIIe siècles*. Patristica 2. Paris: Cerf, 1961.

Nesselrath, Heinz-Günther. *Lukians Parasitendialog: Untersuchungen und Kommentar*. Untersuchungen zur antiken Literatur und Geschichte 22. Berlin: Walter de Gruyter, 1985.

Nicholas, Barry. *An Introduction to Roman Law*. Clarendon Law Series. 1962. Reprinted with corrections. Oxford: Clarendon, 1982.

Niederwimmer, Kurt. *The Didache: A Commentary*. Translated by Linda M. Maloney. Edited by Harold W. Attridge. Hermeneia. Minneapolis: Fortress Press, 1998.

Nisbet, R. G. M. *M. Tulli Ciceronis, In L. Calpurnium Pisonem oratio*. Oxford: Clarendon, 1961.

Nixon, Paul. *Works/Titus Maccius Plautus*. 5 vols. LCL. Cambridge, Mass.:

Harvard University Press, 1966–80.

Noll, Mark A. "The Bible and Slavery." Pages 43–73 in *Religion and the American Civil War*. Edited by Randall M. Miller, Harry S. Stout, and Charles Reagan Wilson. New York: Oxford University Press, 1998.

Nolland, John. *Luke 9:21—18:34*. WBC 35B. Dallas: Word Books, 1993.

Norlin, George. *Works/Isocrates*. 3 vols. LCL. Cambridge, Mass.: Harvard University Press, 1982–91.

Nordling, John G. "Onesimus Fugitivus. A Defense of the Runway Slave Hypothesis in Philemon." *JSNT* 41 (1991): 97–119.

Novick, Peter. *That Noble Dream: The "Objectivity Question" and the American Historical Profession*. Ideas in Context. Cambridge: Cambridge University Press, 1988.

Oakes, James. *The Ruling Race: A History of American Slaveholders*. New York: Vintage Books, 1983.

O'Brien, Peter T. *Colossians, Philemon*. WBC 44. Waco, Tex.: Word Books, 1982.

Olson, S. Douglas. "Names and Naming in Aristophanic Comedy." *CQ* 42 (1992): 304–19.

Origo, Iris. "The Domestic Enemy: The Eastern Slaves in Tuscany in the Fourteenth and Fifteenth Centuries." *Speculum* 30 (1955): 321–66.

Osiek, Carolyn. *The Shepherd of Hermas*. Edited by Helmut Koester. Hermeneia. Minneapolis: Fortress Press, 1999.

Osiek, Carolyn, and David L. Balch. *Families in the New Testament World: Households and House Churches*. The Family, Religion, and Culture. Louisville: Westminster John Knox, 1997.

Owen, Christopher H. "'To Keep the Way Open for Methodism': Georgia Wesleyan Neutrality toward Slavery, 1844–1861." Pages 109–33 in McKivigan and Snay, *Religion and the Antebellum Debate*.

Paget, James Carleton. *The Epistle of Barnabas: Outlook and Background*. WUNT 2/64; Tübingen: Mohr (Siebeck), 1994.

Panayotakis, Costas. *Theatrum Arbitri: Theatrical Elements in the Satyrica of Petronius*. Mnemosyne Suppl. 146. Leiden: Brill, 1995.

Parker, Holt. "Crucially Funny or Tranio on the Couch: The *Servus Callidus* and Jokes about Torture." *TAPA* 119 (1989): 233–46.

———. "Love's Body Anatomized: The Ancient Erotic Handbooks and the Rhetoric of Sexuality." Pages 90–111 in *Pornography and Representation in Greece and Rome*. Edited by Amy Richlin. New York: Oxford University Press, 1992.

———. "Loyal Slaves and Loyal Wives: The Crisis of the Outsider-within and Roman *exemplum* Literature." Pages 152–73 in Murnaghan and Joshel, *Women and Slaves*.

Patillon Michel, with Giancarlo Bolognesi, eds. *Aelius Théon: Progymnasmata*. Budé Series. Paris: Les Belles Lettres, 1997.

Patterson, Orlando. *Slavery and Social Death: A Comparative Study*. Cambridge, Mass.: Harvard University Press, 1982.

Paulding, J. K. *Slavery in the United States.* New York: Harper and Bros., 1836.

Pearson, Brook W. R. "Assumptions in the Criticism and Translation of Philemon." Pages 253–80 in *Translating the Bible: Problems and Prospects.* Edited by Stanley E. Porter and Richard S. Hess. JSNTSup 173. Sheffield: Sheffield Academic Press, 1999.

Penella, Robert J. *The Letters of Apollonius of Tyana: A Critical Text with Prolegomena, Translation and Commentary.* Mnemosyne Suppl. 56. Leiden: Brill, 1979.

Penwill, J. L. "Slavish Pleasures and Profitless Curiosity: Fall and Redemption in Apuleius' Metamorphoses." *Ramus* 4 (1975): 49–82.

Perkins, Judith B. "The Passion of Perpetua: A Narrative of Empowerment." *Latomus* 53 (1994): 837–47.

———. *The Suffering Self: Pain and Narrative Representation in the Early Christian Era.* London: Routledge, 1995.

Perry, Lewis. *Radical Abolitionism: Anarchy and the Government of God in Antislavery Thought.* Ithaca, N.Y.: Cornell University Press, 1973.

Pervo, Richard I. *Profit with Delight: The Literary Genre of the Acts of the Apostles.* Philadelphia: Fortress Press, 1987.

Petersen, Norman. *Rediscovering Paul: Philemon and the Sociology of Paul's Narrative World.* Philadelphia: Fortress Press, 1985.

Petersmann, Hubert. "Zu einem altrömischen Opferritual (Cato de agricultura c. 141)." *Rheinisches Museum für Philologie* 116 (1973): 238–55.

Petzke, G. *Die Traditionen über Apollonius von Tyana und das Neue Testament.* SCHNT 1. Leiden: Brill, 1970.

Pickard-Cambridge, Arthur. *The Dramatic Festivals of Athens.* 2d ed. Revised by John Gould and D. M. Lewis. Oxford: Clarendon, 1968.

Pingree, David, ed. *Vettii Valentis Antiocheni anthologiarum libri novem.* Leipzig: Teubner, 1986.

Plessner, Martin. *Der Oikonomikos des Neupythagoreers "Bryson" und sein Einfluß auf die islamische Wissenschaft.* Orient und Antike 5. Heidelberg: Carl Winter, 1928.

Plummer, Alfred. *A Critical and Exegetical Commentary on the Gospel according to S. Luke.* 5th ed. ICC. Edinburgh: T. & T. Clark, 1922.

———. *A Critical and Exegetical Commentary on the Second Epistle of St. Paul to the Corinthians.* ICC. New York: Charles Scribner's Sons, 1915.

Pomeroy, Sarah B. *Xenophon, Oeconomicus: A Social and Historical Commentary.* Oxford: Clarendon, 1994.

Potter, David. "Martyrdom as Spectacle." Pages 53–88 in Scodel, *Theater and Society.*

Prostmeier, Ferdinand R. *Der Barnabasbrief.* KEK 8. Göttingen: Vandenhoeck & Ruprecht, 1999.

Purcell, N. "Wine and Wealth in Ancient Italy." *JRS* 75 (1985): 1–19.

Raboteau, Albert J. *Slave Religion: The "Invisible Institution" in the Antebellum South.* New York: Oxford University Press, 1978.

Rackham, H. *Politics/Aristotle*. LCL. Cambridge, Mass.: Harvard University Press, 1990.

Radl, Walter. "Befreiung aus dem Gefängnis: Die Darstellung eines biblischen Grundthemas in Apg 12." *BZ* 27 (1983): 81–96.

Rajak, Tessa. "Dying for the Law: The Martyr's Portrait in Jewish-Greek Literature." Pages 39–67 in *Portraits: Biographical Representation in the Greek and Latin Literature of the Roman Empire*. Edited by M. J. Edwards and Simon Swain. Oxford: Clarendon, 1997.

Rahlfs, Alfred, ed. *Septuaginta: Id est, Vetus Testamentum graece iuxta LXX interpretes*. 1935. 2 vols. in 1. Reprint, Stuttgart: Deutsche Bibelgesellschaft, 1979.

Ramsaran, Rollin A. "Paul and Maxims." Pages 429–56 in Sampley, *Paul in the Greco-Roman World*.

Ramsay, G. G. *Works/Juvenal and Persius*. LCL. Cambridge, Mass.: Harvard University Press, 1990.

Ramsay, W. M. *The Bearing of Recent Discovery on the Trustworthiness of the New Testament*. London: Hodder and Stoughton, 1920.

Rankin, H. D. *Anthisthenes Sokratikos*. Amsterdam: Adolf M. Hakkert, 1986.

Rapske, Brian M. *The Book of Acts and Paul in Roman Custody*. Vol. 3 of *The Book of Acts in Its First Century Setting*. Edited by Bruce W. Winter. Grand Rapids, Mich.: Eerdmans; Carlisle: Paternoster Press, 1994.

———. "The Prisoner Paul in the Eyes of Onesimus." *NTS* 37 (1991): 187–203.

Rauh, Nicholas K. *The Sacred Bonds of Commerce: Religion, Economy, and Trade Society at Hellenistic Roman Delos*. Amsterdam: J. C. Gieben, 1993.

Rawski, Conrad H. *Petrarch's Remedies for Fortune Fair and Foul*. 5 vols. Bloomington: Indiana University Press, 1991.

Rawson, Elizabeth. "Freedmen in Roman Comedy." Pages 215–33 in Scodel, *Theater and Society*.

———. *Intellectual Life in the Late Roman Republic*. Baltimore: Johns Hopkins University Press, 1985.

Rea, John. "A Student's Letter to his Father: P.Oxy. XVIII 2190 Revised." *ZPE* 99 (1993): 75–88.

Rei, Annalisa. "Villains, Wives, and Slaves in the Comedies of Platutus." Pages 92–108 in Murnaghan and Joshel, *Women and Slaves*.

Reimer, Ivoni Richter. *Women in the Acts of the Apostles: A Feminist Liberation Perspective*. Translated by Linda M. Maloney. Minneapolis: Fortress Press, 1995.

Rice, N. L. *Lectures on Slavery; Delivered in the North Presbyterian Church, Chicago*. Chicago: Church, Goodman and Cushing, 1860.

Richlin, Amy. "Cicero's Head." Pages 190–211 in *Constructions of the Classical Body*. Edited by James I. Porter. The Body, in Theory: Histories of Cultural Materialism. Ann Arbor: University of Michigan Press, 1999.

Ripley, C. Peter, ed. *The Black Abolitionist Papers*. 5 vols. Chapel Hill: University of North Carolina Press, 1985–92.

Robinson, Armitage. "The Epistle of Barnabas and the Didache." *JTS* 35 (1934): 113–46.

Robinson, Olivia. "Slaves and the Criminal Law." *Zeitschrift der Savigny-Stiftung für Rechtsgeschichte (romanistische Abteilung)* 98 (1981): 213–54.

Roetzel, Calvin J. *Paul: The Man and the Myth.* Columbia: University of South Carolina Press, 1998; Minneapolis: Fortress Press, 1999.

Rorty, Amélie Oksenberg. "Persons and *Personae.*" Pages 1–36 in Gill, *Person and the Human Mind.*

Rosen, F. "The Political Context of Aristotle's Categories of Justice." *Phronesis* 20 (1975): 228–40.

Rosen, Stanley. *Plato's "Statesman": The Web of Politics.* New Haven: Yale University Press, 1995.

Rosivach, Vincent J. "Enslaving *Barbaroi* and the Athenian Ideology of Slavery." *Historia* 48 (1999): 129–57.

Ross, Fred A. *Slavery Ordained of God.* Philadelphia: J. B. Lippincott, 1857.

Rougé, Jean, and Robert Turcan, eds. *Les martyrs de Lyon (177): Lyon 20–23 septembre 1977.* Colloques internationaux du Centre national de la recheche scientifique 575. Paris: Centre national de la recheche scientifique, 1978.

Ruffner, William H. *Lectures on the Evidences of Christianity.* New York: Robert Carter and Bros., 1853.

Rusten, Jeffrey Stuart. "Aesop." *OCD,* 29.

Saillant, John. "Origins of African American Biblical Hermeneutics in Eighteenth-Century Black Opposition to the Slave Trade and Slavery." Pages 236–50 in Wimbush, *African Americans and the Bible.*

Saller, Richard P. "The Family and Society." Pages 95–117 in *Epigraphic Evidence: Ancient History from Inscriptions.* Edited by John Bodel. Approaching the Ancient World. London: Routledge, 2001.

———. "Pater Familias, Mater Familias, and the Gendered Semantics of the Roman Household." *CP* 94 (1999): 182–97.

———. *Patriarchy, Property and Death in the Roman Family.* Cambridge Studies in Population, Economy and Society in Past Time 25. Cambridge: Cambridge University Press, 1994.

———. "Slavery and the Roman Family." Pages 65–87 in Finley, *Classical Slavery.*

———. "Symbols of Gender and Status Hierarchies in the Roman Household." Pages 85–91 in Murnaghan and Joshel, *Women and Slaves.*

Sampley, J. Paul, ed. *Paul in the Greco-Roman World: A Handbook.* Harrisburg, Pa.: Trinity Press International, 2003.

Sandeen, Ernest R. *The Roots of Fundamentalism: British and American Millenarianism, 1800–1930.* Chicago: University of Chicago Press, 1970.

Sanders, E. P. *The Historical Figure of Jesus.* New York: Penguin, 1993.

Sandt, Huub van de, and David Flusser. *The Didache: Its Jewish Sources and Its Place in Early Judaism and Christianity.* CRINT 3/5. Assen: Royal Van

Gorcum; Minneapolis: Fortress Press, 2002.

Sandy, Gerald N. "Serviles Voluptates in Apuleius' Metamorphoses." *Phoenix* 28 (1974): 234–44.

Sargeaunt, John. *Works/Terence.* 2 vols. LCL. Cambridge, Mass.: Harvard University Press, 1986.

Sassi, Maria Michela. *The Science of Man in Ancient Greece.* Translated by Paul Tucker. Chicago: University of Chicago Press, 2001.

Saunders, Trevor J., ed. *Politics: Books I and II/Aristotle.* Clarendon Aristotle Series. Oxford: Clarendon, 1995.

Savage, Timothy B. *Power through Weakness: Paul's Understanding of the Christian Ministry in 2 Corinthians.* SNTSMS 86. Cambridge: Cambridge University Press, 1996.

Schaff, Philip. *Slavery and the Bible: A Tract for the Times.* Chambersburg, Pa.: M. Kieffer, 1861.

Scheidel, Walter. "Finances, Figures and Fiction." *CQ* 46 (1996): 222–38.

———. "Free-born and Manumitted Bailiffs in the Graeco-Roman World." *CQ* 40 (1990): 591–93.

Scherer, Lester B. *Slavery and the Churches in Early America, 1619–1819.* Grand Rapids, Mich.: Eerdmans, 1975.

Schlecht, Joseph. *Doctrina XII Apostolorum: Die Apostellehre in der Liturgie der Katholischen Kirche.* Freiburg: Herder, 1901.

Schmithals, Walter. *Gnosticism in Corinth: An Investigation of the Letters to the Corinthians.* Translated by John E. Steely. Nashville: Abingdon, 1971.

Schneider, André. "Notes critiques sur Tertullian, *Ad Nationes* I." *Museum Helveticum* 19 (1962): 180–89.

Schoedel, William R., ed. *Athenagoras: Legatio and De Resurrectione.* OECT. Oxford: Clarendon, 1972.

Schüssler Fiorenza, Elisabeth. *In Memory of Her: A Feminist Theological Reconstruction of Christian Origins.* New York: Crossroad, 1987.

Schütz, John Howard. *Paul and the Anatomy of Apostolic Authority.* SNTSMS 26. Cambridge: Cambridge University Press, 1975.

Schweiger, Beth Barton. "The Restructuring of Southern Religion: Slavery, Denominations, and the Clerical Profession in Virginia." Pages 296–316 in McKivigan and Snay, *Religion and the Antebellum Debate.*

Schweizer, E. "Traditional Ethical Patterns in the Pauline and Post-Pauline Letters and Their Development (Lists of Vices and House-Tables)." Pages 195–209 in *Text and Interpretation: Studies in the New Testament Presented to Matthew Black.* Edited by Ernest Best and R. McL. Wilson. Cambridge: Cambridge University Press, 1979.

Scobie, Alexander. *Aspects of the Ancient Romance and Its Heritage: Essays on Apuleius, Petronius, and the Greek Romances.* Beiträge zur klassischen Philologie 30. Meisenheim am Glan: Anton Hain, 1969.

Scodel, Ruth. "The Removal of the Arms, the Recognition with Laertes, and

Narrative Tension in the *Odyssey.*" *CP* 93 (1998): 1–18.

————, ed. *Theater and Society in the Classical World.* Ann Arbor: University of Michigan Press, 1993.

Scott, James C. *Domination and the Arts of Resistance: Hidden Transcripts.* New Haven: Yale University Press, 1990.

Segal, Erich. *Roman Laughter: The Comedy of Plautus.* Harvard Studies in Comparative Literature 29. Cambridge, Mass.: Harvard University Press, 1968.

Sellew, Philip. "Interior Monologue as a Narrative Device in the Parables of Luke." *JBL* 111 (1992): 239–53.

Sernett, Milton C. *Black Religion and American Evangelicalism: White Protestants, Plantation Missions, and the Flowering of Negro Christianity, 1787–1865.* ATLA Monograph Series 7. Metuchen, N.J.: Scarecrow Press and ATLA, 1975.

Sevenster, J. N. *Paul and Seneca.* NovTSup 4. Leiden: Brill, 1961.

Shanks, Caroline L. "The Biblical Anti-Slavery Argument of the Decade 1830–1840." *Journal of Negro History* 16 (1931): 132–57.

Shannon, James. *An Address Delivered before the Pro-Slavery Convention of the State of Missouri.* St. Louis: Republican Book and Job Office, 1855.

Shaw, Brent D. "The Bandit." Pages 300–341 in Giardina, *The Romans.*

————. "Body/Power/Identity: Passions of the Martyrs." *JECS* 4 (1996): 296–312.

————. "The Divine Economy: Stoicism as Ideology." *Latomus* 44 (1985): 16–54.

Shelton, Jo-Ann. *As the Romans Did: A Sourcebook in Roman Social History.* 2d ed. New York: Oxford University Press, 1998.

Sher, Richard B. *Church and University in the Scottish Enlightenment: The Moderate Literati of Edinburgh.* Princeton, N.J.: Princeton University Press, 1985.

Sher, Richard B., and Jeffrey R. Smitten, eds. *Scotland and America in the Age of Enlightenment.* Princeton, N.J.: Princeton University Press, 1990.

Simpson, Peter L. Phillips. *A Philosophical Commentary on the Politics of Aristotle.* Chapel Hill: University of North Carolina Press, 1998.

Skidmore, Clive. *Practical Ethics for Roman Gentlemen: The Work of Valerius Maximus.* Exeter: University of Exeter Press, 1996.

Skydsgaard, Jens Erik. *Varro the Scholar: Studies in the First Book of Varro's De Re Rustica.* Analecta Romana Instituti Danici Suppl. 4. Copenhagen: Munksgaard, 1968.

Slater, Niall W. *Plautus in Performance: The Theatre of the Mind.* 2d ed. Greek and Roman Theatre Archive. Amsterdam: Harwood Academic Publishers, 2000.

Sloan, Douglas. *The Scottish Enlightenment and the American College Ideal.* New York: Teachers College, Columbia University, 1971.

Sloan, James A. *The Great Question Answered; or, Is Slavery a Sin in Itself?* Memphis, Tenn.: Hutton, Gallaway, 1857.

Smith, Nicholas D. "Aristotle's Theory of Natural Slavery." Pages 142–55 in *A Companion to Aristotle's Politics.* Edited by David Keyt and Fred D. Miller Jr. Oxford: Blackwell, 1990.

Smith, Theophus H. *Conjuring Culture: Biblical Formations of Black America.* New York: Oxford University Press, 1994.

Smyth, Thomas, gen. ed. *The Christian Doctrine of Human Rights and of Slavery: In Two Articles, from the Southern Presbyterian Review for March, 1849.* Columbia, S.C.: I. C. Morgan, 1849.

Snay, Mitchell. *Gospel of Disunion: Religion and Separatism in the Antebellum South.* Cambridge: Cambridge University Press, 1993.

Soderlund, Jean R. *Quakers and Slavery: A Divided Spirit.* Princeton, N.J.: Princeton University Press, 1985.

Southern Baptist Convention. "The Baptist Faith and Message." Retrieved 24 May 2005, from the official Web site of the Southern Baptist Convention. http://www.sbc.net/bfm/bfm2000.asp.

———. "Resolution on Racial Reconciliation on the 150th Anniversary of The Southern Baptist Convention: June 1995." Retrieved 24 May 2005, from the official Web site of the Southern Baptist Convention. http://www.sbc.net/resolutions/amResolution.asp?ID=899.

Spicq, C. "Le vocabulaire de l'esclavage dans le Nouveau Testament." *RB* 85 (1978): 201–26.

Spranger, Peter P. *Historische Untersuchungen zur den Sklavenfiguren des Plautus und Terenz.* 2d ed. Forschungen zur antiken Sklaverei 17. Stuttgart: Franz Steiner, 1984.

Spurr, M. Stephen. "Columella, Lucius Iunius Moderatus." *OCD,* 367.

Stahl, William H. *Roman Science: Origins, Development, and Influence to the Later Middle Ages.* Madison: University of Wisconsin Press, 1962.

Standhartinger, Angela. "The Origin and Intention of the Household Code in the Letter to the Colossians." *JSNT* 79 (2000): 117–30.

———. *Studien zur Entstehungsgeschichte und Intention des Kolosserbriefs.* NovTSup 94. Leiden: Brill, 1999.

Stendahl, Krister. *Paul among Jews and Gentiles and Other Essays.* Philadelphia: Fortress Press, 1976.

Stewart, James Brewer. "Abolitionists, the Bible, and the Challenge of Slavery." Pages 31–57 in *The Bible and Social Reform.* Edited by Ernest R. Sandeen. The Bible in American Culture. Philadelphia: Fortress Press; Chico, Calif.: Scholars Press, 1982.

Stobaeus. *Ioannis Stobaei Anthologium.* Vol. 4. Edited by Otto Hense. Berlin: Weidmann, 1958.

Stowers, Stanley K. "Apostrophe, *Prosōpopoiia* and Paul's Rhetorical Education." Pages 351–69 in *Early Christianity and Classical Culture: Comparative Studies in Honor of Abraham J. Malherbe.* Edited by John T. Fitzgerald, Thomas H. Olbricht, and L. Michael White. NovTSup 105. Leiden: Brill, 2003.

———. *A Rereading of Romans: Justice, Jews, and Gentiles.* New Haven: Yale University Press, 1994.

———. Review of *Innere Mensch*, by Heckel. *JBL* 114 (1995): 342–44.

———. "Romans 7.7-25 as a Speech-in-Character (*prosōpopoiia*)." Pages 180–202 in *Paul in His Hellenistic Context.* Edited by Troels Engberg-Pedersen. Studies of the New Testament and Its World. Edinburgh: T. & T. Clark, 1994.

Straus, Jean A. "L'esclavage dans l'Égypte romaine." *ANRW* 2.10.1 (1988): 841–911.

Strecker, Georg. "Die neutestamentlichen Haustafeln." Pages 349–75 in *Neues Testament und Ethik für Rudolf Schnackenburg.* Edited by Helmut Merlein. Freiburg: Herder, 1989.

Stringfellow, Thornton. *Scriptural and Statistical Views in Favor of Slavery.* Richmond, Va.: J. W. Randolf, 1856.

Stuart, Moses. *Conscience and the Constitution.* 1850. Reprint, New York: Negro Universities Press, 1969.

Stump, Eleonore, and Thomas P. Flint, eds. *Hermes and Athena: Biblical Exegesis and Philosophical Authority.* University of Notre Dame Studies in the Philosophy of Religion 7. Notre Dame, Ind.: University of Notre Dame Press, 1993.

Suggs, M. J. "The Christian Two Ways Tradition: Its Antiquity, Form, and Function." Pages 60–74 in *Studies in New Testament and Early Christian Literature: Essays in Honor of Allen P. Wikgren.* Edited by David E. Aune. NovTSup 33. Leiden: Brill, 1972.

Sunderland, La Roy. *The Testimony of God against Slavery.* 1835. Reprint, St. Clair Shores, Mich.: Scholarly Press, 1970.

Süss, Wilhelm. *Ethos: Studien zur älteren griechischen Rhetorik.* Leipzig and Berlin: Teubner, 1910.

Swartley, Willard M. *Slavery, Sabbath, War, and Women: Case Issues in Biblical Interpretation.* Scottdale, Pa., and Waterloo, Ont.: Herald Press, 1983.

Synodinou, Ekaterini. "On the Concept of Slavery in Euripides." Ph.D. diss., University of Cincinnati, 1974.

Tadman, Michael. *Speculators and Slaves: Masters, Traders, and Slaves in the Old South.* Madison: University of Wisconsin Press, 1989.

TeSelle, Eugene. "Exploring the Inner Conflict: Augustine's Sermons on Romans 7 and 8." Pages 111–46 in *Engaging Augustine on Romans: Self, Context, and Theology in Interpretation.* Edited by Daniel Patte and Eugene TeSelle. Romans through History and Cultures. Harrisburg, Pa.: Trinity Press International, 2002.

Thalmann, William G. "Versions of Slavery in the Captivi of Plautus." *Ramus* 25 (1996): 112–45.

Theissen, Gerd. *Psychological Aspects of Pauline Theology.* Translated by John P. Calvin. Philadelphia: Fortress Press, 1987.

Thesleff, Holger. *The Pythagorean Texts of the Hellenistic Period.* Acta Academiae Aboensis A. Humaniora 30.1. Åbo: Åbo Akademi, 1965.

Thomas, Garth. "La condition sociale de l'église de Lyon en 177." Pages 93–106 in Rougé and Turcan, *Martyrs de Lyon.*

Thomas, J. A. C. *Textbook of Roman Law.* Amsterdam: North-Holland Publishing Co., 1976.

Thompson, J. Earl, Jr. "Abolitionism and Theological Education at Andover." *New England Quarterly* 47 (1974): 238–61.

Thrall, Margaret E. *A Critical and Exegetical Commentary on the Second Epistle to the Corinthians.* 2 vols. ICC. Edinburgh: T. & T. Clark, 1994–2004.

Tise, Larry E. *Proslavery: A History of the Defense of Slavery in America, 1701–1840.* Athens: University of Georgia Press, 1987.

Toohey, Peter. *Epic Lessons: An Introduction to Didactic Poetry.* London: Routledge, 1996.

Topel, L. John. "On the Injustice of the Unjust Steward: Lk 16:1-13." *CBQ* 37 (1975): 216–27.

Treat, Jay Curry. "Barnabas, Epistle to." *ABD,* 1:611–14.

Treggiari, Susan. *Roman Freedmen during the Late Republic.* Oxford: Clarendon, 1969.

Trevett, Jeremy C. "Xenophon (1)." *OCD,* 1628–31.

Tsouna, Voula. "Doubts about Other Minds and the Science of Physiognomics." *CQ* 48 (1998): 175–86.

Turner, James. *Without God, without Creed: The Origins of Unbelief in America.* Baltimore: Johns Hopkins University Press, 1985.

Turpin, William. "The Epicurean Parasite: Horace, Satires 1.1–3." *Ramus* 27 (1998): 127–40.

Tylawsky, Elizabeth Ivory. *Saturio's Inheritance: The Greek Ancestry of the Roman Comic Parasite.* Artists and Issues in the Theatre 9. New York: Peter Lang, 2002.

Van Broekhoven, Deborah Bingham. "Suffering with Slaveholders: The Limits of Francis Wayland's Antislavery Witness." Pages 196–220 in McKivigan and Snay, *Religion and the Antebellum Debate.*

Varo, F. "El lexico del pecado en la Epistola de San Pablo a los Romanos." *Scripta Theologica (Navarra)* 21 (1989): 99–116.

Vasaly, Ann. *Representations: Images of the World in Ciceronian Oratory.* Berkeley and Los Angeles: University of California Press, 1993.

Vegetti, Mario. *Il coltello e lo stilo: Animali, schiavi, barbari e donne alle origini della razionalita scientifica.* 3d ed. Milan: Il saggiatore, 1996.

Verstraete, Beert C. "Slavery and the Social Dynamics of Male Homosexual Relations in Ancient Rome." *Journal of Homosexuality* 5 (1980): 227–36.

Vlastos, Gregory. "Slavery in Plato's Republic." Pages 133–49 in Finley, *Slavery in Classical Antiquity*.

Vogt, Joseph. *Ancient Slavery and the Ideal of Man*. Translated by Thomas Wiedemann. Cambridge, Mass.: Harvard University Press, 1975.

Vokes, F. E. "Life and Order in an Early Church: The Didache." *ANRW* 2.27.1 (1992): 210–33.

Waldstein, Wolfgang. *Operae Libertorum: Untersuchungen zur Dienstpflicht freigelassener Sklaven*. Forschungen zur antiken Slaverei 19. Stuttgart: Franz Steiner, 1986.

———. "Zum Menschsein von Sklaven." Pages 31–49 in *Fünfzig Jahre Forschungen zur antiken Sklaverei an der Mainzer Akademie, 1950–2000: Miscellanea zum Jubiläum*. Edited by Heinz Bellen and Heinz Heinen. Forschungen zur antiken Sklaverei 35. Stuttgart: Franz Steiner, 2001.

Walhout, M. D. "The Hermeneutical Turn in American Critical Theory: 1830–1860." *JHI* 57 (1996): 683–703.

Wallon, Henri. *Histoire de l'esclavage dans l'antiquité*. 2d ed. 3 vols. Paris: Hachette, 1879.

Walsh, P. G. "The Rights and Wrongs of Curiosity (Plutarch to Augustine)." *GR* 35 (1988): 73–85.

Walters, Kerry S. *The American Deists: Voices of Reason and Dissent in the Early Republic*. Lawrence: University Press of Kansas, 1992.

———. *Rational Infidels: The American Deists*. Durango, Colo.: Longwood Academic, 1992.

Wansink, Craig S. *Chained in Christ: The Experience and Rhetoric of Paul's Imprisonments*. JSNTSup 130. Sheffield: Sheffield Academic Press, 1996.

Washington, Margaret. "The Meanings of Scripture in Gullah Concepts of Liberation and Group Identity." Pages 321–41 in Wimbush, *African Americans and the Bible*.

Watson, Alan. *Roman Slave Law*. Baltimore: Johns Hopkins University Press, 1987.

———. "Roman Slave Law and Romanist Ideology." *Phoenix* 37 (1978): 53–65.

Watts, N. H. *Speeches, Selections: Pro Milone; In Pisonem; Pro Scauro; Pro Fonteio; Pro Rabirio Postumo; Pro Marcello; Pro Ligario; Pro Rege Deiotaro/ Marcus Tulius Cicero*. LCL. Cambridge, Mass.: Harvard University Press, 1979.

Wayland, Francis. *Elements of Moral Science*. 1841. Reprint, New York: Sheldon, 1877.

———. *The Limitations of Human Responsibility*. Boston: Gould, Kendall and Lincoln, 1838.

Weaver, P. R. C. *Familia Caesaris: A Social Study of the Emperor's Freedmen and Slaves*. Cambridge: Cambridge University Press, 1972.

Webster, T. B. L. *Greek Theatre Production*. 2d ed. London Methuen, 1970.

————. "Leading Slaves in New Comedy: 300 B.C.–300 A.D." *JdI* 76 (1961): 100–110.

Weidmann, Frederick W. "The Martyrs of Lyons." Pages 398–412 in *Religions of Late Antiquity in Practice*. Edited by Richard Valantasis. Princeton Readings in Religions. Princeton, N.J.: Princeton University Press, 2000.

Weiser, Alfons. *Die Knechtsgleichnisse der synoptischen Evangelien*. SANT 29. Munich: Kösel, 1971.

Welborn, Laurence L. "The Runaway Paul." *HTR* 92 (1999): 115–63.

Wessner, Paul, ed. *Aeli Donati quod fertur Commentum Terenti*. 3 vols. Bibliotheca scriptorum Graecorum et Romanorum Teubneriana. Scriptores Romani. Leipzig: Teubner, 1902–8.

Westermann, W. L. "Apprentice Contracts and the Apprentice System in Roman Egypt." *CP* 9 (1914): 295–315.

Wheaton, N. S. *A Discourse on St. Paul's Epistle to Philemon*. Hartford, Conn.: Case, Tiffany, 1851.

White, Kenneth D. "Roman Agricultural Writers I: Varro and his Predecessors." *ANRW* 1.4 (1973): 439–95.

White, L. Michael, and O. Larry Yarbrough, eds. *The Social World of the First Christians: Essays in Honor of Wayne A. Meeks*. Minneapolis: Fortress Press, 1995.

Wibbing, Siegfried. *Die Tugend- und Lasterkataloge im Neuen Testament und ihre Traditionsgeschichte unter besonderer Berücksichtigung der Qumran-Texte*. BZNW 25. Berlin: Töpelmann, 1959.

Wiedemann, Thomas E. J. "Duties of Freedmen." *Classical Review*, n.s. 38 (1988): 331–33.

————. *Greek and Roman Slavery*. 1981. Reprint, London: Routledge, 1988.

Wiles, David. "Greek Theatre and the Legitimation of Slavery." Pages 53–67 in *Slavery and Other Forms of Unfree Labour*. Edited by Léonie J. Archer. History Workshop Series. London: Routledge, 1998.

————. *The Masks of Menander: Sign and Meaning in Greek and Roman Performance*. Cambridge: Cambridge University Press, 1991.

Wilken, Robert L. *The Christians as the Romans Saw Them*. New Haven: Yale University Press, 1984.

Wills, Lawrence M. "The Depiction of Slavery in the Ancient Novel." Pages 113–32 in *Slavery in Text and Interpretation*. Edited by Allen Dwight Callahan, Richard A. Horsley, and Abraham Smith. Semeia 83/84. Atlanta: Scholars Press, 1998.

————. *The Jew in the Court of the Foreign King*. HDR 26. Minneapolis: Fortress Press, 1990.

Wilner, Ortha L. "The Character Treatment of Inorganic Rôles in Roman Comedy." *CP* 26 (1931): 264–83.

————. "The Technical Device of Direct Description of Character in Roman Comedy." *CP* 33 (1938): 20–36.

Wilson, Walter T. *Love without Pretense: Romans 12.9-21 and Hellenistic-Jewish Wisdom Literature.* WUNT 2/46. Tübingen: Mohr (Siebeck), 1991.

Wimbush, Vincent L., ed. *African Americans and the Bible: Sacred Texts and Social Textures.* New York: Continuum, 2000.

Windisch, Hans. *Der zweite Korintherbrief.* 9th ed. KEK 6. Göttingen: Vandenhoeck & Ruprecht, 1924.

Winkler, John J. *Auctor and Actor: A Narratological Reading of Apuleius's "The Golden Ass."* Berkeley and Los Angeles: University of California Press, 1985.

Winter, Sara C. "Paul's Letter to Philemon." *NTS* 33 (1987): 1–15.

Winterbottom, Michael. *Declamations/Seneca, the Elder.* 2 vols. LCL. Cambridge, Mass.: Harvard University Press, 1974.

———. *The Minor Declamations Ascribed to Quintilian.* Berlin: Walter de Gruyter, 1984.

Witherington, Ben, III. *Women in the Earliest Churches.* SNTSMS 59. Cambridge: Cambridge University Press, 1988.

Wogaman, J. Philip. *Christian Ethics: A Historical Introduction.* Louisville: Westminster John Knox, 1993.

Woods, Michael. *Eudemian Ethics: Books I, II, and VIII/Aristotle.* 2d ed. Clarendon Aristotle Series. Oxford: Clarendon, 1992.

Woytek, Erich. *T. Maccius Plautus, Persa: Einleitung, Text und Kommentar. Sitzungsberichte.* Österreichische Akademie der Wissenschaften. Philosophisch-Historische Klasse 385. Vienna: Verlag der Österreichischen Akademie der Wissenschaften, 1982.

Wright, Conrad. *The Beginnings of Unitarianism in America.* Boston: Beacon Press, 1955.

Wright, John. *Dancing in Chains: The Stylistic Unity of the Comoedia Palliata.* Papers and Monographs of the American Academy in Rome 25. Rome: American Academy in Rome, 1974.

Wyatt-Brown, Bertram. *Lewis Tappan and the Evangelical War against Slavery.* Cleveland: Press of Case Western Reserve University, 1969.

Yoder, John H. *The Politics of Jesus.* Grand Rapids, Mich.: Eerdmans, 1972.

Yonge, C. D., trans. *The Works of Philo: Complete and Unabridged.* New Updated Edition. Peabody, Mass.: Hendrickson, 1993.

INDEX OF NAMES AND SUBJECTS

INDEX OF BIBLICAL
AND OTHER ANCIENT SOURCES

Apocrypha and Pseudepigrapha, New Testament

Apostolic Fathers

Classical and Ancient Writers